Social Work and Science in the 21st Century

Social Work and Science in the 21st Century

Leon H. Ginsberg

Christopher R. Larrison

Larry Nackerud

John R. Barner

Lauren A. Ricciardelli

OXFORD
UNIVERSITY PRESS

OXFORD
UNIVERSITY PRESS

Oxford University Press is a department of the University of Oxford. It furthers the University's objective of excellence in research, scholarship, and education by publishing worldwide. Oxford is a registered trade mark of Oxford University Press in the UK and certain other countries.

Published in the United States of America by Oxford University Press
198 Madison Avenue, New York, NY 10016, United States of America.

Library of Congress Cataloging-in-Publication Data
Names: Ginsberg, Leon H., author. | Larrison, Christopher R., author.
Title: Social work and science in the 21st century / Leon H. Ginsberg, Christopher R. Larrison, Larry Nackerud, John R. Barner, Lauren A. Ricciardelli.
Description: New York : Oxford University Press, [2019] |
Includes bibliographical references and index.
Identifiers: LCCN 2018045226 (print) | LCCN 2018046735 (ebook) |
ISBN 9780190940416 (updf) | ISBN 9780190940423 (epub) |
ISBN 9780190940409 (alk. paper)
Subjects: LCSH: Social service.
Classification: LCC HV40 (ebook) | LCC HV40 .G557 2019 (print) |
DDC 361.3—dc23
LC record available at https://lccn.loc.gov/2018045226

1 3 5 7 9 8 6 4 2
Printed by Webcom, Inc., Canada

The authors would like to extend a special and heartfelt thank you to Gaurav Ranjan Sinha, Ph.D. student at the University of Illinois School of Social Work, who has been instrumental in organizing and restructuring the images and figures used throughout the book. His valuable contributions are deeply appreciated.

CONTENTS

FOREWORD

The brilliant science writer Siddartha Mukherjee (2016) writes that the three building blocks of science are the atom; the gene, which is the carrier of hereditary information; and the byte or bit, which is the unit that contains digitized information such as one finds in computer data. All three of these are discussed in this book. Social work, in all its dimensions, has long aspired to become more scientific. Dealing with social problems and issues from scientific perspectives has been an objective of social work for the last 50 years. Developments in the sciences make that objective increasingly achievable. The growth of neuroscience, the cracking of the human genome, the growth of climate science, and the beginning of the digital age and big data that includes the widespread use of the computer require most social workers to use scientific instruments and scientific knowledge in almost everything they do. Education for social workers about the social and behavioral sciences, biology, and medicine has long been integrated into social work education. The growth of the natural and physical sciences impacts the practice of the social work profession. Unfortunately, education about STEM (science, technology, engineering, and mathematics) is not a usual part of the preparation of social workers. This book is written to help overcome the lack of attention to the natural and physical sciences and to provide information and ideas that bring those sciences and the related fields, such as climate change, chemistry, and neuroscience, into the emphases of social work education and practice.

There has been significant infusion of the natural and physical sciences into the health care system. Understanding brain chemistry and person-in-environment interactions with chemicals have become mainstays of medical practice in the past decade. These relationships are discussed in Chapter 2. Another example is the use of technology developed in the natural and physical sciences and its application in social work settings, which began to take special prominence in the later decades of the 20th century. Then the state departments of health, mental health, and social services began using computer-based data to maintain records, track client progress, and keep information about programs and services that serve clients. The original computers, which now appear rudimentary, were developed to break codes during World War II and only later were adapted for the kinds of needs social workers and social welfare agencies need. The invention of the transistor made it possible for computer technology to be used in smaller machines, such as the cell phones and laptop computers used today, unlike the original computers, which were large machines that often required their own buildings (Tallack, 2001).

Computer technology is now so pervasive in American life that children and teenagers often seem more proficient in its use than their parents or even eventual employers. The uses of technology in sending messages to one another, and retaining and using music and other digital libraries means that technology is part of the basic knowledge and skill of children and teenagers, almost comparable to earlier generations' uses of typewriters, tape recorders, and landline telephones. Digital devices are so ubiquitous that they pose a challenge to classroom instructors in social work education—attempting to keep student interest in course content, which competes with Facebook, Twitter, and other digital programs that are of great interest to most young adults. As indicated, today, social workers are exposed to more complex computer technology, such as computerized tomography (CT) scans, smartphones, and virtual reality, in the workplace environment. Yet social work students are rarely formally taught about technology coming out of the natural and physical sciences in their bachelor's or master's degree programs.

The growing need for scientific knowledge in social work is a source of many efforts over the years. For example, education about mental health and mental illness, once based almost totally on the psychological theories of Sigmund Freud or, in some social work education programs, Otto Rank, now needs to include material about genetics and neuroscience if their social work graduates are going to be able to succeed in the clinics and hospitals that serve clients with emotional problems or mental illnesses. The *Diagnostic and Statistical Manual of Mental Disorders* (DSM) has attempted to strengthen the underpinning scientific understandings of mental illness by introducing genetic and neuroscience measures. Use of the DSM is essential for insurance reimbursements and decisions about the best ways to treat clients. The issues of science in the mental health field are discussed in the chapter on Mental Health and Science.

This book is designed to fill the gaps for social work students and practitioners. It follows an earlier book by the same authors. *Human Biology for Social Workers*, which came at a time when the Council on Social Work Education, the profession's accrediting body, required that all social work graduates have some instruction in human biology. Social work educators and the authors of this text realized that other sciences such as chemistry, geometry mathematics, and physics were also important to social workers. Much of what social workers now do and will do in the future is based on learnings from the sciences, as discussed earlier.

The focus of this book is on the connections between the sciences and social work knowledge and practice. Of course, it does not purport to provide extensive backgrounds in the sciences. The book intends to provide the reader with the basics of scientific concepts as applicable to social work practice. Introducing social workers to those ideas and helping them understand the connections of what they do with the sciences is the objective. Helping social workers more effectively communicate with scientists about the issues that face clients is a corollary goal. We hope that our efforts will help introduce new emphases in the profession on the natural and physical sciences that are often a progenitor of social work practices, even though their contributions usually are not explicit.

For those readers who want to extend their education in the sciences—or revisit their earlier studies in the sciences—there are many ways to achieve that in addition to taking formal courses in science. Books geared to adults who want to recall or expand their science studies are regularly published independently or as part of series. One of the most accessible for the nonscientists is Isaacson's *Einstein* (2007), which covers the development of modern physics. Two useful series are the titled, "Idiot's ____," and "____ for Dummies," published on many topics in the sciences, and almost any imaginable topic for people who want the basic information on the subject. Although they do not say very much about the applications of the sciences to human services, they provide the foundation information on the sciences in a wider scope and detail than this book. They are not necessary for understanding and using this book, but they are useful resources for those who want to go further with their science education.

Although social work students and practitioners are often well grounded in the social and behavioral sciences, that is not true of the natural and physical sciences such as biology, chemistry, and physics. Even so, much of social work has roots in the sciences, even though those connections are not always explicit in the preparation for and practice of the profession.

This text is designed to help social workers become more current in the use of scientific information, scientific facts, and science-based technology. It parallels the profession's commitment to "evidence-based practice" with an understanding that the evidence upon which practice is increasingly based is scientific evidence. As advances in the natural and physical sciences take place at a rapid pace, changing our understanding of human behavior and the human condition, our hope is this book will serve as a primer for future social work practitioners.

REFERENCES

Isaacson, W. (2007). *Einstein: His life and universe.* New York, NY: Simon and Schuster.

Mukherjee, S. (2016). *The gene: An intimate history.* New York, NY: Scribner.

Tallack, P. (Ed.). (2001). *The science book.* London, UK: Weidenfeld and Nicolson.

ABOUT THE AUTHORS

Leon H. Ginsberg is Dean Emeritus of the University of South Carolina College of Social Work. He also headed social work education programs at West Virginia University and Appalachian State University. He was Commissioner of Human Services for the state of West Virginia in the administration of Governor John D. Rockefeller IV. He has written or edited books on social work management, social welfare policy and services, rural social work, and aging. He served for 2 years as interim chair of the Department of Physics and Astronomy at Appalachian State.

Christopher R. Larrison is Associate Professor at the University of Illinois School of Social Work. His research and teaching focus on the social determinants of, and services for, serious mental illness and health. His work has been shaped by a transdisciplinary approach to research and collecting primary data in rural community-based settings from people receiving and providing services. Dr. Larrison is skilled in utilizing mixed qualitative and quantitative methods. He has studied community-based mental health services in the United States, community development in rural Mexico, and the impact of welfare reform on health in Georgia. Dr. Larrison's research has been funded by the National Institute of Mental Health and a number of foundations, including the Center for Economic Progress and the Research Retirement Foundation. As well, several of his peer-reviewed articles have been placed on suggested reading lists by the US Department of Housing and Urban Development, the US Government Accounting Office, and The World Bank.

Larry Nackerud is Professor of Social Work at the University of Georgia School of Social Work. He has conducted research on social welfare policy and immigration. Part of his work is in program evaluations, which he has conducted in the United States and other nations. He has also worked in state mental health programs in the United States. He is the coauthor with Drs. Ginsberg and Larrison of *Human Biology for Social Workers*.

John R. Barner (PhD, University of Georgia; BS and MSW, University of Minnesota) is on the Public Service Faculty with the Carl Vinson Institute of Government at the University of Georgia. Dr. Barner has published work in journals such as the *British Journal of Social Work, Social Work Education,* and *Research* *on Social Work Practice* on data related to higher education and professional development in social work, psychology, and other behavioral sciences.

Lauren A. Ricciardelli is an Assistant Professor of Social Work at Troy University in Phoenix City, Alabama, and is a licensed Master of Social Work in the state of Georgia. She earned her MSW and PhD from The University of Georgia in 2011 and 2017, respectively. In addition to professional social work experience in the area of disabilities, Dr. Ricciardelli's research focuses on the sociology of disability and policy implications for persons with intellectual disability in the social welfare and criminal justice arenas, including implications for death penalty cases.

Social Work and Science in the 21st Century

Introduction to Social Work and Science
for Students and Practitioners

Natural and physical science concepts are increasingly important to social work education. During the past two decades, the profession of social work has sought to base its concepts and its practice interventions on efforts that are evidenced based, systematically developed, and verified through research. The research methods and rigorous approaches to intervention development are based on models developed to further knowledge in the physical and natural sciences. A primary purpose of this book is to help social workers understand the science that is the basis for what they do and what is done in the health and social services. Although while conceptualizing the book we consulted primary textbooks in the sciences, we often found that it was still necessary to interpret and explain some scientific concepts from a uniquely social work perspective. The McGraw-Hill series elucidates various scientific subjects such as Gibilisco's *Physics Demystified* (2002), and Manga guides to the sciences (Nitta, Yamamoto, & Takatsu, 2011) still require a better understanding of mathematics and science than many social workers have. The tone of this book fits the needs of the social work student with a rudimentary background in the physical and natural sciences.

Carlo Rovelli (2016), famous physicist and author of *Seven Brief Lessons on Physics*, helps us develop perspective about the importance of basic science findings in our everyday lives. He points out that we humans are made of the same atoms and light signals "as are exchanged between pine trees in the mountains and stars in the galaxies" (p. 66). Referring to the genome discoveries and explanations of recent years, he notes that we have great-grandparents in common with butterflies. His brief book on physics (2015) was popular and easy for nonscientists to follow.

Many of us in social work have only partial knowledge of the natural and physical sciences. A large proportion of social workers, both students and practitioners, have stronger backgrounds in the social and behavioral sciences that also constitute a large part of the undergraduate and graduate social work education curriculum. Fields such as sociology and psychology—especially psychology—are parts of the courses in human behavior and the social environment. Courses in research as well as social work–conducted research are often tied to the social and behavioral science fields, all of which have an emphasis on research and utilized methods developed in the physical and natural sciences. To a lesser extent, economics and political science are also part of the knowledge base of most social workers, and content from those fields is part of the curriculum on social welfare policy and services. However, with the increased emphasis on evidence-based practice, knowledge of the natural and physical sciences also plays an important role in understanding the phenomena that are addressed by social work. The understanding of the challenges confronted by social workers has been clarified by science. For example, the profession's understanding of the reasons for poverty or what it means to have a mental illness or how racial disparities in incarceration occur has changed substantially over the past 50 years as a result of findings not only in the social sciences but also in the natural and physical sciences.

Research findings are developed through a complex professional process. This process in social work has been dominated by the social sciences, which often mixes postpositivists and postmodern philosophies. In contrast, the natural and physical sciences are underpinned by the belief that there is an objective and tangible reality that can be directly accessed and measured. There is also an understanding within this paradigm that reality will shift over time, requiring ongoing discovery. This is why scientific knowledge building is an important enterprise for the social work profession to pursue—it allows practitioners to work across systems and be responsive to the changing realities of their clients. Within the natural and physical sciences an experiment or study is done after a hypothesis is defined and promulgated often using qualitative methods such as observation. Data are collected, conclusions drawn, and the information is disseminated, in professional, anonymously reviewed journals. In order to be accepted as valid, the research has to be replicable, which is often successfully performed in the natural and physical sciences through experimentation. Replication in the natural and physical sciences is tied to the concept of "falsification," which states that even scientific knowledge has the inherent possibility that it can be proved false. To facilitate replication in the natural and physical sciences, qualified researchers should be able to access the data used by other scientists to determine the validity of the original research and conclusions.

Within the social sciences replication of findings has been more elusive. *The New York Times* reported on August 27, 2015, that several published psychology studies may be invalid. The Open Science Collaboration attempted to replicate 100 studies that appeared in three major psychology journals, *Psychological Science, The Journal of Personality and Social Psychology,* and *Journal of Experimental Psychology.* The Collaboration called the efforts to replicate the studies as "painstaking." In August 2015, they reported in *Science* (Open Science Collaboration, August 28, 2015) that more than half of the studies could not be replicated. For example, one of the studies that didn't hold up was focused on studying free will; it concluded that if subjects read something suggesting that their behavior was predetermined, those who didn't read the passage were more likely to cheat on an exam. The difficulty with replication and overstatement of results has potentially limited an accurate understanding of human behavior and what practices are evidence based. So quoting research and basing services on it requires a degree of suspicion lest questionable results are treated as valid and reliable.

This text is designed to help social work students bolster their knowledge of science so they can more effectively understand the scientific bases of social work practice, social welfare policy and services, and human behavior and the social environment, and apply that knowledge in their work. Social workers have some education in the sciences. The liberal arts and core curricula of most colleges and universities require exposure to course work in the sciences. Many undergraduate social work programs require biology courses as part of the curriculum. Because they recognized that, these same authors wrote *Human Biology for Social Workers*. We recognized, however, that because the emphases most social work students follow are in the social and behavioral sciences, this kind of text is needed. Many social work students avoided studies in the natural and physical sciences in their undergraduate curricula. Some social work graduate students chose to complete their undergraduate science requirements in fields such as geology, which though they have human services implications, are usually taught without very much attention to those implications.

Those who choose social work as their professional career are often victims of science anxiety because physical and natural sciences instruction in K–12 and undergraduate schools is not readily accessible for students who are not naturally able to assimilate and use mathematics. The sciences rely on mathematical measures for stating their concepts and for defining their facts, which sometimes deters students from pursuing both mathematics and science.

Social work has reached the point of basing more and more of its knowledge base on evidence that is inherently connected to science knowledge. Even when those connections are not emphasized, it is still clear that knowledge of fields such as chemistry, physics, and their person-focused subspecialties is necessary for fully understanding the evidence for evidence-based practice. In fact, evidence-based practice may also be called science-based practice because scientific evidence is what theoreticians often mean when they write about evidence.

The social work literature on evidence-based practice represents the profession's closest connection with the methods utilized in the natural and physical sciences. For many social work educators, evidence-based practice is about systematically incorporating evidence into practice—by formulating a question, analyzing it, and carrying out a specific intervention strategy (Pollio, 2015). Or, in another description, evidence based practices "are interventions and empirically supported treatments that have demonstrated evidence in support of their effectiveness" (O'Neill, 2015, p. 626). The authors of this text agree with the value of that approach and are hoping to further identify its connection with core scientific concepts in the physical and natural sciences while taking into account the unique implications of social work practice.

In this book, we focus on basic concepts that are of immediate use to social workers—both students and practitioners. We attempt to explain those concepts in everyday language, and we avoid loading the reader down with terms. Whenever possible, we avoid presenting the concepts through formulas and, instead, explain them with language. We have created a glossary of terms to assist the reader.

It should also be clear in this text that the bulk of modern scientific ideas have been developed during the past two centuries with an exponential growth since the late 20th century. That is not to discount such historically important scientific endeavors as those of Aristotle, Euclid, Kepler, and, later, Sir Isaac Newton. Many of their ideas are still the bases for extensive scientific developments. But much of what we now know and use—Einstein's theories of relativity, modern meteorology, nuclear power generation, quantum physics, and many others—are fairly recent. In fact, the explosion of scientific knowledge and its use led to the manifestation of and potential responses to some of the serious problems of the 21st century such as climate change, a subject that we also cover in this text.

Despite its growing importance, general information about science is not readily accessible. Media outlets have often discounted science information. Mooney and Kirshenbaum (2009) note that in television news, where many Americans obtain their knowledge of current issues, science is given only 1 minute out of every 300 minutes of news. And the focus of much of the science information is about fitness and exercise, rather than larger science issues.

The consequences of the widespread lack of science knowledge has led to such disturbing phenomena as the rejection of vaccinations for childhood diseases and the use of unproven (or proven to have no bases) health and mental health remedies such as astrology and homeopathic medical treatments. Although there is solid evidence refuting many often popular but dangerous "health" treatments, if they replace proven and valid treatments, they can be injurious, even fatal. Social workers who serve children who are medically neglected may find themselves trying to counter familial beliefs that contradict scientific treatments. For example, theories about the causes of childhood mental illnesses and disabilities such as autism may cause families to reject valid interventions for unproven, sometimes bogus, prevention practices and treatments. So social workers need a basic commitment to the skepticism of scientific inquiry and knowledge about the truth of care for people who are ill or who have a disability.

Scientific knowledge is essential for all human services, including social work. As this book explains, knowledge of chemistry, physics, and several other sciences is fundamental to the care and treatment of social work clients. Biology, specifically human biology, is also critical knowledge for social workers. This text does not focus on human biology because, as mentioned, the authors published a whole textbook on human biology, *Human Biology for Social Workers*, which is still in print and available for use.

Although the emphasis of the text is on natural and physical science, actually science is only one part of the equation for understanding social issues and social programs. Natural and physical sciences are the basis for the development of technology for diagnosing and treating illnesses, for the construction of assistive devices for those who need them, for many health care practices, and for much of social work practice. We use the term "science" because it is the basis for services and equipment. However, much of the actual translation of scientific findings into social interventions is done by other professionals such as engineers and by technicians. Scientists may develop the basic understandings needed for services to people, but a broad range of professionals, including social workers, often implements their ideas.

Essential for social workers is the ability to think scientifically about social behavior and social phenomena. Ideally, social workers need to think as if they were scientists—to be skeptical of ideas that are not factually based and to always think about the science behind intervention methods and social phenomena. In other words, facts should govern our beliefs rather than ideologies.

FUNDAMENTAL IDEAS

Comprehending some of these ideas—no time, no before or after, perhaps no causality—is difficult for most humans to assimilate. They are outside our usual understanding of ourselves and our environments. We think in terms of things happening for a reason and of some things occurring before others, often as causes of those others. But current science doubts the existence of causes, even of time, ideas that are difficult for us to conceive. Astronomers and physicists study the planets and the stars. It is possible to know the composition and movement of the bodies of the universe, even though we only have direct physical evidence about very few celestial bodies—the moon and Mars.

Modern scientific theory even doubts the existence of concepts such as "now" and "here." Now is different for different people in different circumstances or locations. Here is where one may be, but the person being addressed or the object being described is obviously somewhere else. These are some of the complexities of modern scientific theory. Being aware of them is useful, but fully understanding them is not a necessity for social workers learning about the applications of science concepts. They are important issues for scientists and may, someday, be the basis for new understandings of phenomena—so they are far from irrelevant.

FACTS AND FAITH

The age of the universe and the world are generally accepted by scientists. However, those who believe in the literal truth of the Bible would suggest a world that is less than 10,000 years old. For example, in the Jewish calendar, the current year is 5777, dating from the beginning of the world as described in Genesis. Of course, the biblical calculations were made and continue to be made without the tools of modern science. Other data on the ages of the universe and world are presented later in this chapter.

These issues of the world's age help explain such modern phenomena as climate change or, as some call it, global warming, to which a full chapter 6 is devoted. Certainly the world has gone through multiple changes, but many changes are relatively recent and seem to be associated with human beings and modern technology. When the dinosaurs lived, there was no fossil fuel—the dinosaurs became the fossils—from which oil and gas are derived.

There are other mathematical concepts that are especially pertinent to the practice of social work. For example, there is the increasingly used body mass index (BMI) for determining the appropriateness of an individual's weight when calculated in terms of his or her height. It's a mundane idea without a great deal of scientific implications. However, it is widely used by health care providers as diverse as physical therapists and medical practitioners. Insurance providers, schools, athletic programs, and many other institutions use the BMI as an indicator of appropriate weight. Prior to the development of the BMI, weight charts were approximate and associated with age, with little attention to height. Converting the individual's height to inches and dividing that figure into the individual's weight in pounds calculate the BMI. It can also be calculated, of course, with kilograms of weight and centimeters of height. The measure defines obese, overweight, normal weight, and underweight categories. (One of our colleagues said he was not overweight, but undertall!) A complication of the BMI for older adults is that people lose height as they age—through spinal compression. So the same person who may have had an ideal BMI when he or she was 60 may be defined as overweight or obese by the time he or she is 70.

It is worth noting that in the history of the sciences the original developers were typically fascinated by mathematics. A famous example is the theory of Pythagoras that in a triangle A squared times B squared equals C squared—one leg of the triangle is A, a second is B, and the hypotenuse, a line from the top of one leg to the other, is C. Early scientists and today's scientists enjoyed mathematics and conversed with one another through mathematical concepts. Eric Weiner (2016) notes that the ancient Greeks, who developed much of mathematics, always sought elegant solutions and mathematical proofs, such as the Pythagorean theorem (see Fig. 1.1).

Where does it all come from? How were chemistry, geometry, mathematics, and physics "discovered" or developed? Many of the basic ideas for the sciences originated in the fourth century or later. Cultures developed ideas about mathematics or arithmetic, the oldest of the tools of science, along with geometry. There are systems that use base numbers other than 10, which is that used in current Western culture. These developments and alternate systems are explored in many books and on many websites, available to those who want to know more about them. The basics of the sciences are explored in specific chapters throughout this text.

It is somewhat surprising to learn that many scientific principles that even the least sophisticated and youngest people in the United States take for granted are relatively recent, as mentioned earlier. For example, oxygen, as a gas, was only discovered in the 18th century, in 1774 by Joseph Priestley, although we know about it in many ways, as a component of water and the portion of air that we use to sustain

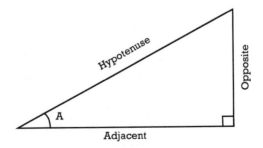

Figure 1.1 Pythagorean theorem Authors' creation

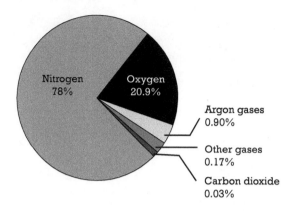

Figure 1.2 Composition of air Authors' creation

life. Air was originally believed to be a single element rather than the combination of elements that Priestley noted. His original name for oxygen was dephlogisticated air (Joseph Priestley and the Discovery of Oxygen, n.d.). Much more about the development of scientific concepts is discussed in Chapter 3. See Figure 1.2.

THE SOCIAL WORK TRADITION IN RESEARCH

Social work began with early efforts to conduct social research and to understand social problems from scientific perspectives. The search for knowledge, wherever the facts lead, should be the focus of practitioners with systems of all sizes. Of course, social workers are expected to behave consistently with certain values—health over illness, well-being over poverty, emotional functioning that helps people perform satisfactorily as family members, employees, and professionals, mental stability over emotional disturbance. Throughout its history, social work has supported various values such as these—but increasingly, the field moves toward scientific, evidence-based ideas, on what social workers should do and how they should do it. Ethically based social work practice is central to modern social work, but a commitment to scientific approaches is an important element of that ethically based practice.

The belief in and ultimate rejection of the ether theory in physics was somewhat comparable to the long-supported theories of Sigmund Freud, which were taught in most schools of social work through the mid-20th century as the primary means for understanding human development and behavior. The id, ego, superego, as components of personality; the Oedipal complex; and other ideas were used (and in a few schools of social work are still used) to explain and assist with teaching human behavior, sometimes called the diagnostic approach. The widely used and accepted theories of psychologist Erik Erikson are related to Freudian theory and are used in many social and behavioral sciences, especially psychology. However, the Freudian theories were not research based and in the past several decades social workers and psychiatrists, among other professions (Lieberman & Ogas, 2015), abandoned them for such systematic concepts of diagnosing mental illness as the *Diagnostic and Statistical*

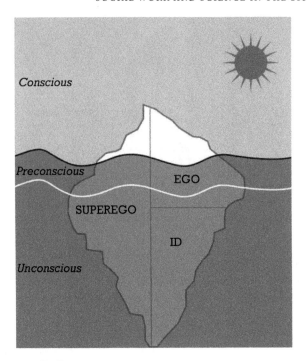

Figure 1.3 Structural iceberg
SOURCE: By en:User:Jordangordanier - en:Image:Structural-Iceberg.png, Public Domain, https://commons.
wikimedia.org/w/index.php?curid=46456585

Manual of Mental Disorders, published in several editions since the mid-20th century by the American Psychiatric Association. Now, instead of relying on a predetermined set of concepts about human development and behavior, the field now relies on statistical analysis of symptoms, evidence of the existence of those symptoms, and establishes criteria for determining whether or not a patient has the described condition. Lists of symptoms are provided and the extent of the condition is determined by the patient's exhibition of some key symptoms as well as a specific number of those symptoms. The science of mental health is discussed in detail in Chapter 13. See Figure 1.3.

PHYSICS, CHEMISTRY, AND PHYSICAL HEALTH

Physics and chemistry, among the sciences, are also fundamental to many physical health issues. Medicines, inoculations, and other treatments are developed by chemists and pharmacologists working in tandem with many other professions. They are also involved in developing treatments for disabilities, as is discussed in Chapter 14.

Physicists also helped develop such diagnostic tools as X-ray, C-scans, and magnetic resonance imaging (MRI; see Figs. 1.4 and 1.5). The continual updating of those devices also requires the knowledge and participation of physicists. Physicists are also essential to the development and use of braces, prostheses for people who have lost limbs, stints for treating heart disease, filters for treating blood clots, and mobility devices such as wheelchairs and walkers. Chapter 11 covers these

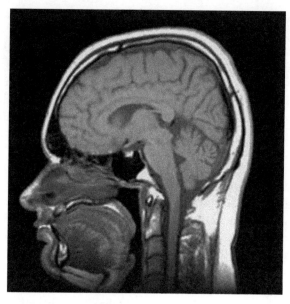

Figure 1.4 Magnetic resonance imaging

contributions in greater detail. A full chapter on chemistry (Chapter 2) is included in this book.

Physicists also assist in the design of ramps, staircases, designs and dimensions of buildings, and other efforts to increase the mobility of those who cannot use traditional sidewalks and stairs. The required angles for ramps, and room for assistance devices in hospital and long-term care corridors, are all part of building codes for such facilities. The specific requirements depend upon research and consultation by

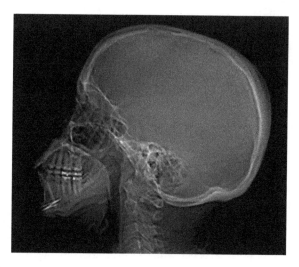

Figure 1.5 X-ray

physicists as are discussed in a later chapter on assistive devices and physical facilities (see Chapter 11).

Climate change, mentioned earlier, is understood and predicted with the use of the scientific concepts of meteorology. The science of meteorology also had its roots in the 19th century, and its development was opposed by such entities as the ship-salvage industry, which relied on maritime accidents such as the 1,914 shipwrecks in the Great Lakes in 1869 (Schultz, 2015). Although weather-related catastrophes continue to affect millions of people each year, scientific predictions of weather events have similarly saved millions of lives.

An interesting dimension of science is that it is for the most part a process of discovery—discovery of truths that are presumed to exist but may not have been known before they were discovered. Unlike social work, in which scholars are able to create theories, scientists discover the dimensions of theories. Facts about science have always existed and scientists discover those facts. Of course, there are stops and starts and diversions from the truth in the sciences, as much of the balance of this text shows, but once discovered and tested and verified, the truths become known and available to the world.

The chapters that follow expand on some of these ideas and introduce others. All are part of the effort to provide a more extensive background for social workers and students of the profession to understand the concepts of science that are important to the study and practice of social work with clients.

FURTHER READING

Berger, A. (2016, June 15). All in his head. *Discover*, 26–31.

Christianity Stack Exchange. (n.d.). Retrieved November 2, 2015, from https://christianity.stackexchange.com/

Engber, D. (2016). Why hasn't the U.S adopted the metric system. *Popular Science*, 96.

Feynman, R. P. (1991). Atoms in motion. In T. Ferris (Ed.), *The world treasury of physics, astronomy and mathematics* (pp. 3–17). Boston, MA: Little, Brown and Company.

Ford, K. W. (1991). The large and the small. In T. Ferris (Ed.), *The world treasury of physics, astronomy and mathematics* (pp. 18–37). Boston, MA: Little, Brown and Company.

Gibilisco, S. (2002). *Physics demystified*. New York, NY: McGraw-Hill.

Hawking, S. W. (1998). *A brief history of time*. xx: Bantam Dell.

Joseph Priestley and the Discovery of Oxygen. (n.d.). Retrieved from http://www.acs.org/content/acs/en/education/whatischemistry/landmarks/josephpriestleyoxygen.html

Karls, J. M. (2008). *Person-in-environment system manual*. Washington, DC: NASW Press.

Kirk, S. A., & Reid, W. J. (2002). *Science and social work: A critical appraisal*. New York, NY: Columbia University Press.

Kirsch, A. (2016). What makes you so sure. *The New Yorker*, 71–75.

Lieberman, J. A., & Ogas, O. (2015). *Shrinks: The untold story of psychiatry*. New York, NY: Hachette.

Lightman, A. (2016). What came before the big bang? *Harpers Magazine*. Retrieved from https://harpers.org/archive/2016/01/what-came-before-the-big-bang/

Mooney, C., & Kirshenbaum, S. (2009). *Unscientific America: How scientific illiteracy threatens our future.* New York, NY: Basic Books.

Nadis, S. (2016). The fall and rise of string theory. *Discover,* 18–20.

Nitta, H., & Yamamoto, M. (2011). *The Manga guide to relativity.* San Francisco, CA: No Starch Press.

O'Neill, M. (2015). Applying critical consciousness and evidence-based practice decision-making: A framework for clinical social work practice. *Journal of Social Work Education, 51*(4), 624–637.

Open Science Collaboration. (2015). Estimating the reproducibility of psychological science. *Science, 349*(6251), aac4716.

Pollio, D. E. (2015). Guest editorial. Evidence-based education: From paradigm shift to social movement—and back again? *Journal of Social Work Education, 51*(4), 619–623.

Rovelli, C. (2016). *Seven brief lessons on physics.* New York, NY: Riverhead Books.

Sanburn, J. (2016, March 10). Greed, politics and the biggest oil boom in decades. *Time,* 35–41.

Schulz, K. (2015, November 23). Writers in the storm. *New Yorker,* 23.

Weiner, E. (2016). *The geography of genius: A search for the world's most creative places from ancient Athens to Silicon Valley.* New York, NY: Simon and Schuster.

Wulf, A. (2015). *The invention of nature: Alexander von Humboldt's new world.* New York, NY: Knopf.

2

Social Work and the Science of Chemistry

We ought, in every instance, to submit our reasoning to the test of experiment, and never to search for truth but by the natural road of experiment and observation.

—ANTOINE-LAURENT DE LAVOISIER

Social workers may address many of the problems facing individuals and so-cieties by paying close attention to the chemical systems that make up those environments (or the chemicals that pollute them), medicines and agricultural chemicals that affect standards of living, and chemical causes or treatments for behavioral and social changes. Social workers may be involved on all levels of practice where a working knowledge of chemistry can bolster their efforts, including (but not limited to) policy analysis on ecology and the environment, mental health therapy and practice, forensic social work, and substance abuse treatment and rehabilitation (Dziegielewski & Jacinto, 2016). As advocates, social workers may also work alongside chemists and other scientists to help improve standards of living in developing nations by helping citizens set up education programs, provide and implement new technologies, and/or create new jobs in areas such as environmental remediation and sustainable agriculture and manufacturing processes where chemistry plays a crucial role in promoting well-being among individuals and their physical and social environments (Hall et al., 2016; Padilla-Rivera, Morgan-Sagastume, Noyola, & Güereca, 2016; Wilson & Schwarzman, 2016).

This chapter presents a historical context for chemistry from a broad social work and social welfare lens, providing introductory material on chemistry for the social work student and practitioner. Sections that follow investigate the integration of chemistry in biological, neurological, and pharmacological aspects of social work theory and practice, as well as environmental aspects of chemistry that inform both clinical and community practice. The chapter concludes with a brief section on the implications that the field of chemistry has for social workers today as well as potential implications for social work in the future. One important caveat for the reader is that this chapter is meant to be taken as an overview rather than a fully probative, methodologically rigorous investigation of chemistry as a scientific discipline. There are several resources cited within this text and provided in the References section that address key mathematical and scientific concepts in greater detail and are therefore recommended additional reading (March & McClure, 2012; Reedy, Wink, & Fetzer-Gislason, 2003; Zumdahl & DeCoste, 2015). Moreover, the reader is encouraged to read chapters in the current volume, such as the chapter on the science of mental illness (chapter 13), for additional information on neurochemistry as well as earlier volumes by the editors on the interrelations between chemistry and genomics, genetics, and the biological sciences (see Ginsberg, Nackerud, & Larrison, 2004).

DEFINING CHEMISTRY

Chemistry can be broadly defined as the branch of the natural sciences dealing with the identification of the substances of which matter is composed and the systematic investigation of their properties and the ways in which they interact, combine, change, and form new substances (Russell, 1980). A chemical is any compound or substance that has been purified or prepared, either organically or artificially. As Reinhardt (2008) noted, chemistry serves as a bridge between the related scientific disciplines of physics and biology, examining the intricate processes that transform matter and energy, and their impacts on biological organisms and the makeup of the physical world.

A simple example of how these three major scientific disciplines work together can be seen by taking a closer look at the human eye (see Fig. 2.1). Examining the eye, a physicist will primarily be interested in how energy (in this case, light) interacts with matter (i.e., the eye), through reflection and refraction on a molecular and atomic level. A biologist will likely first examine the organs of the eye used in vision, such as the lens, cornea, and retina with its attendant rod- and cone-like photoreceptive cells. A chemist will focus on what compounds are present in the eye that aid the light in being reflected, such as retinaldehyde, the light-sensitive molecule found in the rods and cones of the retina that is central in transmitting the molecular light energy into biological information processed by the brain (Wald, 1949).

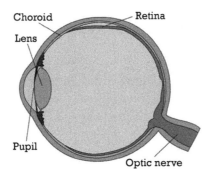

Figure 2.1 The human eye

Due to its ability to bridge between other disciplines, chemistry has been divided into several major subdisciplines and specialized branches in the modern era. These subdivisions continue to specialize, bringing chemical techniques and methods to the study of a variety of phenomena. Subdisciplines and branches of chemistry include biochemistry, inorganic chemistry, nuclear chemistry, phytochemistry, polymer chemistry, radiochemistry, synthetic chemistry, thermochemistry, and many others (Laidlaw et al., 2015).

PHILOSOPHICAL AND HISTORICAL DEVELOPMENTS IN CHEMISTRY

The earliest practical applications of chemical processes were central to the development of metallurgy, pottery, brewing, and dyeing in the ancient world (Partington, 1960). As greater understanding of the natural world and natural processes (i.e., tides, seasons, lunar and planetary orbits) began to be systematized within early (e.g., Arabian, Egyptian, Greek, and Persian) societies around the 3rd century BCE, knowledge and understanding about chemicals and chemical interactions began to be thought of as an extension of religious, philosophical, and esoteric thought, tapping into forces that were often thought to be under supernatural control (Principe, 2013).

The long and diverse history of chemistry and its origins can be found in the etymology of the word itself. From approximately the 3rd century BCE until the 14th century CE, the primary practical applications of chemical processes were found in the pursuit of alchemy (Principe, 2007). *Alchemy* comes from the Arabic word *al-kīmīā*, which can refer both to the ancient Greek word for "Egypt" as well as the Greek word for "casting together" as if combining two substances (Boyle, 1949). Alchemy concerned itself principally with purification, modification, and perfection of objects, often in pursuit of a "sacred" form of matter (Holmyard, 1931). From this pursuit, early alchemists often began with philosophical speculations on the building blocks or crucial elements of matter or the human body. Early Greek philosophers such as Aristotle, in his treatise *On Generation and Corruption*, written in approximately 350 BCE, expound on early alchemical principles around key elements of fire, air, earth, and water (see Fig. 2.2). In 50 BCE, the Roman philosopher Lucretius expanded on alchemical theories in his treatise *On the Nature of Things*.

From these philosophical bases, more applied, experimental practices began throughout the world. Alchemists began to compose texts and records on experimentation with a wide variety of naturally occurring chemicals and found metals, minerals, and plants. As Smith (2016) noted, as with many of the philosophical, mathematical, and scientific practices of these diverse cultures, dissemination occurred through the conquests of lands or migrations of peoples. Thus, alchemy was continually rediscovered and practiced, from the Hellenistic and Arab world and, from there, diffused into medieval and Renaissance Europe through Latin translations of key texts and records of alchemical experiments. This ability to progress

Figure 2.2 Bust of Aristotle (384–322 BCE)
SOURCE: By After Lysippos - Jastrow (2006), Public Domain, https://commons.wikimedia.org/w/index.php?curid=1359807

through the ages was central in the systematic development of a global knowledge base on chemical processes, and it ushered in a move from the occult practice of alchemy to the scientific pursuit of chemistry as we know it today (Principe, 2007).

Building on the discoveries and surviving theories of the ancient world, chemistry was one of the many fields of study that was transformed by the scientific revolutions between the 15th and 17th centuries, with major discoveries by Nicolaus Copernicus, Galileo Galilei, and Sir Isaac Newton. Blossoming under the influence of a new empirical method propounded by Sir Francis Bacon in his *Novum Organum* (1620) and others, scientists ushered in an age of rapid and novel experimentation with various chemical and organic compounds that began to reshape the old alchemical traditions into a testable scientific discipline (Kuhn, 1996; Partington, 1951).

Among these scientific professionals was one of the founding fathers of chemistry, Robert Boyle, who produced *The Sceptical Chymist* in 1661, where he differentiated between the claims of alchemy and the empirical scientific discoveries of the new chemistry (Sootin & Schrotter, 2011). Boyle is best known for contributing to the knowledge and understanding of the behaviors of gases under changing conditions of pressure and temperature, known today as Boyle's Law (see Fig. 2.3). His systematic study of both ancient and modern experiments led him away from the

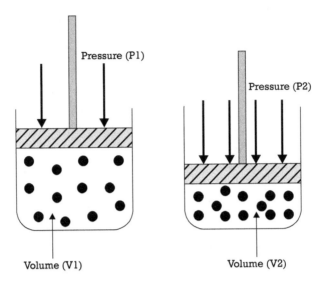

Figure 2.3 An illustration of Boyles' Law
SOURCE: By OpenStax College - Anatomy & Physiology, Connexions Web site. http://cnx.org/content/
col11496/1.6/, Jun 19, 2013., CC BY 3.0, https://commons.wikimedia.org/w/index.php?curid=30148382

classical elements of fire, air, earth, and water and inspired him to offer instead a more mechanistic alternative of atoms and chemical reactions that was conducive to rigorous experimental testing. As a result of Boyle's theories, he produced many tests for chemicals that are still in standard practice today (Kiely, 2002).

A persistent theory that transitioned from alchemical writings into early 18th-century scientific chemistry was that a single substance, called a *phlogiston*, was responsible for combustion (Partington & McKie, 1937). Drawing from the ancient Greeks and early alchemical writings, phlogiston theory was first proposed in 1667 by Johann Joachim Becher, and then restated formally by German chemist Georg Ernst Stahl in the early 18th century (Bowler & Morus, 2010). Phlogiston theory caught the attention of French chemist Antoine Lavoisier, who set about to empirically test the tenets of the theory, which, while disproving the existence of a phlogiston, provided the scientific impetus for the study of oxidation and the role that oxygen consumption plays in both combustion and corrosion of certain metals, producing rust (see Fig. 2.4).

Lavoisier, in addition to these discoveries, brought chemistry into the modern epoch by elucidating the principle of conservation of mass to differentiate elements, the basic atomic building blocks of chemicals occurring naturally, from compounds, those chemicals which are mixtures of various elements. Using this theory, Lavoisier was able to distinguish elements from chemical compounds by assigning a numerical atomic "number" and "weight" to various elements and noticing when the weight changed due to combination with other elements. Lavoisier's theory led to him recognizing and naming oxygen (1778) and hydrogen (1783) and developing a new system of chemical nomenclature used to this day (Eddy, Mauskopf, & Newman, 2014; Guerlac, 1977).

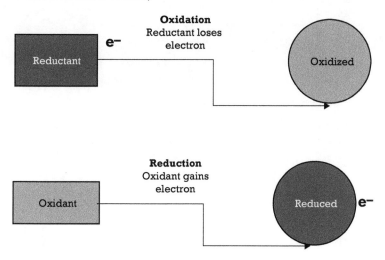

Figure 2.4 The oxidation process Authors' creation

From the 18th to the 20th centuries, chemistry again experienced a period of rapid growth and discovery. This great expansion of chemical discovery was aided by concurrent discoveries in medicine and the physical sciences (such as Louis Pasteur's experiments in the 1860s) as well as technological improvements for the detection and investigation of new elements and chemical compounds (Barnett & Barnett, 2011). One of the great culminations of this vast expansion of knowledge was when Dimitri Mendeleev proposed the periodic law and developed the first *Periodic Table of the Elements* in 1869. Building from the earlier work of Boyle and Lavoisier, Mendeleev's table was arranged according to increasing atomic weight and left holes for elements that were speculated to exist but yet to be discovered.

All elements from atomic numbers 1 (Hydrogen) to 118 (Ununoctium) have been discovered or synthesized. Newly discovered elements are monitored by the International Union of Pure and Applied Chemistry (IUPAC), with the most recent additions (elements 113, 115, 117, and 118) being confirmed by the IUPAC on December 30, 2015 (Karol, Barber, Sherrill, Vardaci, & Yamazaki, 2016). The first 94 elements exist naturally, although some only in trace amounts and synthesized in laboratories prior to their discovery in nature. Elements with atomic numbers from 95 to 118 have only been synthesized in laboratories or nuclear reactors (Emsley, 2011). Synthesis of elements having higher atomic numbers is currently underway by chemists worldwide. Figure 2.5 displays the most recent *Periodic Table of the Elements,* as of 2016.

The elements of the Periodic Table can be viewed basically, from left to right, from metals to gases, with the sole exception of hydrogen, which belongs to no specific category. More specific classifications have emerged in modern times, along with many significant groupings or subgroupings. Elements are commonly divided into metals, semimetals (metalloids), and nonmetals (Emsley, 2011). Within these groups, more specific groups, such as transition metals, rare earths, alkali metals, alkaline earths, halogens, and noble gases, were added. The majority of the classes of

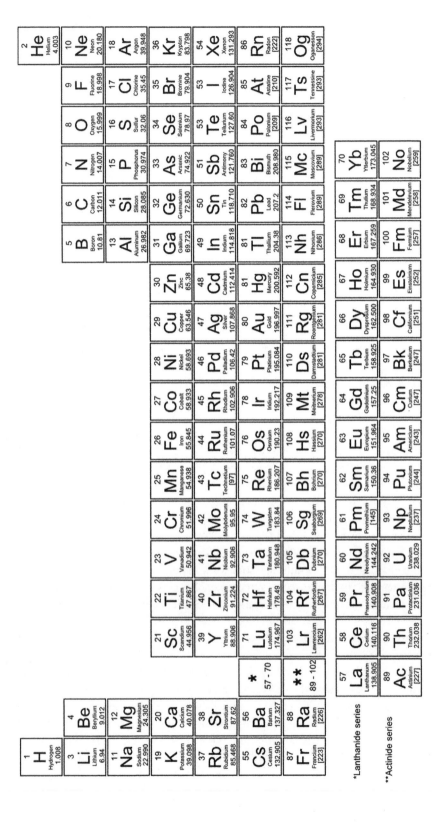

Figure 2.5 The Periodic Table

SOURCE: By Dmarcus100 - Own work, CC BY-SA 4.0, https://commons.wikimedia.org/w/index.php?curid=53071124

elements can be grouped by these specific characteristics, such as their solidity, their metallic luminescence, their atomic structure (such as the number of electrons) and their ability to carry a positive or negative "charge" (in a process called ionization), and their ability to combine with other elements, such as oxygen in the process of oxidation (Zumdahl & DeCoste, 2015). Each of these classes, along with their specific characteristics, is shown in Table 2.1.

The vast history of chemistry, spanning millennia, continues to grow and develop and, as the following sections illustrate, contribute as much to the social environment as to scientific endeavor. The great advances in chemistry by Boyle, Lavoisier, Mendeleev, and many others blazed a path by which the smallest interactions between substances can have tremendous repercussions. By examining the role that chemicals play in our bodies, our brains, and our environment, social work scholars and practitioners can tap into the history and glimpse the potential that chemistry has to shape and define our world and our future.

THE CHEMISTRY OF THE HUMAN BODY

Only six elements account for 99% of the mass of the human body (Emsley, 2011; Uthman, 2000). Carbon, hydrogen, nitrogen, oxygen, phosphorus, and sulfur are these basic "building block" elements that, either alone or combined in compounds such as water, constitute the major masses of the body and provide a vehicle for numerous biological and chemical functions (Hall, 2015). As Uthman (2000) noted, the remainder of elements present in the human body are found in trace amounts, but they play crucial roles in normative biological function.

Oxygen is found in most abundance in the human body, accounting for approximately 65% of a person's mass (Zhu, Traore, Santo, Trush, & Li, 2016). Oxygen is also one of the basic elemental components of water, which accounts for approximately 70% of the composition of the human body (Murray, Granner, Mayes, & Rodwell, 2014; Uthman, 2000). Water as a chemical compound (H_2O) consists of two hydrogen atoms bonded to one oxygen atom, but the mass of each oxygen atom is much higher than the combined mass of the hydrogen (McDowell, 2010). Hydrogen, oxygen's "partner" in the creation of water, is also predominant. However, due to these differences in weight, hydrogen atoms only account for 10% of the human body mass. In addition to being a component of water, oxygen is essential for biological and cellular respiration (Stryer, 1995).

Another essential building block is carbon, found in all organic matter. Carbon is the second most abundant element in the body, accounting for about 18% of body mass (Emsley, 2011; Uthman, 2000). Carbon can be found in proteins, carbohydrates, lipids, and nucleic acids and also plays a crucial role in biological respiration, as a key element in the byproduct of carbon dioxide (CO_2). Nitrogen is about 3.3% of body mass. It is found in proteins and nucleic acids. Calcium accounts for 1.5% of body mass and is used in the development of the teeth, bones, and muscular system (Uthman, 2000; World Health Organization, 1996). Phosphorus, potassium, sulfur, and sodium are found in trace amounts (i.e., less than 2%) in

Table 2.1 CHARACTERISTICS OF ELEMENTS

Class of Element	Characteristics
Alkali metals	Less dense than other metals One loosely bound valence electron Highly reactive, with reactivity increasing moving down the group Largest atomic radius of elements in their period Low ionization energy Low electronegativity
Alkaline earth metals	Two electrons in the valence shell Readily form divalent cations (positive oxidation states) Low electron affinity Low electronegativity
Transition metals*	Very hard, usually shiny, ductile, and malleable High melting and boiling points High thermal and electrical conductivity Form cations Tend to exhibit more than one oxidation state Low ionization energy
Metalloids or semimetals	Electronegativity and ionization energy intermediate between that of metals and nonmetals May possess a metallic luster Variable density, hardness, conductivity, and other properties Often make good semiconductors Reactivity depends on nature of other elements in the reaction
Nonmetals	High ionization energy High electronegativity Poor electrical and thermal conductors Form brittle solids Little if any metallic luster Readily gain electrons
Halogens**	Extremely high electronegativity Very reactive Seven valence electrons, so elements from this group typically exhibit a −1 oxidation state
Noble gases	The noble gases have complete valence electron shells, so they act differently. Unlike other groups, noble gases are unreactive and have very low electronegativity or electron affinity.

Authors' creation* The lanthanides (rare earths) and actinides are also transition metals. The basic metals are similar to transition metals, but they tend to be softer and to have nonmetallic properties. In a pure state, all of these elements tend to have a shiny, metallic appearance. Although there are radioisotopes of other elements, all of the actinides are radioactive.
** The halogens exhibit different physical properties from each other, but they do share chemical properties.

the human body but are key to molecular reactions in all the major body systems (World Health Organization, 1996).

As a result of these elements and their interactions, there are tens of trillions of chemical reactions happening simultaneously in the body that constitute a "living," organic being (Gropper & Smith, 2012). This collection of chemical reactions and biochemical processes is known as metabolism (see Fig. 2.6). Metabolism functions through typical patterns or pathways that chemicals take throughout the body, changing and combining as encoded within specialized chemical compounds such as deoxyribonucleic acid, or DNA (Watson & Berry, 2009). Such processes include sensitivity to environmental factors, such as temperature, nutrition and energy production, respiration, excretion or eliminating waste products from the body, growth, movement, and reproduction.

Through these processes, chemical compounds can enter and exit the body. Chemicals are breathed, swallowed, absorbed through the skin or hair, or other membranes of the body. While many chemicals that are taken in by the body are broken down and used by these processes, others can disrupt the metabolism, or lead to illness or disease. Metabolism can be anabolic, which builds molecules in the body, or catabolic, which breaks molecules down in the body (Gropper & Smith, 2012). These types of reactions are controlled by a group of proteins called enzymes. Enzymes function to maintain a healthy set of conditions inside the body needed to support these many chemical reactions. This maintenance is called homeostasis (Gropper & Smith, 2012).

Disturbing the homeostasis within the body may cause illness. Every illness results from chemical reactions that give rise to characteristic symptoms. Sometimes the body's own defenses cause changes that make us feel ill, for example, by a fever causing the body's internal temperature to rise above normal levels. The chemical compounds that make up medicines are often used to either address the symptoms that may be causing a person to feel ill or to attempt to return the body to homeostasis by encouraging one or more chemical reactions to take place within the body (Herlihy, 2013). Other social, cultural, and environmental factors. including living conditions, diet, exercise regimen, and body temperature, contribute directly to the chemical composition and reactions within an individual (Gropper & Smith, 2012).

CHEMISTRY AND THE BRAIN

Within the brain, both electrical impulses and chemical reactions impact different parts of the brain and provide a communication network between the brain and the rest of the nervous system. When a neuron is activated, a small difference in electrical charge occurs, causing the release of chemicals called neurotransmitters, which may stimulate a cell or trigger a new set of electrochemical reactions (Lajtha, Tettamanti, & Goracci, 2009).

Neurotransmitters include serotonin, dopamine, and glutamate (see Fig. 2.7). Serotonin controls functioning in mood, appetite, and sleep. Research shows that people with depression often have lower than normal levels of serotonin (National

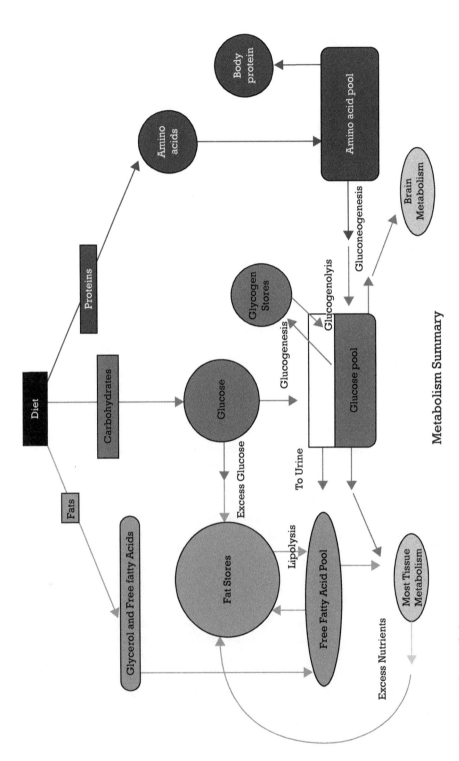

Figure 2.6 The metabolic process

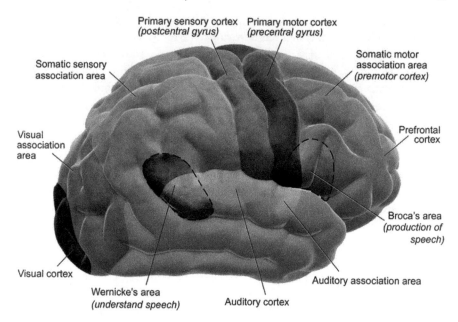

Figure 2.7 Chemical production in the human brain
SOURCE: Blausen.com staff (2014). "Medical gallery of Blausen Medical 2014". WikiJournal of Medicine 1 (2). DOI:10.15347/wjm/2014.010. ISSN 2002–4436. - Own work, CC BY 3.0, https://commons.wikimedia.org/w/index.php?curid=60100749

Alliance on Mental Illness, 2015). Dopamine is mainly involved in controlling movement and aiding the flow of information to the front of the brain, which is linked to thought and emotion. It is also linked to reward systems in the brain. Problems in producing dopamine can result in Parkinson's disease and may play a role in disorders like schizophrenia or attention-deficit/hyperactivity disorder (ADHD) (Howes et al., 2012). Glutamate—the most common neurotransmitter—may assist in learning and memory. Problems in making or using glutamate have been linked to many mental disorders, including autism, depression, obsessive-compulsive disorder (OCD), and schizophrenia (Beck, Javitt, & Howes, 2016).

These neurochemical reactions (as seen in Chapter 13) can also be disturbed and may require medication or change in the social or lived environment to cause positive change or restore equilibrium in the chemical reactions occurring in an individual's brain. Psychotropic medications may be used to adjust perceived chemical imbalances and strengthen the pathways that enable chemical reactions to naturally occur. As seen in the following section, these same pathways may be affected or permanently damaged through the repeated use or abuse of illegal drugs.

SUBSTANCE USE, MISUSE, AND ABUSE

Drugs and medicines are the chemicals that are most likely to be encountered by social work practitioners and the clients they serve. The National Institute on Drug Abuse (2014) defines drugs as follows:

Chemicals that affect the brain by tapping into its communication system and interfering with the way neurons normally send, receive, and process information. Some drugs, such as marijuana and heroin, can activate neurons because their chemical structure mimics that of a natural neurotransmitter. This similarity in structure "fools" receptors and allows the drugs to attach onto and activate the neurons. Although these drugs mimic the brain's own chemicals, they don't activate neurons in the same way as a natural neurotransmitter, and they lead to abnormal messages being transmitted through the network.

While this definition may comport most readily to illicit drugs, it is important to note that virtually any consumed chemical, including alcohol, tobacco, or food supplements, can be used to the point at which they interact directly with the body's normal chemical makeup. Drugs directly or indirectly interact with the chemistry of the brain and can impact the release or reabsorption of neurotransmission chemicals, such as dopamine (Nutt, Lingford-Hughes, Erritzoe, & Stokes, 2015). Overstimulation of the brain and nervous system with drugs, however, produces effects that are commonly held to be positive, like euphoria and energy, which strongly reinforce the behavior of drug use or cause repeated drug interaction, thus creating a pathway from substance use to misuse or abuse (Straussner, 2013). As drugs are used more frequently, impacted chemicals in the brain deregulate and more drugs are required to return the brain chemistry to its homeostasis. This cycle produces what is commonly known as physical addiction to the chemical, with consonant changes in mood, attitude, and behavior (American Society of Addiction Medicine, 2011). These broader changes to the person will typically create changes in interpersonal relationships and interactions between the addicted individual and the broader social environment, leading to addiction as both a malady and a social problem (Elster, 2012).

An addicted individual will also develop a tolerance for a particular drug of abuse, in which an increased amount of the drug or a rapid escalation in time between doses is needed to produce the same desired effects. Such increases in amounts or frequency of use can lead to profound changes in brain and body activity and may severely compromise the long-term health of the brain (The National Institute on Drug Abuse, 2014). The impact of tolerance on the brain and body can manifest in a variety of ways. Physical symptoms may mirror that of illness, with increased perspiration, increased respiratory rate, nausea, or mild to moderate body tremors. Brain and neurotransmitter-based impacts of drug tolerance may include anxiety, depression, confusion, rapid cycling of mood, diminished short-term or long-term memory, and disturbance in speech, hearing, or eyesight (Butcher, Mineka, & Hooley, 2013; Julien, 2001).

Social work researchers and practitioners working within the field of substance abuse and recovery are encouraged to gain an active working knowledge and understanding of the chemical reactions that are at work in the mind of an active or recovering drug-addicted individual (Senker & Green, 2016; Straussner, 2013). This specialized knowledge of the brain and body chemistry at work can inform treatment planning and practice decisions, and it can enable the social worker to better relate to the client's needs, offset potential difficulties in recovery, and provide direct, timely, and empirically informed treatment.

CHEMISTRY AND THE ENVIRONMENT

In addition to the chemicals that provide the building blocks for the physical environment, the human body, the brain, and those that are used for medicinal purposes, the past three decades have seen greater attention focused on those chemicals produced within the workplace, industry, and manufacturing (Kent, 2012; Thomas, DiCosimo, & Nagarajan, 2002). As Dominelli (2012) noted, ecological crises, pollution of the environment, and potential hazards to public health have galvanized both public awareness and the need for a concerted social work response to these issues. Concurrently, research in biology and chemistry has shown that innovation, technological improvement, and a strong regulatory and policy stance can provide a significant impact in both educating the public-at-large and developing ecologically sound and scientifically informed alternatives and solutions to existing environmental problems such as climate change, air and water safety, waste management, and efficient sources of renewable energy (Gray, Coates, & Hetherington, 2012).

Environmental chemistry takes as its primary focus chemical reactions that are occurring naturally on the planet—including its atmosphere, its soil, and its water supply (Williams, 2001). The focus shifted somewhat as time progressed and human society moved from agrarian means of cultivation and use of hand tools for industries like mining, brewing, dyeing, and paving to large industry. As Hudson (2014) noted, with the advent of both the Industrial Revolution throughout Western Europe and America from approximately 1750 until approximately 1840 and the development and widespread adoption of the internal combustion engine by the 1870s, attention was paid by chemists and scientists to the impact burning fuels and chemicals would have on the larger environment. Thus, scientists began to look at the chemical reactions related to both contamination and pollution within the environment.

As Chapman noted:

> Contamination is simply the presence of a substance where it should not be or at concentrations above background. Pollution is contamination that results in or can result in adverse biological effects to resident communities. All pollutants are contaminants, but not all contaminants are pollutants. (p. 492)

Today, society continues to face environmental problems created by reliance upon internal combustion of carbon-based or "fossil" fuels like coal, oil, and natural gas (see Fig. 2.8). Because the chemical reactions needed to create combustion of these substances rely on the process of oxidation discussed earlier, the byproducts (including carbon dioxide and other potential pollutants) must be considered for potential adverse effects on the air and water quality around the area of combustion,

Petrochemical and Chemical Industry

Petroleum Industry etc.

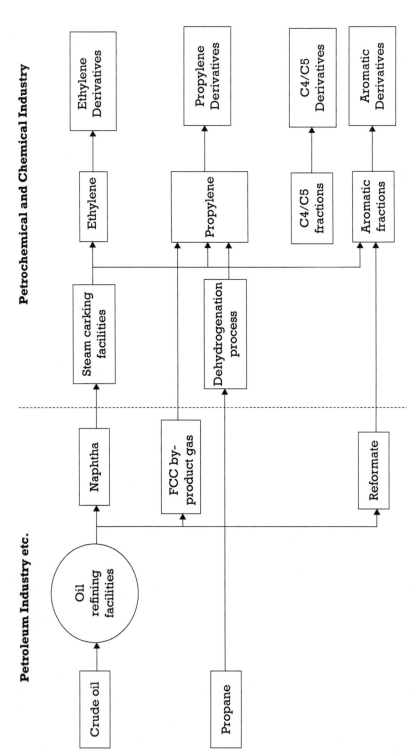

Figure 2.8 Petrochemistry Authors' creation

where any waste products are being deposited, and the lasting impact this may have in terms of temperature rise and climatological impact (Harper, 2015).

Both chemists working in large industries like fuel development (known as petrochemistry), energy, and environmental science and social workers operating in the fields of medicine, public health, social welfare policy, and ecological or environmental social work are united in their overarching professional mission for chemicals to be used in the safest and most environmentally friendly way (Dominelli, 2012; Gray et al., 2012). Recently, research in chemistry has produced new methods and materials that are more sustainable and environmentally friendly while retaining viability within the respective industries and the global marketplace. Some examples of these types of chemicals and compounds are included in Table 2.2.

Strengthening the science of chemistry through research and development is a necessary component to reducing potential negative impacts arising from our technological and societal advancements. As Steffen, Crutzen, and McNeill (2007) noted:

An alternative pathway into the future is based on the recognition that the threat of further global change is serious enough that it must be dealt with proactively . . . by vastly improved technology and management, wise use of Earth's resources, control of human and domestic animal population, and overall careful use and restoration of the natural environment. The ultimate goal is to

Table 2.2 CHARACTERISTICS OF ENVIRONMENTALLY FRIENDLY CHEMICALS

Type of Environmental Chemical	Characteristics
Biofuels	Transportation fuel derived from biomass. A wide range of biomass products such as sugar cane, rapeseed, corn, straw, wood, animal and agriculture residues, and waste can be transformed into fuels for transport.
Bioplastics	Production of plastic materials using natural sources such as plants, which are then biodegradable.
Insulation	Enhanced insulating materials to enable more energy-efficient homes and buildings.
Lightweight plastic composites	Help reduce cars' and airplanes' fuel consumption.
Fuel cells	Used to power cars or motorbikes, hydrogen fuel cells produce water vapor instead of exhaust gases.
New lighting technologies	Organic light-emitting diodes (OLEDS) produce more light with less electricity.
Wind turbines and solar paneling	Although both of these traditionally rely on materials produced by the chemical industry, recently the metal blades of wind turbines have largely been replaced by blades made of more environmentally friendly fiberglass-reinforced polyester to stand up to the severest weather.

Authors' creation

reduce the human modification of the global environment to avoid dangerous or difficult-to-control levels and rates of change. (p. 619)

CONCLUSIONS

As an educational component of social work practice, a working knowledge of chemistry and the biological sciences is important for all students, researchers, and practitioners. These fields provide evidence and empirical data that inform and ground the biopsychosocial perspective that informs a great deal of practice knowledge and technique (Engel, 1980; Schwartz, 1982). As Urberg (1989) noted, the use of "basic scientific principles derived from chemistry in conjunction with the model ... will assure successful results" (p. 644). Social workers should be encouraged to have an understanding and to continue to cultivate an understanding of the underlying science that impacts the persons they serve and the environments in which they practice (Dominelli, 2012; Ginsberg et al., 2004).

According to the Bureau of Labor Statistics (2016), of the over 600,000 social workers, approximately 20% work directly in issues of substance abuse and mental health, where a knowledge of the chemical and biological antecedents to social and behavioral issues is a necessary component of ethical practice. Although this percentage may seem small, it is accepted that many social work practitioners are likely to encounter issues related to substance abuse regardless of their settings, from hospitals and private clinics to neighborhood associations, nonprofit organizations, and school systems, and regardless of their particular field of practice, from clinical to community centered, or even in the areas of public policy and advocacy (Smith, Whitaker, & Weismiller, 2006). Social workers trained in the biopsychosocial model will very likely rely upon a background in the natural sciences to execute treatment plans and inform diagnostic, strategic, or policy-based decisions.

One of the fastest growing areas of social work practice is environmental social work. As Teixeira and Krings (2015) noted, "social workers, traditionally concerned with the promotion of human rights and social justice, are primed to be strong partners in environmental justice movements" (p. 515). Social work educators, practitioners, and researchers with a pronounced interest in environmental issues can utilize a knowledge of chemical interactions and environmental impact. This information can inform various avenues for community organizing, advocacy, and policy work within several arenas of social work practice.

This chapter provided a basic overview of the philosophical, historical, and present-day conceptions of chemistry with particular focus on where these concepts inform social work theory and practice. The reader is provided with a solid foundation in chemical processes, related terminology, and areas where social work and chemistry intersect. As stated in the introductory paragraphs of this chapter, the reader is encouraged to seek out additional references to continue to inform knowledge building and to continue education in the areas of chemistry, biochemistry, neurochemistry, environmental chemistry, or drug interactions that comport best with his or her chosen field of practice.

REFERENCES

American Society of Addiction Medicine. (2011). Definition of addiction. Retrieved from http://www.asam.org/quality-practice/definition-of-addiction

Barnett, J. A., & Barnett, L. (2011). *Yeast research: A historical overview*. Washington, DC: American Society of Microbiology Press.

Beck, K., Javitt, D. C., & Howes, O. D. (2016). Targeting glutamate to treat schizophrenia: Lessons from recent clinical studies. *Psychopharmacology, 233*(13), 2425–2428. https://doi.org/10.1007/s00213-016-4318-6

Bowler, P. J., & Morus, I. R. (2010). *Making modern science: A historical survey*. Chicago, IL: University of Chicago Press.

Boyle, R. (1949). *The sceptical chymist or, Chymico-physical doubts and paradoxes*. PLOS. https://doi.org/10.5479/sil.140935.39088002863561

Bureau of Labor Statistics. (2016). *Social workers: Occupational outlook handbook*. Retrieved from http://www.bls.gov/ooh/community-and-social-service/social-workers.htm.

Butcher, J. N., Mineka, S., & Hooley, J. M. (2013). *Abnormal psychology*. New York, NY: Pearson.

Dominelli, L. (2012). *Green social work: From environmental crises to environmental justice*. Cambridge, MA: Polity.

Dziegielewski, S. F., & Jacinto, G. A. (2016). *Social work practice and psychopharmacology: A person-in-environment approach*. New York, NY: Springer.

Eddy, M. D., Mauskopf, S. H., & Newman, W. R. (2014). An introduction to chemical knowledge in the early modern world. *Osiris, 29*(1), 1–15. https://doi.org/10.1086/678110

Elster, J. (2012). *Strong feelings: Emotion, addiction and human behavior*. Cambridge, MA: MIT Press.

Emsley, J. (2011). *Nature's building blocks: An A to Z guide to the elements*. Oxford, UK: Oxford University Press.

Engel, G. L. (1980). The clinical application of the biopsychosocial model. *American Journal of Psychiatry, 137*(5), 535–544. https://doi.org/10.1176/ajp.137.5.535

Ginsberg, L. H., Nackerud, L. G., & Larrison, C. R. (2004). *Human biology for social workers: Development, ecology, genetics, and health*. Boston, MA: Pearson/Allyn and Bacon.

Gray, M., Coates, J., & Hetherington, T. (2012). *Environmental social work*. New York, NY: Routledge.

Gropper, S. S., & Smith, J. L. (2012). *Advanced nutrition and human metabolism*. Cengage Learning. www.cengage.com.

Guerlac, H. (1977). *Essays and papers in the history of modern science*. Baltimore, MD: Johns Hopkins University Press.

Hall, J. E. (2015). *Guyton and Hall textbook of medical physiology*. Amsterdam: Elsevier Health Sciences.

Hall, T. E., Engebretson, J., O'Rourke, M., Piso, Z., Whyte, K., & Valles, S. (2016). The need for social ethics in interdisciplinary environmental science graduate programs: Results from a nation-wide survey in the United States. *Science and Engineering Ethics, 23*(2), 565–588. https://doi.org/10.1007/s11948-016-9775-0

Harper, C. (2015). *Environment and society.* London, UK: Routledge.

Herlihy, B. (2013). *The human body in health and illness.* Amsterdam: Elsevier Health Sciences.

Holmyard, E. J. (1931). *Makers of chemistry.* Oxford, UK: Clarendon Press.

Howes, O. D., Kambeitz, J., Kim, E., Stahl, D., Slifstein, M., Abi-Dargham, A., & Kapur, S. (2012). The nature of dopamine dysfunction in schizophrenia and what this means for treatment. *Archives of General Psychiatry, 69*(8). https://doi.org/10.1001/archgenpsychiatry.2012.169

Hudson, P. (2014). *The industrial revolution.* Xxx: Bloomsbury.

Julien, R. M. (2001). *A primer of drug action: A concise nontechnical guide to the actions, uses, and side effects of psychoactive drugs, revised and updated.* New York, NY: Holt. https://doi.org/10.1111/j.1465-3362.2008.00046_2.x

Karol, P. J., Barber, R. C., Sherrill, B. M., Vardaci, E., & Yamazaki, T. (2016). Discovery of the elements with atomic numbers Z = 113, 115 and 117 (IUPAC Technical Report). *Pure and Applied Chemistry, 88*(1–2). https://doi.org/10.1515/pac-2015-0502

Kent, J. A. (2012). *Riegel's handbook of industrial chemistry.* Washington, DC: Springer Science & Business Media.

Kiely, T. (2002). *Science and litigation.* Boca Raton, FL: CRC Press. https://doi.org/10.1201/9781420042610

Kuhn, T. S. (1996). *The structure of scientific revolutions.* Chicago, IL: University of Chicago Press.

Laidlaw, W. G., Ryan, D. E., Horlick, G., Clark, H. C., Takats, J., Cowie, M., & Lemieux, R. U. (2015). Chemistry subdisciplines. Retrieved from http://www.thecanadianencyclopedia.com/en/article/chemistry-subdisciplines/

Lajtha, A., Tettamanti, G., & Goracci, G. (2009). *Handbook of neurochemistry and molecular neurobiology.* Berlin, Germany: Springer.

March, J. L., & McClure, C. P. (2012). *Introductory chemistry: A guided inquiry approach.* Belmont, CA: Brooks/Cole.

McDowell, J. (2010). *Encyclopedia of human body systems.* Xxx: ABC-CLIO.

Murray, R. K., Granner, D. K., Mayes, P. A., & Rodwell, V. W. (2014). *Harper's illustrated biochemistry.* New York, NY: McGraw-Hill.

National Alliance on Mental Illness. (2015). Mental health facts in America. Retrieved from https://www.nami.org/NAMI/media/NAMI-Media/Infographics/GeneralMHFacts.pdf

National Institute on Drug Abuse. (2014). Drugs, brains, and behavior: The science of addiction. Retrieved from https://www.drugabuse.gov/publications/drugs-brains-behavior-science-addiction/drugs-brain

Nutt, D. J., Lingford-Hughes, A., Erritzoe, D., & Stokes, P. R. A. (2015). The dopamine theory of addiction: 40 years of highs and lows. *Nature Reviews Neuroscience, 16*(5), 305–312. https://doi.org/10.1038/nrn3939

Padilla-Rivera, A., Morgan-Sagastume, J. M., Noyola, A., & Güereca, L. P. (2016). Addressing social aspects associated with wastewater treatment facilities. *Environmental Impact Assessment Review, 57,* 101–113. https://doi.org/10.1016/j.eiar.2015.11.007

Partington, J. R. (1960). Short reviews. *Nature, 188*(4753), 837. https://doi.org/10.1038/188837c0

Partington, J. R. (1951). Chemistry as rationalised alchemy. *Bulletin of the British Society for the History of Science, 1*(6), 129. https://doi.org/10.1017/s0950563600000543

Partington, J. R., & McKie, D. (1937). Historical studies on the phlogiston theory—I. The levity of phlogiston. *Annals of Science, 2*(4), 361–404. https://doi.org/10.1080/00033793700200691

Principe, L. M. (2007). *Chymists and chymistry: Studies in the history of alchemy and early modern chemistry.* Sagamore Beach, MA: Watson.

Principe, L. M. (2013). *The secrets of alchemy.* Chicago, IL: University of Chicago Press.

Reedy, P., Wink, D., & Fetzer-Gislason, (2003). *Lab experiments in introductory chemistry.* San Franciso, CA: W.H. Freeman.

Reinhardt, C. (2008). *Chemical sciences in the 20th century: Bridging boundaries.* Birmingham, AL: John Wiley & Sons.

Russell, J. B. (1980). *General chemistry.* Columbus, OH: McGraw-Hill.

Schwartz, G. E. (1982). Testing the biopsychosocial model: The ultimate challenge facing behavioral medicine? *Journal of Consulting and Clinical Psychology, 50*(6), 1040.

Senker, S., & Green, G. (2016). Understanding recovery: The perspective of substance misusing offenders. *Drugs and Alcohol Today, 16*(1), 16–28.

Smith, M. J. W., Whitaker, T., & Weismiller, T. (2006). Social workers in the substance abuse treatment field: A snapshot of service activities. *Health & Social Work, 31*(2), 109–115.

Smith, P. H. (2016). *The business of alchemy: Science and culture in the Holy Roman Empire.* Princeton, NJ: Princeton University Press.

Sooton, H., & Schrotter, G. (2011). *Robert Boyle, founder of modern chemistry.* Whitefish, MT: Literary Licensing, LLC.

Steffen, W., Crutzen, P. J., & McNeill, J. R. (2007). The Anthropocene: Are humans now overwhelming the great forces of nature. *AMBIO: A Journal of the Human Environment, 36*(8), 614–621.

Straussner, S. L. A. (2013). *Clinical work with substance-abusing clients.* New York, NY: Guilford.

Stryer, L. (1995). *Biochemistry.* San Francisco, CA: W. H. Freeman.

Teixeira, S., & Krings, A. (2015). Sustainable social work: An environmental justice framework for social work education. *Social Work Education, 34*(5), 513–527.

Thomas, S. M., DiCosimo, R., & Nagarajan, V. (2002). Biocatalysis: Applications and potentials for the chemical industry. *TRENDS in Biotechnology, 20*(6), 238–242.

Urberg, M. (1989). Chemistry—a scientific model for family medicine? *Journal of Family Practice, 29*(6), 644–649.

Uthman, E. (2000). Elemental composition of the human body. *American Board of Pathology.* https://www.scribd.com/document/387307102/elemental-composition-of-the-human-body

Wald, G. (1949). The photochemistry of vision. *Documenta Ophthalmologica, 3*(1), 94–137.

Watson, J. D., & Berry, A. (2009). *DNA: The secret of life.* New York, NY: Knopf.

Williams, I. D. (2001). *Environmental chemistry: a modular approach.* Hoboken, NJ: Wiley.

Wilson, M. P., & Schwarzman, M. R. (2016). Toward a new US chemicals policy: rebuilding the foundation to advance new science, green chemistry, and environmental health. *Industrial Chemistry: New Applications, Processes and Systems, 117*(8), 176.

World Health Organization. (1996). *Trace elements in human nutrition and health.* Geneva, Switzerland: World Health Organization.

Zhu, H., Traore, K., Santo, A., Trush, M. A., & Li, Y. R. (2016). Oxygen and oxygen toxicity: The birth of concepts. *Reactive Oxygen Species, 1*(1), 1–8.

Zumdahl, S. S., & DeCoste, D. J. (2015). *Basic chemistry.* Scarborough, Ontario: Nelson Education.

3

Social Work and the "Far-Out Sciences"

of Physics, Astronomy, and Geometry

The physical sciences have a good bit to offer human services professionals—if nothing else, they help organize their thinking and show a model for being skeptical and objective in what they think and do.

—LEON H. GINSBERG

The purpose of this chapter is to aid social work students and practitioners to peer into the scientific world of the "far-out sciences" of physics, astronomy, and geometry. It is a gross understatement to claim that these areas of scientific study and thought are of great significance and complication. Physicists, astronomers, and advanced mathematicians who specialize in or practice geometry devote their lives to the study of these complex and often difficult-to-understand areas of scientific wonder. Physics and astronomy, in particular, have helped people understand (and wonder about) the nature of the world and the universe around us. Astronomers assist us with knowledge and understanding of the architecture of the cosmos that surrounds us. Those who advance the study of geometry assist us in understanding the properties and relationships of points, lines, angles, surfaces, and solids (Rovelli, 2016; Tallack, 2001). Taken together, these areas of scientific study are the source of explanations of almost all physical phenomena—gravity, light, movement, space, electronics, magnetism—and just about anything else one can think of. Of course, the chapter does not fully explain all these phenomena. It focuses, instead, on the application of a number of the major tenets of physics, astronomy, and geometry to the practice of social work as a means of both helping social work practitioners and their clients, at all systems levels, understand the world around them and how science is a constant source of discovery and advance. Enhanced, restored, and/or achieved functioning of persons, at all systems levels, is better achieved with a more informed understanding of the world around us. The sciences of physics, astronomy, and geometry assist us in understanding the presence of uncertainty in our lives and the central idea that it is interaction that serves as a cornerstone of existence—between particles so small we can never see them

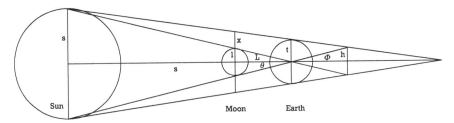

Figure 3.1 Hipparchus construction illustrates the link between physics, astronomy, and geometry
Source: By Dedwarmo - Own work, CC BY-SA 4.0, https://commons.wikimedia.org/w/index.php?curid=49189083

and planets so distant that they can only be observed with super telescopes, and ideas so big and complex that we can only ponder them (Rovelli, 2016). And, yes, even interactions between and among people matter to our understanding of the world around us, and even the universe that surrounds us.

A major premise of the chapter, and one hopes a major takeaway for the social work reader, is that these major sciences, physics, astronomy, and geometry, are interrelated (see Fig. 3.1). For example, a number of major theoretical formulations in physics and astronomy use axioms central to geometry in drawing their conclusions. In fact, all physical and natural sciences use mathematics in defining their laws and theories. Although this book illustrates scientific concepts in words, a complete text in any of the fields discussed, astronomy, geometry, and physics, will use mathematical explanations, especially equations.

ENERGY

Physics from its earliest development has studied and developed concepts of energy. Like water, energy is a finite resource. Again, there is the same amount of energy in the world today as there was at the beginning. Of course, energy takes many forms such as matter or things, which always contain potential energy. The famous Albert Einstein formula, $e = mc^2$, essentially illustrates that energy is mass (or matter) times squared (Rovelli, 2016).

How to provide the nation with sufficient energy is an ongoing political, economic, and social concern (see Fig. 3.2). The fossil fuels that have historically provided electricity are a source of climate change and global warming, which are discussed in more detail in Chapter 6. Nuclear energy is used in some parts of the nation, but there are concerns about possible hazards from the use of atomic energy, and the disposition and storage of nuclear fuel are issues wherever nuclear power is used. Illnesses that affect those who work in the nuclear industry result from exposure to nuclear power. For example, the incidence of cancer among employees of the Savannah River Plant in South Carolina, which has produced chemicals for the construction of atomic and hydrogen bombs since World War II, is higher than would normally be expected in a population. The hope is that power generated by wind and sun will replace or at least minimize the use of

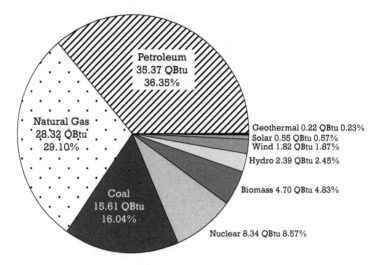

Figure 3.2 Energy consumption in the United States
SOURCE: By Delphi234 - Own work, CC0, https://commons.wikimedia.org/w/index.php?curid=37193359

fossil and nuclear fuels in the future. In some parts of the United States, the generation of power is the most important social issue. One of the major present-day controversies in energy production is the practice of fracking, a process for extracting oil and natural gas from deposits that were once considered inaccessible. Obtaining oil from great depths with new technology increased the production of oil and natural gas in many parts of the United States. The high costs of drilling so deeply were offset by the increased scarcity and value of petroleum. Although it is not a major contributor to global warming, the process causes new problems, especially earthquakes. Oklahoma, a state whose economy had long been based on oil and natural gas extraction, uses fracking extensively. The state had scarcely experienced earthquakes for much of its history, but in 2014 it had 900 (Sanburn, March 21, 2016) The seismic faults, according to Sanburn, that lie under Oklahoma were dormant for 300 million years—and active in causing earthquakes in the 2000s.

It is useful to keep in mind how the sciences of physics and astronomy and their relationship with the existent finite amount of energy may impact the lives of persons, particularly those persons in positions of societal disadvantage all around the world. In fact, these disciplines explain much of what happens in the modern world.

PRINCIPLES AND IDEAS

Physics is the science that deals with matter and motion—essentially everything in the world. The academic study of physics is a complex field with many subdivisions. Theoretical physicists, for example, such as Albert Einstein, conceptualize and develop mathematical formulas that describe and explain the ways in which things—from tiny atoms through whole planets and the universe—work and change over time.

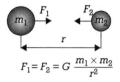

$$F_1 = F_2 = G\,\frac{m_1 \times m_2}{r^2}$$

Figure 3.3 Laws of gravitation

The origins of physics are tied to the origins of astronomy. Drawing conclusions about the motions of the planets and stars; understanding gravity and its effects on all things; learning such fundamental facts as the size of the world, the patterns of planetary circling of the sun, the ways in which seasons change, and the methods for determining time all originated with physics and the work of physicists (see Fig. 3.3). The learnings of physics made chemistry, nuclear energy, modern transportation, and virtually all other science-based developments possible. However, engineers, many of whom are, in many ways, applied physicists, do not always note their contributions from physics, although much of modern technology, science, and engineering is based on the discoveries of physics. Much of medicine and dentistry has procedures and treatments that involve physics. Modern acoustic systems have bases in physics as do modern optics, including cameras and their lenses. Computers and the storage devices that make them work such as magnetic tape and disks have roots in physics. So without the discoveries of physics the modern world would be much different—and not nearly so modern.

NEWTON'S LAW OF UNIVERSAL GRAVITATION

A few basic ideas and principles within physics are important for the social work reader to achieve a modicum of understanding of this important scientific area. Carlo Rovelli (2016), an Italian theoretical physicist, has written a wonderfully approachable book, *Seven Brief Lessons on Physics*. In only 81 pages of text Rovelli explains to the nonscientist reader (1) Einstein's theory of relativity, (2) quantum mechanics, (3) the architecture of the cosmos, (4) elementary particles, (5) quantum gravity, (6) probability and black holes, and (7) how people can even begin to understand these complex, often befuddling ideas. Even though these brief lessons and their divergent topics may seem daunting, it is considered essential by the authors of this book that social work students and practitioners try to gain a basic understanding of physics. And even though seemingly a bit less complex (but not really so), the premise of the constant speed of light, actually discovered by Albert Einstein (1879–1955), seems a bit more approachable for the nonscientist to accept and begin to understand (see Fig. 3.4). Some of the other basic truth premises about the world are considered to have been first promulgated by Sir Isaac Newton (1643–1727), even though Aristotle, the Greek philosopher, mentioned some of his basic and quite similar ideas centuries before.

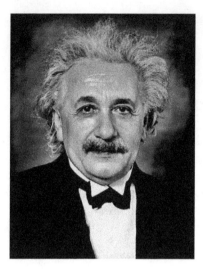

Figure 3.4 Albert Einstein circa 1935
SOURCE: By Sophie Delar, photographer; published in 1955 by "unknown press organization" per source - RR Auction and Einstein's World, Public Domain, https://commons.wikimedia.org/w/index.php?curid=23932774

Newton's laws of motion, outlined later, are fundamental. But he is also the promulgator or discoverer of gravitation, which is fundamental to all physics. Gravity is often thought of in terms of things being attracted to the ground, which keeps us and the things we possess from floating around. We recognize that if we drop something, gravity makes it fall downward. But gravity is universal and is not only a gravitational field, but rather the gravitation field is the space itself. This is the eventual idea of the general theory of relativity put forth later by Einstein (Rovelli, 2016). The Earth to which we dropped an object is also exerting gravity on the object. Newton also applied the universal idea of gravity to the planets and stars, which were a basic interest of all the early scientists. He explained that the gravity that we understand on Earth was also the force that kept the planets in relationships with each other. Gravity was the force that affected the orbits around the sun and the physical relationships of all other planets and stars. These change as the Earth spins and the tilt of the Earth at varying angles and varying times of the year causes seasons. But it is gravity that keeps it all together and in relationships among all the stars and planets.

The universality of gravity means that all things—from atoms and their constituent parts up to planets—have impact on all other things and are impacted by all other things. Most people have learned by the time they have completed basic studies in school that gravity makes objects fall to the ground, because the ground is pulling them downward through gravity. Less well understood is that the opposite is also true: the ground pushes upward because of gravity. So the dropped object is attracted through gravity to the ground, but the ground is also pushing upward because of its gravity. Of course, the results of the pushing are less obvious than the dropping because the ground is extremely large and the dropped object is small. However, it is worth noting that both are exerting influence on the other. Another way of discussing gravity is to note that all things have an impact on all other things.

This focus on the relationships among planets and things, all affected by gravity, is central to Einstein's famous theory of general relativity, which he applied to the planets, space, and relationships among all things.

SPECIAL AND GENERAL RELATIVITY

Special and general relativity are the names of Einstein's discoveries, and they are different. Despite the language usage, special relativity is less complicated than general relativity (see Fig. 3.5). Special relativity can ignore the effects of gravity and acceleration, while general relativity incorporates them into its calculations. In essence, when considering general relativity, one must look at the observer as well as the observed. Since both are moving (the observer is on a moving planet and the objects, such as planets are also moving), they have effects on one another. We are not aware of these processes from simple observation—the speeds are so great that we can't encompass them in our minds. The measurements of general and special relativity are made in specialized, laboratory facilities. But they are important in everyday life, nevertheless. Such phenomena as GPS and even lasers, compact discs,

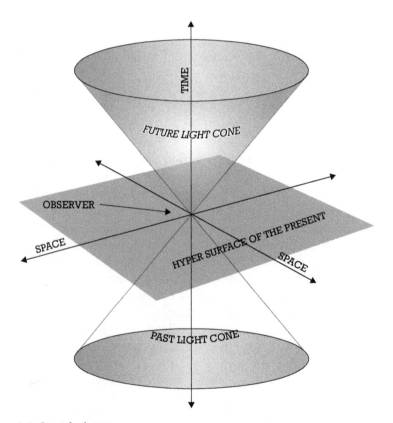

Figure 3.5 Special relativity
SOURCE: By SVG version: K. Aainsqatsi at en.wikipediaOriginal PNG version: Stib at en.wikipedia - Transferred from en.wikipedia to Commons.(Original text: self-made), CC BY-SA 3.0, https://commons.wikimedia.org/w/index.php?curid=2210907

and cell phones, are all based on understanding and applying the Einstein laws of relativity (Nitta, Yamamoto, & Takatsu, 2011).

MATTER AND MASS

A key principle of physics is that everything is composed of atoms (see Fig. 3.6). These contain smaller parts, neutrons, electrons, protons, and a nucleus, which is a dense, though small, central region. Although much of the space within an atom is empty, the electrons and neutrons contain even smaller matter, which is known as quarks. How big—or how small—are atoms? Some physicists explain that if all the atoms in a grapefruit were the size of a blueberry, the grapefruit would have to be the size of Earth. (One of the better and more accessible sources of basic ideas in physics is Holzner's [2010] *Physics Essentials for Dummies.*)

Model of an Atom

Although physicists and chemists know a good deal about atoms and molecules, much of the matter in the universe's space is not known and is referred to as "dark matter." And parts of the universe consist of "black holes," which are remnants of stars that exploded in the past. Other elements of dark matter are particles that are too weak to measure and neutrinos, which seem numerous but very small. Faint stars and other forms of known matter may make up the rest. (Dinwiddie,

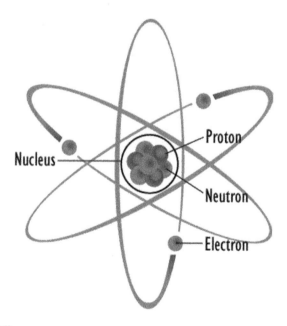

Figure 3.6 Atom

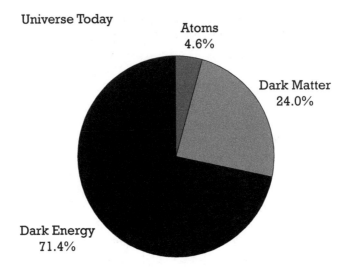

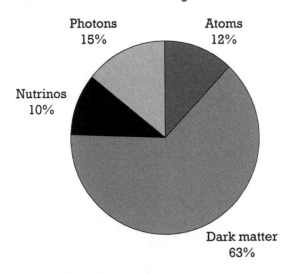

Figure 3.7 Universe today and long ago
SOURCE: Redrawn based on data by NASA: Data Credit: ASA / WMAP Science Team (https://map.gsfc.nasa.gov/media/080998/index.html)

2009) Essentially, scientists are unable to see definitively much of what exists in the universe, so the theory of dark matter filling the unmeasurable space is the basis for understanding the whole universe. Dark matter may be 23% of the universe. The universe is so vast that it is no surprise that only some small parts of it are known definitively by scientists (see Fig. 3.7).

In 2016, our understanding of black holes was dramatically changed (Overbye, 2016). The earliest theories purported that black holes "swallowed" all that may have been around them. Later studies, reported by Stephen Hawking, a legendary theoretical physicist, and some colleagues suggested that the holes had leakages and

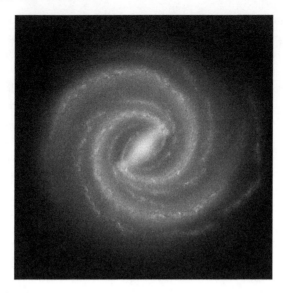

Figure 3.8 Black hole
SOURCE: NASA/JPL-Caltech https://www.nasa.gov/audience/forstudents/k-4/stories/nasa-knows/what-is-a-black-hole-k4.html

that their contents were likely to eventually escape the holes and enter the universe (see Fig. 3.8). While the black holes concepts and controversies have no apparent immediate application to social work education and practice, it is important to remember that being curious about the principles and ideas put forth in physics is essential to helping others understand the world around them, and it may have application to the attempts by persons to understand their own lives. For even though physics and astronomy assist us in attempting to understand highly complex ideas, one of the things that we understand the least about is ourselves, and how it is that people function, exist, and thrive in a complex world. The good thing is that it is people (as far as we know) who do most of the observing of all things, from the complex to the seemingly simple (Rovelli, 2016).

THE PLANETS AND ROTATION

Richard Feynman (1991), one of the most highly regarded physicists, points out that rotation is a characteristic of most structures in the universe. This scientific theoretical premise is thought to be true for the smallest structures to the largest. The Earth rotates on an axis once every 26 days and once around the sun every year. The sun rotates, as do the other stars in our galaxy, once around the galaxy every 230 million years. And, of course, the electrons in atoms rotate continuously. This concept of a constantly spinning universe is a useful and nonintuitive fact about our lives and our universe.

Some of Newton's most important contributions to understanding the world include these laws of motion:

1. Every object in a state of uniform motion tends to remain in that state of motion unless an external force is applied to it. That means that if an object is moving it will continue to move until something slows it down and stops it. Without some force, objects will remain still.

2. Objects, regardless of their size or weight, dropped from a height will reach the bottom at the same time, because of gravity, unless something slows them down. An old favorite childhood debate—whether a feather or a brick thrown out an upstairs window would reach the ground at different times—was answered by Newton. They would arrive at the same time unless some force (wind, for example) would slow one of them, most likely the feather, down.

3. For every action, there is an equal and opposite reaction.

Social workers may follow that principle as matters of human behavior, but Newton meant physical things. It is important to note that the forces of gravity, following this principle or law, mean that everything has an effect on every other thing. So the feather or brick being attracted to the ground is also a phenomenon of the earth acting on the feather or brick. It's not possible to see the attraction of the earth to the item that falls, but it is important to understand that both affect each other as opposed to only the brick or the feather being attracted to the earth.

Newton also invented calculus, a mathematical process that lends itself to quantifying physical properties (Feynman, 1991; Simmons, 1996).

There are several other ideas, principles, and theoretical notions germane to physics that can ideally be known to learned persons such as undergraduate and graduate students in social work, even though they may not take courses in or otherwise study the physical or natural sciences extensively. For example, most social work students know, from their K–12 studies, that the planets in the solar system "orbit" around the sun on a fixed basis with varying orbits among the planets. Many hold the erroneous belief that the orbits are in regular circles. However, Johannes Kepler (1571–1630) discovered, in the early 17th century that, in fact, the orbits are elliptical, flattened circles, rather than fully circular. Kepler used geometric measures to define and explain the movements of the planets (Chaisson & McMillan, 2010; see Fig. 3.9). Early astronomers with very weak telescopes were able to confirm

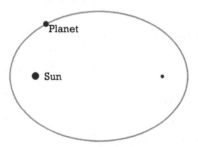

Figure 3.9 Kepler (1571–1630) discovered in the early 17th century that orbits are elliptical

that and explain it through their observations of the planets and the movements among them.

Another common misperception among those with only a casual knowledge of the physical and natural sciences is that the changes in seasons are related to the changing distance of the Earth from the sun. In fact, the changes relate to the tipping of the angle of the Earth to the sun—not the distance from the sun. These kinds of observed truths were also developed by early astronomers who were able to define the planetary world with little more than telescopes that today would be simply toys or useful for sporting and theatrical events. Galileo Galilei made some of the most important early discoveries in the 16th and 17th centuries (see Fig. 3.10). He was charged with heresy by church leaders in part because he disproved the religious doctrine that Earth was the center of the universe and that the planets, including the sun, orbited around the Earth.

Galileo's early conflicts with religious authorities are strikingly similar to today's disagreements between scientists and politicians on the fact of and the implications of climate change, which is discussed in detail in Chapter 6. Conflicts between scientists and religious institutions have a long history. The religious pushback against scientific discoveries is perhaps best exemplified by the Creation Museum in Hebron, Kentucky. Visitors to the museum see exhibits of humans interacting with dinosaurs, illustrating the Museum founders' beliefs that the world is about 6,000 years old, based on the writings in Genesis. The Bible dates the ages of Adam and Eve and patriarchs such as Abraham so that the periods covered in the Old

Figure 3.10 Portrait of GalileBy
SOURCE: By Justus Sustermans - http://www.nmm.ac.uk/mag/pages/mnuExplore/PaintingDetail.
cfm?ID=BHC2700, Public Domain, https://commons.wikimedia.org/w/index.php?curid=230543

Testament constitute a theory of a "Young Earth," certainly not an Earth that is as old as billions of years, discussed later in this chapter. In the Creation Museum, visitors may have their photos taken in the company of dinosaurs, which the founders believe coexisted with humans. The Museum is completing a reconstruction of Noah's Ark, another of the major events discussed in Genesis in response to the great flood of those times. So the Creationist movement, including its museum and its publication, *Answers*, believes in a Young Earth, based upon the historical writings in the Old Testament, and counters the beliefs of modern scientists, who consider the Earth to be over 4 billion years old.

Of course, the major target of the creationists is Charles Darwin, whose book *Origin of Species* was published in 1859. It is the most often credited source of the concepts of evolution and "natural selection," theories that Darwin published jointly with Alfred Russell Wallace in 1858 (Tallack, 2001) As mentioned, these ideas conflicted, in the minds of some, with established religious doctrine about the development of the world and the species within it. However, Darwin did not think of his theories as alternatives to religion but as complements to religious understandings (Tallack, 2001).

TIME

Physics and astronomy also help us attempt to understand the concept of time. We are principally satisfied to understand that time, using a base 60 system, divides hours into 60 minutes, minutes into 60 seconds, and so forth. Since 1967, however, a second has been scientifically defined in terms of the time an electron spins on its own axis in an atom of cesium. An international body, the Commission on Weights

Figure 3.11 Louis Essen (right) and Jack Parry (left) standing next to the world's first caesium-133 atomic clock

SOURCE: By National Physical Laboratory - http://www.npl.co.uk/upload/img/essen-experiment_1.jpg, Public Domain, https://commons.wikimedia.org/w/index.php?curid=5543813

and Measures, created that definition. Now atomic clocks can measure a second with an accuracy of 13 decimal places (see Fig. 3.11). There are now "atomic clocks" that correct themselves by synchronizing with the standards of the Commission on Weights and Measures. Wrist watches also self-correct daily in terms of the international standards of time (Trefil, 1992).

QUANTUM PHYSICS

Classical physics, of the kind defined by Newton, proposes certainties—persuasive descriptions of what occurs and will occur given specific variables, materials, and forces. The certainty of the classic physics is supplanted by modern physics, also called quantum physics, which focuses on randomness and probabilities. Modern physicists deal with randomness and conclusions that are focused on probabilities and uncertainties. Rather than believing in certainties, quantum physics deals with statistical predictions. So the modern study of physics deals with uncertainties (Rovelli, 2016). One of the more famous theorists of modern physics was Werner Heisenberg, who developed, among other concepts, the uncertainty principle. It suggests that when something is observed or measured, the observation or measuring changes the nature of the matter being examined (Pagels, 1991). So today's physics and today's physicists do not define absolutes but report probabilities. That is similar, of course, even to an area of the applied social sciences, like modern social work research. Research findings are reported in terms of levels of confidence about conclusions, typically concluding that results are significant when the researcher would expect the same results 95% of the time or more. Confidence levels are expressed in percentages—typically 1% or 5% (see Fig. 3.12). All sciences, natural, physical, and social, have moved in the same direction for forming conclusions.

One of the important and newer concepts of physics has limited importance for social workers in their everyday practice of the profession but certainly has application to our philosophy about the world and universe and how people move through and relate to the philosophical world of our constructed reality. That is the central concept of quantum mechanics (see Fig. 3.13). Quanta are the items that cannot

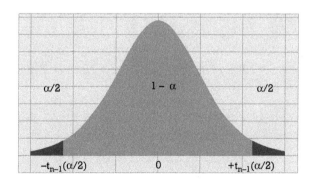

Figure 3.12 Confidence interval

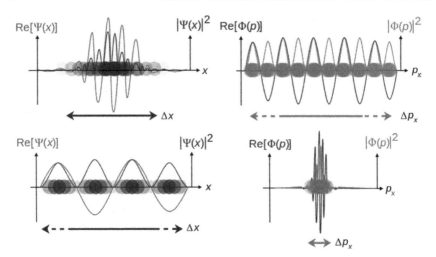

Figure 3.13 Quantum mechanics traveling wave functions
SOURCE: By Maschen - Own work, Public Domain, https://commons.wikimedia.org/w/index.php?curid=16199957

be further subdivided. And quantum mechanics explains how atoms combine to make molecules along with many other important theoretical constructs. Quantum mechanics lay the bases for such familiar items as computers, lasers, MP3 players, and much else in the modern world. The theory also demonstrates such hard-to-imagine ideas as how electrons, parts of atoms, can rotate both clockwise and counterclockwise at the same time. It also suggests that an atom can exist at more than one place at the same time (Parsons, 2009). Fortunately, we need not fully explain all of these concepts, and social workers, in the normal course of their responsibilities, need not fully understand them. Teaching about them and understanding them fully could possibly only be achieved with several courses over several years of study.

GEOMETRY AND SCIENCE

Another set of scientific theoretical notions are those of geometry, a science that was used by astronomers and physicists in defining the positions of the planets. Geometry is a high school course in its fundamental form and often the favorite of high school students not inclined to go on further and study such complex areas as calculus. Geometry has progressed significantly since it was first developed. Although the origins of geometry can be traced to the 3rd century, the clearest definition of "axioms" that define the science come from the Greek philosopher Euclid, whose postulates are still taught and consulted by scientists. Readers may recall some of these ideas from their studies of geometry in precollege courses or as part of their undergraduate studies. The Euclidean postulates include the following:

1. A straight line segment can be drawn joining any two points.
2. Any straight line segment can be extended indefinitely in a straight line.

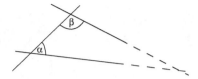

Figure 3.14 An illustration of the parallel postulate in Euclidean geometry
SOURCE: By 6054 - Edit of http://pl.wikipedia.org/wiki/Grafika:Parallel_postulate.svg by User:Harkonnen2, CC
BY-SA 3.0, https://commons.wikimedia.org/w/index.php?curid=4559984

3. Given any straight line segment, a circle can be drawn having the segment as radius and one endpoint as center.
4. All right angles are congruent—that is, the same.
5. If two lines are drawn which intersect a third in such a way that the sum of the inner angles on one side is less than two right angles, then the two lines inevitably must intersect each other on that side if extended far enough. This postulate is equivalent to what is known as the parallel postulate (https://www.wolframalpha.com/; see Fig. 3.14).

These are the "axiomatic" geometry concepts that are the scaffolding for the original form of the science. Geometry has moved on to other kinds of study, sometimes called "non-Euclidean" geometry, for understanding much more complex problems of shape, volume, and analyses of space and figures. Euclid's work, *Elements*, was published in the third and fourth centuries (Tallack, 2001). It was not until the 19th century that it was concluded that Euclid's principles were not absolute—but he discovered a great deal in a very early time in world history.

This book, of course, does not teach geometry or any other basic sciences. However, it is worthwhile to understand that astronomy and physics made, and continue to make, use of geometry, calculus, and algebra, in their study of planets, space, and other phenomena, that help explain the world and universe. Geometry is also useful to social workers involved in the planning and managing of physical facilities. Room sizes, building accesses, hallway dimensions, and other physical space issues are all related to geometrical measures and processes.

Although it is beyond the scope of this book, it is useful to mention that astronomy, as a science, is different than most nonastronomers think of it. For example, most astronomical activities are carried out with computer programs that identify the constellations, stars, and planets known to astronomers. The pointing of telescopes is achieved by moving about those programs, and the results are understood through the programs, rather than through observations with the eye through telescopes. Telescopes are not single scientific instruments. Astronomers and astronomy organizations purchase time on distant telescopes that may be thousands of miles away. Their observing is remote, through the use of distant astronomy organizations. For US astronomers, for example, much of their observing is through telescopes in Hawaii and Chile, through organizations that have exceptional instruments and favorable environments for observation. Another paradox in astronomy is that many of the discoveries and ongoing observations of astronomical phenomena are achieved by amateur astronomers. Thousands of people

Figure 3.15 Telescope
SOURCE: By Timwether - Own work, CC BY-SA 3.0, https://commons.wikimedia.org/w/index.php?curid=14691679

are astronomy hobbyists, often with powerful telescopes (see Fig. 3.15), which are often within the economic resources of individuals. Because the sky is too large for any individual astronomer or astronomy center to observe everything all the time, amateurs often make important astronomical discoveries by studying portions of the sky.

PHYSICS AND HEALTH CARE

Physics and health care are important considerations in understanding the role of physics in much of what is done. Enkhjargl (2012) wrote about the importance of physics and physical scientists in the development of the noninvasive procedures and equipment in diagnosing and treating illnesses. Without the diagnostic

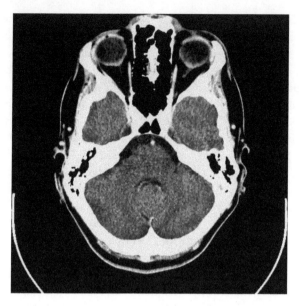

Figure 3.16 Computed tomography of human brain
SOURCE: By Department of Radiology, Uppsala University Hospital. Uploaded by Mikael Häggström. - Radiology, Uppsala University Hospital. Uploaded by Mikael Häggström., CC0, https://commons.wikimedia.org/w/index. php?curid=3484310

tools developed by physicists and other scientists, surgery would have been more common and more necessary for understanding health problems.

Among the most important contributions of physics to social work practice and health services was the development of X-ray, magnetic resonance imaging, and computerized tomography (see Fig. 3.16). These three resources and the procedures arising from them have revolutionized the diagnosis and ultimately the treatment of illnesses. They not only make it possible to more accurately diagnose conditions but also make it possible to monitor treatments, including surgery, which would have been done blind before the creation of these devices. Diagnostic procedures such as mammograms and virtually all kinds of medical interventions involve one or more of these diagnostic devices.

The problems that arise from these diagnostic tools include cancer, resulting from the radiation used by some of them. Dental offices typically take regular X-rays of patients' teeth and some patients are nervous about the possibility of developing cancer because of excess radiation from X-rays. However, one can be exposed to as much radiation as in a single X-ray by standing outside for an hour or so. In other words, what is important to remember is that radiation occurs naturally and is all around us. The treatment of illnesses is also accomplished with radiation. Treatment of both malignant and nonmalignant tumors and cancer often involves radiation. The X-ray was developed from Madame Marie Curie (1867–1934) and her husband Pierre Curie's (1859–1906) discovery of radiation, which Madame Curie named. She discovered the elements of radium and polonium, the latter of which she named for her native country, Poland (Simmons, 1996). Their daughter Marie, along with her parents, won the Nobel Prize (Curie, 1991). She essentially invented the X-ray, a tool for examining the human body with radioactive rays. She actually died from anemia caused by carrying radioactive elements in test tubes in her pockets.

Of course, as mentioned earlier, X-ray is widely used in modern health care, especially for diagnosing cancers, fractures, and dental problems. The excessive use of X-rays has been a potential health problem for patients, although modern X-rays are much less powerful than when they were originally developed. They were also used for a variety of efforts for which they are no longer used now that the dangers of extensive exposure to radiation are better understood. One of the older authors of this text recalls that as a child a dermatologist used radiation to destroy a skin cyst. He also remembered that shoe stores routinely checked the fit of shoes on children with X-ray machines that showed the shoes and the feet to determine they were of the proper size.

A magnetic resonance imaging (MRI) device uses a 1.5 ton magnet, which has magnetic power 21,000 times that of the regular magnetic field. Objects can be accelerated 40 miles per hour so an inadvertent paper clip could become a dangerous weapon to a patient being examined by an MRI (www.mayoclinic.org/tests-procedures/mri). The dangers of MRIs are related to items left in the pocket or in the machine harming the patient. Radiation, however, is not a problem with the MRI. The computerized tomography scan is also widely used in health care. The machine takes a series of X-rays from different angles at different times. Together they give a complete, cross-sectional picture of the patient (American Association of Physicists in Medicine, https://www.aapm.org/). Physicists in medicine have a national organization, a journal, and professional meetings. Their work is somewhat different than but related to what social workers do in using physics. Social workers must often collaborate with health physicists in the diagnosis and treatment of health problems.

MEDICAL PHYSICISTS, CLINICAL SERVICE, AND CONSULTATION

Health care professionals, called medical physicists, are heavily involved with responsibilities in the areas of diagnosis and treatment, often with specific patients with special needs or conditions. These activities take the form of consultations with physician colleagues. In radiation oncology departments, one important example is the planning of radiation treatments for cancer patients, using either external radiation beams or internal radioactive sources. An indispensable service is the accurate measurement of the radiation output from radiation sources employed in cancer therapy. In the specialty of nuclear medicine, physicists collaborate with physicians in procedures utilizing radionuclides for delineating internal organs and determining important physiological variables, such as metabolic rates and blood flow. Other important services are rendered through investigation of equipment performance, organization of quality control in imaging systems, design of radiation installations, and control of radiation hazards. The medical physicist is called upon to contribute clinical and scientific advice and resources to solve the numerous and diverse physical problems that arise continually in many specialized medical areas.

PHYSICISTS IN MEDICINE

Medical physicists also play a vital and often leading role on the medical research team. Their activities cover wide frontiers, including such key areas as cancer, heart disease, and mental illness. In cancer, they work primarily on issues involving radiation, such as the basic mechanisms of biological change after irradiation, the application of new high-energy machines to patient treatment, and the development of new techniques for precise measurement of radiation. Significant computer developments continue in the area of dose calculation for patient treatment and video display of this treatment information. Particle irradiation is an area of active research with promising biological advantages over traditional photon treatment. In heart disease, physicists work on the measurement of blood flow and oxygenation. In mental illness, they work on the recording, correlation, and interpretation of bioelectric potentials.

Medical physicists are also concerned with research of general medical significance, including the applications of digital computers in medicine and applications of information theory to diagnostic problems; processing, storing, and retrieving medical images; measuring the amount of radioactivity in the human body and foodstuffs; and studying the anatomical and temporal distribution of radioactive substances in the body.

Medical physicists are also involved in the development of new instrumentation and technology for use in diagnostic radiology. These include the use of magnetic and electro-optical storage devices for the manipulation of X-ray images, quantitative analysis of both static and dynamic images using digital computer techniques, radiation methods for the analysis of tissue characteristics and composition, and the exciting new areas of computerized tomography and MRI for displaying detailed cross-sectional images of the anatomy. Medical physicists are also engaged in research and development on imaging procedures utilizing infrared and ultrasound sources. Typical examples of the various research areas presently under active investigation may be found in scientific journals dedicated to this field. The journal *Medical Physics* is published by the AAPM (from the American Association of Physicists in Medicine website, https://www.acr.org/).

There are also related organizations for professionals who deal with radiology. The Radiology Society of North America is one (https://www.acr.org/). The American College of Radiology and the American Board of Radiology are physician organizations that specify credentials in radiology diagnosis and treatment. As the medical physicists explain, one of the major functions of their professionals and of other health physicists is guaranteeing the safety of patients who are evaluated with and treated with radiation. They also work with organizations that are involved in radioactive organizations, including manufacturing, nuclear power companies, and many other organizations that routinely use radiation in their work. Often, they equip employees with docimeters, devices that measure the extent of exposure

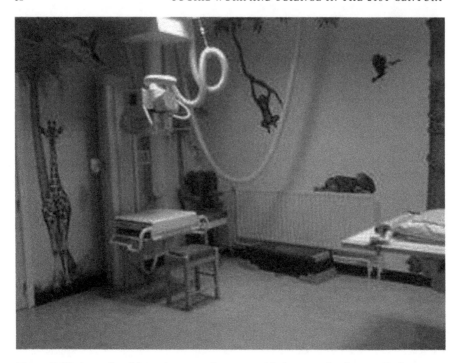

Figure 3.17 A comfortable environment is an essential element of pediatric radiology
SOURCE: http://www.childrenshospital.org/centers-and-services/departments-and-divisions/department-of-radiology/programs-and-services/nuclear-medicine-and-molecular-imaging

that the employees may have in their regular work (Radiology Society of North America, www.rsna.org).

SOCIAL WORKERS AND RADIATION

Of course, medical social workers often have extensive contact with patients who are undergoing radiation therapy as well as diagnosis (see Fig. 3.17). They work with physicians and nurses as part of the treatment teams in oncological (cancer) diagnosis and treatment. They also work with family members helping them discuss radiological diagnosis and treatment. There are social workers who identify as oncology social workers, but most social workers employed in medical settings become involved in radiation services. Social workers may also help with pain and other side effects of radiology as well as arrange transportation and other practical aspects of radiology treatment. Helping patients and their families make arrangements for posttreatment placements, such as long-term care, is also often a role for the social worker who deals with radiation services (Ginsberg, 1998).

DENTISTS

The field of dentistry uses physics extensively. Although the basics of physics—motion, gravity, and the like—may not be a conscious part of a dentist's professional training and work, dentists use physics and physical principles in their everyday work. For instance, the spacing of teeth, the use of fillings to treat cavities, the construction of crowns and caps, and the placement of tooth implants and other natural tooth replacements all involve principles of physics. These may differ in magnitude, but they are not necessarily different in basic concepts to the construction of bridges to span rivers or buildings for housing, manufacturing, and other personal and enterprise functions. One might conclude that wherever and whenever material objects are involved that some principles of physics need to be applied. The American Dental Association website points to the need for dental students to obtain prerequisite study in physics and also describes the multiple ways in which dental care requires a knowledge of and use of physics.

PHYSICS AND PERSONS WITH SENSORY LOSSES IN HEARING

For much of American history, social policies have created provision for specialized services for persons with sensory losses in hearing. This is especially true in the provision of education for persons with severe hearing loss and/or who might be completely void of hearing. For example, and something that social workers are quite familiar with, the US government assisted with the founding and continuing operation of Gallaudet University in Washington, DC, an educational setting specifically

Figure 3.18 Gallaudet University
SOURCE: By AgnosticPreachersKid - Own work, CC BY-SA 3.0, https://commons.wikimedia.org/w/index.php?curid=6013953

designed for persons with mild to severe hearing loss (see Fig. 3.18). The university has its own accredited bachelor of social work and master of social work programs.

Additionally, most states founded, early in their histories, special schools for deaf and blind students. Of course, social and education policy shifted and now tends to favor the "mainstreaming" of students with those sensory losses, although the special schools continue and are favored by some leaders in the Deaf community. Deaf people note that deafness is not just a disability but is also a culture, with its own language. In the United States, American Sign Language is the preferred mode of communication for people who have been without hearing since childhood. It is typically acquired in the same ways children learn all languages—by being exposed to it. Each other language group also has a sign language and they are not all the same. Translation is practiced for Spanish Sign Language, for example, in the same way English is translated into other languages. Sign language is a total language. It is much more than the spelling out of words, letter by letter, with hand signs, a process for which sign language users have disdain (www.gallaudet.edu/).

A primary application of physics is to help develop equipment for people with the two main sensory losses, vision and hearing. For those with hearing loss, which includes large numbers of older adults but children and younger people as well, there are hearing aids, small microphones placed in one ear or both ears. These devices make it possible for people with hearing loss to converse with others, listen to media, hold jobs, and otherwise participate more fully in society. These electroacoustic devices rely on the learnings of physics, which has special knowledge of acoustics, to invent and improve devices for those with hearing loss. They originally simply augmented sounds, but as they have become more scientifically sophisticated, they are able to help clarify sounds and speech. Many are programmable by the users, who can select various modes—speech in crowded rooms, audio from televisions,

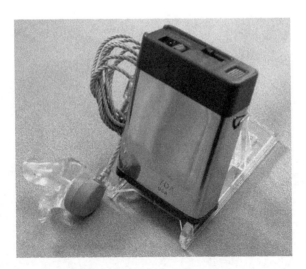

Figure 3.19 Body-worn aids were the first type of hearing aids
SOURCE: By Joe Haupt from USA - Vintage Telex Transistor (Body) Hearing Aid, Model 70A, Made in the USA, CC BY-SA 2.0, https://commons.wikimedia.org/w/index.php?curid=35547849

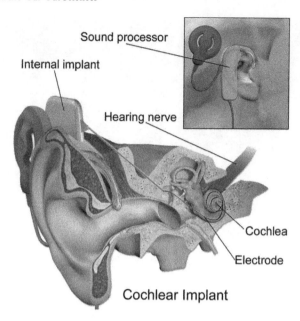

Figure 3.20 How a cochlear implant works

SOURCE: By BruceBlaus. When using this image in external sources it can be cited as:Blausen.com staff (2014).
"Medical gallery of Blausen Medical 2014". WikiJournal of Medicine 1 (2). DOI:10.15347/wjm/2014.010. ISSN
2002-4436. -Own work, CC BY 3.0, https://commons.wikimedia.org/w/index.php?curid=29025007

movies, and radio, to simply increase the volume heard by the user (Beukelman & Mirenda, 2013).

Hearing aids, in their first designs, were relatively large. Users had to suspend machines that were about the size and shape of modern transistor portable radios (Fig. 3.19). Connecting wires from these devices to the user's ear or ears made the use of hearing aids obvious and cumbersome. However, as the technology has developed, often using the acoustic engineering developed with better understanding of physics, hearing aids are now relatively small. Some fit into the ear canal and are barely visible. Others combine microphones placed over the ear with hearing devices placed within the ear. They have become and are becoming both more effective and less noticeable.

For some reason, eyeglasses have had a much longer and positive response from those with visual needs. The stigma, for reasons that are more sociological and psychological than technical, of hearing aids is much greater. People who are quite willing to wear eyeglasses, which are often even fashionable items, are reluctant to even consider wearing hearing aids. Designers such as Ralph Lauren market eyeglass frames, but Ralph Lauren hearing aids are unlikely future products. Telephone systems are usually equipped with telecommunication device for the deaf (TDD), which provides messages in written form for those who cannot hear as well as its corollary, devices that allow those who cannot speak to send messages in written form through the same kinds of devices.

Of course, social workers need to understand the varieties of hearing devices and the ways they can be used. More than a few clients are likely to experience reduced

Figure 3.21 Cochlear implants are controversial in infants and children, pictured here
SOURCE: By Bjorn Knetsch from The Netherlands - 2009_01_20_2352Uploaded by tabercil, CC BY 2.0, https://
commons.wikimedia.org/w/index.php?curid=19058175

involvement in their environments because of hearing losses and the reluctance to
make use of modern audio technology. Social workers need not completely understand the physics behind various devices, but knowing what is available and how it
can serve clients is a necessity in an increasing mix of older clients.

A relatively new approach to providing hearing for persons who are deaf or hard
of hearing is the cochlear implant, a device connected directly to the inner ears and
which actually begin or restore hearing (see Fig. 3.20). Surgical procedures are involved and the result is actual hearing through the deaf or hard-of-hearing person's
body. As an actual modification in the body of the person, ideas such as a Deaf culture are bypassed, especially with cochlear implants for young children, who may
never learn or need to learn sign language (Fig. 3.21). Again, scientists of all kinds
were involved in designing the implants and the devices to which they are connected in the brain (www.nicdh.nih.gov/cochlearimplants).

Social workers with clients who are deaf or hard of hearing need to understand
the availability of the various kinds of hearing devices and procedures. Some social
workers who serve clients who are deaf master sign language and communicate
effectively in that fashion (Fig. 3.22). Although they may not need to know the
science involved in hearing solutions, some awareness of it is helpful in communicating with clients and their families about the available solutions. For a variety of
reasons, persons who are deaf or hard of hearing do not receive the same kinds of
empathy as those with more visible disabilities. Deaf people largely do not have any
physical manifestations of their conditions. It is only when they do not understand
communications from hearing persons that their disability becomes manifest. In
difficult situations, they may be stereotyped as slow or mentally disabled when, in
fact, they are not. Those who serve persons who are deaf and hard of hearing can
usually recite multiple examples of those clients being misunderstood or shunned
through no fault of their own other than their limited hearing.

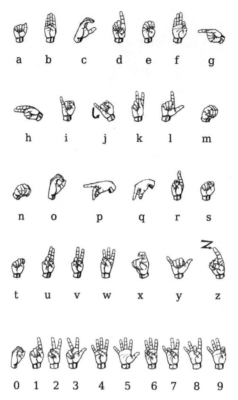

Figure 3.22 The letters of the American Sign Language (ASL) fingerspelling with the equivalent Latin character

SOURCE: By User:Marnanel based on image by User:Dancor~commonswiki based on image by en:user:Ds13 - Vectorised version of Image:Asl alphabet gallaudet ann.png which is annotated version of Image:Asl_alphabet_ gallaudet.png, Public Domain, https://commons.wikimedia.org/w/index.php?curid=3108474

PHYSICS AND PERSONS WITH SENSORY LOSSES IN VISION

Optics is a major field of study that is of interest to social workers. Optics integrates principles of physics and its related discipline astronomy and has done so from the beginnings of their development. Seeing and analyzing the motions of the planets, and the sizes and composition of the planets, has its transfer and application value in micro applications in optics. Studying the smaller elements of the world's material by physicists has assisted in the development of such scientific instruments as the microscope. Microscopes enable scientists to study and learn about cell structure, in both animals and plants, the ages of objects, and the ways in which they develop. So optics in physics leads to understandings of the largest matter in the universe, through telescopes, and the smallest, through microscopes. More modern microscopes such as electron microscopes have even enabled scientists to actually see items too small in the past for study by microscopes (Fig. 3.23).

The application of the ideas and principles of physics and astronomy led directly to advances in optic theory and were basic to the creation and further refinement of visual aids such as eyeglasses and contact lenses. Corrective

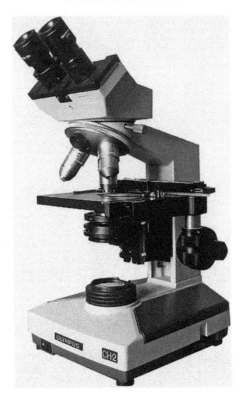

Figure 3.23 Olympus CH2 microscope
SOURCE: By Amada44 - Own work, CC BY-SA 3.0, https://commons.wikimedia.org/w/index.php?curid=30166589

lenses are based upon the scientific applications of optics theory to the practical problems of vision correction. The technology resources of people who
have lost or never had vision or whose vision is failing are somewhat different
than the resources of people who have experienced hearing loss. The American
Federation of the Blind even publishes a magazine, *Access World*, which updates
the resources available to people who are blind. Blindness is readily apparent
to the seeing population and, therefore, people who are blind are less likely to
encounter misunderstandings about their disability than people who are deaf
or hard of hearing.

Social workers have also played a part in advocating for other advances in technical supports and solutions such as traffic signals that are both sonic and visual to
help people who are blind negotiate intersections. Guide dogs for persons who are
blind are sponsored by a variety of organizations and provide persons with the kind
of mobility assistance that makes it possible for them to live and work in a society
that is primarily organized for those who can see more fully (Fig. 3.24). Perhaps
most important are the recordings of books, magazines, and other media, made
available for persons who are blind. These recorded materials have a long history
and are perhaps the first technological, scientific services for people with disabilities. Many popular magazines and newspapers are regularly available to persons
who are blind at little or no charge. Public libraries have extensive collections of

Figure 3.24 A person receives assistance from a guide dog
SOURCE: By Conrad Poirier - This file has been scanned and uploaded to Wikimedia Commons with the gracious permission and cooperation of Bibliothèque et Archives nationales du Québec and Wikimedia Canada under the Poirier Project., Public Domain, https://commons.wikimedia.org/w/index.php?curid=34363675

books, both fiction and nonfiction, for people who have vision losses, usually at no cost and with library-provided players and free postage for receiving and returning materials. Recording technology has a long history. Therefore, these kinds of services are long-standing and extensive. Stenographers with vision losses and others who carry out word processing assignments are able to type from recorded dictation and other recorded materials.

Persons who are blind also have a special language, braille, which translates written words into raised formats which are read by touch. There are writing resources for typing in braille and writing devices that produce materials in the language. Braille is an important resource for people who have been blind since birth or early childhood. However, for adults who lose their vision in their later years, learning braille is actually the learning of a new language with new characters, often a difficult requirement. One of the more remarkable innovations, optical character recognition devices, was developed by Ray Kurzweil. These permit persons who are blind to place almost any written material into a machine, which translates the written materials into touch-sensitive figures. Therefore, people who are blind are able to "read" anything that can be placed into the optical character recognition device, thus expanding their knowledge sources well beyond materials that are produced in braille. The optical character recognition (OCR) devices are able to read handwritten documents as well as those that are printed. They can also translate computer documents, such as portable document format (pdf) materials into OCR, allowing persons who are blind to read computer-generated documents.

Again, social workers need to be aware of the various resources—developed with the basics of physics playing a major role—available to people who are blind so they can advise clients and client families of the services they may use for work, family life, and education. It is interesting to note that although people, especially children, who have sensory losses such as blindness and deafness were historically treated in special schools with special instruction in the use of devices designed to assist them. Learning braille and learning sign language (often taught to one another as part of peer relationships) may be less important now and may be replaced by technological developments. With the availability of cochlear implants and OCR devices, learning the traditional means of communicating may be emphasized less for people who cannot see and hear. The other significant social policies in these areas are those of "mainstreaming" children—placing children who cannot see and hear—in classrooms with children who can. Avoiding separating and isolating children with special learning needs, a policy also applied to children with learning disabilities, is a current focus of public education.

The emphasis on special schools is in some places diminished as more and more students are mainstreamed. Such developments are not without controversy. Children may feel singled out in the mainstream classroom and may also wish for opportunities to be leaders among their peers. Some educators point out that children in schools for the deaf and blind may rise to student body leadership positions and important roles in sports, theatre, and music, which may be less likely in schools where the majority of students can see and hear at higher levels.

CONCLUSION

Although they may not always seem to be related, social work and the "far-out" sciences of astronomy, geometry, and physics, are in many ways closely related. Physics, especially, is tied closely to many social work functions, especially in health and to services to people with disabilities. Of course, social workers need not know all that these scientists know and use in their daily work, and the scientists need not know all that social workers know about human relations and human problems. However, the solutions to many problems are scientific solutions. The health and medical care of clients, the mobility of people with physical disabilities, and technologies such as optical readers and cochlear implants all exist at the nexus of social work and varying technologies. Knowing how science is used in serving people is a useful part of the knowledge base of all social workers. This brief introduction to the sciences of astronomy, physics, and geometry provides basic information and some ideas for future study of the scientific concepts that affect the practice of social work in modern times.

REFERENCES

Beukelman, D., & Mirenda, P. (2013). *Augmentative and alternative communication: Supporting children and adults with complex communication needs.* Baltimore, MD: Paul H. Brookes.

Chaisson, E., & McMillan, S. (2010). *Astronomy* (6th ed.). New York, NY: Addison-Wesley.

Curie, P. (1991). Radioactive substances. In T. Ferris (Ed.), *The world treasury of physics, astronomy and mathematics* (pp. 50–79). Boston, MA: Little, Brown and Company.

Dinwiddie, R. (2009). *How science works: Everything you need to know about science in small, easily-digestible portions.* New York, NY: Chartwell Books.

Enkhjargl, B. (2012). World Congress on Medical Physics and Biomedical Engineering, Beijing, China. In *IFMBE Proceedings* (pp. 1698–1699). New York, NY: Springer Link.

Feynman, R. P. (1991). Atoms in motion. In T. Ferris (Ed.), *The world treasury of physics, astronomy and mathematics* (pp. 3–17). Boston, MA: Little, Brown and Company.

Ginsberg, L. (1998). *Careers in social work* (2nd ed.). New York, NY: Pearson.

Holzner, S. (2010). *Physics II for dummies.* Hoboken, NJ: John Wiley & Sons.

Nitta, H., Yamamoto, M., & Takatsu, K. (2011). *The Manga guide to relativity.* San Francisco, CA: No Starch Press.

Overbye, D. (2016). No escape from black holes? Stephen Hawking points to a possible exit. *The New York Times.* Retrieved from https://www.nytimes.com/2016/06/07/science/stephen-hawking-black-holes.html

Pagels, J. R. (1991). Uncertainty and complementarity. In T. Ferris (Ed.), *The world treasury of physics, astronomy and mathematics* (pp. 97–115). Boston, MA: xxx.

Parsons, P.-E. (2009). *30-second theories: The 50 most thought-provoking theories in science, each explained in half a minute.* New York, NY: Metro Books.

Rovelli, C. (2016). *Seven brief lessons on physics.* New York, NY: Riverhead Books.

Sanburn, J. (2016, March 21). Greed, politics and the biggest oil boom in decades. *Time,* 35–41.

Simmons, J. G. (1996). *The scientific 100: A ranking of the most influential scientists, past and present.* New York, NY: Citadel Press.

Tallack, P. (2001). *The science book.* London, UK: Weidenfeld and Nicolson.

Trefil, J. S. (1992). *1001 things everyone should know about science.* New York, NY: Doubleday Books.

4

Social Work and the Science of Numbers

Virtually all human experiences are reducible to numbers—how many, how much, how often. Is it possible to practice human services without thinking about them numerically?

—LEON H. GINSBERG

D ealing with science and its applications to social work practice requires some basic skills and knowledge that are important in the sciences. Of course, scientists use a language that is somewhat different than that employed in most social work practice. The language of science is typically based upon numerical concepts. Dealing with scientific reports and scientific ideas requires some understanding of the mathematics scientists use in describing their information and in reporting their ideas. Those numbers are not typically those we use in everyday life or even in the professional practice of social work. We are more likely to center our quantitative concepts on measures that are familiar to us from the English system of weights and measures. We deal with ounces and pounds, inches, feet, yards, and miles. That is how we think as Americans. We can be easily impressed when traveling to most other nations to hear everyone, including young children, describe everything numerical in metric terms—"Go about 50 meters and you'll be there"; "The distance is 40 kilometers"; "It just weighs about 10 kilograms"; "It's very hot today, about 38 degrees." Tables 4.1 and 4.2 are conversion charts that show the equivalents of our usual system of weights, temperatures, and lengths, which are called the English system, in SI. Scientists throughout the world have long used the metric system, adapted as the SI or international system. For most purposes, the SI (the adjective "international" comes after the noun, "system," as is the pattern in French and other Romance languages) is the system used when calculating results of study and when reporting those results. So a large portion of this chapter is designed to help readers acclimate to and use SI, rather than the English system, in studying and reporting results of study and the measurements of the life around them. Tables 4.1 and 4.2 provide conversion charts, which explain the ways in which the conversions are made.

Table 4.1 METRIC/ENGLISH CONVERSION FACTORS

ENGLISH TO METRIC		METRIC TO ENGLISH	
LENGTH (APPROXIMATE)		LENGTH (APPROXIMATE)	
1 inch (in)	= 2.5 centimeters (cm)	1 millimeter (mm)	= 0.04 inch (in)
1 foot (ft)	= 30 centimeters (cm)	1 centimeter (cm)	= 0.4 inch (in)
1 yard (yd)	= 0.9 meter (m)	1 meter (m)	= 3.3 feet (ft)
1 mile (mi)	= 1.6 kilometers (km)	1 meter (m)	= 1.1 yards (yd)
		1 kilometer (km)	= 0.6 mile (mi)
AREA (APPROXIMATE)		AREA (APPROXIMATE)	
1 square inch (sq in, in^2)	= 6.5 square centimeters (cm^2)	1 square centimeter (cm^2)	= 0.16 square inch (sq in, in^2)
1 square foot (sq ft, ft^2)	= 0.09 square meter (m^2)	1 square meter (m^2)	= 1.2 square yards (sq yd, yd^2)
1 square yard (sq yd, yd^2)	= 0.8 square meter (m^2)	1 square kilometer (km^2)	= 0.4 square mile (sq mi, mi^2)
1 square mile (sq mi, mi^2)	= 2.6 square kilometers (km^2)	10,000 square meters (m^2)	= 1 hectare (ha) = 2.5 acres
1 acre = 0.4 hectare (he)	= 4,000 square meters (m^2)		

Source: Authors' creation

Table 4.2 METRIC/ENGLISH CONVERSION FACTORS

MASS - WEIGHT (APPROXIMATE)			MASS - WEIGHT (APPROXIMATE)		
1 ounce (oz)	=	28 grams (gm)	1 gram (gm)	=	0.036 ounce (oz)
1 pound (lb)	=	0.45 kilogram (kg)	1 kilogram (kg)	=	2.2 pounds (lb)
1 short ton = 2,000 pounds (lb)	=	0.9 tonne (t)	1 tonne (t)	=	1,000 kilograms (kg)
				=	1.1 short tons
VOLUME (APPROXIMATE)			**VOLUME (APPROXIMATE)**		
1 teaspoon (tsp)	=	5 milliliters (ml)	1 milliliter (ml)	=	0.03 fluid ounce (fl oz)
1 tablespoon (tbsp)	=	15 milliliters (ml)	1 liter (l)	=	2.1 pints (pt)
1 fluid ounce (fl oz)	=	30 milliliters (ml)	1 liter (l)	=	1.06 quarts (qt)
1 cup (c)	=	0.24 liter (l)	1 liter (l)	=	0.26 gallon (gal)
1 pint (pt)	=	0.47 liter (l)			
1 quart (qt)	=	0.96 liter (l)			
1 gallon (gal)	=	3.8 liters (l)			
1 cubic foot (cu ft, ft^3)	=	0.03 cubic meter (m^3)	1 cubic meter (m^3)	=	36 cubic feet (cu ft, ft^3)
1 cubic yard (cu yd, yd^3)	=	0.76 cubic meter (m^3)	1 cubic meter (m^3)	=	1.3 cubic yards (cu yd, yd^3)
TEMPERATURE (EXACT)			**TEMPERATURE (EXACT)**		
$[(x-32)(5/9)]°F$	=	y°C	$[(9/5)y + 32]°C$	=	x°F

Source: Authors' creation

Social workers need to understand and be able to use the SI international system of measurements or metric systems of measurement and calculation. Being conversant with SI is essential to understanding many of the scientific bases of human services diagnosis and treatment as well as for communicating with scientists about their work on human services interventions and solutions. Although some sporadic efforts are made to convert the United States to the metric system or at least to bring it to the attention of Americans as an alternative set of measurements, for the most part it has never taken hold, except among scientists, health care providers, and a few others who cannot get along without using the metric measures. Occasionally highways mark distances in kilometers as well as miles. Our medicines are usually prescribed in milligrams, although most of us don't have a feel for exactly what a milligram—or a gram—is. Gold and other precious metals as well as diamonds are often measured metrically.

Daniel Engber (2016) dealt with the question of why the United States has not adopted the metric system. He says that Thomas Jefferson proposed its adoption in 1789, as did Alexander Graham Bell in 1906. The US Congress authorized a study of its adoption and recommended the change over 10 years. However, it was not made mandatory, and the adoption did not happen. A Gallup poll found 45% of Americans opposed its adoption (Engber, 2016). Manufacturers thought the cost of converting all its sizes of products and its tools would be prohibitively expensive. Scientists deal often with numbers to describe the phenomena that are critical to them just as the larger US public does in their everyday activities. We discuss the daily climate in terms of degrees; we measure rainfall in inches; we calculate our resources in terms of dollars credited to our accounts or in our pockets and purses; we evaluate our class work in percentages.

SOCIAL WORK RESEARCH

All professionally educated social workers study social research, which has been a component of the profession throughout its history. The principles for understanding the scientific data that are often needed are the same as those used in social research. Data are arrayed in a frequency distribution; measures of central tendency such as the mean, mode, and median, are calculated (see Fig. 4.1). Statistical tests such as chi square, the correlation coefficient, and many others that are taught in statistics and research methods courses are essentially the same as used in the sciences. Of course, the means of study are often different because social research is different than research in the sciences. Scientists may study single cases and may use trials to determine the efficacy of a substance or a treatment in medicine. They may use double-blind approaches to determine the effects of an intervention, just as social workers might. Of course, the trials may be different in a study such as testing the efficacy of a new chemically based medicine. Subjects may be given the substance while others receive a placebo. In social

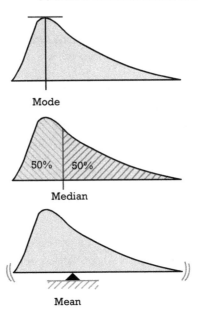

Figure 4.1 Example of the statistical mode, median, and mean
SOURCE: By Cmglee - Own work, CC BY-SA 3.0, https://commons.wikimedia.org/w/index.php?curid=38969094

work research, the intervention or treatment is provided, but in much of science an actual substance is introduced into the subject. The procedures and concepts are similar but the tolerance of error may be smaller. In testing a treatment for a disease, the researchers will expect their subjects to benefit but will also be especially cautious about the substance doing harm. That may be less true for social work interventions that may or may not be effective—but ineffective treatments (group therapy, structured counseling, for example) will ordinarily cause the end of the subject's life. But scientific research should be seen as a parallel to social research, using similar methods, procedures, and criteria. The "confidence" levels may be the same, although in social research a result that is true 95% of the time may be considered a significant and positive result while in much scientific research, especially medical research, the scientist will not want to accept a 5% failure or ineffectiveness rate in most cases.

SOURCES OF INFORMATION

Social workers often have to understand the validity of problems reported by clients and evaluations of those issues by other social workers, psychologists, and physicians. For those reasons, it is important for social workers to understand the reliability of the science behind the evaluations and diagnoses of client concerns. At times, social workers are faced with a barrage of information, some of it conflicting, which they may not be able to evaluate responsibly. This section provides some suggestions for evaluating information and understanding the science behind conclusions that are reported.

Information From the Media

The media (newspapers, magazine, the Internet, radio, and television) may often be the source of scientific information and ideas. Scientists differ in the degree of confidence they have in the media and make varying use of them. In general, daily newspapers are the best media sources of information. That is because they are usually carefully edited and staffed by professional journalists. They generally adhere to professional standards which make their information reliable. Newspapers follow such procedures as working to achieve the accuracy of their information by consulting multiple sources or official sources that have information adequate to draw the conclusions they report. Often, before the reporters' work is printed, it is examined and evaluated by editors who are also experts in journalism and typically anxious to guarantee the truth of what the newspaper prints.

Some newspapers are probably more worthy of consultation and use in understanding science. The *New York Times*, which has a weekly special section on science, and the *Washington Post* are usually reliable sources of science information. They often include lengthy articles on science subjects. But most other newspapers, including local papers, often subscribe to these two major national newspapers and include stories from them on science. Virtually all local papers also subscribe to and have access to the Associated Press and United Press International, which have reporters who cover major stories, including those about science, and also transmit articles from the major papers as well as stories of national importance from local papers. As such, newspapers can and do provide good science information for social workers and others who have an interest in it.

Magazines are often good sources of information about science. Specialized magazines such as *Popular Science* and *Science* regularly provide articles on current science issues and information, often before newspapers. Some general interest magazines are also sound sources of science information. The *New Yorker* regularly provides specialized science information. It has been particularly strong in writing about environmental issues. Some other general interest magazines such as *The Atlantic Monthly*, and Harper's and *Time*, are also good sources. The better magazines such as those mentioned here have some of the same characteristics as good newspapers, such as professionally educated and talented reporters whose work is carefully edited. Some magazines include not only narrative information but also tables and charts that deal with science.

Sometimes a carefully written article in publications such as *Rolling Stone* may be valid for research or for documenting information. However, the information should be identified as such, as a product of journalistic reporting, so that the reader can properly evaluate the material.

Radio and television are often good beginning points for dealing with science issues. However, their stories often come from newspapers or other written sources, including the wire services, Associated Press and United Press International, and newspapers.

The Internet is different than the other possible sources and requires more diligence by those who use it for information on science. One of the limitations, for those seeking to draw on Internet information, is the ease with which anyone or any group of people may disseminate information on the Internet through blogs that they create and with comments on other stories or exchanges. Sites may include blatantly false information. Some sites are sponsored by prejudiced organizations such as the Ku Klux Klan and others of similar persuasions. On the other hand, some Internet sites are simply reporters of information from professional journals or exact copies of scientific newsletters or research findings. Some websites are carefully documented and sources are cited. For some of those reasons, this book relies on several websites for basic information.

One site that requires special attention is Wikipedia, an online encyclopedia, on almost all topics. Pick a topic, search for it with Google or another search engine, and a Wikipedia entry will appear. Wikipedia has a function that allows the editing, often augmenting, sometimes correcting, of its entries. Because of that, some believe Wikipedia is unreliable. That doesn't seem true. Controls on editing are such that it is not the case that anyone, on a whim, can significantly edit a Wikipedia entry. Generally, Wikipedia is reliable on all of its entries and includes citations and documentation that assure accuracy. In order to know when to use information from a website, book, or professional journal, some rules are helpful to those deciding on the validity of the information for the task they are conducting. Being careful about the validity of the information you find can make the difference between a strong case and information that is questionable or invalid. The following are some of the principal ways in which professional scientists analyze and evaluate what they read or are told:

Peer Review

In general, it is important to note when an article, a chapter in a book, a book itself, or information presented on a website is "peer reviewed." That means that the material has been reviewed objectively and anonymously by at least two people and often more who have some expertise in the subject matter. Editors and authors of journals and books make certain to ascertain that people who are peers of the author of the material being presented have reviewed the information. That is, they are members of the same profession or otherwise have some expert knowledge of the subject matter. Material that has been peer reviewed would usually be identified as such. If the material simply reflects the beliefs or opinions of the author or authors, it should be identified in that way. For example, reporting a researched conclusion about social work students that appears to be reliable could be as follows: "Professor Jones of ABC University reported that students who understand the importance of peer review in scholarship are more likely than others to become doctoral students in their field. Her findings were based on a questionnaire administered to 150 randomly selected Master of Social Work students in the United States." However, a statement that Professor Jones in an opinion editorial published in the same journal could be identified as follows: "In Professor Jones's work on the likely transition from master's to doctoral education, she concluded that students who appreciate

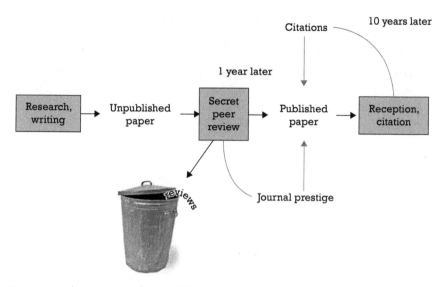

Figure 4.2 The current academic publishing system
By Nikolaus Kriegeskorte - Kriegeskorte N (2012) Open evaluation: a vision for entirely transparent post-publication peer review and rating for science. Front. Comput. Neurosci. 6:79. doi:10.3389/fncom.2012.00079, CC BY 3.0, https://commons.wikimedia.org/w/index.php?curid=22690346

the importance of peer review in research are more likely than others to become doctoral students." It is acceptable, in other words, to quote opinions but opinions should not be confused with accomplished and verified research (see Fig. 4.2).

The quality of the publication in which the information is found is one indicator. Scanning the information at the beginning of a professional journal should tell the reader whether or not the contents are peer reviewed. A journal's sponsorship by professional organizations is another indicator. In the case of social work, *Social Work, Social Service Review*, and *the Journal of Social Work Education* as well as many others are clearly reliable and the contents are likely to have been rigorously reviewed. Other measures of reliability include whether there is a board of directors or editors, whether the journal specifies that it uses peer review in its evaluation of submitted articles, and whether the journal is regularly published. Of course, citing the source of the material gives the reader an opportunity to evaluate the materials.

Sample Size and Selection

If the information is part of a scientifically researched study, information on the number of subjects who were studied and how they were selected is important. An author may provide a convincing report, but it may be based on only a handful of subjects, all of whom are personally known to the author. The insights of the author may be worth reporting, but the limitations on the research have to be mentioned.

If the subject is controversial, look at other studies of the same subject for an additional way to judge veracity of the reported findings. For example, treatment of schizophrenia by social workers may be reported to be effective. But do other articles on the same subject come to opposite conclusions? One need not say which is correct, but it is important to note the existence of various alternative reports and conclusions.

EVALUATE THE RELIABILITY OF RESEARCH AND ANALYSIS METHODS

The report should show how it collected and analyzed the data. The use of such statistical analysis methods as Statistical Package for the Social Sciences (SPSS) is often a good indication that the research was reliably collected and presented.

EVALUATE REPLICABILITY AS ANOTHER INDICATOR

Reliable research reports should make their data available for restudying the same issues. As mentioned earlier, there was a good bit of discussion in 2015 about the lack of replicability of psychology studies. The Open Science Collaborative used 270 researchers to examine 100 psychology articles, attempting to obtain the same results as the original studies found. The papers that were studied reported significant results in 97% of the cases. But the reproduced studies found that only 36% of the studies yielded significant results (Aschwanden, 2015; Open Science Collaboration, 2015).

Some conclusions are based on trials, especially clinical trials in medical research that deals with medicines and pharmaceuticals. The standard for determining the effectiveness—as well as the dangers and side effects—is typically found through clinical trials. These may include studies of the effects of a product on animals or human subjects.

"I HEARD" OR "PEOPLE ARE SAYING"

It should not be necessary to mention to professionals with some background in research and the sciences that much of what passes for factual statements is not. Political leaders and other advocates for policy positions may introduce ideas by saying that "they heard" or "people are saying." Whatever. The role of public discourse is not often enabled by such assertions. Interestingly, the proliferation of information in print and online sometimes confuses what the researcher is finding. Rumors and prejudiced data may appear legitimate but may not be. There are clear hoaxes and misstated "facts" about critical issues in American life.

A case in point was the World Trade Center and Pentagon attacks on September 11, 2001. More than a few advocates for one cause or another developed and spread rumors that no Jewish people who worked in the World Trade Center went to work that day—implying that the attacks were part of a Jewish plot. Other rumors suggested that crowds of persons of the Islamic faith were seen cheering the attack. Neither rumor had any truth to it (Wiedeman, 2016). An additional propagated idea was that the Sandy Hook Elementary School killing of 20 children and seven adults was a hoax. Conspiracy theorists asserted that there had been no such killings—that reports of the event were used for political motives just as the rumor that the US moon landings were faked. In 2016, the winning candidate for President, Donald Trump, said he would have had a majority of the votes cast if illegally invited voters had not voted for his opponent. But there were no facts provided to support the assertion that nonauthorized voters participated in the election. A social work professor reported to one of the authors that he had given an assignment on minority relations in the U.S. Several of the papers that were submitted by his students were carefully documented. However, when the professor examined them more carefully, he discovered that many of the sources cited were from Ku Klux Klan websites and other racist sources with points of view far removed from what he sought. Being careful about evaluating data and verifying it, sometimes with multiple sources, especially sources that seem reliable on the bases of the discussions in this chapter, is critical for reporting scientific facts and research.

NUMBERS AND SCIENCE

For scientists, numbers are a bit different than numbers are for most Americans. For example, they often deal with very small quantities. One author (Ford, 1991) illustrates the smallness of scientific numbers by suggesting that the quantity of atoms in a few drops of water would be the equivalent of 10 million billion airports, reaching to the sky. Or it would take 2 million hydrogen atoms to cover the period at the end of this sentence. Some of the mathematical procedures scientists use are made necessary because of the small numbers inherent in much of science. Of course, as Feynman notes (1991), the metric system, although logical, was not created as an obvious scientific fact. It was originally calculated as one ten-millionth of the distance from the Earth's poles to the Equator. A gram is based on the mass of a cube of water that is one centimeter in length on each side. So, Feynman observes, measures, even in the SI system, are based on the size of the Earth, which was not, at the time the numbers were agreed upon, as well understood as it now is. Feynman, a Nobel Prize winner, was one of the most engaging science writers and a good resource for those who want to develop a feel for and a general understanding of physics. A good introduction to his work, among several accessible works about his theories, is 1994's *Six Easy Pieces*.

Because so much of science is international, scientists have to use a common measuring system in order to communicate with one another. Because scientists often have to deal with exceedingly small numbers, as mentioned earlier, SI is much more convenient in calculating quantities. For example, our ounce is 28.34952312 grams—a difficult amount to calculate when trying to communicate with people accustomed to the metric system. A pound is 453.59237 grams. A milligram is 0.00003527396195. A prescription for 10 milligrams of a medicine is much easier to state in metric than in the English system terms. Dividing and multiplying portions of ounces and pounds is difficult. The very small amounts that are relatively easy to quantify with SI are cumbersome in the English system.

Memorizing a few key SI terms is helpful in daily life, especially daily life overseas, where everyone is able to speak in terms of metric measures that are often incomprehensible to Americans. A kilogram is 2.2 pounds, so a person who weighs 100 kilograms weighs 220 pounds, in terms more familiar to us. Of course, the British are likely to confuse us even further because they often state body weight in terms of "stones," which are 14 pounds each. So a 150-pound person would weight 10.7 stones or a little more than 10.5 stones.

In terms of lengths, a kilometer is 0.6213711922, but when long-distance runners convert the often kilometer-measured routes set for races, they round off the conversion and simply use 0.6 miles per kilometer. So a 5-kilometer race is 3 miles, and the popular "10K" is 6 miles. A meter is 1.093613298 yards, but for most nonscientific purposes yards and meters are treated as equivalent.

The SI system is valuable because it moves systematically with decimal measurements. A milligram is one-thousandth of a gram; a kilogram is one thousand grams; a centimeter is one hundredth of a meter; a kilometer is one thousand meters, and so on. See Tables 4.1 and 4.2, and there are also several conversion applications in the application stores on computers and smartphones, most of them free of charge.

Effective social workers learn to calculate and evaluate numbers in their heads in order to better understand what they are doing and what they need to do. A basic orientation to understanding numbers is essential to modern social workers. Being able to analyze a social agency budget, for example, is a needed skill. That is especially true when trying to determine the adequacy of the budget for meeting the agency's objectives. Knowing how to analyze statistical reports—in order to roughly calculate per-service costs—is another common skill for effective social workers. Social workers who are able to perform most efficiently are likely to think statistically and mathematically about the work they encounter. Although those skills are most pertinent to social work managers and large system workers such as community organizers, they are equally valuable for direct service workers who want to more systematically analyze the work that they do or of which they are a part. For example, one of the authors of this text was involved in the development of a planned national organization to improve services to children in the United States. The goals were lofty and the plans were idealistic. However, the budget was just enough to perhaps improve services in one city or one county. Rather than embarking on a project that was unlikely to reach its objectives, the planners of the program would have been more likely to succeed if they had structured the effort as a demonstration project, or a guide to improving services that could be distributed throughout the nation, or an evaluation of a few existing programs. Of course, the project failed and frustrated those who were involved. Some extensive expenditures were wasted on an effort that could not possibly achieve what it set out to do. A well-informed social worker would be able to estimate the numbers of agencies that serve children in the nation, the cost of intervening with and assisting all of those agencies, and the funds that could be allocated for each of them—an analysis that would demand major modifications in the plan (see Fig. 4.3).

SOURCES OF IDEAS ABOUT NUMBERS

Aryabhata wrote down the Hindu mathematical procedures, including algebra, long division, and multiplication in 470 CE, which are essentially the same as the methods we use today (Schwartz & McGuinness, 1979). Schwartz and McGuinness

Relationship of Data, Information, and Intelligence

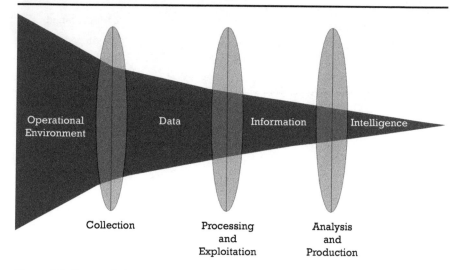

Figure 4.3 Data analysis
SOURCE: By U.S. Joint Chiefs of Staff JP2-0 - http://www.dtic.mil/doctrine/new_pubs/jp2_0.pdf, Public Domain, https://commons.wikimedia.org/w/index.php?curid=47853614

(1979) also say that more complex mathematical concepts such as calculus, decimals, and algorithms were developed by several thinkers in the 16th and 17th centuries. For example, although Newton is credited with the development of calculus, Gottfried Leibniz independently developed calculus (the mathematics of change) at about the same time as Newton (Kirsch, 2016).

Scientists have always been concerned with numbers, and the elegance of scientific concepts is often related to numerical systems of designing and calculating them. Science and mathematics have always been closely related, and the great scientists and great scientific theories are also mathematic models developed by people with a consuming interest in mathematics. The importance of mathematical literacy is discussed in an accessible way by John Allan Paulos (1988) in in his book, *Innumeracy: Mathematical Illiteracy and Its Consequences.*

OTHER USEFUL NUMBERS

Another valuable number is the speed of light. This particular speed is fundamental for understanding many other theories, especially those in physics. There are no instantaneous transmissions, even conversations. When we speak and are heard, the transmission time is slower than the speed of light, which is the fastest speed in the universe, 299,792,458 meters per second, a measurement discovered by Albert Einstein. Time is required for moving anything—light waves, sound— from one place to another. Nothing is instantaneous, although it seems that way in the normal course of our activities. That knowledge helped Einstein develop his famous theories. The establishment of the speed of light was first developed by classical researchers using telescopes to determine the speed by triangulating through

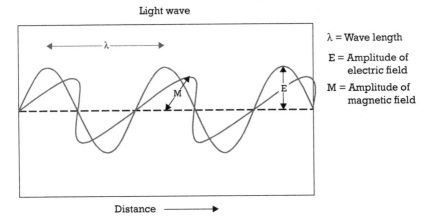

Figure 4.4 Light wave
SOURCE: CC BY-SA 3.0, https://commons.wikimedia.org/w/index.php?curid=1864272

geometrical studies the speed of light between different points among the planets, which move at constant rates. The speed was refined early in the 20th century by Einstein and other physicists.

The speed of light, as mentioned, is 299,792,458 meters per second, which is often rounded off for discussion purposes to 300 million meters per second— which is also 186,000 miles per second. A person at the Equator traveling at the maximum speed of light would circle the Earth about 7.5 times in a second. The speed of light is what scientists call a constant. It doesn't matter who is looking at what or where they are; it's always that speed. Consider that a modern jet airplane, traveling between the coasts of the United States, requires at least 4 hours to travel from one coast to the other. Of course, an airplane travels much, much slower than the speed of light (see Fig. 4.4).

CONCLUSION

Researchers do their best work when they validate the sources they quote and the research on which they rely. Scientific rigor is a critical element in determining whether or not to credit existing research to one's own work and to ensuring the reliability of the research one includes in his or her work. Researching the vast fields of science and determining how it does or does not stand up in one's writing requires the ability to separate quality research from studies of lesser quality. Using some of the criteria suggested in this chapter is a useful guide for evaluating the data one encounters. The chapter has also covered the systems science uses in its calculations, especially the SI measurement, which is standard for the sciences.

REFERENCES

Aschwanden, C. (2015, November 30). Psychology's inner demons. *Discover*. Retrieved at http://discovermagazine.com/2016/janfeb/8-psychologys-inner-demons

Engber, D. (2016, May/June). Why hasn't the U.S adopted the metric system. *Popular Science, 96.*

Feynman, R. P. (1991). Atoms in motion. In T. Ferris (Ed.), *The world treasury of physics, astronomy and mathematics.* Boston, MA: Little, Brown and Company.

Ford, K. W. (1991). The large and the small. In T. Ferris (Ed.), *The world treasury of physics, astronomy and mathematics* (pp. 3–17). Boston, MA: Little, Brown and Company.

Kirsch, A. (2016, September 05). Are we really so modern. *The New Yorker.* Retrieved from https://www.newyorker.com/magazine/2016/09/05/the-dream-of-enlightenment-by-anthony-gottlieb

Open Science Collaboration. (2015). Estimating the reproducibility of psychological science. *Science, 349*(6251), aac4716. Retrieved from http://nymag.com/intelligencer/2016/09/the-sandy-hook-hoax.html

Paulos, J. A. (1988). *Innumeracy: Mathematical illiteracy and its consequences.* New York, NY: Macmillan.

Schwartz, J., & McGuinness, M. (1979). *Einstein for beginners.* New York, NY: Pantheon.

Wiedeman, R. (2016, September). The Sandy Hook hoax. *New York Magazine.* Retrieved from http://nymag.com/daily/intelligencer/2016/09/the-sandy-hook-hoax.html

5

Social Work and the Science of Big Data

You might periodically hear the term "big data" when listening to the news or reading about technology in the popular press and wonder what it means. The idea of "data" is fairly well understood to mean a wide array of information gathered together for analysis. The information may take the form of numbers from surveys, EKG readings, self-report measures of depression, or narratives from interviews and case notes from a child welfare case manager. Typically, data are placed in databases that allow for analysis. Databases are assembled all the time for purposes of research or business analytics. In fact, at the website datahub (https://datahub.io/dataset) there are nearly 11,000 publically available databases open for analysis.

These conceptions of databases predate the technological revolution in data collection and storage that started in 2002 with the advent of the digital age (see Fig. 5.1). A number of important factors contributed to the possibility of big data, including the decreasing cost of digital storage and the expansion of data collected electronically by almost every bureaucracy and business we interact with—whether filing your taxes with the US Internal Revenue Service via the Web or having your health data collected during doctors' appointments and entered into an electronic health record (EHR). Even in most social services agencies, data are now collected and entered into electronic databases. For example, in Illinois, the Department of Children and Family Services works closely with Chapin Hall, the Center for State Child Welfare Data and the University of Illinois Child and Family Research Center to organize, analyze, and utilize findings to shape services. Community mental health agencies like Centerstone, a national nonprofit behavioral health organization, and Chestnut Health Systems, a highly innovative organization in central Illinois, are utilizing robust EHR systems. Most professional social workers are familiar with the basic technology that makes big data possible and interact with it professionally and personally on a daily basis.

It is funny to note that we still have not defined "big data" and how it differs from the types of databases typically encountered by social workers in their professional and personal lives. You probably intuitively understand that the datasets are bigger than all of the data in an EHR system used by a hospital, for example. But how much bigger? Think of the amount of data used to predict the weather or stock markets or how long someone is likely to live. The data used for these types of analyses

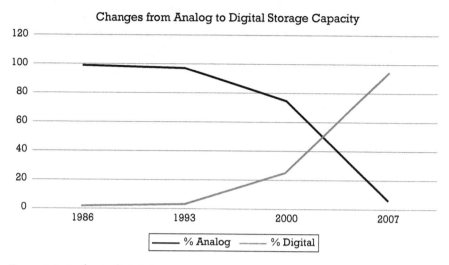

Figure 5.1 Analog to digital storage
SOURCE: Authors' creation; Data source: Hilbert, M., & López, P. (2011). The world's technological capacity to store, communicate, and compute information. Science, 1200970.

considers tens of thousands of factors and the interactions of those factors in the context of historical data about the phenomenon. If you use Facebook, Instagram, Twitter, or LinkedIn; have had your genome analyzed; receive Medicare; or pay taxes, then you are contributing to big data. Google search data have been used to predict flu outbreaks, Medicare data are used to predict the duration and type of treatment that is most successful for the most patients, and our tax data are used to understand our economy. For some of these big data aggregators, such as social media companies, the purpose is to create big data that can be analyzed and used to attract advertisers. For others such as Medicare, the data are aggregated because it is the best and most efficient way to track and bill services. The big data aspect is the result of moving to electronic files. In both cases the data sets are enormous by any historical standard and growing exponentially. To get a better understanding of big data beyond size, we will take a brief look at the history of the concept and the first big data project.

HISTORY

The term "big data" appears to have originated in Silicon Valley and is associated with Web search companies such as Google (Sanchez & Verspoor, 2014). In 2001, Gartner, an American research and advisory firm that focuses on information technology (https://en.wikipedia.org/wiki/Gartner), issued a widely cited white paper that is used to define the term "big data." Interestingly, the paper never uses the term "big data." Beyond size, which is typically defined as "high volume," the paper also identifies high velocity and high variety as important factors in understanding the future of data (Sanchez & Verspoor, 2014; Ward & Barker, 2013). Together, volume, velocity, and variety are known as the "three Vs." Gartner revised the three

Vs in 2012 to include a fourth, veracity, which refers to the level of trust in the accuracy of the data and the outcomes from analyzing the data (Sanchez & Verspoor, 2014; Ward & Barker, 2013).

Although Gartner's four Vs are widely cited as the defining features of big data, there are other definitions offered by technology experts and companies. Ward and Baker (2013) conducted a survey of definitions and found some slightly different takes on the term. For example, Oracle, an American multinational computer technology corporation that specializes in cloud computing and data platforms, does not utilize Gartner's Vs but instead focuses on the addition of new and complex data sources to traditional databases. This might include the data from social media or images from video. Intel, the computer chip maker, put a specific number on the size of big data, which from their perspective is data linked to organizations producing a median of 300 terabytes of data per week. Finally, Microsoft defines "big data" as a "term increasingly used to describe the process of applying serious computing power—the latest machine learning and artificial intelligence—to seriously massive and often complex sets of information." You get the sense that two descriptions of big data are true—it is massive in size and extraordinary in complexity.

The other widely discussed concept that is useful to understanding big data is whether the data are structured or unstructured. Traditionally, data contained in databases were structured by a defined model or schema that made the data easily accessible for analysis by computer programs (Sanchez & Verspoor, 2014). Financial transactions are an example of structured big data that provide insights into the trends in the US and world economies. Unstructured data include information that does not have a data schema. The most typical form of unstructured data is text or image related, such as included in Wikipedia. The traditional analytic programs are not well equipped to analyze all of the text related to race relations from newspapers in the United States produced between 1800 and 2016, YouTube videos from hundreds of millions of users, or the MRI images from thousands of people with brain cancer.

One of the first big data projects, sequencing the human genome, fits the bill for massive and complex. Starting in 1986 when the Department of Energy allocated funding for genomic studies, one of the significant barriers to the sequencing project was the technology needed to store and analyze massive amounts of complex data. The term used was "bioinformatics" and the goal was to build the data storage and analysis capacities beyond what was currently available at the time. An example of early work in this area that presages big data is BLAST (Basic Local Alignment Search Tool), which was a computer program developed to search for genes that are common across different genomes (Ginsberg, Nackerud, & Larrison, 2004). By 2001 when the drafts of the human genome were published in *Science* and *Nature*, the technology necessary for big data to develop in other realms such as in health care or social media was well underway to being widely available for many applications beyond genome sequencing. For more about the history of the human genome and the technology developed as a result of the race to sequence it, refer to our book *Human Biology for Social Workers* (2001).

SOCIAL MEDIA, SEARCH ENGINES, AND
SILICON VALLEY

The future of big data seems most strongly linked to social media and search engine companies, two types of company that purposefully generate massive amounts of unstructured data. If you or a relative or a friend uses social media such as Facebook, Twitter, LinkedIn, YouTube, and Instagram, think about the amount of information entered into these platform—photos, links to your social network, narrative about your feelings and thoughts, and your likes and dislikes of products and popular trends. Further, think about how much narrative data companies like Google generate by tracking the types of searches and websites reviewed by people who access their service. Multiply this by hundreds of millions, sometimes billions of people around the world, and you get a sense of the opportunities to better understand human behavior and the barriers to analyzing this data.

The data generated by social media and Web search companies are central to their business model. This means for now most of the analyses coming from these companies focus on increasing the amount of time individuals use their service and selling advertising. Periodically these companies have begun to delve into larger questions of human behavior by leveraging their user data. The idea of social media research is growing interest in general because of the size and uniqueness of data generated by social media. Social media research allows for tracking conversations in real time, identifying trending topics of interest, finding key influencers in social networks, researching hard-to-access populations that may be hidden or small and dispersed over a wide geographic area, and pursuing inductive approaches that discover previously unanticipated observations (MRA, 2016). Companies such as Google and Facebook have developed their own research teams. Some examples of interesting research that moves beyond marketing include Facebook's examination of the diffusion of social movements by analyzing the factors that contribute to users adopting a symbol that indicated their support for marriage equality and studying how the adoption of an "I Voted" sticker increased voter participation across the nation (Monnappa, 2017).

Reliability and validity of information from social media and Web search data are open to much debate (the fourth V, veracity). The range of reliability and validity of big data is wide. Some of the common problems are associated with most measurement methods. One of the most common pitfalls of big data is its representativeness (MRA, 2016). Because the number of users and amount of data are enormous in scale, it is easy to forget that size does not replace good sampling techniques. Understanding who is represented by the users of Facebook or Google, for instance, is important to applying the meaning of findings from big data research properly. An early and public failure of big data research was the Google flu trend project. The idea was that by tracking people's search terms you could understand in real time the overall prevalence of flu outbreak. A Google team published a paper in *Nature*, one of the premier science journals, about the success of the method in 2008. However, in a follow-up analysis the method misjudged the peak of the 2013 flu outbreak by 140% (https://www.wired.com/2015/10/can-learn-epic-failure-google-flu-trends/).

HEALTH

Speaking of the flu, one of the largest untapped big data areas that is likely to have an impact on social work practice is health care. Disparate and widely collected health care data have been growing since the introduction of health information technology in 2001 when the Institute of Medicine issued a call to implement electronic prescription services (Shekelle, Morton, & Keeler, 2006). Since 2001 there have been substantial resources spent by the federal government—first under President Bush when he signed the executive order of President's Health Information Technology Plan in 2004 and as part of President Obama's American Recovery and Reinvestment Act in 2009 (Chiu & Fitzgerald, 2013; Hillestad et al., 2005). It represents the next significant big data frontier.

Three issues are barriers to realizing the full potential of health care big data. Because of these issues, the process is likely to be slow moving and to take longer than expected. However, like other technology leaps experienced throughout the 2000s, once these issues are addressed there will be substantial and unpredictable changes to how we approach personal health and health care services. The first substantial barrier is that 80% of health care data is unstructured and wide ranging, including clinical notes from providers, medications, data from medical devices, lab results, images (e.g., CT, X-ray, or MRI), correspondences between medical professions, genomic data, and services data (McDonald, 2016). The technology and applications needed to bring together these disparate unstructured data are growing in sophistication (in the next section we will discuss some of these fascinating new approaches to data) and are already being applied to the similarly complex data found on Facebook pages, which leads us to the second barrier. Unlike Facebook, health care data do not share a common platform that provides commonly shared home for the unstructured data. In fact, EHR systems, which are where most of the untapped health care data in the nation are located, tend to be idiosyncratic to the organization. Hospitals located in the same city may use substantially different EHR systems that are not necessarily meant to be combined for analysis. Issues as simple as how different EHR systems code particular diseases, services, and the content of clinical notes represents another layer of complexity that has not been addressed as of yet. At the insurer level (both private and Medicaid/Medicare), there is a substantial aggregating of data across providers, but in private insurance, which in 2015 insured 67.2% of the US population, data are not widely available for public analysis (Barnett & Vornovitsky, 2016). The third and final barrier to big data analytics of health care data is related to confidentiality and the legal issues associated with accessing personal health information. These issues will be discussed in a later section.

Once the three aforementioned barriers are addressed, the progress on improving areas such as personalized medicine, preventative interventions, and chronic disease care will be substantial. Sanchez and Verspoor (2014) noted three areas of structured data and three areas of unstructured health care data that are likely to see growth during the upcoming decade. The structure data areas include (1) molecular databases, bioinformatics, and systems biology; (2) clinical health care applications in EHR systems; and (3) population and global health policy applications that use infectious disease risk maps or trends in health disparities experienced by minority populations. The unstructured data areas include (1) text mining published bio-medical literature—the growth in this literature has been incredible with nearly a million citations added in 2013 alone and this is growing every year; (2) clinical narratives in EHR systems; and (3) social media and Web-based information (e.g., Web queries, blogs, news aggregating sites), which may allow for tracking conta-gious diseases, identifying evidence-based interventions that are developed by pa-tients, and identifying the side effects of interventions such as pharmaceuticals that are not currently identified in the scholarly literature. An example of the latter type of research was conducted by Dr. Russ Altman at Stanford University in 2012 when he and his colleagues identified the unknown side effect of diabetic level increases in blood glucose. He found that this side effect was created by taking a popular anti-depressant along with a popular cholesterol-reducing drug, and he discovered this by using big data techniques to mine 30 years of adverse medication events reported by doctors, patients, and drug companies in an FDA database (Tene & Polonetsky, 2013). Beyond these opportunities there is the possibility to use smartphones to monitor patient health in real time and the ability to use EHR data for predictive modeling using machine learning. For example, Optum Labs, a health care research collaborative, has assembled the EHR files of 30 million people to develop predictive analytic tools for doctors and other medical professionals (McDonald, 2016).

It is not hard to imagine the benefits of defragmented communication among health care providers who are presented with meaningful interpretations of your health based on data collected directly from you throughout your life starting with data collected during your mother's prenatal appointments. Further, it is interesting to ponder how individuals' health-related behaviors (e.g., exercise, healthy eating, sleep) might change when they have access to the same data. Currently, anyone who has experienced a complex chronic health problem such as cancer, a serious mental illness, diabetes, or cardiovascular disease that requires multiple longitudinal inter-ventions provided by different professionals located in multiple organizations knows that communication is rarely seamless and the massive amounts of infor-mation gathered during appointments is not organized in meaningful ways for pro-viders and patients. The complexity of some of the aforementioned health problems requires case management by social workers to help the individual experiencing the problem navigate the health care system. As health care organizations better lever-ages big data analytics, there may be decreasing needs for case management services provided by social workers.

BIG DATA ANALYTICS: TECHNOLOGIES AND APPLICATIONS

At this point in the chapter, we should have a better understanding of what "big data" is and its potential to change what we know about human behavior in all sorts of realms, but we might know little about the analytic applications that make this potential possible. Without being too technical we will identify a couple of the prominent analytic tools in big data and explain in nontechnical language how they work. One of the easiest ways to imagine how big data are analyzed is to think of a process of systematically identifying positive signals (e.g., a tiny local radio station) in a sea of white noise—sort of like looking for "a needle in a haystack." This process is typically referred to as data mining. The two most widely discussed and used big data applications are Hadoop and MapR. Hadoop is an open-sourced and Java-based programming framework that supports the processing of big data. The easiest way to think of it is as an ecosystem for big data. MapR works within the Hadoop ecosystem and was developed by Google. Both products have multiple tools for data storage and analysis that allow for structured and unstructured data from multiple sources to be streamed, organized, stored, and made usable for analysis.

Two other technologies are important to big data: One is new and the other old. Traditionally, data have been housed in devices like your desktop computer (in some ways) called servers, which are located physically onsite at the business or agency using them. Maintaining physical servers can be an expensive cost barrier to social service agencies and most small businesses interested in storing and analyzing data that are too big to fit in the memory space typically found on a desktop computer. Cloud computing represents a new technological advance that uses a network of remote servers connected to the Internet to store and analyze data. Amazon, Google, and Apple (to name a few) offer Cloud computer services to individual users and businesses. If you own an iPhone, you may already be using a cloud computing service to store, share, and access music, videos, photos, and word documents without filling the hard drive memory on your phone.

An older idea that has found new meaning in big data is machine learning. Arthur Samuel, a famous research who worked on artificial intelligence (and was briefly a professor at the University of Illinois, the home institution of one of the authors of this book) first used the phrase "machine learning" in 1959. The concept means to providing computers with the capability to learn without human programing (Samuel, 1959). The abstract of his interesting paper, which used the game of checkers to explore the concept of machine learning, follows. It clearly explains the basics of the concept:

> Abstract: Two machine-learning procedures have been investigated in some detail using the game of checkers. Enough work has been done to verify the fact that a computer can be programmed so that it will learn to play a better game of checkers than can be played by the person who wrote the program. Furthermore, it can learn to do this in a remarkably short period of time (8 or 10 hours of machine-playing time) when given only the rules of the game, a sense of direction, and a redundant and incomplete list of parameters which are thought to have something to do with the game, but whose correct signs and relative weights are unknown and unspecified. The principles of machine learning verified by these experiments are, of course, applicable to many other situations. (p. ii)

Combining big data with machine learning is occurring in a number of different areas with interesting results confirming the last line of Samuel's abstract.

An example that will resonate with social workers relates to hospital readmission rates. Medicare and private insurers penalize hospitals for high readmission rates. In response, the Carolinas Healthcare System (CHS) used machine learning to understand patients' level of risk. This information was then used by case managers in discharge decisions by helping them to prioritize patients according to risk and complexity. The system lowered readmission rate by 30% (Ambati, 2015). One machine learning experiment by Microsoft that went terribly wrong was Tay, a Twitter bot that was programmed to act like a millennial teen. The public taught Tay to be a racist Holocaust-denier within 24 hours, thereby demonstrating the potential to further institutionalize prejudices by relying on biased algorithms and data (Larson, Angwin, & Parris, 2016).

PRIVACY, CONFIDENTIALITY, AND ETHICS

The growth of data in general, its perceived economic value, and the rapidly developing technology to mine and use data in ways that may impact the everyday lives of individual citizens produce the potential ethical issues, particularly in regard to privacy. These concerns, which are proper and important to pay attention to, need to be balanced with providing the necessary space for innovations to arise in areas such as health care and transportation.

The Fourth Amendment to the US Constitution states: "The right of the people to be secure in their persons, houses, papers, and effects, against unreasonable searches and seizures, shall not be violated, and no Warrants shall issue, but upon probable cause, supported by Oath or affirmation, and particularly describing the place to be searched, and the persons or things to be seized." You probably can begin to think of problems that might arise. Two particularly sticky issues have to do with cell phones, which contain an incredible amount of personal data (e.g., emails, texts, contacts, location tracking), and social media, where there can be a blurring of private versus public unlike historic experiences of papers, houses, and physical effects (e.g., a trunk or safe). To give you a sense of how complex this might be from a legal standpoint, think of all the case law devoted to searching an automobile, which is thought to be different from a house, papers, or effects. Even now, the rules of search and seizure related to automobiles remain open to interpretation. Recently in California there was significant debate over opening an Apple iPhone owned by a person implicated in a terrorist attack that killed 14 individuals working at a social service agency. The conflict between privacy and the government's right to search a citizen's effects was not resolved legally, but technologically, which means the next time this occurs, the same basic legal conflicts about privacy will remain (Rubin, Queally, & Dave, 2016).

In general, there are significant questions about who owns data, who has access to data, who can grant access to data, and how data are used. The expanding personalization of product advertising and newsfeeds by Google and Facebook are examples of how individual data are being leveraged for economic reasons. The Arab Spring, Occupy Wall Street, Black Lives Matter, and President Trump's campaign have all used Twitter to shape the narrative of events and to build a reservoir of data/information that is leveraged to support their movement. Who beyond the company Twitter should have access to these data and how the data are analyzed to create meaning that may shape public perceptions of events is not entirely clear. In Europe there has been a growing movement to recognize that data generated by social media or Web searches belongs in part to the individual citizens who generated it. An example of this is 2014 ruling by the Court of Justice of the European Union that allows individuals the "right to be forgotten," which allows users to remove links that are false or out of date (see Box 5.1 for more information). However, this right is only available to citizens of the European Union. In a more general move toward transparency, Google in recent years has provided access to a dashboard that allows users to see most of their data, again providing some level of ownership to individual citizens.

Literature has long explored the issues related to data-driven societies. The first to leap to mind is George Orwell's *1984*, which was written in 1949. Two strong parallels between the world created by Orwell and today's world of big data are the collection of data for surveillance of people's behaviors, whether this is the use of face recognition software at airports or the use of phone metadata, which include the date, time, call duration, both parties involved in the call, and geographic location of call participants by the U.S. National Security Agency (NSA), or Facebook's personalizing your advertisement and newsfeeds. These are instances of beginning

---

Box 5.1

THE RIGHT TO BE FORGOTTEN

The following is a search removal request under data protection law in Europe.

Background

In May 2014, a ruling by the Court of Justice of the European Union (C-131/12, 13 May 2014) found that certain people can ask search engines to remove specific results for queries that include their name, where the interests in those results appearing are outweighed by the person's privacy rights.

When you make such a request, we will balance the privacy rights of the individual with the public's interest to know and the right to distribute information. When evaluating your request, we will look at whether the results include outdated information about you, as well as whether there's a public interest in the information—for example, we may decline to remove certain information about financial scams, professional malpractice, criminal convictions, or public conduct of government officials.

You will need a digital copy of a form of identification to complete this form. If you are submitting this request on behalf of someone else, you will need to supply identification for them. Fields marked with an asterisk * must be completed for your request to be submitted.

---

tracked and monitored that were never available before the advent of big data. As Orwell states about society in *1984*:

> The telescreen received and transmitted simultaneously. Any sound that Winston made, above the level of a very low whisper, would be picked up by it; moreover, so long as he remained within the field of vision which the metal plaque commanded, he could be seen as well as heard.... How often, or on what system, the Thought Police plugged in on any individual wire was guess-work. It was even conceivable that they watched everybody all the time. You had to live—did live, from habit that became instinct—in the assumption that every sound you made was overheard ... every movement scrutinized. (pp. 6–7)

The second parallel is the growing use of what Orwell called "Newspeak": "Newspeak is the only language in the world whose vocabulary gets smaller every year ... the whole aim of Newspeak is to narrow the range of thought. In the end we shall make thought crime literally impossible, because there will be no words in which to express it. Every concept that can ever be needed will be ex-pressed by exactly one word, with its meaning rigidly defined and all its subsidiary meanings rubbed out and forgotten.... Every year fewer and fewer words and the range of consciousness always a little smaller" (p. 46). The ability to access a con-stant stream of information that confirms your beliefs and never interacts with in-formation that is contrary is thought to be one of the central reasons for fragmenting society in the United States, leading to isolation and extremism.

In a modern update, the television show *Black Mirror* (BBC and Netflix) has been examining some of these same issues. In the first episode of the third season titled "Nose Dive," people are constantly ranked by their behavior via a social media–type app on their smartphones and assigned numeric ratings that define their access to all kinds of services (e.g., health care, airplane tickets, hotel rooms, jobs, housing). In the episode, these numbers are always changing, like the changes in ratings you might experience as a Twitter or Instagram user. All the time your behavior is moni-tored and rated by others. Some of this is also occurring in Silicon Valley businesses like Airbnb, which helps people rent their extra house space to travelers, or Uber, which allows people to use their own cars like a taxi. Both of these companies have rating systems that are used by all parties involved in the exchange. Needless to say, in both *1984* and *Black Mirror*, we are offered cautionary tales of using big data to improve society.

HOW WILL BIG DATA IMPACT SOCIAL WORK?

There are three impacts of big data on the profession of social work that are worth discussing briefly before we close out the chapter. First, big data is going to change our understanding of human behaviors greatly. As we have discussed throughout the chapter, the technology and data are now beginning to be available to understand the complex interaction between genes and the environment. For example, the cost of genomic sequencing has decreased from $10 million in 2008 to approximately $1,000 today. This means the number of sequenced human genomes is growing daily and increasing our understanding of genetics in a way that was never possible before. Currently human behavior is understood from a variety of fragmented perspectives represented broadly by the nature-versus-nurture approach to research. When genetic data begin to be connected to unstructured individual health data and social media data, we are a likely to see significant growth in understanding human behavior. With a better understanding of human behavior and the root causes of problems such as mental illness or diabetes or family violence, there are likely to be improved interventions. Social work professionals and researchers will have an opportunity to lead the development of these interventions by bringing a human voice to the data.

Second, there are opportunities to better understand how families and friends interact to create communities and human capital. Community development, a historic part of social work practice that attracts less than 20% students, may become more important as this information is leveraged to improve community relations and decrease the modern propensity toward tribalism, fragmentation, and isolation. Additionally, there may be opportunities for clinical social workers to counsel or coach people around issues related to social media usage and privacy in the world of big data. In response to these changes, university programs training social workers will have to begin to develop classes related to big data and social media.

Finally, as mentioned under the health care section, big data may have a negative impact on the need for case management services by people who are experiencing complex, chronic health problems. If this comes to pass, it will mean a loss of jobs traditionally held by social workers in the health care system. But these same systems will also improve the monitoring of client progress in real time and increase the amount of data coming from clients about their experiences with interventions. As you think about the ways big data might change and reshape the profession of social work, we will hope that you find the introductory information contained in this chapter helpful.

REFERENCES

Ambati, S. (2015). Machine learning: A practical introduction—How new tools and techniques are extracting business insights from massive data sets. Retrieved from http://www.infoworld.com/article/3010401/big-data/machine-learning-a-practical-introduction.html

Barnett, J. C., & Vornovitsky, M. S. (2016). *Health insurance coverage in the United States: 2015.* Washington, DC: US Government Printing Office.

Chiu, S.-H., & Fitzgerald, K. M. (2013). Electronic medical/health record and pediatric behavioral health providers: progress and problems. *Archives of Psychiatric Nursing,* 27(2), 108–109.

Ginsberg, L., Nackerud, L., & Larrison, C. (2004). *Human biology for social workers: Development, ecology, genetics, and health.* Needham Hts., MA: Allyn & Bacon.

Hillestad, R., Bigelow, J., Bower, A., Girosi, F., Meili, R., Scoville, R., & Taylor, R. (2005). Can electronic medical record systems transform health care? Potential health benefits, savings, and costs. *Health Affairs, 24*(5), 1103–1117.

Larson, J., Angwin, J., & Parris Jr, T. (2016). *Breaking the black box: How machines learn to be racist.* New York, NY: ProPublica.

Marketing Research Association. (2016). *IMRO guide to the top 16 social media research questions.* Retrieved from https://www.insightsassociation.org/issues-policies/best-practice/mra-guide-top-16-social-media-research-questions

Martin-Sanchez, F., & Verspoor, K. (2014). Big data in medicine is driving big changes. *Yearbook of Medical Informatics, 9*(1), 14.

McDonald, C. (2016). How big data is reducing costs and improving outcomes in health care. Retrieved from https://www.slideshare.net/caroljmcdonald/how-big-data-is-reducing-costs-and-improving-outcomes-in-health-care

Monnappa, A. (2017). How Facebook is using big data—The good, the bad, and the ugly. Retrieved from https://www.simplilearn.com/how-facebook-is-using-big-data-article

Orwell, G. (1949). *1984.* New York, NY: Signet.

Rubin, J., Queally, J., & Dave, P. (2016, March 28). FBI unlocks San Bernardino shooter's iPhone and ends legal battle with Apple, for now. *LA Times.* Retrieved from http://www.latimes.com/local/lanow/la-me-ln-fbi-drops-fight-to-force-apple-to-unlock-san-bernardino-terrorist-iphone-20160328-story.html

Samuel, A. L. (1959). Some studies in machine learning using the game of checkers. *IBM Journal of Research and Development, 3*(3), 210–229.

Shekelle, P., Morton, S. C., & Keeler, E. B. (2006). Costs and benefits of health information technology. Retrieved from https://healthit.ahrq.gov/sites/default/files/docs/page/hitsys.pdf

Tableau. (2016). Top ten big data trends for 2017. Retrieved from https://www.tableau.com/sites/default/files/media/Whitepapers/whitepaper_top_10_big_data_trends_2017.pdf

Tene, O., & Polonetsky, J. (2013, April). Big data for all: Privacy and user control in the age of analytics. *Northwestern Journal of Technology and Intellectual Property, 11*, 240–272.

Ward, J. S., & Barker, A. (2013). Undefined by data: A survey of big data definitions. *arXiv Preprint arXiv:1309.5821.*

6

Social Work and the Science

of Climate Change

If you take care of the birds, you take care of most of the big problems in the world.
—Dr. THOMAS LOVEJOY, Professor of Environmental Science
and Policy at George Mason University

One of the more important and contentious current subjects in the sciences is climate change or, for those who emphasize its most important elements, "global warming." The potential changes, it is not unrealistic to suggest, are more likely than other phenomena to change the way life is lived in the next two centuries. For several years, scientists have noted that the world is warming—that the warmest weather in all the history of recorded weather reports has been in recent years. The highest world temperatures ever recorded were in 2015. Each year, the weather, on average, has been consistently warmer than the year before, and each year sets a new record for warmth. Observers have noted the melting of glaciers in frigid parts of the world such as Greenland and the North and South Poles. Habitats for cold-weather animals such as penguins, seals, and polar bears have disappeared. Lifestyles of peoples such as the Inuit, which are organized around frozen territory, have necessarily changed. The melting ice has raised the depth of oceans so that many island communities are being flooded and made uninhabitable, requiring people living in cold-weather climates to relocate. Similarly, people in warm-weather ocean communities such as Miami Beach face the potential flooding of their property. Unless the trend to flooding is abated, many island communities and beachfront areas will disappear into the sea.

The reasons for controversy are largely based on what is assumed to be the cause of the changes in the climate, which is typically connected to the release of carbon into the atmosphere by manufacturing, electric power generation, agriculture, automobile exhausts, and other activities that rely in part on gasoline and coal for energy. If the changes in the climate are a result of the use of fossil fuels, then major changes would be indicated for human activity in fields such as manufacturing and transportation. However, those who deny that the climate is changing insist that the changes are not a result of human activity, that they are natural phenomena, reflecting the regular changes in temperatures and other climate indicators over the centuries, or the result of other factors.

Governments take a variety of measures to reduce the "greenhouse gases" that are associated with climate change and global warming. For example, US automobiles and those of other nations require the installation of catalytic converters, which reduce the emission of some greenhouse gases. Gasoline is now sold without the addition of some substances that increase the problem of greenhouse gases. However, these measures do not eliminate greenhouse gases, and therefore other steps need to be taken to reduce them.

Climate change is worldwide, with some regions encountering more problems than others. For much of the world, it is the melting of the polar ice caps and glaciers that presents the biggest problem. According to Justin Gillis (2016, March 30), citing several science journals, the melting is likely to disrupt the lives of millions of people, some of whom are children as this is written, by 2100. A major article on the subject was published in *Nature* by Robert DeConte of the University of Massachusetts and David Pollard of Pennsylvania State University, which is the basis for the article by Gillis, who notes that models of climate change in the West Atlantic ice sheet, which is larger than Mexico, could melt rapidly and flood 95,000 miles of the US coastline. New York City, which has existed for some 400 years, is not likely to last for another 400. The total rise in the sea levels could total 3 feet and much more in some areas. The predictions of 3 years earlier did not predict such disastrous consequences, but climate change is so great that the estimates are being revised upward. Miami Beach, Florida, has experienced serious floods, with puddles that remain in local roadways often have swimming fish. One of the major problems with climate change, according to Gillis, is that there is not necessarily time to prepare for its disasters. The climate can change abruptly and the consequences may occur with little or no notice—unlike other problems in social policy. The specific changes are often unpredictable. Living at higher elevations does not necessarily protect people from floods, which can occur anywhere at any time.

Charles P. Pierce of Esquire.com (2016) reported that the expected rise in sea levels is twice as great as the United Nations predicted 3 years ago. That is because the breaking up of the great ice sheets responds to only small amounts of global warming. He notes, as do others, that dealing with climate change is the kind of problem nations such as the United States have difficulty addressing. The consequences are relatively far in the future, but action has to begin early to prevent those consequences. The physical laws, Pierce notes, do not care who wins the debate—they just go inexorably on. He suggests that epidemic disease, food riots, and massive dislocations are some of the potential results of not dealing with climate change.

The consequences of climate change throughout the world are already being felt in many places and have multiple impacts. Dexter Filkins (2016) reported on a visit he made with a group of scientists to assess the melting of a glacier, Chhoga Shigri, in the Himalayans. The glacier had lost 20 feet of its surface since 2002. The glacier has affected the water supply and climates of Bangladesh, India, and Pakistan throughout the history of the region. Already, the villages in those nations were experiencing more frequent flooding and changes in the monsoons, which make farming possible in the thousands of villages that contain most of the populations of those nations. A change in the rain patterns will affect many who rely on steady patterns for their livelihoods. One of the authors of this book remembered visiting India and, after looking at the sky, believed that rain was on the way, in February. The Indian counterparts said, "It will rain in October," which it always did. But now rains are coming at quite different times and monsoons are not coming when they have been predicted for thousands of years. They come sporadically. Perhaps worse, rain has led to the disruption of village life, which is likely to become more severe. The 2015 monsoon season was the driest in decades.

Of course, oceans are international. A rise in ocean levels in Asia has effects in North America and everywhere else. Although the rises are largely a result of melting glaciers, the seas rise both where there are glaciers and where there are none. Elizabeth Kolbert (2016), a noted environmental writer, says that the melting of the ice cap studied by Filkins would cause difficulty for anyone who lives near an ocean—New York, New Orleans, much of Florida, coastal North Carolina, the Texas Gulf Coast—anywhere. Tidal flooding in cities such as Charleston, South Carolina, is a reality. When there is rain at high tide, many areas of the city become impassable.

As Filkins describes, the histories of glaciers are typically identified by drilling into them to study the changes over years in their composition. That process is made more difficult because of the melting of the glaciers, which prevents them from being stable and drillable.

In 2016, scientists began discovering that coral reefs around the world were being destroyed by the warming of the oceans and other weather events. Innis (2016) reported in the *New York Times* that there was massive "bleaching" of the coral reefs. One third of the world's coral reefs, which are surfaces in the oceans made up of tiny marine organisms called polyps, were in danger of disappearing. The reefs produce food and shelter for marine life, including organisms such as fish and other seafood. Some 30 million people earn their living by harvesting seafood from the reefs and 1 billion people's diets are primarily from seafood. The extent of the loss of coral reefs worldwide appears to be greater than any other seen in world history, according to Innis (2016). For example, Australia's Great Barrier Reef is composed of 520 coral reefs. In studying them, scientists found that only four had not been damaged and bleached. Those losses in Australia could lead to the loss or reduction of some 620 miles of coral reefs.

New York City, which is surrounded by water from rivers and the Atlantic Ocean, is especially vulnerable to the consequences of climate change. Andrew Rice (2016) points to the need for the city to elevate many of its services and facilities. Houses located on waterways may need to be rebuilt with stilts to deal with the rising waters that are associated with the warming of the oceans. He notes that the years 2014, 2015, and 2016 were the warmest on record and that the temperatures are rising even more rapidly than had been predicted. He suggests that the New York subway system might have to be modified to an elevated train system if it is to survive. The authority that operates the subways is unable to buy flood insurance—because the major insurance companies are taking steps to protect themselves from greater claims than they can handle without major changes in what they insure. These kinds of warnings are long-standing. In 2010, the New York Museum of Modern Art created an exhibit called *Rising Currents* that modeled what was in the offing for the city. Whole sections of the city would be surrounded by water and could not be reached by the bridges and highways currently available. The exhibit showed a possible set of solutions—watercraft that would be used for commuting in the city and for making access to stores, hospitals, and work, in the likely changes that were predictable.

This chapter is really focused on the weather—something that all of us, social workers included, attend to every day. We do so directly through observational or experiential data gathering or indirectly via interactive forums as varied as conversations with those around us, hearing and reading about the weather on our favorite news outlet—print or electronic, or watching the highly popular Weather Channel. We take note of how our daily activities are impacted by the weather. In this technological era, we are able with ease to take note of how persons at great distances from us are influenced in myriad ways by the weather—think big storms, floods, and hurricanes. We all are impacted by the oft times uncertain or mistaken outcomes in weather predictions. Attending to the weather falls within a broad spectrum of science focused on climate, the study of which is referred to as climatology (Henson, 2014).

Two empirically well-established ideas central to present-day climatology serve as a conceptual anchor for this chapter. The first of these foundational ideas is that there can be no doubt that the Earth's climate is changing. The second foundational idea is that the activities of people are a major causal element in theoretical understandings of climate change (Smallwood, 2016; Williams, 2009). These two foundational ideas have become so well accepted that there is a scientific debate occurring right now about whether the current time period should be labeled a new epoch (period in time), potentially labeling it the Anthropocene—meaning an epoch that is characterized primarily by the changes and impacts upon the Earth's environment caused by the development and activity of people (Smallwood, 2016). Of course, there are scientists, a number of geologists for example, who argue the data are just not there yet—meaning there is still not enough data to support the decision to rename the current epoch. It is important to note, however, that while the belief that the Earth's climate is changing appears irrefutable and that people-driven development and activity are major causal elements, there remain a host of climate change naysayers focused on challenging, in particular, scientific claims about climate change projections and the use of computer-based modeling as the main predictive methodology (Weart, 2008). Of course, we as social workers welcome the voice of the naysayers into the dialogue about climate change, even as we hope to change their minds.

Climate change is a scientifically complex concept—with claims by adherents of the concept that it is the most important social, ecological, and economic issue of our times (Henson, 2014; Weart, 2008). Following in that line of reasoning is the claim that if climate change and its accompanying harmful effects are not confronted in the present and steps taken now to offset its predicted outcomes, the results will be apocalyptic—the eventual ruin of us all is ensured. Of course, not everyone is a believer in such dark predictions. With an attempt to set aside the too often vitriolic dialogue attached to climate change and the embedded concept of global warming, this chapter is focused on the basics of the science of climate change and how and why, particularly in regard to the social justice issues involved, climate change matters for social workers. The major question to be raised for the social work reader is where and what is the intersection between climate change and social work? A preliminary answer appears to fall somewhere in the mix of the certainty/uncertainty of the science of climate change and the achievement of enough knowledge acquisition to allow for a thoughtful analysis of the social justice issues involved in advocacy for those populations that might be unjustly impacted by climate change. Importantly, social workers must try to figure out what can be done about this injustice. Questions for consideration include the following: What populations will be most impacted by climate change? Where do these persons live, and what can be done about it all—be it research, advocacy, and/or policy analysis? Can the big producers of climate-changing contributors—particularly those countries with the production of high levels of global warming gases—be convinced, coaxed, or coerced into changing their ways? And if the ice continues to melt and the seas continue to rise as the Earth warms, how much adaptation will be expected of people? How much can be achieved?

Consideration of climate change is now firmly ensconced in the domestic and international public policy arenas. In 2015, the United Nations organized an international meeting on climate change and the nations that participated agreed to take steps to reduce climate change. It included most of the world's nations, including China and the United States, the two nations that produce the largest amount of emissions that cause global warming. The benchmark is 2 degrees Celsius, or 35.6 degrees Fahrenheit in total, beyond the preindustrial levels. In another 10 or 20 years, emissions would have to be reduced to zero. The agreement stated that when 55 nations agreed to the changes, they would become legally binding. Although President Barack Obama participated and indicated US agreement with the goals of the conference, the US Congress includes a large number of climate change "deniers," who disagree that the problems of climate change are real.

Climate is a massive area of science, and a full rendition of it all falls beyond the purview of this chapter. Our hope is to assist the social work reader in better understanding the scientific basics of climate change, including how much we know about it, what scientific evidence supports climate change, what is happening scientifically and politically with climate change, and what steps might be taken to offset the impact of climate change. And, to further aid the reader, the author of this chapter has chosen to look at climate change through a set of sequential lenses. First, the science of climate change is presented in the chapter, and then in a modified case study approach, the chapter looks at how birds are being impacted as climate change progresses and quite possibly intensifies. Then perhaps we can overlay that knowledge on the present and the future for people and climate change. By combining the science of climate change with ornithology, the science of birds, pertinent scientific concepts, theories, and ideas are made more conceptually accessible to the social work reader. So the chapter includes a review of the science of climate change and then looks specifically at ornithology, the impact of climate change on bird species, and finally how that hypothesized impact might ring true as well for climate change and people. The chapter begins with a section focused on the basics of the science of climate change and includes a segment on the issue of social justice and how climate change matters for social work.

THE SCIENCE OF CLIMATE CHANGE

This section includes two main scientific claims about climate change and includes a segment focused on the intersection of climate change, social justice, and social work. The first claim is that it took a long time, more than a century, for a scientific consensus about climate change to be achieved. How could the climate, such a huge and uncontrollable feature of existence, be undeniably altered by the actions and the activities of people? It was believed previous to this scientific consensus that the climate was just too complex, too large, and too diffuse to be influenced by what people did or did not do. Another ancillary reason that it took so long was that to take up such an idea was to confront the long-held philosophical belief of the "balance of nature." It was akin to heretical thinking to propose that the behavior of mere people was enough to offset the powerful balance of nature that purportedly governed the planet as a whole—with its interlocking balance of all the natural elements. But undoubtedly that belief has been altered. Even scientific naysayers about the dire prospects of global warming and climate change now admit to the claim that the activities of people can and have changed the climate (Weart, 2008).

The good news is that a great deal is now known about climate change, its progression, and how people are disturbing the climate system (Henson, 2014). Multiple independent lines of research and subsequent evidence support the claim. These independent lines of research include, but are not limited to, (1) longitudinal measurement of temperatures at the Earth's surface measured by thermometers, (2) longitudinal measurement of temperatures throughout the atmosphere by satellites and balloon-borne thermometers, (3) longitudinal measurement of ocean temperatures (i.e., greater heat content), (4) physical measurement of glaciers throughout the world observed to be melting, and (5) as will be mentioned in a later section of the chapter via the use of the examples of the tundra swan, the puffin, and the red knot, bird and animal species migrating and undergoing changes in the timing of key biological life events. To support claims of climate change, two types of studies are commonly used: detection studies and attribution studies. Detection studies attempt to establish only that unusual change in climate has occurred. Attribution studies try to discover the likelihood that particular factors, including the activities of people, are directly involved (Henson, 2014).

An important team of international climate researchers, the Intergovernmental Panel on Climate Change (IPCC), constituting the work of more than 1,000 scientists over more than 20 years, has conclusively concluded the same. And their assessments have become progressively more strongly stated. In 1995, the IPCC assessment statement was that the balance of evidence suggests a discernible human influence on global climate. In 2013, the IPCC concluded that it is extremely likely that human influence has been the dominant cause of the observed warming since the mid-20th century. Conclusively and undoubtedly, the suggestion that climate is not changing or that people are not a major causal variable in climate change is a rejection of science (Henson, 2014). And the scientific evidence is pretty solid that as climate change progresses, more frequent and quite possibly more severe weather disruptions in the future are a certainty (Khanna, 2016).

The second scientific claim of this section is that the temperature of Earth is slowly but gradually rising. All evidence supports the notion that the temperature of the Earth is warming. All analyses point to temperature rise. While estimates of temperature rise may vary, there is general agreement that there has been a rise of around 0.8 degrees Celsius in the average surface air temperature of Earth when comparing the period of 2003–2012 to 1850–1900. The estimated linear trend from 1800 to 2012 is a bit higher—roughly, 0.85 degrees Celsius. In recent decades, global temperatures have spiked. The first decade of the 21st century was the hottest on record. Ice is melting and Arctic temperatures have risen a full 4 degrees Celsius in just the past half-century. Conversely, the rise in temperature has lengthened the growing season across North America. Birds, mosquitoes, and other creatures are being pushed into new territories, driven to higher altitudes and latitudes by increasing warmth. And many forms of marine life are moving away from the Equator and toward the North and South Poles (Henson, 2014).

An understanding of what constitutes global warming is essential to understanding what climate change is. Put simply, the greenhouse effect is the antecedent to global warming and is the actual warming of the Earth by greenhouse gases in the atmosphere (Williams, 2009). Use of the term "greenhouse effect" comes from the early 19th-century work of a French mathematician, Joseph Fourier. Fourier experimentally showed the distinct temperature contrast between an airless Earth and the one people actually inhabit. He speculated that energy reaching the Earth as sunlight must be balanced by energy returning to space, some of it in a different form. While Fourier could not figure out the exact process, he rightfully suspected that some outgoing energy is continually intercepted by the atmosphere and thus keeping us warmer than we would be otherwise. It was Fourier, while experimenting, who labeled the warmed atmosphere and likened it to a hothouse or a greenhouse. But the atmosphere does not imprison the air in a glass box, like in Fourier's experiments, but rather it absorbs infrared radiation rising from the Earth's sun-warmed surface. All else being equal, the more greenhouse gas there is, less radiation can escape from the Earth to space, and the warmer we get (Henson, 2014).

Of the sunlight that reaches Earth, about 30% gets reflected back or scattered back to space by clouds, dust, or the Earth's surface. More than 20% is absorbed in the atmosphere, mainly by clouds and water vapor. Close to 50% of the sunlight gets absorbed by the Earth's surface—land, forest, pavement, oceans, and the rest (Williams, 2009). Figure 6.1 is an illustration of the greenhouse effect.

Greenhouse gases are those that absorb and reradiate radiation from the Earth, bouncing radiation back instead of letting the energy from the sun escape and go back into space. This differential results in a warming of the Earth's atmosphere (Williams, 2009). People have transformed Earth's atmosphere by adding enormous quantities of carbon dioxide (CO_2) and other greenhouse gases to it over the last 150 years. These gases warm the atmosphere, though not literally in the same way a greenhouse does. The gases absorb heat that is radiated by Earth,

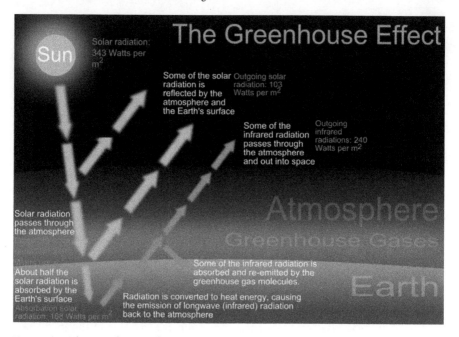

Figure 6.1 The greenhouse effect
SOURCE: By ZooFari - Own work, CC BY-SA 3.0, https://commons.wikimedia.org/w/index.php?curid=5776439

but they release only part of that heat to space, which results in a warmer atmosphere (Henson, 2014). Krishna AchutaRao, a climate scientist in the Centre for Atmospheric Sciences at the Indian Institute of Technology Delhi, a member of the IPCC and a recipient of the Nobel Peace Prize for his work on climate change, is convinced that the evidence for the warming of the Earth's atmosphere is mounting. He believes scientists now have a fairly precise accounting of where the extra heat that is being trapped by the greenhouse effect has gone and what the impacts are. The extra heat is being absorbed into the oceans, it is melting our ice caps, and it is warming the atmosphere (Carde, 2016). The atmosphere's greatest trick is to intercept a part of the infrared radiation emitted from the surface, preventing it from escaping into space (Weart, 2008).

Greenhouse gases are numerous, but carbon dioxide is of great concern as it makes up about 64% of the total. Carbon dioxide is created when fossil fuels are burned, when people and animals breathe, and when plants decompose. Plants and the oceans soak up lots of carbon dioxide, but they cannot do it all. A major concern is the prevalence and molecular ability to trap energy of each greenhouse gas. Additionally, levels of carbon dioxide were pretty steady until the Industrial Revolution but are now on the increase. It is important to also consider another major greenhouse gas, methane. Although methane accounts for only about 17% of the total greenhouse gases, a third of the amount attributed to carbon dioxide, it has a multitude of sources—rice paddies, peat bogs, belching cows, insect guts, vehicles, homes, factories, wastewater, and landfills (Henson, 2014).

Globally, agriculture is the number-one source of methane emissions. According to a recent Environmental Protection Agency report, in 2014, 8% of US methane emissions connected to the activities of people were due to the management or mismanagement of animal waste. Twenty-three percent of methane emissions were produced by enteric fermentation—the digestive process in which cows produce methane, mostly released through burping and, while often left out of most scientific reports, farting as well. A typical dairy cow can emit 145 kilograms of methane per year (Smallwood, 2016). Waste from cows is a big problem. It is ammonia that makes manure smell bad and is a by-product of its natural decomposition. When manure is collected and stored in an oxygen-free environment, it produces several other gases, but lots of methane production is included (Smallwood, 2016). Figure 6.2 presents global greenhouse gas emissions by type of gas.

Even though greenhouse gases do not really act like a greenhouse, which keeps inside air warm by preventing convection currents from carrying heat away, the term "greenhouse effect" has been around since the 19th century and we are stuck with it. A better referent or descriptor would be the Callendar effect. The Callendar effect refers to the direct relationship between the amount of carbon dioxide in the air and temperature. It was Guy Stewart Callendar (1897–1964), a British scientist who laid the foundation for our current understanding of greenhouse gases. Callendar, in 1938, scientifically linked the three key elements of global warming: rising temperatures, rising levels of anthropogenic carbon dioxide (released by the activities of people), and infrared sky radiation. The direct relationship between levels of carbon dioxide and temperature is thus better called the Callendar effect (Williams, 2009).

The Earth also generates some of its own heat, primarily via geothermal heat from the planet's interior. Additionally, ozone is an almost colorless, gaseous form of oxygen that is not emitted when fossil fuels are burned, but it forms when sunlight hits other pollutants and triggers ozone-making reactions. Ozone levels spike when stagnant air takes hold near ground level where people and animals live and breathe (Henson, 2014).

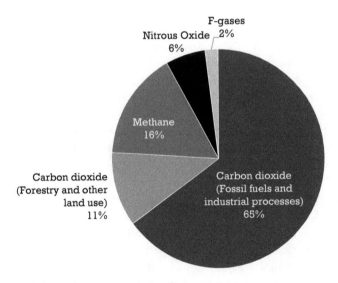

Figure 6.2 Global greenhouse gas emissions by gas

Redrawn based on data from IPCC, 2014, available at USEPA; Data Source: IPCC (2014), Available at US Environmental Protection Agency. https://www.epa.gov/ghgemissions/global-greenhouse-gas-emissions-data

To further knowledge acquisition, we suggest that social workers read all, or parts of, three books recommended by the state climatologist of Georgia. The books are designed for the nonscientist reader and include *The AMS Weather Book: The Ultimate Guide to America's Weather* written in 2009 by J. Williams, *The Thinking Person's Guide to Climate Change* written in 2014 by R. Henson, and *The Discovery of Global Warming* written in 2008 by D. Weart.

CLIMATE CHANGE, SOCIAL JUSTICE, AND SOCIAL WORK

Climate change and its science matter for social work. Although uncertainty remains in the speculated long-term impacts of climate change, consideration of what to do about it now is important, for climatologists, environmental scientists, and social workers. Of concern to social workers is that to do nothing now is to passively accept the injustice of climate change, particularly its uneven impacts on people around the world struggling with poverty. What to do? For eons, geophysical phenomena as dissimilar as meteor strikes and the ice ages have profoundly shaped the Earth and thus the relationship of people to their planet. The fundamental geology of plate tectonics is always in motion, with earthquakes and tsunamis constantly shifting coastlines. But people have attempted to tame the impacts of naturally occurring geophysical phenomena with a variety of technologies such as land reclamation, sea barriers, and earthquake-resistant architecture. Geo-engineering techniques such as carbon dioxide removal and solar radiation management have also been used to attempt to slow climate change impacts (Khanna, 2016). But through it all climate change appears to be advancing.

The impacts of climate change are a major concern for social workers because billions of people who have done little to contribute to the creation or the progression of global warming, and thus climate change, will be adversely impacted. Consider that today in 2016 more than 1.5 billion of Asia's 4 billion people live within a hundred kilometers of the Indian or Pacific Ocean, where rising sea levels could overwhelm existing coastal barriers. Countries termed low-elevation coastal zones with the most exposed territory and population centers include countries with highly challenged infrastructures such as Egypt, Nigeria, Thailand, Bangladesh, Vietnam, India, and China (Khanna, 2016). While the Netherlands and the United States are also on the low-elevation coastal zones list, it is easy to recognize their possession of stronger infrastructures and the resources to better respond to climate change impacts. Climate change scientists long ago concluded that the practice of people voluntarily concentrating into a dense coastal civilization around the world has proven efficient, but it may not have been futuristically wise (Khanna, 2016).

The need to deurbanize as people retreat from the submerged coastlines will be highly disruptive to the lives of millions of persons living in poverty around the world. The IPCC 2013 warned that shifting oceanic currents and the increased frequency of extreme weather events will most likely result in flooding, crop failure, heat waves, and escalating poverty in countries without the robust infrastructure and safety nets needed to ride out such ecosystem imbalances. The IPCC 2014 report formally recommended that countries invest in relocation strategies such as evacuation routes for the populations of cities and establish new inland settlements in higher elevation areas, and urban cooling centers. The old climate diplomacy that focused on mitigating greenhouse gas emissions may certainly need to be maintained. However, today's social workers also may need to consider the resettlement of massive numbers of people living in poverty and the development of adaptive infrastructure into their thinking about climate change initiatives (Khanna, 2016).

Weather is always important to people forced to make desperate journeys. While flooding from melting glaciers and coastal inundation from sea-level rise are problems of too much water, droughts and desertification, problems of too little water, will also create climate refugees of many of the world's most vulnerable people. Already the growing ranks of climate refugees may outnumber the number of the world's political refugees. Climate refugees unfortunately will experience climate change impacts but also often the vestiges of political refugeedom, such as civil war and generalized violence (Khanna, 2016). For example, the warmer weather experienced across the Mediterranean this spring and early summer, according to representatives of the International Organization for Migration, helped to put 2016 on track to be the deadliest year ever for asylum seekers fleeing from northern Africa to Europe—3,770 died in 2015. The warmer weather has calmed the Mediterranean and has served to trick those people fleeing from Eritrea, Nigeria, Gambia, and Somalia into thinking the journey across the sea is safer than it is (Vitkovskays, 2016).

If you look specifically at the United States, it is important to keep in mind that the country has more than 88,000 miles of shoreline and that 5.6 million people and 2.6 million homes are situated less than 4 feet above high tide (Gertner, 2016). Based on estimated sea-level rise as a function of climate change, 316 American cities and towns will be submerged before the end of this century (Khanna, 2016). The United States will also experience the development of its own internal climate refugees. As climate change causes sea levels to rise, the United States will have to decide which coastal towns should be saved from the rising sea and which should be surrendered to the sea (Gertner, 2016). Large parts of Miami Beach may be uninhabitable by around 2050. And there will be dozens of Miami Beaches—the Outer Banks, the Delmarva Peninsula (i.e., most of Delaware and parts of Maryland and Virginia), Long Island, and the Jersey Shore (Gertner, 2016). And a never-ending supply of money to defend the coastal settlements from the rising sea will not be available.

Climate science suggests that it may soon be time to consider more conclusively which towns, which islands, and which cities, both within the United States and around the world, can (or cannot) be saved. From a social justice perspective, importantly, is the question of what criteria will be used to make decisions about where money and other resources are spent (or not) to combat the impacts of climate change. Will it be economic wealth, population density, natural appeal, or historical value that should weigh most heavily in these decisions (Gertner, 2016)? Will poverty and living in a position of societal disadvantage play a part at all (Rawls, 1999)?

Looking outward from the United States, it is important to remember that half of the world's population lives within 35 miles of the sea. An inordinate number of people, the vast majority of whom will have limited means to adjust their geographic location, will be totally displaced (Carde, 2016). The continued release of enormous amounts of greenhouse gases must be controlled or the consequences will be difficult to endure for the world's poor (Carde, 2016). A major social justice issue is whether the people and institutions responsible for producing greenhouse gases will bear the impacts of their choices, or will those who had no say in the matter bear a greater burden. It is likely that people in the poorest parts of the world, such as a number of locations in the countries of Africa, will be generally least equipped to deal with climate change. Ironically, these regions are releasing only a small fraction of the greenhouse gases causing the changes in climate. The greatest impacts will be where land meets sea. Rising seas will force people to migrate. While crop production may actually rise in developed areas—due primarily to the fertilizing effect of rising carbon dioxide levels, millions of subsistence farmers around the world in less developed regions are sure to suffer inordinately (Henson, 2014).

The overarching claim made by the author of this chapter is that climate change is a social justice issue and is germane to social work. If so, we (all the authors of this book) believe climate change is wholly worthy of placement on the national and international public policy agenda. Inclusion of two social justice guideposts, John Rawls's Second Principle and Jane Addams's concept of "lateral progression," are helpful to understanding a social work perspective of social justice applied to climate change. Rawls, the most famous American philosopher, captures a concept of social justice central to social work in his Second Principle of justice—stated as "social and economic inequalities are to be arranged so that they are both: a) to the greatest benefit of the least advantaged, consistent with the just savings principle, and b) attached to positions and offices open to all under considerations of fair equality of opportunity" (Rawls, 1999, p. 266). Social workers are committed to the ideal that societal resources need to be made available to the least advantaged among us. This social work value certainly is applicable to any theoretical or applied discussion of social justice and climate change. Like Rawls, Jane Addams was a considered an American pragmatist but was also a public philosopher. Her social justice fame was secured for social workers by her mix of thought and action associated with the neighborhood-based Hull House and, of course, her pacifist stance which led to being awarded the Nobel Prize for Peace in 1931. Addams advocated for the betterment of all persons in what she called "lateral progress." For Addams, lateral progress meant that social advancement and justice could not be achieved by just noting the achievements of a few, but could only be found in social gains held in common (Hamington, 2014). Social workers can take Addams's concept of lateral progress and sympathetic knowledge, a caring borne out of empiricism and standpoint analysis, and use it as a point of intervention to offset the unjust burden of climate change being thrust upon the most vulnerable people of the world (Hamington, 2014).

Social justice concern for climate change prompts a need for speculation of assessment of proposed action plans and the possible intended and unintended consequences of whatever actions may be selected (Ginsberg & Miller-Cribbs, 2005). Promoting awareness of climate change as a social justice issue and amplifying an awareness of the injustice of climate change is a good place for social workers to begin or continue their work. Central to that proposed awareness-raising work is an accurate assessment of how strong is the belief that climate change is a social justice issue. How many people actually do, or do not, embrace the idea that climate change needs our immediate attention? A study recently published in *Nature Climate Change* and titled "Predictors of Public Climate Change Awareness and Risk Perception Around the World" found that nearly 2 billion adults worldwide have never even heard of climate change (Lee, Markowitz, Howe, Ying Ko, & Leiserowitz, 2015). The data used in the study were assembled from the 2007–2008 Gallup World Poll, and the study was conducted in 119 countries of the world. A major study finding was that there existed a dramatic contrast between people living in what the authors of the study referred to as differentially as developed and developing countries. For example, in North America, Europe, and Japan, more than 90% of the public was found to be aware of climate change. But awareness declines to more than 65% of the public in countries with major infrastructure challenges, like Egypt, Bangladesh, and India. Yet, ironically, many persons in these resource- and infrastructure-depleted countries were able to note changes in their local weather and climate conditions. These changes often caused them concern, because many were closely tied to the land through subsistence farming (Lee et al., 2015). Certainly, consideration of climate change and the varied impact on persons in different environments will be a major element in any future sense of global social justice (Rawls, 1971; Weart, 2008).

Action in response to or in anticipation of the impacts of climate change is the next step for social workers to either participate in or advocate for. Basic, well-accepted solutions for climate change have been and continue to be focused on controlling/limiting greenhouse gas emissions. Reducing one's carbon footprint—from the national to the individual level—is a reasonable goal. And there are plenty of like-minded steps that can have an impact. Simple policy adjustments favored by some economists and environmental activists in the United States could include such things as an increase in the gas tax, which hasn't been raised since 1993. Others suggest taxing carbon emissions. Or create what just a few years ago seemed impossible: an electric car that actually offers more value than its gas-powered competitor (Worland, 2016). Fuel emissions account for more than 16% of total US greenhouse-gas emissions, making the car you drive and the choice to drive at all—the simple greatest variable affecting your carbon footprint. Put simply, the more gas America guzzles, the more it is warming the climate. For a week in June 2016, US drivers consumed more than 9.8 million barrels of gas every day, eclipsing a record set in 2007. In recent years since, as the economy recovered post the economic collapse in 2008 and as gas prices dropped, so has demand for more fuel-efficient cars. In 2016, electric and hybrids now make up less than 3% of new car purchases (Worland, 2016).

Social workers should not despair, however. Instead of just falling in line with the massive dark predictions that sometimes lead to inaction regarding climate change, social workers should more broadly ask: What can be done? Let social workers lead, or at least participate in consideration of some new alternatives: moving from the seemingly obvious, such as the goal of controlling one's carbon footprint, to the radical, such as developing new frontiers of living, particularly for the world's poor in previously harsh environments, like northern Canada, Russia, and Sweden. These areas, as a result of climate change, may become the new tropical paradises (Khanna, 2016).

Believe it or not, optimism is present in the community of scientists and advocates whose focus is on climate change and doing something about it. The 2016 landmark Paris Agreement on climate change was a major leap forward. And the Paris Agreement will now have more political force as a coalition of the world's largest polluters and small island nations threatened by rising seas pushed past a key threshold on October 5, 2016. The European Union and 10 countries ratified the Paris Agreement, and the percentage of greenhouse gas emissions they account for topped the 55% threshold needed for the treaty to actually take effect. The countries submitting that day were Austria, Bolivia, Canada, France, Germany, Hungary, Malta, Nepal, Portugal, and Slovakia (Davenport, 2016).

And on October 16, 2016, just under 200 nations signed a legally binding agreement to limit the use of hydrofluorocarbons (HCFs). These greenhouse gases used in refrigerators and air conditioners, also found in inhalers and insulating foams, are the world's fastest growing climate pollutant. Cutting HCFs may be the fastest way to reduce global warming. The agreement caps the use of HCFs in a gradual process beginning by 2019 with action by the most developed countries, including the United States, the world's second worst polluter. More than 100 developing countries, including China, the world's top carbon emitter, will start taking action by 2024. Estimates are that the agreement will cut the global levels of HFCs by 80%–85% by 2047. Small island states and many African countries had pushed for earlier timeframes, saying they face the biggest threat from climate change. The new agreement is equal to stopping the entire world's fossil fuel carbon dioxide emissions for more than 2 years (Klapper & Ssuuna, 2016). Radical considerations for action fall directly within the purview of social workers prepared to consider new alternative solutions to climate change impacts. Urbanization, the major demographic trend in the world, with estimates as high as 70% of the world's population living in cities or megacities by 2030, may require new thinking to face new challenges (Swanson, 2016). Urbanization has, from a social justice perspective, accelerated the domestic inequality that globalization has enabled. The more populous and connected cities become, the more their countries feature a doubled stratification—not only between urban and rural but also between these wealthy, globalized cores and the expanding peripheries with concentrations of persons living with the vestiges of poverty. Urbanization and inequality are a combustible mix for social justice considerations and climate change. The vast majority of the world's population spends much of its disposable income on the basics of food and water, health and education, services that weak governments scarcely provide. With the right investments in 2016, the 9 billion people on Earth in 2050 could be more evenly distributed across the hemispheres while also being more mobile and adaptable to the unpredictable forces of nature, particularly the anticipated problematic weather, big storms, floods, and hurricanes associated with intensifying climate change. Indeed, in the coming decades countries may need to build new inland cities to resettle populations affected by coastal flooding as sea levels rise. Also, thinking differently about the relational geography of the world may assist social workers to conceive more broadly and radically about solutions for persons in disadvantaged societal position as climate change progresses. A common Arctic culture may be one answer. The advantaged may already be making such a move. Consider that in 2013 Facebook opened its biggest data center outside the United States in Sweden's Artic Circle to leverage naturally low temperatures to cool its thousands of servers. Cities all across the Arctic, from Canada, to Sweden, to Russia are flourishing (Khanna, 2016).

And political advocacy by social workers will be an important part of addressing the social justice issues of climate change. For example, the platforms of the two US-based major political parties take starkly different positions on education, immigration, health care, and criminal justice, though their opposing worldviews are most plainly seen in their thinking on energy and climate change. The GOP platform claims coal is an abundant, clean, affordable, reliable domestic energy resource and questions the scientific integrity of the United Nations' IPCC, the global authority on climate science. Democrats say climate change is an urgent threat and call for an 80% cut in carbon emissions. Another stark difference is support for the Paris climate accord, an international agreement adopted by 195 countries which aims to keep global temperature increases to well below 2 degrees Celsius, something the Republican Party platform flatly rejects (McKenna, 2016).

Social agencies and social workers will have to deal with many dimensions of the global climate change issues. At the macro level, social policy advocacy organizations will find it desirable to work toward recognition of climate change and to support the policies necessary to prevent its direst consequences. That may involve coalitions with groups such as the Natural Resources Defense Council and others that will take on the issues of climate change. Macro social workers will find themselves organizing groups to deal with climate change. In the 21st century, energy companies that use coal and petroleum are not sharing the concerns of environmental activists about climate change. In fact, many public officials deny its impact and respond to questions about what they will do by noting that they are not scientists. If the severe problems that people will face because of climate change are to be prevented, nonscientists and public officials will have to come to the side of those who want to prevent and resolve the problems. Community organizers may well find it necessary to help build the kinds of organizations and efforts that can deal with the problems, advocating for social and environmental policies that may reduce the impact of climate change or further delay its worst consequences.

Obviously, direct practice social workers will need to help with residential issues, including homelessness, when rising seas may destroy homes, and the necessity to move to higher elevations is realized. The diseases and food shortages suggested by Pierce will require more efforts by agencies and more extensive efforts to sustain people with food insecurity. Although the full consequences of climate change are not yet known, it will be useful for agencies to begin preparing staff and volunteers to deal with the effects that will come during the next decades unless changes are made soon.

In September 2015, Jonathan Chait wrote a cover story in *New York* magazine. He acknowledged that climate change was "a problem politics is almost designed not to solve" (p. 28). Politics is designed to deal with immediate problems and the climate change problem is far in the future. However, in 2014, he notes, the world economy grew but carbon emissions did not grow. Coal plants in the United States have declined from 523 to 323, and coal usage has reduced by 21%. The price of solar energy is rapidly falling. It fell from $101 per watt in 1975 to 61 cents in 2015. In fact, in sunnier areas, building a solar power plant is less expensive than building a coal or natural gas plant. The number of electric cars is growing significantly, and more jobs, 125,000 in clean energy, have been added since 2013. Chait was writing in anticipation of the United Nations Paris summit on climate change mentioned earlier—in which most of the world's nations agreed to reduce greenhouse emissions and head off the problems of climate change.

Another possible development is the achievement of power generation through fusion (Grossman, 2015). Companies are working to develop energy through the merging of atomic nuclei. Nuclear fusion is the opposite of nuclear fission, which is the way nuclear bombs explode and current nuclear power plants create energy. The fusion process releases immense amounts of energy, and it is comparable to the creation of energy by the sun and other stars. Of course, the process is complicated, but if the efforts are successful, fusion may be a source of large amounts of clean energy—another potential means for preventing the dangerous consequences of climate change through the release of greenhouse gases.

It is technically possible to arrest the major climate changes observed by scientists, but the consequences of climate change will still be significant. In the political discussions of climate change, those who doubt it and question the conclusions of climate scientists remind us that climate cycles have occurred regularly throughout recorded history and that they are a normal phenomenon. That has some truth, but the current changes may be more significant. Although the world might recover from the immediate effects of climate change, the dislocations and suffering that would result are not choices that modern government officials are likely to ignore. Social work's task may be that of making sure the positive changes continue. If the negatives of climate change actually occur, the results could be the most serious social and health problems imaginable.

BIRD SCIENCE AND CLIMATE CHANGE

Birds can be used in a meaningful way to help us better understand climate change. Ornithologists and bird enthusiasts of every ilk have long advocated for attending to birds as a way to capture the intensity of climate change, its progression, and possible impacts, and in the process hopefully also create action plans for ameliorating the impact of climate change on bird species. Observations of birds and their changes in behaviors, such as changes in migration patterns, and the need for adaptation to environmental impacts, such as habitat loss, can also help us contemplate the future of climate change impacts on people. Studying changes in the migration patterns of birds and the adaptive challenges faced by birds as they experience habitat loss can be easily overlaid on the changes in behaviors people may need to undertake as a function of climate change impacts, particularly rising sea levels and the flooding of some inhabited places (Henson, 2014; Weart, 2008). The adaptive challenges birds face as a result of habitat loss parallel the adaptations people will be forced to make as habitat loss occurs for them. Think of the flooding of many seaside cities, such as Miami, as the oceans rise just a few feet and how people will be forced to adapt (Khanna, 2016).

The 2016–2020 Strategic Plan of the Audubon Society, an internationally based conservation organization, uses science, advocacy, and education in a three-pronged approach to address the needs of all bird species. Audubon's scientists state unequivocally that climate change is the greatest single threat of modern times to the birds of North America. Their peer-reviewed research highlights how 314 bird species—roughly half of all North American bird species—are threatened by the impacts of climate change with the loss of at least 50% of their habitat by 2080. Audubon's "Climate" initiative has two key elements: protecting the habitats that birds will need as the world becomes warmer, and advocating for significant public policy changes at the local, state, and federal levels (Audubon Strategic Plan). David O'Neil, Senior Vice President of Audubon, Conservation, states unequivocally that birds will face a number of major threats over the next 5 years, including, but not limited to, sharp declines in critical habitat ecosystems like the Everglades and the Arctic. Also sharp declines in critical habitat ecosystems for people will certainly extend to include the residents of major North American cities such as Miami, Boston, and New York (Khanna, 2016).

Birds are used to being in the sights of people when it comes to concern about negative environmental impacts. The general public of the United States embraced environmental knowledge about both the decades-long demise of the American bald eagle and the bird's successful resurgence in the past few years. As the bald eagle's demise became general public knowledge, eventually we all became wholly convinced that the grand bird's demise, like climate change, was attributable to the activities of people. Human activities as diverse as hunting, habitat destruction, and pesticide use all were conclusively accepted as not just correlative but causal factors in the decline of the bald eagle's numbers. This belief, which grew to be nearly in-contestable, contributed mightily to the passage of a major piece of environmental public policy, the Endangered Species Act of 1973 (Byrne, 2016).

Other bird species have stories equally compelling as that of the bald eagle. The tundra swan, a bird that migrates a long distance and has a distinct breeding and feeding pattern, has faced adaptive challenges as a result of climate change (see Fig. 6.3). Every spring, the tundra swan makes a marathon-like journey, migrating from the marshes of the Atlantic Coast and the western United States to the frozen tundra of the North American Arctic to breed. When it is time to return to its winter home, the tundra swan gathers in flocks as large as 100 for the trip back south with its young. The swans feed primarily on seeds and plants, sometimes paddling with their feet to stir up food from below the water's surface (Audubon's *Climate Report* and *Field Guide*, 2016a, b). However, the food sources in some of its wintering areas have now been reduced by the destruction of southern wetlands, and the tundra swan has been forced to adapt by shifting to feeding on agricultural waste.

While the tundra swan appears to be successful in making current adaptive ad-justments, greater adaptive challenges loom for the bird in the future. By 2080, the tundra swan is predicted to lose 61% of its current winter range, according to Audubon's climate model. Additionally, its summer range in the Arctic, which is

Figure 6.3 Tundra swan
SOURCE: By Maga-chan - photo taken by Maga-chan, CC BY-SA 2.5, https://commons.wikimedia.org/w/index.php?curid=504419

being disproportionately impacted by climate change, will also contract. It's not known how or whether the swans will be able to respond to such dramatic changes in both of its primary ranges (Audubon's *Climate Report*, 2016a).

Puffins are a favorite bird species among birdwatchers for their colorful beaks and playful nickname as the "parrots of the sea" (see Fig. 6.4). But, alas, all three varieties of the puffin, the Atlantic, the horned, and the tufted, have known dramatic population variance due to climate change. Their numbers have been dwindling off the coast of Maine since the use of agri fisheries in the late 1880s. But in this

Figure 6.4 Puffins are referred to as the "parrots of the sea"
SOURCE: By Richard Bartz - Own work, CC BY-SA 3.0, https://commons.wikimedia.org/w/index.php?curid=27624174

century an ornithologist, Stephen Kress, demonstrated through a scientific conservation project that in one particular island context, Easter Egg Rock, and through implemented intervention activities such as hand feeding and hand rearing that puffins could be assisted in making a population-based comeback. That was until an environmental feature, attributable to the global warming associated with climate change, occurred. Mr. Kress was able to verify empirically that the temperature of the waters of the Gulf of Maine was rising faster than 99% of the Earth's oceans. This contextually based temperature rise threw delicate fish populations in the Gulf of Maine out of balance. Subsequent to the temperature rise in the waters of the Gulf, the weight of puffin chicks began to decline. This inverse correlation between the rising water temperature and the weight of puffin chicks was believed to be a direct result of climate change. While changes in the overall water temperature may have been difficult to assess within the massive entity we call the ocean, the impact of water temperature change in the Gulf of Maine on the puffin chicks was observable in a fairly noninvasive manner (Byrne, 2016).

As mentioned earlier in the chapter, the study of bird migrations is another mechanism by which ornithologists are able to link the impact of climate change with bird species. Birds often combine staggering endurance and superb timing in their migration journey. The vulnerability of a bird species can be exacerbated by climate change before, during, and after that migration journey (van Gils et al., 2016; Zimmer, 2016). Consider the migration journey of a shorebird known as the red knot (see Fig. 6.5). Each spring, flocks of the red knots fly up to 9,300 miles from the tropics to their high Arctic breeding ground.

Figure 6.5 Red knot
SOURCE: By DickDaniels (http://carolinabirds.org/) - Own work, CC BY-SA 3.0, https://commons.wikimedia.org/w/index.php?curid=19507052

As the snow melts in the Artic breeding grounds, the red knots mate and produce a new generation of chicks. The chicks gorge themselves on insects, and then all the red knots head back south to the tropics. According to Dr. van Gils, an ecologist at the Royal Netherlands Institute for Sea Research, and his colleagues, it is important to note that the birds are up north for a very short period of time, only 2 months (Zimmer, 2016). In their recent study just published in the journal *Science*, Dr. van Gils and his colleagues hypothesized that a disturbing reduction in the body size of the red knots, particularly the young juveniles, could be increasingly identified as a response to climate warming. Analyzed data showed that a long-distant bird migrant, like the red knot, experiencing unmatched warming rates at their Artic breeding grounds was producing smaller offspring with shorter bills when early snowmelt was occurring. And the negative consequence half a world away at the bird's tropical wintering grounds was that shorter billed red knots had reduced survival rates. Phenological changes in biological phenomena such as breeding and migration are a well-known response to climate change. Shifts in geographical range are an additional well-known response to climate change. But the migratory study of the red knots lent credence to the idea that a third response to global warming in birds might be body shrinkage. Body shrinkage in a bird species might be considered a micro evolutionary response to global warming—due to smaller individuals being better able to dissipate body heat because of the larger surface/volume ratio of their bodies. Dr. Gils and his colleagues concluded that changes in climate and corresponding changes in beak size, body size, and food source were responsible for the changes in size in the juvenile red knots. On average, today's juvenile red knots are about 15% smaller today than in 1985. Especially in the Arctic, warming has been observed at unprecedented rates and this has proven to be problematic for the red knots (van Gils et al., 2016; Zimmer, 2016). The Arctic's chilly environment is becoming less so every year. Stoked by human-accelerated climate change, Arctic temperatures have risen a full 4 degrees Celsius in just the past half-century. The summer ice coverage is only half what it was in 1979 (Khanna, 2016).

Birds have been used for decades to assess gradations in environmental conditions, but particularly in regard to the quality of atmospheric conditions. We need look no further than the well-known example of a canary in a coal mine: If the canary dies inside the mine, the quality of the air is deemed toxic for humans. The canary in the coal mine relationship is a mainstay in modern popular culture. For example, the song "Canary in a Coal Mine," by the rock group The Police, was released in 1980 and included on their album *Zenyatta Mondata*. The lyrics of the song herald to us how birds may be viewed as an index for how climate change may impact our lives:

> First to fall over when the atmosphere is less than perfect
> Your sensibilities are shaken by the slightest defect
> You live your life like a canary in a coalmine
> You get so dizzy even walking in a straight line

While it may have been merely folklore in the early 19th century that hinted at the relationship between the canary and the air in the coal mine, it was scientific study in the late 1880s that cemented the veracity of the relationship (Burton, 2014). The renowned Scottish scientist J. S. Haldane first published scientific studies that advocated for the use of birds in coal mining rescue operations. Beginning in the 1880s, Haldane was intent on creating protocols for safely dealing with the dangerous gases that were responsible for so many coal mine-based casualties. He honed in on "afterdamp"—a poisonous mixture of gases, most notably carbon monoxide, often left behind after an explosion of methane or coal dust—as one of the most deadly and least preventable risks of rescue attempts after a coal mine disaster. Haldane's contemporary, American scientist and mining researcher George A. Burrell, called carbon monoxide the most feared and the most difficult to detect of all the gases produced in mines.

Previous to the work of Haldane and Burrell, 19th-century miners relied on simple sensors such as lamps to alert them to possible threats of other poisonous gases, but no sensor existed to detect the presence of carbon monoxide. After determining how carbon monoxide worked physiologically, Haldane hypothesized that the purposeful presence of oxygen-dependent species was a scientifically based and more expedient manner in which to quickly identify the presence of the virtually undetectable fumes of carbon monoxide. He speculated that canaries and mice—highly sensitive and easily portable—would make excellent living carbon monoxide detectors. Canaries, in particular, he pointed out, were affected by much lower levels of the gas than were the people working alongside them in the mines. If the birds exhibited signs of distress, miners would thus be alerted to the danger and could evacuate before being overcome themselves. Haldane published the first official recommendation of the use of canaries in rescue efforts in an 1894 report of the Tylorstown, Wales, and mining disaster of the same year. Haldane concluded convincingly that a dangerous percentage of carbon monoxide in the air, which would require nearly an hour to affect a man at rest, would affect the canary within about 5 minutes. With more than a hint of irony, canaries were also preferred because their distress was so highly visible (Burton, 2014; see Fig. 6.6).

In a way similar to how canaries were used in the coal mines of the 19th century as a warning tool, modern-day scientific estimates of the impact of climate change on birds—their habitats, their feeding and breeding habits, and, importantly, alterations in migratory flight patterns—can also serve as a early warning mechanism for the eventual influences of climate change on people. Birds can show us the way—maybe, hopefully.

The National Audubon Society collects copious scientific data on birds and excitedly does so with the help of what they refer to as "citizen scientists." Citizen scientists are just regular folks who go out of their way to report bird sightings and hearings from within data collection efforts and sampling strategies designed by Audubon scientists. Two of the most well-known Audubon-sponsored data collection efforts, the North American Breeding Bird Survey and the Christmas Bird Count, are not only used to count birds but also used by Audubon scientists to complete a continental analysis of how North America's birds may respond to future climate change. Detailed climate layers are used to create predictive models that characterize the relationship between bird species and future climate change. The climate change estimates are based on the work of the IPCC. In the 2015 effort, predictive analysis of the North American Breeding Bird Survey and the Christmas

Figure 6.6 Coal miner with canary
SOURCE: US Bureau of Mines Call Number TICL-00203; Hollinger Mine, Timmons, Ontario, Canada. Mine Fire February 10, 1928. Photo credit: George S. McCaa

Bird Count databases showed that 314 of 588 bird species modeled will lose more than half of their current geographic range. And that for 126 bird species this loss will occur without accompanying range expansion. However, a less bleak finding predicts that for 188 bird species, loss in current geographic range may be coupled with the potential to colonize new areas. A major conclusion arising from the data analysis is that the persistence of many North American bird species will depend on their ability to colonize climatically suitable areas outside of current ranges and habitat management actions by environmental and wildlife experts that target climate change adaptation (Langham et al., 2015).

The empirical bird data derived from the Christmas Bird Count have a strong and rigorous basis of comparison over time that enhances its scientific consideration (Rubin & Babbie, 2014). The Christmas Bird Count started in 1900 and has been a successful venture in documenting early winter bird assemblages from year to year all across North America. Conducted by citizen scientists (bird enthusiasts like the authors of this book), the data collection effort includes observation-based data (both sight and sound) and the use of time and place sampling, sometimes referred to as time-in-point sampling (Rubin & Babbie, 2014). Interestingly, time and place sampling is a scientific sampling methodology that is actually now used successfully by applied social scientists, like social work academics and social work practitioners, to "count" the number of persons who are homeless within a particular geographic context (e.g., city, metropolitan area, county). Time and place sampling can be used effectively whenever a complete enumeration of all elements of the population, as with birds whose location is elusive and persons who are unsheltered or without a home, is impossible. In the Christmas Bird Count, citizen scientists within 24.1 km diameter circles observe bird species for one 24-hour period during a 2-week interval centered on December 25. The North American Breeding Bird Survey, initiated in 1966, does it just a bit differently. This data collection effort also attempts to empirically assess bird populations but takes place in the summer months. Most of the data comes from surveys completed in June, but some data come as early as May or as late as mid-July. Survey routes are 24.5 miles long with stops at 0.5 mile intervals (sampling of place), and at each stop a 3-minute point count of birds is conducted (sampling of time) and a scientifically based, reportable record of birds seen or heard is the result (Langham et al., 2015).

A recognized value of the two Audubon bird databases is that they are translatable into action plans. Analyses of the databases by ornithologists point the way for broad-scale bird conservation plans. They also hint at what responsive conservation plans might need to be undertaken for people (Khanna, 2016). The bird data analyses highlight three important considerations: (1) the impact of climate change on bird species diversity in the United States and Canada, (2) the identification of habitats that are expected to remain important to birds when future climate change takes place, and (3) the potential climate change impact on 314 bird species. Increasingly for ornithologists, people-induced climate change is recognized as a fundamental driver of biological processes and patterns in birds. Biological response is concluded for each bird species as the tendency or the ability to (1) track and move, (2) suffer in place, or (3) adapt in place (Langham et al., 2015). And this is a conclusion that sounds similar to the old axiom oft times attributed, but not ever actually established as such, to Charles Darwin in *On the Origin of Species*: for a species to survive, it must "mutate, migrate, or die." Climate action plans for people may need to be primarily focused on resettlement of people as the seas rise, as well as adaptive infrastructure development as environmental change, such as the continued melting of the Arctic's permafrost, takes place (Khanna, 2016).

To build a foundation for action plans to assist birds as they attempt to adapt to climate change, Audubon's bird scientists first built spatial prioritizations based on shifts in climatic suitability for each of the 588 bird species in North America. Additionally, the scientists developed a multispecies spatial prioritization for the 314 climate-endangered and threatened species. Arising from the bird data was the identification of priority bird species—those *climate-endangered* bird species in need of help within the environment they currently occupy and then *climate-threatened* bird species in need of help where they are but also in need of help with moving to new environmental sites in the future. Furthermore, a network of 2,600 Important Bird Areas (essentially environmental sites where a lot of birds live) across the United States was identified. These bird recognition and location variables were combined with other variables, such as extinction, extent, climate maps, habitat, sea-level rise, predation, competition, dispersal, and migratory species. Predictions about the future impact of climate change on bird species were based on the development of forecasting models (see Fig. 6.7). The models can be depicted, often visually (Langham et al., 2015).

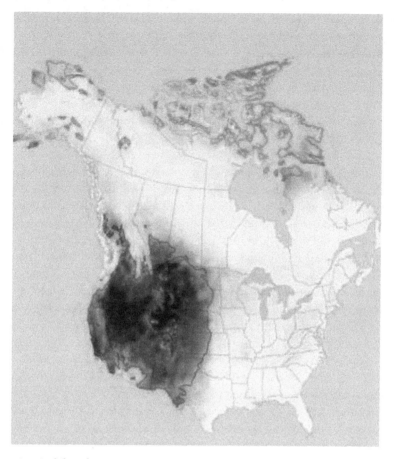

Figure 6.7 Audubon forecasting model
DATA SOURCE: Authors' creation; Data source: http://climate.audubon.org/birds/goleag/golden-eagle

Predictive models help us understand climate change in important ways. They reduce complexity in any scientific effort to achieve understanding and they highlight
selected major points of scientific inquiry. However, as critics of the modeling efforts
state with great emphasis, it is important to keep in mind that all predictive models
have an inherent feature of distortion, commonly referred to as uncertainty (Dye,
2016). In the case of climate change and forecasting bird species responses, there are
at least three sources of uncertainty: (1) future climate uncertainty, (2) modeling
uncertainty stemming from the quality of the data (remember those citizen scientists), and (3) biological uncertainty nested in the question of whether a species
can persist in place or colonize newly suitable environmental areas. In other words,
to more fully understand the intersection of future climate change and the ability of
any bird species to adapt, we must gain a fuller understanding of how bird populations persist. The persistence of a bird population is heavily dependent on such variables as the overall birth rates, death rates, immigration, emigration, competition,
foraging, and life span characteristics of members of that population (Langham
et al., 2015). Of course, any human geographer or population demographer with

work focused on the people of the world will recognize all of these variables as important to their own work (Knox & Marston, 2003).

For the reader wishing to pursue further the link between bird species and climate change, there are a number of peer-reviewed journals and databases that will prove helpful: Auk, Avian Conservation and Ecology, Condor, Ibis, Journal of Avian Biology, and databases, BIOSIS, Zoological Record, and the Birds of North America Online. All are resources used by bird study scientists and enthusiasts and accessible, either directly or indirectly, through the Adelson Library of the Cornell University Lab of Ornithology.

To conclude this section on birds and climate change, the reader is encouraged once again to consider the applicability of ornithology to the situation of people as climate change impact progresses and intensifies. People may need to do exactly as bird species have demonstrated a tendency to do: (1) track and move, (2) suffer in place, or (3) adapt in place. Put a bit more harshly, climate change may force people to "migrate, mutate, or die." And as Audubon scientists concluded about priority bird species, in a similar way some people may be endangered and in need of help within the environment they currently occupy, and some people may need help with moving to new environmental sites in the future (Khanna, 2016; Langham, 2015). In conclusion, coming to terms with science for the nonscientist, in this case the science of climate change for the social worker, is not getting any easier. The challenges include (1) the fact that there is more and more science to explain, particularly as scientists expand their reach and embrace an ever-widening range of phenomena and (2) that scientific theories in abstractness and magnitude can be a bit overwhelming (Carroll, 2017). But in regard to global warming, climate change, and the social justice implications for the millions of people living in poverty around the world, ignoring science is to reject both the value of science and the values of social work. And don't forget the birds.

In late 2018 the U.S. government released the annual National Climate Assessment which is mandated by the U.S. Congress. It warns of the dangers to the environment that are discussed in this chapter.

REFERENCES

Audubon. (2016a). Tundra Swan. *The Climate Report.* Retrieved from http://climate.audubon.org/birds/tunswa/tundra-swan

Audubon. (2016b). Tundra Swan. *Field Guide.* Retrieved from https://www.audubon.org/field-guide/bird/tundra-swan

Burton, C. (2014). Risking life and wing: Victorian and Edwardian conceptions of coal-mine canaries. *Victorian Review, 40*(2), 143–159.

Byrne, T. (2016, July 28). A bird's eye view of climate change. *USA Today.* Retrieved from https://www.usatoday.com/story/opinion/voices/2016/07/27/voices-puffins-climate-change-audubon-birds/87522316/

Cardé, L. (2016, June). Dispatch Krishna AchutaRao. *Tulane Magazine,* 33.

Carroll, S. (2017). *The big picture: On the origins of life, meaning, and the universe itself.* New York, NY: Penguin.

Davenport, C. (2016, October 16). Nations agree to cut use of harmful coolant. *New York Times*, 1.

Dye, T. R. (2016). *Understanding public policy* (15th ed.). Englewood Cliffs, NJ: Prentice Hall.

Filkins, D. (2016, April 4). Exploring a Himalayan glacier. *The New Yorker*. Retrieved from https://www.newyorker.com/magazine/2016/04/04/investigating-chhota-shigri-glacier

Gertner, J. (2016, July 10). Should the United States save Tangier Island from oblivion? *The New York Times Magazine*, 42–49.

Gillis, J. (2016, March 30). Climate model predicts West Antarctic ice sheet could melt rapidly. *New York Times*. Retrieved from https://www.nytimes.com/2016/03/31/science/global-warming-antarctica-ice-sheet-sea-level-rise.html

Ginsberg, L. H., & Miller-Cribbs, J. (2005). *Understanding social problems, policies, and programs*. Xxx: Columbia, SC: University of South Carolina Press.

Grossman, L. (2015, November 02). Inside the quest for fusion, clean energy's holy grail. *TIME*. Retrieved from http://web.mit.edu/nse/pdf/news/2015/TimeMagazine_11-2-15_Fusion.pdf

Hamington, Maurice. (2014). "Jane Addams." *Stanford Encyclopedia of Philosophy Archive*. Retrieved from https://stanford.library.sydney.edu.au/archives/sum2014/entries/addams-jane/

Henson, R. (2014). *The thinking person's guide to climate change*. Boston, MA: American Meterological Society.

Klapper, B., & Ssuuna, I. (2016). Global deal reached to limit powerful greenhouse gases. Retrieved from https://apnews.com/5b168e763e184c65b1afdd06c6e4fff2

Khanna, P. (2016). *Connectography: Mapping the future of global civilization*. New York, NY: Random House.

Knox, P., & Marston, S. (2003). *Human geography: Places and regions in global context*. London: Pearson.

Kolbert, E. (2016, March 31). Climate catastrophe, coming even sooner. *The New Yorker*. Retrieved from https://www.newyorker.com/news/daily-comment/climate-catastrophe-coming-even-sooner

Langham, G., Schuetz, J., Distler, T., Soykan, C., & Wilsey, C. (2015, September 2). Conservation status of North American birds in the face of future climate change. *Climate Change and Health: Special Issue*. Retrieved from https://doi.org/10.1371/journal.pone.0135350

Lee, T. M., Markowitz, E. M., Howe, P. D., Ko, C.-Y., & Leiserowitz, A. A. (2015). Predictors of public climate change awareness and risk perception around the world. *Nature Climate Change*, 5(11), 1014.

McKenna, P. (2016). GOP and Democratic platforms highlight stark differences on energy and climate. *Inside Climate News*. https://insideclimatenews.org/news/26072016/democrat-republican-party-platforms-energy-climate-change-hillary-clinton-donald-trump

Pierce, C.P. (2016, April 5). Climate change is not about temperature. It's about dying, starving, displaced people. *Esquire*. Retrieved from https://www.esquire.com/news-politics/politics/news/a43648/climate-change-slavery/

Rawls, J. (1971). *The theory of justice*. Cambridge, MA: Belknap Press of Harvard University Press.

Rawls, J. (1999). *A theory of justice,* revised edition. Cambridge, MA: Harvard University Press.

Rice, A. (2016, September 05). This is New York in the not-so-distant future. *New York Magazine.* Retrieved from http://nymag.com/intelligencer/2016/09/new-york-future-flooding-climate-change.html

Rubin, A., & Babbie, E. (2014). *Research methods for social work* (8th ed.). Belmont, CA: Brooks/Cole, Cengage Learning.

Smallwood, C. (2016). Manure: A sage. *The New York Times Style Magazine,* 141–161.

van Gils, J. A., Lisovski, S., Lok, T., Meissner, W., Ożarowska, A., de Fouw, J., ... Klaassen, M. (2016). Body shrinkage due to Arctic warming reduces red knot fitness in tropical wintering range. *Science, 352*(6287), 819–821.

Vitkovskays, J. (2016, June 26). Immigration to Europe: Weather, greed have helped to make this the deadliest year for migrants. *Atlanta Journal Constitution,* A17.

Weart, S. R. (2008). *The discovery of global warming.* Cambridge, MA: Harvard University Press.

Williams, J. (2009). Mesoscale weather. In *The AMS Weather Book: The Ultimate Guide to America's Weather* (pp. 204–227). New York, NY: Springer.

Worland, J. (2016, July 28). Low gas prices are stalling the green-car revolution. *Time,* 19. Retrieved from http://time.com/4428012/low-gas-prices-are-stalling-the-green-car-revolution/

Zimmer, C. (2016, May 12). Climate change and the case of the shrinking Red Knots. *New York Times.* Retrieved from https://www.nytimes.com/2016/05/17/science/climate-change-bird-red-knots.html

7

Social Work and the Science of Water

This is a story of government failure, intransigence, unpreparedness, delay, inaction, and environmental injustice.

—Flint Water Advisory Task Force

There are few claims that achieve a standard of absolute acceptance, but there can be no disagreement that water is important to people. Water is the single most important substance that people consume. You can survive for quite a while without food—some estimates are as long as 2 months, but you would die without water in a matter of days. Estimates of life viability without water, depending on environmental and personal variables, range from a low of 3 days to a theoretically possible 7 days. Again, even though estimates vary, the human body is known to be made up of a large percentage of water: 75% of an infant's weight and 55% and upward of an older person's weight. The well-being of people, at every level from the cellular to a community of neighbors in a subdivision, is dependent on water. Human cells simply cannot function without water (Brody, 2016). And the concept of internationally based sustainable development is completely contingent upon clean water for drinking and the availability of water in some systemic manner for the attainment and maintenance of sanitation and hygiene (WaterAid, 2016).

Yes, we accept all of these claims and not just propositionally but absolutely. But what is less clear is whether people (and, in this case, social workers) really know much about the science of water. What is water? What is water composed of? How has the creation of water supply systems altered how people can, and do, live? How has the systemic treatment of water (e.g., chlorination and fluoridation) changed our lives? How do proponents and opponents of water system treatment vary in opinion? And what happened with the water in Flint, Michigan? What is the relationship of water to poverty and subsequently to the concept of internationally based sustainable development? How is water and its availability linked to sanitation, hygiene, health, and disease worldwide? Is access to clean, drinkable water a basic human right? And, if so, how do we get there for all people?

This chapter is intended to familiarize the social work reader with the salient features of a science of water. Included is consideration of the sources of that scientific knowledge and discussion of the great discoveries and advances regarding water. Of import is how research outcomes have affected our understanding and knowledge of water, including those that highlight points of agreement and contention in water management, such as Flint, Michigan, and their drinking water crisis. Additionally, the chapter includes a descriptive section with a focus on development issues regarding water availability, water use, and worldwide efforts to positively influence the relationship between poverty, internationally based sustainable development, and water. It is important to note, though, that by focusing on the science of water in this chapter some important considerations of water need to be set aside—for example, how important water is to religious thinking; how important water is to the concepts of spirituality, purification, and mysticism; and/or how central water is to a number of creationist stories.

WATER AND EPIDEMIOLOGY: *THE GHOST MAP*

A good place to start our discussion of the science of water and its relationship to social work is by pointing the social work reader to a most approachable book, *The Ghost Map: The Story of London's Most Terrifying Epidemic—And How It Changed Science, Cities, and the Modern World*. This 2006 book is written by a talented investigative storyteller, Steven Johnson, and dramatically describes the critical role played by water, wastewater, and animal and human waste removal via water in the London cholera epidemic of 1854. While London had at that time become one of the first modern cities of the world, what the city lacked was a system for the provision of clean water to its residents. Accordingly, its leaders lacked an understanding of how reliance on water for the haphazard removal of human and animal waste could spread disease. What the story of the book reveals is how water, and particularly contaminated water, was discovered to be the main carrier of the bacteria that cause cholera (Johnson, 2006) (Figure 7.1).

As Londoners began dying in massive numbers during the cholera epidemic of 1854, the story in the book follows the joint efforts of a local pastor, Henry Whitehead, and a physician/researcher, Dr. John Snow, to understand and arrest the epidemic. It was the combination of qualitative and community-based methods on the part of Pastor Whitehead and the quantitative methods, including "disease mapping" on the part of Dr. Snow, that carried the day. This combination of "mixed methods" of scientific pursuit (Chaumba, 2013) led first to discarding the theory of miasmas (i.e., the misunderstanding of a causal association between the stench associated with faulty waste removal often experienced in poor London neighborhoods and the incidence of cholera). The scientifically based mixed research methods led secondly to the startling discovery of contaminated water as the cause of cholera (Johnson, 2006). In fact, as suppositional evidence became less speculative, the association of cholera with contaminated water drew more and more attention. Eradication efforts eventually became focused on a particular neighborhood water pump and well: the Broad Street Pump (McGuire, 2013) (Figure 7.2).

The disease mapping of people's location that had suffered and/or died from cholera in relationship to water sources strengthened previously speculative claims. Following the removal of the handle from the suspected water pump and well, subsequent mapping showed a dramatic decrease in incidence and death from cholera in the immediate area (Figure 7.3).

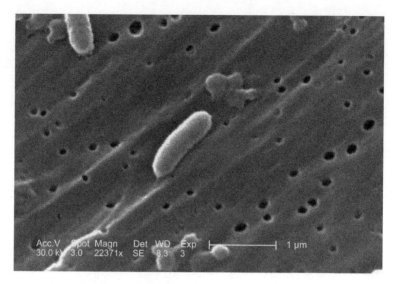

Figure 7.1 Vibrio Cholerae
Photo Credit: Janice Haney Carr, Centers for Disease Control and Prevention (https://phil.cdc.gov/Details.aspx?pid=7819)

Figure 7.2 "Death's Dispensary" showing the pump with handle
SOURCE: "Death's Dispensary" This sketch was drawn in 1866, around the same time that John Snow published his definitive studies on cholera transmission. The contaminated water supply of London, like that of other major European capitals, was untreated river water. (Illustration: John Pinwell). https://openi.nlm.nih.gov/detailedresult.php?img=PMC1360632_pmed.0030042.g001&req=4

Figure 7.3 After pump handle removed – John Snow's memorial and public house
SOURCE: After pump handle removal (Image: From Wikipedia Commons, link: https://commons.wikimedia.org/w/index.php?curid=357998)

The Ghost Map captures well how scientific understanding that includes multidisciplinary thinking can result in scientific advances. For example, the author of the book claims that early "disease mapping" signaled the beginnings of the formal public health field of epidemiology. In this London-based neighborhood, scientific advances in the understanding of water, wastewater, and water systems also helped shape the world we live in (Johnson, 2006). And in a most ironic manner, the social work reader of *The Ghost Map* will come to realize that while water, and its ability to carry contaminants to people, is a leading cause of cholera, it is also important to understand more fully that drinking clean water and lots of it, with its ability to rehydrate the sickened individual, is a main curative agent for cholera. The human body's dependence on water is so profound that almost all the major systems begin to fail when so much fluid is evacuated in such a short period of time as is the case with cholera. Cholera victims who are given water and electrolytes via intravenous and oral therapies reliably survive the illness, but only with lots of water (Johnson, 2006).

The need to counteract the heightened occurrence of waterborne diseases, particularly as a rural-to-urban migration occurred in Europe in the mid-1700s, was solved primarily through the patchwork development of privately owned water pipes that provided running water to homes. It is impossible to overestimate the impact of this scientific structural development. Eventually, in Europe and throughout the developed world, the spread of water delivery systems to private and public water pipes increased and helped push forward the development of such modern-day standards as showers, flush toilets, and washing machines (Johnson, 2006). All, however, depend on a reliable supply of water. Johnson's book has justifiably enjoyed a wide audience of readers that includes students and practitioners in a number of fields: hydrology, epidemiology, the physical sciences, engineering, urban planners and developers, research methodologists, and, of course, readers who just like a chilling medical mystery story. To that list of readers we recommend that social work scholars, practitioners, and students give the book, with its central focus on water, a try.

WHAT IS THE SCIENCE OF WATER?

Even though water has been studied for decades, water scientists still ponder big questions—questions with difficult answers and always with a hint of uncertainty. For example, how did water arise from the Big Bang? How did water get to Earth? Hypotheses still abound about both questions. Three primary hypotheses or speculations about how water got to Earth are wet accretion, gas from the solar nebula, and late impact of comets and asteroids. But how much water came from each hypothesized etiology is unclear, even today, and a subject for current research (Finney, 2015). Physical scientists, particularly astronomers, know that interstellar water was abundantly available to a young planetary system and it is obvious that Earth, sometimes referred to as the blue planet due to an abundance of surface water, collected (or accreted) plenty of it. Still, the answer to how water moved about an emerging interstellar system is elusive. Additional big questions, like how and when life emerged on Earth, and possible answers are seemingly forever linked to the science of water (Sarafian, Nielson, Marschall, McCubbin, & Montelone, 2014).

Even in the face of scientific uncertainty, the Big Bang theory still appears to be the best scientific model we have to ascertain and explain the beginnings of our universe and the planet Earth. The important theoretical premise to keep in mind here is that as the Big Bang explosion occurred, the temperature would have been in the region of a billion, billion degrees (or somewhere around there). But with rapid expansion of matter the temperature of the universe dropped rapidly and quite possibly the conditions were then available for water to have come to Earth or come into existence on Earth (Ball, 1999).

Additionally, scientific understanding of the distribution and history of Earth's water from the time of its arrival following the Big Bang to the present day is a most intractable question. Through the centuries and decades, water scientists have established a great deal of knowledge about water on our planet—but not about everything. What water scientists do know is that water dominates the Earth's surface. Seventy percent of the Earth's surface is covered by water via the oceans. Five percent of the Earth's water (and shrinking) is the ice caps (sometimes referred to as frozen oceans) (Finney, 2015). More than two thirds of the planet's surface is covered by liquid water and more than one twentieth is covered by ice (Ball, 1999).

A good deal of the Earth's additional water is what makes up rivers, groundwater, and organic matter. There is also lots of water in the Earth's mantle; however, it is fresh water that people primarily need and that amount, available to us, is really quite small, with estimates generally in the range of only 0.1 of the grand total of water (Finney, 2015).

A point of scientific certainty in water science is a thorough understanding of the constant overturn of water between the Earth, the oceans, and the sky. The label for this churning of water is the hydrological cycle (Ball, 1999). The hydrological cycle (Figure 7.4) consists of evaporation and transpiration followed by precipitation, and this cycle is critical to life on Earth. It is responsible for the continued existence of water on Earth and the ability of water to serve as a purification mechanism with a resultant massive influence on our climate (Finney, 2015).

The very existence of the hydrological cycle is a consequence of water's unique ability to exist in more than one state—solid, liquid, or gas—under the conditions that prevail at the surface of the planet. Scientific discoveries help us understand that these changes in physical states—condensation, evaporation, freezing, and melting—are triggered by variations in temperature and pressure (Ball, 1999). And with that scientific awareness comes an accompanying understanding that water is a truly unusual liquid. The vast majority of the theoretical work on liquids is concerned with so-called simple liquids, but the tools of the theory of simple liquids are often inadequate to understand how water behaves. For example, water has a constant ability to change states, sometimes referred to as phases, and to have innumerable phase transitions. Water's idiosyncratic behaviors include the ability while in a solid state/phase (ice) to float in its own liquid state/phase. Water is also quite different in regard to cooling and density. The vast majority of liquids become denser as they cool. But water is different. Water scientists have known for about 300 years that water is densest not when it is at its coldest, 32 degrees Fahrenheit

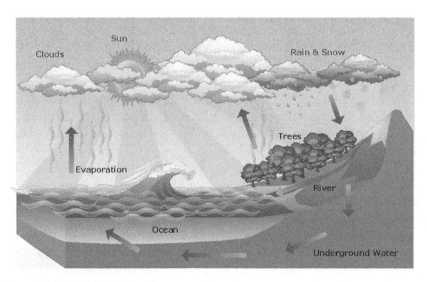

Figure 7.4 The hydrological cycle
SOURCE: Image from Wikipedia, By K.Tapdıqova, link: https://commons.wikimedia.org/w/index.php?curid=59406993

(0 degree Celsius), but at 4 degrees above the freezing mark. Only at about 30 degrees Fahrenheit does water behave like most other liquids: declining density with increasing temperature. The relationship of cooling temperature and density is a mysterious characteristic of water (Ball, 1999).

WHAT IS WATER?

A poor schoolmaster, in rags, introduced himself to a scientific friend with whom I was talking, and announced that he had found out the composition of the sun. "How was that done? —by consideration of the four elements" — "What are they?"—"Of course, fire, air, earth, and water."—"Did you know that air, earth, and water have long been known to be no elements at all, but compounds?"—"What do you mean, sir? Who ever heard of such a thing? (Augustus De Morgan, *A Budget of Paradoxes*, 1872 [reprinted in Ball, 1999])

This quote, used in a well-known book, *A Biography of Water*, focused on the science and knowledge base of water studies, helping us understand that water and the eventual scientific understanding of its makeup was a long journey. For centuries water was considered an element—one of the basic elements presented in folklore, religion, and mysticism. It was only as water science progressed did we learn that water is actually a compound. It was the French scientist Lavoisier who primarily helped us understand that water is a compound, not a single element, and actually made up of two elements, oxygen and hydrogen. But it was not until 1826 that water scientists set aside the notion of one atom of each in combination and arrived finally at the formula of H_2O for water (Finney, 2015).

Chemically, water is an inorganic compound formed by the union of the elements of oxygen and hydrogen (Figure 7.5). Oxygen is one of the most important and

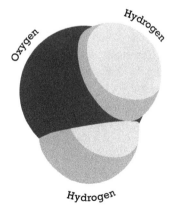

Figure 7.5 Water molecule
SOURCE: Image: From Wikipedia, by Booyabazooka, link: https://commons.wikimedia.org/w/index.php?curid=16278333

plentiful chemical elements on our planet. Oxygen, with three atomic isotopes of 16, 17, and 18, furnishes about eight ninths of the weight of water and one fifth of the volume of air. Uncombined oxygen is always found as a gas (colorless, odorless, and tasteless) and contributes mightily to those preferred qualities in water. Oxygen is also a very social element, always ready to combine with others (King, 1955). Hydrogen, oxygen's partner in water, is the number-one element of the atomic table. Hydrogen has one proton and one electron, and this is the simplest composition possible for an atom or element. The very simple structure of the atom makes hydrogen the lightest of the elements with a weight of only one. Hydrogen is also very social and ready to combine with other elements, in the case of water with oxygen. Hydrogen forms innumerable compounds and one of its favorite mixings is with oxygen—one molecule of oxygen and two molecules of hydrogen combine to form water (King, 1955). It is important to note, however, that the conclusion that water is a molecule made up of one oxygen atom and two hydrogen atoms was based on a number of major advances in science, including atomic theory itself and the recognition of the existence of elements. Getting to this stage of knowledge about water took a long time: It wasn't until the second quarter of the 19th century that water was recognized as H_2O (Finney, 2015). Hydrogen, helium, and oxygen are the most abundant elements within the universe. So it is not surprising that with oxygen and hydrogen's propensity for combining with another element, we get a lot of the compound of water: H_2O. In fact, it is the most abundant compound on Earth (Finney, 2015).

Water also has some unusual characteristics at the molecular level. Water is a "bent" molecule, with a characteristic kink at an angle of 104.5 degrees. Water molecules also have an unusual stickiness to them and that is how they get high melting and boiling points. Water molecules also link up in a bit of an unusual manner (Ball, 1999).

WHAT IS CLEAN WATER?

As stated earlier, pure, distilled water is composed of two hydrogen atoms and one oxygen atom. If the sample of water is not "pure," the composition of the sample can be different. For example, salt water obviously contains salt, but it can contain many other trace elements. Fresh water from different sources will also contain different elements and minerals. These trace elements can come from the rocks the water washes over and/or from agricultural or industrial pollutants. In modern times, water presented as clean, pure, and wholesome and available for drinking will usually contain several additives used for purification plus the fluoride that is added for our dental health. Rainwater will have any number of pollutants that have accumulated in the atmosphere. At high temperatures and pressures, like those in the interior of large planets, scientists think that water exists as ionic water in which the molecules break down into a soup of hydrogen and oxygen ions, and at even higher pressures as superionic water in which the oxygen crystallizes but the hydrogen ions float around freely within the oxygen framework (Coffey, 2015). There are many interesting features about water. Water is a tasteless, odorless liquid. And although water appears colorless in small quantities, in large quantities the color of water and ice appears slightly blue. Ice also appears colorless, and water vapor is essentially invisible as a gas. Since the water molecule is not linear and the oxygen atom has a higher electronegativity than hydrogen atoms, water carries a slight negative charge. As a result, water has an electrical dipole moment, with separate but equal point charges. Water can form a large number of intermolecular hydrogen bonds (four). These factors lead to water's high surface tension and capillary forces (Coffey, 2015). Water is the greatest solvent. Life and water on Earth are inseparable. A huge mass of plants and animals actually live in water. Interestingly, there are forms of life that can exist without a fresh supply of water for years. Grains, seeds, and nuts, after years of no exposure to water, have the capability of germination and growth after being kept in a dry place and then exposed to water (King, 1955).

Ultimately, defining good or clean water is like a social worker in the mental health field attempting to define good mental health. Actually, it is easier for the mental health social worker to describe the attributes of poor mental health and the accompanying observable symptoms rather than to be able to say with a sense of certainty what good mental health is. In the same sense it is bit easier to say what bad water is like than what good water is like. But let's try. Good water looks pure and attractive. That is, it looks clear, colorless (even though water itself has slightly blue hue—think of the color of frozen water in mountain glaciers), and sparkles in sunlight. There is no disagreeable taste and that generally means good water has no taste at all to the consumer. And, for certain a disagreeable odor leads the consumer of water to feel at odds with the question of water quality. Yet, with all that, water might look good, taste good, smell good, and still contain germs of disease (King, 1955). Typhoid and cholera (water contaminated by human sewage) are but two well-known waterborne diseases (Johnson, 2006; King, 1955). And it is important to note that water and the terms used to identify it are of almost innumerable manifestations. A list including a few of those identifiers might include precipitation, rain, sleet, hail, dew, snow pack, watersheds, runoff, surface water, storm and rainfall types and characteristics, floods, groundwater, rivers, lakes, and ponds, to name just a few (The Committee on Hydrology, 1949).

But the ultimate answer of what is acceptable water quality, at least in the United States, comes from the Environmental Protection Agency (EPA). The EPA is responsible for the assessment of water quality and sets limits for drinking water on more than 90 contaminants. As new contaminants are identified, they may or may not be added to the list for scientific scrutiny. Water scientists are constantly studying newly identified contaminants and ascertaining at what levels they are acceptable in water, particularly drinking water and water to cook with. The federal government and state governments regulate the quality of water while water scientists test for temperature, chlorine, and pH levels as well as certain chemicals that prevent pipe erosion. Scientists, as well, look for *E. coli*, which would indicate sewage contamination (Reub, 2016).

ADVANCES IN THE SCIENCE OF WATER—WATER SYSTEMS, WATER TREATMENT

Two major advances in the science of water were chlorination and fluoridation of water and particularly public drinking water supply systems. This section outlines the foundation for these advances and a bit of the science, describes a number of the people responsible for these advances, and while noting the success of both chlorination and fluoridation also briefly presents opposing views.

Chlorination

Chlorination of water systems has been often recognized as one of the greatest innovations of the 20th century. A noted "water wonk," Michael McGuire notes this claim and additional merits of placing chlorine in water systems by titling his well-known 2013 book, *The Chlorine Revolution: Water Disinfection and the Fight to Save Lives*. To understand the impact of systemic infusion of chlorination into water supply systems, it is important to remember how commonplace disease and death were in the United States in the late 1800s and early 1900s. Life expectancy hovered around 47 years of age in 1900. Persons who survived infancy tended not to die of what we now know as the aging process; rather, they died of disease. And the big killer diseases were epidemic and waterborne. The most common of the waterborne diseases were cholera, typhoid, and diarrheal diseases. The data are nearly irrefutable that the placement of chlorine in water systems directly resulted in a containment of the disease of cholera, a near eradication of the disease of typhoid, and dramatic reduction in the incidence of diarrheal diseases (McGuire, 2013).

It is important to note that scientific theorists as they came to appreciate the impact of chlorination as a form of disinfection needed to reject such folly as the theory of miasma. At its best, miasma was the idea that the cycle of epidemic diseases was due to weather change and seasonal characteristics, but at its worst, it was the idea that the stench, the foul odor associated with filth often found in the poorer neighborhoods in the burgeoning urban cities of the world, was the cause for disease. To understand the etiology of that eventual rejection, we must harken back to the French chemist and microbiologist Louis Pasteur and recognize him as the originator of germ theory as the source explanation of waterborne diseases. For it was Pasteur's germ theory of disease proffered in the mid- to late 1800s that gave rise to the tools to identify contamination in water supplies and to figure out ways to eliminate that contamination, and most importantly, how to protect human health (McGuire, 2013). Pasteur actually came up with a germ theory of fermentation first, and eventually application was extended to the creation of a germ theory of disease applicable to human health. It was germ theory that ultimately helped explain the etiology of several diseases. And consistent with Thomas Kuhn's ideas about paradigm shifts, it was not so much the data about waterborne diseases, but Pasteur's interpretation of the data in new and informed ways that caused a paradigm shift, with germ theory moving to the foreground of scientific understanding (McGuire, 2013). Nancy Tomes, in her 1998 book, *Gospel of Germs: Men, Women, and the Microbe in American Life*, articulated that germ theory consisted of two related propositions: first, that animal and human diseases were caused by distinctive microorganisms, which were widely present in the air and water; and second, that these germs could not generate spontaneously, but rather always came from a previous case of exactly the same disease (McGuire, 2013). The germ theory of disease began to attract popular interest even as physicians remained doubtful. But the causal link between germs and the deadly diseases of the era grew stronger and stronger. The general principle that microorganisms played a central role in causing communicable diseases had by 1900 achieved widespread acceptance in the United States and Europe. Bacteriology as a field of scientific study and a profession was born (Tomes, 1998). The rise of the specialized area of water bacteriology took place mainly from 1880 to 1905 (McGuire, 2013). Water bacteriologists identified disease agents, demonstrated how disease agents were carried by water, and tracked how they spread from the diseased person to the well, resulting in more diseased persons (Tomes, 1998). The following timeline, in a somewhat reductionist fashion, highlights the point of discovery of waterborne disease organisms, the actual disease agent, and the person primarily identified with the discovery. It is important to realize though that these discoveries, while often aligned with the name of one individual, usually represent the combined contributory work of a number of water scientists who often did their work in disparate fields of science (McGuire, 2013, p. 55).

1880	typhoid fever	*Salmonella typhi*	C. J. Eberth
1883	cholera	*Vibrio cholera*	Robert Koch
1885	diarrheal disease	*Escherichia coli*	Theordor Escherich
1898	dysentery	*Shigella dysenteriae*	Kiyoushi Shiga

Once water bacteriologists identified these disease agents, and really even before complete faith in the scientific findings was established, there was a belief that water could be purposefully disinfected with the simple aim of killing, selectively if necessary, those living organisms that had the capability of spreading or transmitting infections through or in the water (McGuire, 2006). And, in a somewhat counterintuitive manner, as cities became larger and centralized drinking water systems were developed, contaminated water was actually being distributed more widely to even larger populations. This distribution of contaminated water resulted in recurring and frequent large-scale epidemics. However, even before widespread acceptance that diseases could be caused by bacteria or other pathogens, early public health pioneers hypothesized correctly that, in fact, it could be the drinking water supply that was the actual source of disease epidemics (McGuire, 2006). This was particularly true during the latter half of the 19th century and can be directly attributed to the misinformed construction of sewer pipes to remove human wastes as quickly as possible to sources of drinking water, such as lakes, rivers, and constructed reservoirs (McGuire, 2006).

A disinfection revolution required acceptance of the notion that bacteria and other microorganisms in water could cause disease in humans. The 19th century saw a bitterly fought battle between those scientists who believed in the concept of spontaneous generation of disease and innovators such as the previously mentioned Louis Pasteur, who developed the germ theory of disease and its primary proposition that spontaneous generation of disease was not possible. It was Pasteur's work in fermentation of wine and beer that rightfully set the stage for his understanding of how the actions of microorganisms affected life processes. His 1857 publication on fermentation contained all of the elements necessary to eventually explain what entailed a germ theory of disease (McGuire, 2006). Disinfection via chlorination won out, but it was not without a struggle.

Chlorine, an element with the symbol of Cl, first discovered by the Swedish chemist Carl W. Scheele in 1774, had always been known to have disinfecting and deodorizing qualities. The mantra was, however, that while a little bit of chlorine might be beneficial, in too large a quantity or too strong a dose, chlorine could be quite harmful. Hydrochloric acid was, indeed, harmful to people, particularly if ingested. To actually accomplish the first chlorination of a water supply in Jersey City, New Jersey, required the work and insights of two great figures in water science innovation, from 1890 to 1910. These figures were Dr. John Leal, a physician turned water scientist, and Mr. George Warren Fuller, a sanitary engineer of almost mythical status, who at one point became the president of the American Public Health Association (McGuire, 2013). Previous to disinfection via chlorination, attempts to purify water were achieved primarily via filtration of two major types, slow sand filters and subsequent mechanical filters. Even though filtration had some impact on the goal of cleansing water, it was the subsequent scientific venture of understanding how heat and chemicals, in this case chlorine, could overcome waterborne disease agents that signaled a huge leap forward. It was not until cities across the country began disinfecting drinking water with chlorine that the sewer pipe and water pipe intertwinement and its death spiral of contamination was broken. The results were impressive. For example, with the introduction of chlorine to water systems, the typhoid death rate in the United States declined until it was ultimately eradicated (McGuire, 2013). The major advance of chlorination took place in the years between 1906 and 1918 and the advances in filtration from 1906 to 1922 (Gordon, 2016). With a great sense of courage and conviction, Dr. Leal and others instituted the first US base chlorinated water system in Jersey City, New Jersey. A new dam, a reservoir, and a pipeline were constructed. A revolutionary water treatment process using chloride lime was conceived, designed, and implemented at the Boonton Reservoir in 1908. The contract called for the chlorinated water to be "pure and wholesome," language that still gets used today to describe treated water and also in claims made about naturally occurring water that is believed to be of good enough quality for people to drink (McGuire, 2013).

Dr. Leal and the others knew that the historical transfer of human and animal sewage, no matter how well intended, to a river or lake that served as somebody else's water supply was not the solution. He promulgated the idea that there had to be a way of killing disease-causing organisms, even if that method was not perfect and did not kill all bacteria, and this method was disinfection using chloride of lime. A key feature of any water disinfection system using chlorine, and Dr. Leal knew this as well, was setting the chlorine dosage (McGuire, 2013). Full-scale and continuous implementation of disinfection for the first time in Jersey City, New Jersey, ignited a disinfection revolution in the United States that reverberated around the world.

Seeds of revolution were planted in the ideas of the innovators, but it was the law-suits based on contractual issues in Jersey City that brought all to fruition.

Scientific studies of disinfection to kill or inactivate waterborne pathogens were underway at the turn of the 20th century. In 1896, George W. Fuller tried the first experimental applications of chlorine and hypochlorite to soda in the Louisville, Kentucky. The first permanent application of chlorine to drinking water in the world occurred in Belgium in 1902. A second implementation of chemical disin-fection with chlorine did not occur until 1905 in Lincoln, England (Baker, 1981). As with all revolutions, it takes time for everyone to recognize what is happening and for additional volunteers to get on board. At the beginning of the 20th century, it took the court dispute in Jersey City, New Jersey, and a legal deadline to clear away the objections and to apply what was until then only an experimental treat-ment method in the United States. Little progress was made in applying processes of disinfection to public water supplies until that year, 1908. By adding chlorite of lime to the Boonton reservoir supply, a great reduction in bacteria was obtained, and the result was reached with a smaller amount of the disinfectant than could have been anticipated from any previous experience on a small scale. The "pure and wholesome" water promised by the East Jersey Water Company to Jersey City was delivered as a function of chlorination. The Boonton chlorination plant began op-erations September 26, 1908. For the first time in US history, chlorine was used for disinfection on a large scale and as part of a permanent installation for drinking water treatment. By the 1920s, chlorination was well established as the primary means of disinfecting drinking water (McGuire, 2006).

With the obvious disease suppression success of the Boonton reservoir and pipe-line of the drinking water supplied to Jersey City, the use of chlorine as a disinfecting agent in the United States exploded. In 1914, just over 40 million people were served by municipal water systems and fully 53% were drinking water treated with chlorine (McGuire, 2013). Shortly thereafter, the US Public Health Service estimated that 85% of US drinking water supplies were chlorinated (McGuire, 2013).

Disinfection, as a scientific-based intervention, continued to develop new tools to target disease prevention. In 1931, all of the elements were in place in the United States for serving water that did not cause disease to the public. The germ theory of disease was an accepted fact. Filtration could reduce bacterial concentrations, but chlorine's efficacy in disease prevention and even elimination had been demon-strated in laboratory and full- scale applications in hundreds of US cities by effect-ively killing disease-causing bacteria and pathogens. Practical methods of applying chlorine were in wide use. Pipeline disinfection became common practice. As soon as pipes were used to transfer water, drinking water utilities recognized the need to physically clean pipes (McGuire, 2006).

However, not all is peaceful in the world of disinfection and the presence of chlorination in public drinking water supplies. While proponents of disinfection via chlorination are strongly supported by scientific evidence, opponents of chlor-ination still flourish. Opponents question the need for continued chlorination and raise the question of whether chlorination has links to disease protocols of a dif-ferent nature, such as cancer. Furthermore, the question of civil rights, particularly individual rights, are often put forward as a point of discussion by opponents, as chlorination of a water system does not allow for the individual, a family, a household, or a collective, such as the homes in a subdivision, to opt out of a systemic infusion of chlorine into a water supply (McGuire, 2006, 2013).

There, however, can be no scientific doubt of the veracity of the prediction of Dr. John Leal in the early 1900s regarding the positive effect of chlorine uses on water treatment. Even though he at first just believed in an idea, subsequent data-generating studies confirmed the veracity of his belief: that the practical application of the use of a bleaching substance, chlorine, for the purpose of disinfecting a water supply would be a great advance in the science of water. He and his fellow pioneers in water science were right.

Fluoridation

A second major advance in water science and the issue of water treatment is fluoridation of a water supply. The proponents make strong claims. Burt and Tomar (2007) in their writings claim that water fluoridation is one of the major public health achievements of the 20th century. Water fluoridation was named in by the Centers for Disease Control as one of the ten great public health achievements of the 20th century. It was described as a major contributor to the decline of the rate of tooth decay, and particularly so for children. Studies cited in a report by the Surgeon General attribute water fluoridation with a 18%–40% reduction in the incidence of decay in children's teeth (US Department of Health and Human Services, 2000).

Adding fluoride to water was first carried out in the 1930s. Fluoridation research tended to focus on the right amount or balance of fluoride in water as a means to prevent tooth decay but not stain one's teeth. Grand Rapids, Michigan, in January of 1945, was the first city to have its water supply fluoridated. Fluoridation became the official policy of the US Public Health Service in 1951. Fluoridation now reaches 64% of the US population—one of the highest percentages in the world (Gordon, 2016). From the beginning, there had always been two lines of thought on how best to get fluoride to the teeth. First, there was the systemic approach, whereby fluoride reaches the teeth only after it is metabolized into our bodily system following the ingestion of fluoridated water or secondly through topical applications of fluoride directly onto the teeth (Freeze & Lehr, 2009). There seems little doubt, based on current scientific and medical understanding, that fluoridation does more good than harm. Data, arising from epidemiological studies, laboratory studies, physiologic-based medical reasoning, and longitudinal data from studies with children, all affirm 70 years of public policy with respect to the fluoridation of public water supplies. There has been a dramatic decline in the incidence of tooth decay among children in the years since World War II. Dental caries, particularly tooth decay, is no longer considered a major public health problem in the resource-rich countries of the world. And the evidence is indisputable that the increased fluoride intake via fluoridation of drinking water supplies has been a major factor in this success (Freeze, & Lehr, 2009).

In any discussion of the scientific basis for the use of fluoride in a water supply, it is important to recall that during the early to mid-1900s in the United States, severe decline in dental health was prevalent and a near certainty of life. Tooth decay and the loss of teeth, and in many cases all of one's teeth, were commonplace. As science progressed, it was not surprising that confirmation of the idea that dental caries and cavities, the most common being tooth decay, were caused by a breakdown of the tooth enamel. This breakdown was the result of bacteria on teeth during the breakdown of foods. Acids were produced with the resultant destruction of tooth enamel, and this process often resulted in tooth decay (US Department of Health and Human Services, 2000). Dentists really carried the ball in regard to consideration of fluoride as a means to fight this acidic buildup, particularly following a Colorado dentist's use of the term "mottled enamel" in the 1910s and the possibility that this tooth discoloring was linked to fluoride in some naturally occurring water sources. So, counterintuitively (at least for the sake of this chapter), fluoride was thought initially to be a problem. Dr. Trendley Dean, also a dentist, changed the term "mottled enamel" to "fluorosis," and the study of the efficacy of fluoride as a preventative treatment for tooth decay was off and running. Dr. Dean created a numerical scale for assessing fluorosis. And even though the scale was of questionable validity due to the ordinal nature of the numerical scale and his use of weighted measure from mostly descriptive work, Dr. Dean's work laid the groundwork for later more rigorous analysis of tooth discoloration and the link to fluoride. Later, via his scaling and disease mapping, Dr. Dean's data also suggested a relationship between mild fluorosis levels and low occurrence and severity of caries and tooth decay. His later 21 cities study confirmed the association between fluoridated water systems and reduced prevalence and severity of caries (Burt & Tomar, 2007). After the stage was set by increasing awareness of mottled enamel, fluorosis, and the possibility of a link to fluoride, a series of epidemiologic studies of persons living in areas with naturally occurring fluoride in their drinking water was undertaken. These studies led to the hypothesis that routine exposure to fluoride would reduce the prevalence and severity of dental caries, particularly tooth decay, and this was eventually to be proven correct (Burt & Tomar, 2007).

The toxicology of fluoride has been well understood and detailed in numerous books, review papers, and literally hundreds of journal articles for decades. The pros and cons on every harmful health impact that could possibly be laid at the door of fluoride have been thoroughly discussed in the scientific literature and popular press. Major questions about fluoride intake format, dosage, duration of exposure, and the differing impact on adults and children, particularly as to the difference in size of the fluoride recipient's body, are seemingly under continuous study. Proponents of fluoridation see fluoride compounds as beneficial to human health in small amounts but harmful in large amounts. Fluorides, in this sense, are similar to many other chemical compounds, including chlorine, as discussed in the previous section of this chapter on chlorination of water supplies (Freeze & Lehr, 2009). The mechanism of fluoride action on tooth enamel is now understood to be primarily topical and posteruptive, rather than systemic and pre-eruptive. This refers to the idea of when fluoride should be present to be effective—before teeth emerge in the mouth (pre-eruptive) or after teeth emerge in the mouth (posteruptive)

(Freeze & Lehr, 2009). By the end of the 20th century, the topical effect of low-concentration fluoride, by drinking fluoridated water and/or brushing one's teeth with fluoridated toothpaste in enhancing remineralization in the early stages of the tooth decay process, was well understood (Burt & Tomar, 2007). By the start of the 21st century, more than half of the US population had access to fluoridated water, and virtually all mass-marketed toothpastes contained fluoride. Additionally, dentists were using fluoride in topical treatments and many processing companies used fluoridated water in the production of food (Burt & Tomar, 2007). While the positive effects of fluoridation of water systems in reducing tooth decay and tooth loss have been convincingly demonstrated, there are other contributing variables to consider—improvement in oral health through the brushing and flossing of teeth, a rise in the standard of living for millions of Americans, and better dental treatment technology. These have all combined with fluoridation of water supplies to achieve massively improved dental health for the US population (Burt & Tomar, 2007).

After the first urban-based ventures, fluoridation of water supplies just grew and grew. By the 1960s, major cities, New York and San Francisco for example, had fluoridated water systems. In 2000, just under 70% of Americans were drinking fluoridated water from the tap (Burt & Tomar, 2007). Subsequently, since the mid-1970s the prevalence and severity of dental problems in US children, particularly tooth decay as observed via the occurrence of cavities, has declined steadily. While how much of that decline is solely attributable to fluoridation of the drinking water supply is difficult to pinpoint, the correlative feature with the decline and fluoridation of the water supply is quite robust (Burt & Tomar, 2007). There have been numerous gains in dental health and much can be easily attributed to fluoride in community drinking water supplies (Freeze & Lehr, 2009).

However, even with strong data about the efficacy of fluoridation of water supplies, controversy exists about whether fluoridating the drinking water supply should continue. This is particularly true when questions arise about whether the fluoride intervention should be in the pre-eruptive phase of tooth development or in the posteruptive phase. An additional ongoing question is whether the fluoride intervention should be a systemic application or topical application. One strong piece of empirical data for those opposing the systemic intervention of fluoride via the drinking water supply is that there have been noted declines in dental caries, tooth decay, and tooth loss in both fluoridated and nonfluoridated communities over the past few years. Furthermore, opponents of fluoridation of the drinking water supply are fearful of the unknown harmful health effects for even the smallest dose of fluoride on a continual basis (Freeze & Lehr, 2009).

When opponents question the continued use of systemic fluoridation of drinking water supplies, social workers are urged to consider the positive impacts of systemic fluoridation on dental disease, particularly with children, and the potential impacts on reduction of health disparities supported by empirical data. It is also important to consider that not all children in the United States see a dentist, and thus fluoridation via a water supply might be their only source of dental treatment. Also, there are almost no school-based dental programs in the United States, unlike the social welfare democracies of Western Europe. And for economically disadvantaged children, the drinking water might be their sole source of fluoride. The major reason to say yes to the fluoridation of drinking water supplies in the United States, at least for social workers, is that fluoridated drinking water supply systems have been shown to reduce dental health disparities that exist between socioeconomic groups (Burt & Tomar, 2007). Opposition to fluoridation of a water supply system rests primarily on the question of whether it necessary and whether it infringes on individual rights. Of course, even though there is little, if any empirical data to support the idea that fluoridation of the drinking water supply system is linked to disease protocols and developmental delays and disabilities, opponents continue to raise these issues. Undeniably so, systemic fluoridation of drinking water systems has been shown scientifically to be a major positive advance in water science, particularly for children.

WATER TODAY, WATER IN THE UNITED STATES

An additional and highly informative source highlighting the impact of water in the lives of people who reside in the United States is R. J. Gordon's 2016 book, *The Rise and Fall of American Growth: The U.S. Standard of Living Since the Civil War*. Gordon convincingly includes water availability, particularly safe drinking water piped into the home and the management of human waste via indoor plumbing, among a host of life-altering innovations over the last 100 years, including electric lighting, home appliances, motor vehicles, air travel, air conditioning, and television. A central thesis of Gordon's is that some innovations and inventions, like water systems, are more important than others. Furthermore, what helped make the last 100 years so unique was not only the magnitude of its transitions, but also the speed at which they were completed. For example, from 1880 to 1940, almost no urban homes in the United States had clean running piped water and sewer pipes for waste disposal, but within a little more than a hundred years the percentage of urban homes with those water-based developments had risen to 94%. Public health indicators, including longer life expectancy, increased noticeably from the mid-1940s to the 1970s. The conquest of infant mortality was an additional quantitative indicator. Public water systems, and their extension into the home, not only revolutionized the daily routine of the persons living in the home but also helped protect nearly every family against waterborne diseases (Gordon, 2016).

By 1880, only one third of urban households in the United States were equipped with water closets—generally considered to have consisted of a flush toilet and a sink with running water (Gordon, 2016). Most important, prior to the development of urban sewer waste systems, these water closets drained directly into existing privy vaults and cesspools—often located in the basement of homes or tenements. Remember Johnson's book, *The Ghost Map*, and the grisly description of these awful living and disease-promoting conditions (Johnson, 2006).

Clear recognition of the health benefits of keeping such bodily wastes as urine and feces rigidly separated from food and drink became scientifically a near absolute. The provision of running water and sanitary sewage systems is directly (and positively) linked to the decline in mortality rates in the first half of the 20th century in the United States. In fact, centralized water supplies and sanitary sewers may outweigh both improvements in medical practice or genetic changes in the virulence of disease organisms in the improvement of health outcomes for all, and the reduction of health disparities between persons of high socioeconomic status and those of lower socioeconomic status. In fact, clean water technologies have been labeled as likely the most important public health intervention of the 20th century (Gordon, 2016).

However, not all is well in the world of drinking water in the United States, and the next section examines the Flint, Michigan, drinking water crisis.

SCIENCE AND THE FLINT DRINKING WATER CRISIS

The drinking water crisis in Flint, Michigan, began when the city switched its water supply from the Detroit Water Sewerage Department to the Karegnondi Water Authority in an effort to cut cost (Kennedy, 2016). Flint, a city with a majority of Black persons and located 66 miles northwest of Detroit, has a federal poverty rate of 40% (US Census Bureau, 2015). Flint residents began expressing concern over the quality of their drinking water when the city began using water from the Flint River. According to officials, an interim source of water (i.e., the Flint River) was necessary until the city could connect water pipelines to the Karegnondi Water Authority of Genesee County, the county in which the city of Flint is located. Mistakes in treating the corrosive river water damaged pipes, which presently continue to leach lead, and have resulted in increased blood lead levels in Flint's children (Camody, 2016; Kennedy, 2016). According to the Centers for Disease Control and Prevention, high blood lead levels are especially harmful to children and women who are pregnant, and they can cause learning and intellectual disabilities (CDC, 2016).

Michigan has spent more than $200 million in Flint to distribute over 3 million cases of bottled water and approximately 145,000 water filters (Camody, 2016). In the beginning of November 2016, a federal judge ordered Michigan to deliver safe bottled drinking water to all Flint residents who did not have functioning water filters, as per the State's earlier plan of action (Wertheimer, 2016). However, Michigan challenged the ruling, stating that it would cost approximately $10 million per month to deliver the amount of water ordered by the federal court (Wertheimer, 2016). The state further countered that the measure was unnecessary because it already delivered bottled water to anyone who asked for it (Wertheimer, 2016). Following the federal ruling, in the beginning of December 2016, the US Congress approved $170 million in aid; however, state officials reported that they would need tens of millions more to replace all of the city's lead pipe infrastructure. Many Flint residents report that Flint's decades of economic challenges have been exacerbated by the continued drinking water crisis (Carmody, 2016). More than 400 civil lawsuits have been filed thus far amid multiple claims by officials, including Michigan's Governor Rick Snyder's own admission, that the local and state government's response—and the federal response—to the Flint water crisis was alarmingly negligent (Carmody, 2016; Kennedy, 2016). It remains unseen if the governor himself will face charges

(Henry, 2016). Table 7.1 presents a timeline of the Flint, Michigan, drinking water crisis (Henry, 2016; Kennedy, 2016).

While we all watch the drinking water crisis in Flint, Michigan, continue to play itself out, we as social workers can learn a lot about how important drinking water and drinking water systems are to the quality of life for people. From a scientific perspective it is noted that it was the testing of water, particularly by water scientists from outside Flint, that resulted in empirical data that confirmed the lived experience of the people of Flint, who were forced to drink unsafe, lead-filled water.

WATER TODAY: WATER AND SUSTAINABLE
DEVELOPMENT AROUND THE WORLD

This final section of the chapter is focused on development issues regarding water availability, water use, and worldwide efforts to positively influence the relationship between poverty, internationally based sustainable development, and water. First, it is important to note that international efforts aimed at water-related issues such as the improving the availability of clean drinking water, diminishing the mixing of animal and human wastes with potential surface drinking water, limiting open defecation, and increasing water availability to promote sanitation and hygiene concerns, to name some of the more prominent ones, have been underway for quite some time. For example, in 1977, the United Nations proclaimed: "all peoples have the right to have access to drinking water in quantities and of a quality equal to the basic needs." The 1980s were declared the International Decade of Drinking Water Supply and Sanitation (Ball, 1999). On July 28, 2010, through *Resolution 64/292*, the United Nations General Assembly explicitly recognized the human right to water and sanitation and acknowledged that clean drinking water and sanitation are essential to the realization of all human rights. The resolution calls upon states and international organizations to provide financial resources that will help capacity-building and technology transfer to countries, in particular developing countries, to provide safe, clean, accessible, and affordable drinking water and sanitation for all. In November 2002, the Committee on Economic, Social, and Cultural Rights adopted *General Comment No. 15* on the right to water. Article I.1 states that "The human right to water is indispensable for leading a life in human dignity. It is a prerequisite for the realization of other human rights." Comment No. 15 also defined the right to water as the right of everyone to sufficient, safe, acceptable, and physically accessible and affordable water for personal and domestic uses (United Nations General Assembly, 2010).

Secondly, while much has being done, there can be no doubt, particularly for those who aspire to practice international social work and participate in internationally based development efforts, there is much more to do. But the major point of this section of this chapter is to emphasize how the concept of internationally based sustainable development is completely contingent upon clean water for drinking

Table 7.1 TIMELINE OF THE DRINKING WATER CRISIS IN FLINT, MICHIGAN

Date	Event	Description
June 2012 – April 2013	Officials begin to look for less expensive water sources	1. Officials in Flint, Michigan, explore cost savings related to a switch in the city's water provider, the Detroit Water and Sewerage Department (DWSD) 2. City and state officials look to build a pipeline connecting to the Karegnondi Water Authority (KWA), a move projected to save the region $200 million over 25 years 3. On April 16, Ed Kurtz, Flint Emergency Manager, informs the state treasurer that Flint is joining KWA 4. On April 17, Detroit's water system informs Kurtz it is terminating service effective April 2014
April 25, 2014	Flint tapped as interim source of water	1. Until the Flint pipeline to the KWA becomes operational, an alternate, interim source of water is required 2. Water from the Flint River, the main water source for the city until the 1960s, once again begins flowing to Flint 3. Officials do not immediately treat the Flint River water to ensure it didn't cause corrosion in the pipes
May 2014	Flint residents begin to complain about water quality	1. Some residents complain about the smell and color of the new water, which is 70% hsarder than its previous water source
August 2014	Dangerous bacteria detected in water supply	2. *E. coli* and total coliform bacteria are detected in water, prompting multiple advisories to boil water before use 3. According to the Michigan Department of Environmental Quality (MDEQ), Flint addresses the issue by increasing chlorine levels
October 13, 2014	General Motors stops using Flint River water	1. General Motors announces it will stop using Flint River water, fearing corrosion in its machines from the chlorine

Table 7.1 CONTINUED

Date	Event	Description
January 2, 2015	Disinfection byproducts are detected in Flint River water	1. Flint is found to be in violation of the Safe Drinking Water Act owing to the high level of trihalomethanes (TTHM), which are disinfection byproducts that occur when chlorine interacts with organic matter in the water; some types of TTHM are possible cancer agents for humans according to the Centers for Disease Control and Prevention (CDC) 2. In response to the TTHM finding, the State of Michigan buys bottled water for its employees at government offices; the needs of residents remain unaddressed
February 25, 2015	Tests reveal high lead levels in a Flint home	1. The water at Lee Anne Waters's home indicates a lead content of 104 parts per billion (ppb); in April, Walters reports that her child has been diagnosed with lead poisoning 2. 15 ppb is the Environmental Protection Agency (EPA)'s limit for lead in drinking water; 5,000 ppb is considered hazardous waste 3. An independent test conducted by researchers at Virginia Tech find lead levels at 13,200 ppb
April 24, 2015	State Agency reports Flint did not implement corrosion controls	1. The MDEQ notifies the EPA that there was no corrosion control treatment in place at the Flint Water Treatment Plant
July 13, 2015	State spokesperson dismisses concerns	1. The American Civil Liberties Union (ACLU) obtains a leaked internal memo from the EPA expressing concern for lead levels 2. In response to the leaked memo, Michigan Radio reaches out to Brad Wurfel, spokesperson for the MDEQ; Wurfel states, "Let me start here—anyone who is concerned about lead in the drinking water in Flint can relax […] It does not look like there is any broad problem with the water supply freeing up lead as it goes to homes" 3. Wurfel issues this statement in spite of a lack of corrosion controls; according to Dr. Marc Edwards in a subsequent interview, who is a member of the Virginia Tech research team, "Flint is the only city in America that I'm aware of that does not have a corrosion control plan"

(continued)

Table 7.1 CONTINUED

Date	Event	Description
August 20, 2015	Lead-level samples are excluded from report and accusations of data cherry-picking emerge	1. In a controversial move, the MDEQ drops two outlier samples from its initial report, putting the results within the federally mandated levels 2. According to Michigan Radio, if the MDEQ had dropped just one of the high samples, Flint would still have been over the federal action level; however, dropping the two samples placed the state below the action level 3. According to the MDEQ, the two samples did not meet federal inclusion criteria: one sample had a water filter and the other came from a place of business and not a home
September 2015	Virginia Tech research team reports "serious" lead levels in Flint River water	1. The research team from Virginia Tech tests hundreds of Flint homes for lead, finding that preliminary tests show "serious levels of lead in city water" 2. Spokesperson Brad Wurfel from the MDEQ dismisses the research team's preliminary findings: "I don't know how they're getting the results they're getting"
September 24, 2015	Study finds elevated levels of lead in children	1. A study conducted by the Hurley Medical Center in Flint, Michigan found that 2.1% of children under the age of 5 years had elevated blood lead levels prior to the city's switch to Flint River water; post switch, this figure nearly doubled to 4% 2. In a response to Hurley Medical Center findings, a spokesperson for the Michigan Department of Health and Human Services (DHHS) suggests that elevated blood lead levels may be a result of seasonal changes
September 25, 2015	Flint issues lead advisory, then cautions about politicizing interests	1. The city of Flint issues a lead advisory to residents 2. On the same day, Michigan Governor Rick Snyder's Chief of Staff, Dennis Muchmore, expresses in an email that the MDEQ and the Michigan DHHS "feel that some in Flint are taking the very sensitive issue of children's exposure to lead and trying to turn it into a political football claiming the departments are underestimating the impacts on the population and particularly trying to shift responsibility to the state"

Table 7.1 CONTINUED

Date	Event	Description
October 2, 2015	Action plan released	1. Gov. Rick Snyder issues a plan of action calling for the city and state to provide free water filters and testing for Flint residents
October 16, 2015	Flint switches from Flint River water back to the Detroit water supply	1. After announcing in 2012 a plan to switch from the Detroit Water and Sewerage Department (DSWD) to the KWA, Flint again switches back to the Detroit water supplier, now called the Great Lakes Water Authority
October 18, 2015	Michigan State Regulator cites confusion about federal regulations	1. Dan Wyant, director of the MDEQ, addresses the lack of corrosion control in an email to a Detroit News reporter: "What the staff did would have been the proper protocol for a community under 50,000 people […] it's increasingly clear there is confusion here, but it also is increasingly clear that [M]DEQ staff believed they were using the proper federal protocol here and they were not" 2. According to the US Census Bureau, the estimated population of Flint, Michigan, for July 1, 2015 was 98,310—a decrease of 4% since April 1, 2010 3. According to the US Census Bureau, the estimated population of Genesee County, Michigan (home of Flint), for July 1, 2015 was 410,849—a decrease of 3.5% since April 1, 2010
December 14, 2015	Newly elected Flint mayor declares state of emergency	1. Karen Weaver, who won against incumbent Dayne Walling in the previous month's Flint mayoral election, vows to fix the water crisis and declares a state of emergency due to elevated lead levels in the city's water
December 29, 2015	State regulation officials resign	1. Dan Wyant, director, and Brad Warful, spokesperson, resign from their positions with the MDEQ 2. Their resignations come 1 day following the Flint Water Advisory Task Force preliminary finding that primary responsibility of the water crisis rests with the MDEQ; the Task Force was created by Gov. Rick Snyder 3. The Task Force reported that the MDEQ's interactions with the public about their concerns "was often one of aggressive dismissal, belittlement, and attempts to discredit these efforts and the individuals involved"

(continued)

Table 7.1 CONTINUED

Date	Event	Description
January 2016	President Obama and Governor Snyder declare state of emergency	1. Gov. Rick Snyder declares a state of emergency in Genesee County due to the lead in Flint's water 2. Less than 2 weeks later, Pres. Barack Obama followed suit, meaning that the Federal Emergency Management Agency (FEMA) "is authorized to provide equipment and resources to the people affected. Federal funding will help cover the cost of providing water, water filters and other items"
January 21, 2016	The EPA issues emergency order	1. The EPA issues an emergency order to take action on the Flint water crisis, stating that the "EPA has determined that the City of Flint's and the State of Michigan's responses to the drinking water crisis in Flint have been inadequate and that these failures continue"
February 3, 2016	House Committee hears testimony	1. The House Committee on Oversight and Government Reform hears testimony from several Flint officials and experts 2. Gov. Rick Snyder is not present to testify
February 17, 2016	Governor testimony	1. Gov. Rick Snyder testifies before the House Committee on Oversight and Government Reform and states, "This was a failure of government at all levels"
March 21, 2016	Next steps	1. Gov. Rick Snyder outlines state agencies' goals in handling the Flint water crisis, which include providing professional support for children under the age of 6 years with elevated blood lead levels; replacing water fixtures in public facilities; replacing the city's 8,000 lead service lines; and increasing resources for schools
April 12, 2016	Researchers report that Flint's water is still unsafe	1. According to results released from the Virginia Tech research team, Flint's water remains unsafe to drink
April 20, 2016	Criminal charges are filed against three officials	1. Charges are filed against Stephen Busch and Michael Prysby of the MDEQ and Flint city's water quality supervisor, Michael Glasgow 2. Charges include misconduct, neglect of duty, and conspiracy to tamper with evidence; they are also charged with violating Michigan's Safe Drinking Water Act

Table 7.1 CONTINUED

Date	Event	Description
June 22, 2016	Civil lawsuits are filed against two corporations	1. Michigan Attorney General, Bill Shuette, announces that his office is filing a civil suit against two corporations: Veolia and Lockwood, Andrews, & Newman 2. Veolia, a French company, was hired by the city as a water-quality consultant in 2015; the Texas-based Lockwood, Andrews, & Newman was originally hired in 2011 and helped to operate the water treatment plant using the Flint River 3. The suit accuses both corporations of negligence and public nuisance with an additional accusation of fraud levied against Veolia
July 29, 2016	Criminal charges are filed against six officials	1. Charges are filed against Liane Shekter-Smith, Adam Rosenthal, and Patrick Cook of the MDEQ for allegedly misleading officials about Flint's treatment plant 2. Charges are also filed against Nancy Peeler, Robert Scott, and Corinne Miller with the Michigan DHHS for allegedly failing to release a report that showed unsafe lead levels in the blood of Flint children 3. All six are charged with misconduct in office, conspiracy, and willful neglect of duty 4. Adam Rosenthal is additionally charged with tampering with evidence; it is alleged that he requested water tests that did not evidence elevated lead levels
December 20, 2016	Felony charges are brought	1. Michigan Attorney General, Bill Schuette, brings felony charges against two former emergency managers, Darnell Earley and Jerry Ambrose 2. Flint city employees Daugherty Johnson and Howard Croft are charged with false pretenses and conspiracy 3. With these latest charges, 13 people have been formally accused criminally in connection with the Flint water crisis; while some have pleaded guilty, others are currently fighting their charges in court.

and the availability of water in some systemic manner for the attainment and maintenance of sanitation and hygiene (WaterAid, 2016).

Next, let's take a look at some successes and then take a look at the major
challenges in the world of water internationally. While there continues to be a
large number of people in the world without clean drinking water—estimates
range as high as 6.5 million people—there have been tremendous gains over
the last decade. Take, for example, the early achievement of the Millennium
Development Goal related to water. The Millennium Development Goal's target
for cutting in half the proportion of the planet's population without safe drinking
water was met in 2010, well ahead of the 2015 deadline. At present, more than
90% of people in the world now have access to sources of noncontaminated
drinking water (Burgess et al., 2016). More than 2.5 billion people have gained
access to improved drinking water sources since 1990. Between 1990 and 2015,
the proportion of the global population using an improved drinking water source
has increased from 76% to 91% (http://www.un.org/sustainabledevelopment/
water-and-sanitation/#c52bbb43eb4dfe500).

Even with notable progress, serious problems remain for millions of people in the
world. Today more than 650 million of the world's poorest people are living without
access to an "improved" source of drinking water, such as public taps, protected wells,
rainwater, and/or water piped into a household. These millions of people continue
to rely on "unimproved" water sources that include rivers, ponds, unprotected wells,
tankers, and bottled water only (Burgess et al., 2016). In 16 countries, more than
40% of the population does not have access to even a basic water facility such as a
protected well. This water is always a health risk. Globally, diarrheal diseases caused
by dirty water and poor sanitation are the second biggest child killer after pneumonia, taking 315,000 young lives every year (Burgess et al., 2016). Worldwide 2.1
billion people have gained access to improved sanitation. Despite this progress, 2.4
billion are still using unimproved sanitation facilities, including 946 million people
who are still practicing open defecation (The Millenium, 2015). At least 1.8 billion people globally use a source of drinking water that is contaminated with fecal
material. Approximately 2.4 billion people lack access to basic sanitation services,
such as toilets or latrines. More than 80% of wastewater resulting from human activities is discharged into rivers or seas without any pollution removal. Each day,
nearly 1,000 children die due to preventable water- and sanitation-related diarrheal
diseases   (http://www.un.org/sustainabledevelopment/water-and-sanitation/
#c52bbb43eb4dfe500).

A major problem is that water quality insecurity is becoming more and more con-
centrated in specific locations, many of which are countries with weak infrastructures, tremendous demands on resources, and some of the world's poorest people.
Listed next are, as of 2016, the top 10 countries with the greatest percentage of
people living without access to safe water:

1	Papua New Guinea	60%
2	Equatorial Guinea	52%
3	Angola	51%
4	Chad	49%
5	Mozambique	48%
6	Madagascar	48%
7	Dem. Rep.Congo	47%
8	Afghanistan	45%
9	Tanzania	44%
10	Ethiopia	43%

Here are the top 10 countries with the greatest numbers of people living without access to safe water:

1	India	75,777,997
2	China	63,166,533
3	Nigeria	57,757,141
4	Ethiopia	42,251,031
5	Dem. Rep. Congo	33,906,771
6	Indonesia	32,286,276
7	Tanzania	23,239,992
8	Bangladesh	21,088,119
9	Kenya	17,205,557
10	Pakistan	16,096,404

Considerations for internationally based social workers and the issue of water's place in any internationally based sustainable development work might include the following.

Sufficient

The water supply for each person must be sufficient and continuous for personal and domestic uses. These uses ordinarily include drinking, personal sanitation, washing of clothes, food preparation, and personal and household hygiene. According to the World Health Organization (WHO), between *50 and 100 litres* of water per person per day are needed to ensure that most basic needs are met and few health concerns arise.

Safe

The water required for each personal or domestic use must be safe and therefore free from microorganisms, chemical substances, and radiological hazards that constitute a threat to a person's health. Measures of drinking water safety are usually defined by national and/or local standards for drinking water quality. The *World Health Organization (WHO) Guidelines for Drinking-Water Quality* provide a basis for the development of national standards that, if properly implemented, will ensure the safety of drinking water.

Acceptable

Water should be of an acceptable color, odor, and taste for each personal or domestic use. All water facilities and services must be culturally appropriate and sensitive to gender, lifecycle, and privacy requirements.

Physically Accessible

Everyone has the right to a water and sanitation service that is physically accessible within or in the immediate vicinity of the household, educational institution, workplace, or health institution. According to WHO, the water source has to be within 1,000 meters of the home and collection time should not exceed 30 minutes.

Affordable

Water, and water facilities and services, must be affordable for all. The United Nations Development Program (UNDP) suggests that water costs should not exceed 3% of household income (Human Development Report, 2006).

And now the creation of the new international Sustainable Development Goals shows even greater promise for water enthusiasts with the inclusion of a specific goal, Goal 6, completely focused on water, within the total 17 goals. Goal 6 reads: Ensure access to water and sanitation for all (http://www.un.org/sustainabledevelopment/water-and-sanitation/#c52bbb43eb4dfe500)

Furthermore, Goal 6 has specific targets that align closely with the ideals and objectives of water scientists around the world:

1. By 2030, achieve access to adequate and equitable sanitation and hygiene for all and end open defecation, paying special attention to the needs of women and girls and those in vulnerable situations.
2. By 2030, improve water quality by reducing pollution, eliminating dumping, and minimizing release of hazardous chemicals and materials,

halving the proportion of untreated wastewater and substantially increasing recycling and safe reuse globally.

3. By 2030, substantially increase water-use efficiency across all sectors and ensure sustainable withdrawals and supply of freshwater to address water scarcity and substantially reduce the number of people suffering from water scarcity.

4. By 2030, implement integrated water resources management at all levels, including through transboundary cooperation as appropriate.

5. By 2020, protect and restore water-related ecosystems, including mountains, forests, wetlands, rivers, aquifers, and lakes.

6. By 2030, expand international cooperation and capacity-building support to developing countries in water- and sanitation-related activities and programs, including water harvesting, desalination, water efficiency, wastewater treatment, and recycling and reuse technologies.

Water scarcity, poor water quality, and inadequate sanitation negatively impact food security, livelihood choices, and educational opportunities for poor families across the world. Drought afflicts some of the world's poorest countries, worsening hunger and malnutrition (http://www.un.org/sustainabledevelopment/water-and-sanitation/#c52bbb43eb4dfe500).

On the positive side of things, there is no shortage of well-constructed, well-presented materials available to the social worker with a focus on the work of internationally based sustainable development, with water as a significant additional consideration. Scientific information is available in reports constructed by scientists, policy makers, and advocates from such diverse entities as the US Agency for International Development, WASH (Water, Sanitation, and Hygiene), and a host of agencies/programs linked with the United Nations, such as the World Bank Group, the World Food Program, UNESCO (United Nations Educational, Scientific, and Cultural Organization), and UNICEF (known originally as the United Nations International Children's Emergency Fund, but now known as the United Nation's Children Fund). But a marvelous resource for water scientists and water advocates is the World Health Organization's "WHO International Scheme to Evaluate Household Water Treatment Technologies." And the Scheme does exactly what its title presumes: It provides scientific, but approachable information on types and performance evaluations on a host of household water treatment (HWT) technologies measures assessed against WHO performance recommendations. It includes consideration of a range of technologies, including solar, chemical, filtration, and ultraviolet (WHO, 2016).

CONCLUSION

The easy conclusion for this chapter is merely to repeat the opening claim: Water is important to people. But for the social work reader, this chapter ends instead with a more difficult, but important point of professional consideration and encouragement. Yes, water, and the key elements of water science, are important. Yes, there has been much success experienced worldwide as a result of advances in water science. Included in a list of successes would be the observation that clean drinking water is now available to more than 90% of the world's population. Also water systems worldwide are disinfected of microorganisms via chlorination and systemic efforts to combat other contaminants, such as lead in pipes. And there can be no doubt of the obvious positive impact of water fluoridation on reduction of tooth decay, particularly in children, and tooth loss for adults. There is, however, much left to do. Water, clean water, and its availability for all are social justice and social equity issues. The social, economic, and health disparities that are associated with water availability or water of suspect quality should serve as a siren call to the profession of social work and to the individual social worker. And this is not just true of persons in resource-depleted environments. System anomalies that occur in resource-rich environments, like in Flint, Michigan, are deeply troubling for social workers. However, it is the intense challenges in water availability and water quality, particularly in water intended for drinking, cooking, sanitation, and hygiene experienced by the world's poorest persons, that are the most troubling. The final premise of this chapter is that social workers can be more effective in both environments, resource rich and resource depleted, where water is a problem if they have an enhanced awareness of the key elements of water science and a sustained vigilance for the inclusion of the key elements of water science in implementation of their advocacy and development efforts. The elements of the science of water can serve for social workers as a crucial point of reference when addressing the prodigious social, economic, and health disparities of the world. For the current century, it will be important for social workers to know about water issues—the safety and availability of water, waterborne illnesses, and transportation of and accessibility of social agencies, which may be disrupted because of water issues. Social workers should endeavor to apply their required involvement in social policy to the current and emerging water issues.

REFERENCES

Baker, M. N. (1981). *The quest for pure water: The history of water purification from the earliest records in the twentieth century.* vol. 1, 2nd ed. (M.J. Taras, editor), pp. 341–342. Denver: AWWA.

Ball, P. (1999). *Life's matrix: A biography of water.* New York, NY: Farrar, Straus, and Giroux.

Brody, J. E. (2016, May 10). Dehydration: Risks and myths. *New York Times*, D5.

Burgess, T., Wheeler, C., Brewer, T., Jones, D., Wicken, J., Gudo, H. S., ... Maunder, T. (2016). *Water: At what cost? The state of the world's water 2016 briefing.* Retrieved from https://www.womenforwater.org/uploads/7/7/5/1/77516286/water_at_ what_cost_wateraid_2016.pdf

Burt, B. A., & Tomar, S. L. (2007). Changing the face of America: Water fluoridation and oral health. In Ward, J.W., & Warren, C. (Eds.), *Silent victories: The history and practice of public health in twentieth-century America* (p. 307). New York, NY: Oxford University Press.

Carmody, S. (2016, December 14). A year later, unfiltered Flint tap water is still unsafe to drink. National Public Radio (NPR). Retrieved from https://www.npr.org/2016/12/14/505478931/a-year-later-unfiltered-flint-tap-water-is-still-unsafe-to-drink

Centers for Disease Control and Prevention (CDC). (2016, December 12). Saving lives, protecting people. What people need to know to protect their children. *CDC 24/7* Retrieved from https://www.cdc.gov/cdctv/emergencypreparednessandresponse/cdc-24-7.html.

Chaumba, J. (2013). The use and value of mixed methods research in social work. *Advances in Social Work, 14*(2), 307–333.

Coffey, J. (2015, December). What is water made of. *Guide to Space: Universe Today.* Retrieved from https://www.universetoday.com/74209/what-is-water-made-of/

The Committee on Hydrology of the Hydraulics Division. (1949). *Hydrology handbook.* New York: The American Society of Civil Engineers.

The Millenium Development Goals 2015 Report. (2015). UN Department of Public Information. Retrieved from http://www.un.org/millenniumgoals/2015_MDG_Report/pdf/MDG%202015%20PR%20FAQs.pdf

Finney, J. (2015). *Water: A very short introduction* (vol. 440). New York, NY: Oxford University Press.

Freeze, R. A., & Lehr, J. H. (2009). *The fluoride wars: How a modest public health measure became America's longest running political melodrama.* Hoboken, NJ: John Wiley & Sons.

Gordon, R. J. (2016). *The rise and fall of American growth: The US standard of living since the civil war.* Princeton, NJ: Princeton University Press.

Henry, D. (2016, December 22). Michigan governor not concerned about being charged over Flint. *The Hill.* Retrieved from https://thehill.com/policy/energy-environment/311533-michigan-gov-not-concerned-about-being-charged-for-flint.

Human Development Report. (2006). *Beyond scarcity: Power, poverty and the global water crisis* (Vol. 11). New York: Palgrave Macmillan. Retrieved from: http://www.undp.org/content/dam/undp/library/corporate/HDR/2006%20Global%20HDR/HDR-2006-Beyond%20scarcity-Power-poverty-and-the-global-water-crisis.pdf.

Johnson, S. (2006). *The ghost map: The story of London's most terrifying epidemic—and how it changed science, cities, and the modern world.* New York, NY: Penguin.

Kennedy, M. (2016). Michigan ends water subsidies to Flint despite Mayor's opposition. Retrieved from https://www.npr.org/sections/thetwo-way/2017/03/01/517932477/michigan-ends-water-subsidies-to-flint-despite-mayors-opposition

King, T. (1955). *Water, miracle of nature.* New York, NY: Macmillan.

McGuire, M. (2006). Eight revolutions in the history of US drinking water disinfection. *Journal (American Water Works Association), 98*(3), 123–149. Retrieved from http://www.jstor.org/stable/41314572

McGuire, M. J. (2013). *The chlorine revolution: Water disinfection and the fight to save lives* (Vol. 1942686209). Denver, CO: American Water Works Association.

Rueb, E. S. (2016, April 3). Keeping New York City's water clean. *The New York Times, 29.*

Sarafian, A. R., Nielsen, S. G., Marschall, H. R., McCubbin, F. M., & Monteleone, B. D. (2014). Early accretion of water in the inner solar system from a carbonaceous chondrite-like source. *Science, 346*(6209), 623–626.

Tomes, N. (1998). *The gospel of germs: Men, women, and the microbe in American life.* Cambridge, MA: Harvard University Press.

US Census Bureau. (2015). *Quick facts, Flint City, Michigan.* Retrieved from https://www.
census.gov/quickfacts/fact/table/flintcitymichigan/PST045217

US Department of Health and Human Services. (2000). *Oral health in America: A report
of the Surgeon General.* Washington, DC: Government Printing Office.

WaterAid. (2016). *UK annual report and financial statements. WaterAid American.*
New York, NY: Author.

Wertheimer, L. (2016, November 19). Water crisis continues in Flint after judge
orders water delivery. National Public Radio (NPR). Retrieved from https://
www.npr.org/2016/11/19/502717949/water-crisis-continues-in-flint-after-
judge-orders-water-delivery.

WHO. (2016). Water and sanitation. Retrieved from http://www.un.org/
sustainabledevelopment/water-and-sanitation/#c52bbb43eb4dfe500

8

Social Work and the Science

of Human Geography

The dynamics and variables important to the relationship of people with a land or a place is a long-standing concern in the physical and social sciences. Central to that concern is how each shapes the other. How do people shape the land or place around them? How does the land or a place shape the people who inhabit it, travel through it, live in harmony with it, or attempt to dominate it? To partially address the struggle with questions arising from this relationship, the applied social sciences field of social work settled on the person-in-environment approach, often referred to as the ecological model (Zastrow & Kirst-Ashman, 2006).

While the person-in-environment dynamic is, indeed, a valuable resource for social work, this chapter argues that human geography is a more broad-based field of science. It can help social work educators, students, and practitioners to achieve an enhanced understanding of the relationship between people and the land or a place and thus expand the scientific knowledge base of social work—all the while making it scientifically stronger. Like social workers, human geographers tend to explore social, economic, cultural, political, and demographic dimensions of human existence. But they strengthen the focus of their study and help specify the process of inquiry when they situate analysis in geographical space (conceptualized across and between scales from the individual to the city, nation, and globe). While diversity of fields and subfields of interest defines contemporary human geography, there are common questions of geographical scale, causality, agency and structure, interrelationships and networks, and place and movements. Human geographers are concerned with observed distributions and analytical explanation. They tend to focus on the spatial and, whether implicit or explicit, have a great deal to say about the activities of people and the moral and political dimensions of such (Gibson, 2009).

It is important to note, however, that the desire by social scientists to understand the complexity of the relationship between people and the land or a place has a long history—quite possibly one that cannot even be documented. A good beginning, however, is one of the most famous pieces ever written, the seminal work of Thomas Malthus, titled "An Essay on the Principle of Population." The essay was first published in 1789, republished, tweaked by the author a number of times in response to criticisms, and has served as a fulcrum of debate since its initial penning. In the first chapter of that essay, quite aptly named, "Question Stated," Malthus asserts the complexity of the relationship of the variables under study: the Earth and its people. Malthus situates his assertion directly upon the idea of what number of people can be sustained by the Earth. He asks how much population increase can the Earth sustain? Is the Earth to be overwhelmed with populace, particularly as our ability to feed people continues to increase? The Malthus essay also helped create and extend interplay between philosophy and the burgeoning social sciences, particularly sociology. He states famously:

> I say, that the power of population is indefinitely greater than the power in the earth to produce subsistence for man. Population, when unchecked, increases in a geometrical ratio. Subsistence increases only in an arithmetical ratio. A slight acquaintance with numbers will skew the immensity of the first power in comparison of the second. By that law of our nature which makes food necessary to the life of man, the effects of these two unequal powers must be kept equal. This implies a strong and constantly operating check on population from the difficulty of subsistence. This difficulty must fall somewhere; and must necessarily be severely felt by a large portion of mankind. (Malthus, 1789, pp. 4–5)

While Malthus asked a question of seemingly great importance—Can the Earth sustain an ever-increasing population?—he failed to provide enough substantive ideas about how to answer the question. Interestingly also, at least for us social workers, was the contention put forward by Malthus that it was the discomforts of poverty that drove persons within a particular geographic bounded location, in this case England, to be industrious. He put into question as early as the late 1700s whether the provision of assistance to the poor robs them of motivation and instead inculcates them with a sense of dependency that might last a lifetime. While that question is of keen interest, it is not the focus of this chapter. Instead, the representation of science in human geography is—with a particular focus on its definition, its place in the broader area of physical science, its theory base, its tools of instrumentation and measurement, and its explosion of areas of study. The first sections of this chapter are presented with consideration of the following conceptual areas: sources and history of knowledge about human geography, how scientific knowledge informs human geography, great discoveries, research and how it affects the knowledge base of human geography, measurement and instrumentation, and points of contention and unsettled issues. The final section of the chapter chooses a particular focus of human geography—an aim to understand the movement of people from one physical location to another physical location (migration)—and exemplifies how including the tenets of human geography may serve to strengthen social work's scientific base. In this case, it will provide an enhanced theoretical and scientific understanding of immigrants, refugees, and internally and regionally displaced persons.

Traditionally, geography is considered the study of the Earth's environments and peoples, and the interactions between them. *Geography* is a term with ancient Greek origins, literally translating as "to write or describe the world." In classical and Enlightenment geography, humans and the "natural" world were usually described in juxtaposition, often in a regional fashion, as Europeans stormed about the world and encountered unfamiliar places all the while exploring and building their colonial empires. Since the late 19th century, this conjoint understanding of geography—as describing the natural and human world, region by region—has gradually been augmented by more precise subdisciplinary pursuits and identities. The most basic of these disciplinary debates describes geography as consisting of two fundamental halves: physical and human geography. Physical geography generally means the science of the Earth's surface, while human geography usually refers to the study of its peoples, and geographical interpretations of economies, cultural identities, political territories, and societies. In contrast, physical geographers classify and analyze landforms and ecosystems; explain hydrological, geomorphological, and coastal processes; and examine problems such as erosion, pollution, and climatic variability (Gibson, 2009). Social workers could benefit by adopting concepts and technology used by human geographers.

Just as the field of social work education and practice struggle with deciding what is the right emphasis for the elements of macro and micro focus, geographers spend a good bit of time trying to decide if human geography has enough strength to stand alone as a separate discipline. Human geography can sometimes be seen as on par with physical geography and sometimes as a part of or a major subdiscipline within the wider field of geography (Gibson, 2009). But unlike social workers, the vast majority of whom are out there in the world of applied practice, the vast majority of human geographers are found on the faculties of Departments of Geography in university and college settings.

Nonetheless, human geographers analyze population trends, theorize social and cultural change, interpret geopolitical conflict, and seek to explain the geography of human economic activities around the world. How exactly the division of labor between physical and human geographers came to be is a pivotal story in contemporary geography. It is a story about 20th-century scientific fragmentation and about different theories on the status of humans vis-à-vis nonhuman nature. It is also a slippery and difficult story about how academic knowledges are produced, mutate, and move about (and how this happens in particular places), and how knowledges find popularity, fade away, or are challenged in time and across space. The central division of labor in geography—produced by these means over more than a hundred years—has established and defined the space within which most human geographical practice now occurs. Thomas Kuhn, the author of *The Structure of Scientific Revolutions*, and his coining of the term "paradigm" come to mind as one struggles to understand how human geography has become, in the modern era, a distinct phenomenon (Kuhn, 2012). Rather than viewing human geography as a completely new paradigm with a whole new set of beliefs about the world and distinct from physical geography, the reader is advised to view the sides, issues, and faces of physical and human geography as complementary areas of research, analysis, and teaching (Gibson, 2009).

However, there have been significant shifts in knowledge in regard to human geography that have prompted the inclusion of more than a singular organizing theory and instead an array of competing theories. Additionally, methods of data collection and analysis were altered—the qualitative paradigm emerging, competing with, and then coming to coexist in a more peaceful fashion with the quantitative paradigm (Manzo & Devine-Wright, 2013). Factors that complicated an understanding of human geography include the late professionalization of the discipline; variations in human geography written in different languages; and the difficulty of being able to identify definitive research questions, sequential paradigms, or key thinkers (Gibson, 2009, p. 18). In other words, human geography is an area of social science, like social work, that prompts a good number of self-directed, self-examining questions.

Human geographers distinguish groups of people according to important cultural characteristics that describe where particular cultural groups are distributed, and they offer reasons to explain the observed distribution. Human geographers study why the customary ideas, beliefs, and values of a people produce a distinctive culture in a particular place. Human geographers refer to culture as a collective of beliefs, material traits, and social forms that together constitute the distinct tradition of a people. Especially important cultural values derive from a group's language, religion, and ethnicity (Rubenstein, 2014). Of course, there have been highly influential theorists and practitioners in every era, but human geography has been a remarkably open field, particularly since the 1960s, when especially diverse ideas and political practices found traction (Gibson, 2009).

The openness of the field of human geography and the diversity of attempted scientific coverage are easily exemplified. Just take a look at the table of contents of any introductory human geography textbook, for instance, Rubenstein's, currently in its 11th edition, published in 2014 by Pearson Education, and prepare to witness the diversity of topical coverage in human geography. Rubenstein's table of contents for this well-known introductory text includes an initial chapter on Basic Concepts and then 12 chapters linking human geography with the study of Population and Health, Migration, Folk and Popular Culture, Languages, Religions, Ethnicities, Political Geography, Development, Food and Agriculture, Industry and Manufacturing, Services and Settlements, and finally Urban Patterns. The major scholarly journals in the field of human geography also reflect the diversity of coverage in the field, as displayed in Table 8.1.

The major mistake to be avoided for those unfamiliar with human geography as an area of social science is to think of human geography as merely the study of how people are spatially arranged around the world. The field of human geography is much more robust. Human geography is better interpreted as the study of the geography of humans: when, where, and how humans evolved, developed strategies for survival, and dispersed to literally all parts of the world (Gibson, 2009). And human geography, while often possessed of a historical focus, is also adept in the area of speculation—responding to the desire of people to find meaning in what is happening in their current lives and in the world around them more and more characterized as a global process. Thinking, researching, and coming to know more about life as lived in a place, pursuing it in real time, and speculative pondering as people live their lives all fall under the purview of human geography. Eric Weiner's (2016) book, *The Geography of Genius: A Search for the World's Most Creative Places From Ancient Athens to Silicon Valley*, is a fascinating read and proffers the conclusion that "great minds don't necessarily think alike, but they do gravitate to one another,

Table 8.1 Major Scholarly Journals in Human Geography

Journal Title	Description	Publisher	Impact Factor
Asian and Pacific Migration Journal	Publishes research and analysis on the sociodemographic, economic, political, psychological, historical, legislative, and religious aspects of human migration and refugee movements from and within Asia.	Sage	.409
Economic Geography	This is an internationally peer-reviewed journal with a specialization in theoretically based empirical articles that deepen the understanding of significant economic geography issues around the world.	Wiley	2.735
International Migration Review	This is a new peer-reviewed, public policy publication of the Center for Migration Studies devoted to US and international policy debates on migration.	Wiley	1.033
Journal of Historical Geography	Themes include geographies of places and environments in the past; the dynamics of place, space, and landscape; historiography and philosophy of historical geography; methodological challenges and problems in historical geography; and landscape, memory, and environment.	Elsevier	1.028
Political Geography	The focus of this journal is on research on the spatial dimensions of politics. Themes include critical, feminist, and popular geopolitics; electoral geography and policy analysis; identity, landscapes, and representation; peace and conflict studies, states, and territoriality; political ecology and politics of the environment; political economy; and quantitative methodologies/spatial analyses based on GIS.	Elsevier	2.676
Population and Development Review	Includes population studies, the relationships between population and social, economic, and environmental change, and related thinking on public policy.	Wiley	1.667
Population, Space and Place	Seeks to inform population researchers of the best theoretical and empirical research on topics related to population, space, and place.	Wiley	1.781

(continued)

Table 8.1 CONTINUED

Journal Title	Description	Publisher	Impact Factor
Social & Cultural Geography	Its articles are especially focused on space, place, and nature in relation to social and/or cultural issues, including inequalities, poverty, housing, crime, work, and leisure; as well as everyday life, consumption, identity, community, and neighborhood.	Taylor & Francis	1.315
Urban Geography	Focuses on problem-oriented current research by geographers and other social scientists on urban policy; race, poverty, and ethnicity in the city; international differences in urban form and function; historical preservation; the urban housing market; and provision of services and urban economic activity.	Taylor & Francis	1.355

drawn by some powerful, unnamed force" (p. 97). A strong proponent of appreciating place diversity, he studies the geography of genius in locations as dispersed as Athens, Greece; Hangzhou, China; Florence, Italy; Edinburgh, Scotland; Calcutta, India; Vienna, Austria; and Silicon Valley, California.

Social work educators and social work students can relate quite closely to a central idea in human geography: place attachment. Social workers value greatly the attachment of persons to their homes, the places of their birth, the place where they have made a home, and the legacy of people feeling as if a place is a part of them. Meaning often comes from the interpretation of place attachment (Manzo & Devine-Wright, 2013). Place attachment was central to a landmark book for human geographers, *Place Attachment*, by Altman and Low in the early 1990s as part of a series on human behavior and environment. All social work students can recall with differing degrees of awareness and satisfaction their own coursework in Human Behavior and the Social Environment (HBSE). In fact, HBSE coursework, distinguishing the relationship of people, their behavior, and the social environment around them, is required in all social work programs accredited by the Council on Social Work Education (Zastrow & Kirst-Ashman, 2006). What human geography can add, however, is an important emphasis and specificity on the relationship of human behavior to the physical environment. And how each influences the other—the person influencing the place and the place influencing the person.

Altman and Low moved forward a discourse on place attachment as that conceptual variable was fully emerging in human geography. Those human geographers offered a working definition on place attachment as the "bonding of people to places" (1992, p. 2). Place identity, sense of place, and place dependence moved since that time from the conceptual phase to an application/action phase. Topics as diverse as pro-environmental engagement, social housing, and community design emerged as the scientific purview of human geography became a bit more politicized. Theory, methods, and applications were explicated. Place attachment, though, remained a variable with a good deal of inference and/or uncertainty. Place attachment has been notably applied by human geographers to the study of natural resource management, alternative energy sources, pro-environmental behavior, responses to disasters and flood preparedness, social housing policy and displacement, and socially responsive community design. Consideration of place attachment has facilitated an understanding of global climate change, urban restructuring programs, and increased mobility in a context of globalization (Manzo & Devine-Wright, 2013). Again, human geographers, like social work educators and students in the study and teaching of Human Behavior and the Social Environment, also embrace a concern for oppression. Human geographers often include social ontology, questions about the nature of existence and how people relate to one another, as a form of social and philosophical geography that brings together ideology with place. As such, they attempt to understand social, economic, and political power that invariably results in forms of oppression and, in many instances, exploitation (Allman, 2013).

MEASUREMENT AND INSTRUMENTATION

A focus on precise positional measurement and the availability of instrumentation enhances the scientific nature of human geography. In addition, specificity of positional measurement and relatively complex instrumentation are major contributors to the ability of human geographers to produce scholarly scientific work. Social workers could easily use these measurement and instrumentation tools to enhance the scholarly nature of their work—particularly that work that includes any focus on positionality, space, and finality of measurement. Social work researchers and practitioners doing community-based work, where knowledge of the availability, or the lack thereof, of community-based resources and an understanding of the distance from user to resource, could truly benefit from these tools of human geography (Zastrow & Kirst-Ashman, 2006).

The ability to understand the more sophisticated positional measurement and instrumentations that contribute to the science of human geography, such as mapping, the Global Positioning System (GPS), the Geographic Information System (GIS), and remote sensing techniques require first the understanding of a few scientific basics, such as understanding the workings of the compass and the system measurement designation of latitude and longitude.

A complex thought for most folks not well versed in physics, and often one of a challenging nature, is that the Earth has a magnetic field. And that through the years scientists, particularly physical scientists, have come to understand that the Earth's magnetic field is not a static entity but a dynamic one. Change in the Earth's magnetic field is a constant. An additionally misguided notion is that the magnetic field of the Earth sits directly atop the geographic North Pole (see Fig. 8.1).

In fact, it is the magnetic compass reportedly invented a couple of thousand years ago by the Chinese that allows data collectors, physicists, and those lost in

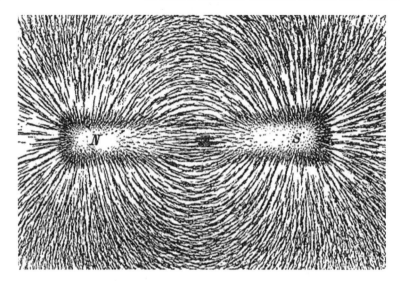

Figure 8.1 The magnetic field
SOURCE: By Newton Henry Black - Newton Henry Black, Harvey N. Davis (1913) Practical Physics, The MacMillan Co., USA, p. 242, fig. 200, Public Domain, https://commons.wikimedia.org/w/index.php?curid=73846

the woods to assess the angle between true magnetic north and the North Pole. Referred to at various times as magnetic variation, compass variation, magnetic declination, or simply "the variation," it allows for use of the compass to point to a specific direction and assist the individual wanderer to determine the affiliated location of any particular site. It is also important to note that the Earth's magnetic field is additionally affected by variation in the composition and movement of the Earth's outer core (Egbert & King, 2003). The ability to read a compass has for centuries assisted explorers, travelers, and navigators as they try to find their way in the world (see Fig. 8.2).

Figure 8.2 The face of a compass
SOURCE: By User:Bios~commonswiki - Own work, CC BY-SA 3.0, https://commons.wikimedia.org/w/index. php?curid=342457

Mapping is also an important tool used by human geographers. Mapping at its most basic helps us all, including students and teachers in the social sciences, to enhance our scientific understanding of the ultimate place attachment that we have: our place attachment to Earth. Mapping can capture all the sizes, shapes, and changes in the structure of the Earth over time. The Earth is an oblate sphere (flattened a bit at the poles) with a circumference of 24,901.55 miles compared to a circumference of 24,859.82 miles for a vertical ring passing through both the North and the South Poles. The Earth is 0.168% greater in circumference at the Equator than around the poles, thus giving the Earth a bit of a squished feature, like stepping slightly on the top of a motionless basketball. The bulge at the Equator is the result of gravitational pull from the moon and sun (Egbert & King, 2003).

Now let's take a stab at understanding the entire Earth as a function of parallels of latitude and meridians of longitude (Egbert & King, 2003). Latitude is the angular distance from the Equator to any point on the surface of the Earth as measured north or south of the Equator. The Equator is latitude 0 degrees. The North Pole is latitude 90 degree N, North. The South Pole is latitude 90 degrees S, South. One degree of latitude is approximately equal to 69 miles. The value of the numeric as stated in degrees increases slightly as we move toward the poles due to the "squished" shape (mentioned earlier) of the Earth near the poles.

Longitude is an angular distance on the surface of the Earth, measured along any latitude line east or west of the prime meridian. A meridian of longitude is a vertical line passing from pole to pole. By international agreement, the meridian that passes through the original site of the Royal Greenwich Observatory at Greenwich, England, is designated the prime meridian. Points east or west of the prime meridian have longitudes ranging from 0 degrees to 180 degrees east or 0 degrees to 180 degrees west. Parallels of latitude and meridians of longitude together form a grid that covers the entire Earth (see Fig. 8.3). This then allows for specification of the latitude and longitude coordinates of any spatial position on the Earth's surface (Egbert & King, 2003, p. 40). And as Stephen Hawking, the great astrophysicist,

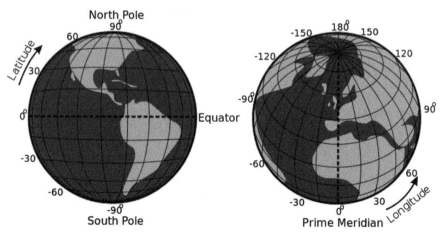

Figure 8.3 Parallels and meridians (latitude and longitude)
SOURCE: By Djexplo - Own work, CC0, https://commons.wikimedia.org/w/index.php?curid=15351129

helped us understand, one key to the achievement of a better understanding of life is to be able to comprehend how "space and time" are central to all (1998). The compass and the grid system of latitudes and longitudes are just two rudimentary pieces of conceptual measurement that help human geographers, and potentially social workers, to understand how space and time relate to how people live on Earth.

And now we are ready to take a step up in scientific understanding to two more complex, sophisticated methods of positionality measurement, the Global Positioning System (GPS) and the Geographic Information System (GIS), both capable of enhancing the specificity of measurement, particularly of location, in the work of social workers. While the GPS system is probably more helpful in social work situations where the focus in on the individual, such as an older person living alone who might have an attached alert that will facilitate responders locating her in a time of emergency, the GIS system is much more valuable in creating community-based understandings of the relationship of entities and resources within a bounded context, such as a neighborhood or designated community.

GLOBAL POSITIONING SYSTEM AND GEOGRAPHIC INFORMATION SYSTEM

Scientists working for the US Department of Defense conceived the idea of GPS in the 1970s. The initial purpose of the GPS system was to allow ballistic missile submarines to accurately determine their position before launching the on-board missiles. The GPS system is anchored by a constellation of 24 satellites located in precise orbits (Rubenstein, 2014). The GPS satellites began in the 1970s and continue to this day to orbit the Earth every 12 hours. Scientists calculate the estimated life of the satellites and there are ongoing plans for continual replacement. Ground stations monitor the satellites for the adherence to orbit, plus error, and positioning. GPS satellites contain a high-frequency transmitter and relay information via signals back to Earth. A GPS receiver on Earth locks on to the signals and by a process of "triangulation" of signals from a small number of satellites can accurately determine its own location anywhere on Earth. This allows GPS to be used, for example, to achieve precise navigation. While social workers may often feel the need for assistance in navigating troubled waters, either for themselves or for those they are working with, the GPS system can most notably help scientists, even applied social scientists like social workers, to assess movement and location. In understanding the science of the GPS system, it is important to understand how time is used to determine the distances between an unknown location and the GPS satellites. A GPS receiver measures the time it takes for the radio signal transmitted from each triangulated satellite to reach the location of the GPS receiver. Since radio waves travel at the speed of light, 186,000 miles per second, measuring the time it takes for the signal from each satellite to travel to the receiver helps pinpoint the location of the receiver. Even though there can be measurement error, the distance from the receiver to the satellite can be calculated by multiplying the travel time by the speed of the radio waves. It is important, however, that all measurement can, and probably does, include some error. For example, variance in predetermined orbits and even

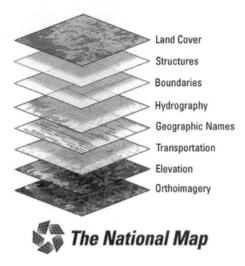

Figure 8.4 Geographic information system (GIS) layered map
SOURCE: By United States Geological Survey - USGS Center of Excellence for Geospatial Information Science (CEGIS) Image: http://cegis.usgs.gov/images/national_map_layers.jpg, Public Domain, https://commons.wikimedia.org/w/index.php?curid=19219765

obstructions like tall buildings can be a problem in accuracy of GPS determinations (Egbert & King, 2003).

The GIS allows for the layering of spatially referenced data and the creation of layered maps. The GIS system owes its strength and viability to a computer system that captures, stores, queries, analyzes, and displays geographic data. The position of any object on Earth can be measured and recorded with mathematical precision and then stored on a computer. The applicability of the GIS system is immense and its uses are quite varied. GIS maps of single layers or multiple layers can be used to depict almost anything and the spatial relationship between almost anything—available housing, grocery stores, police substations, or schools (see Fig. 8.4). For example, a social work community advocate could use a GIS layered map to show where health disparities exist—where cancer rates are relatively high and medical care facilities quite sparse—and then combine that data with another layer showing the location of people with various incomes and ethnicities. The mixing of data within a GIS map, sometimes referred to as mashups, highlights the practice of overlaying data from one source on another for the purpose of enhancing understanding of the physical, social, and demographic variables found in combination in a particular geographic space. For example, a mashup GIS map could display all the day care centers within a 5-mile radius of a neighborhood of families with low socioeconomic status (Rubenstein, 2014) and then overlay all the bus routes of the city to help community members understand transportation possibilities or advocate for more.

HUMAN GEOGRAPHY AND MIGRATION

This final section chooses a particular focus of human geography—human migration, the movement of people from one physical location to another. Two goals are primary in this section: (1) understanding more fully how human geographers theorize, research, and understand migration as a world, regional, and local phenomenon; and (2) exemplifying how social work educators, researchers, and practitioners might benefit from a greater understanding of migration via the tenets of human geography and consequently strengthen the scientific knowledge base of social work. While social workers do a lot of applied work with immigrants, refugees, and internally and regionally displaced persons (Zayas, 2016), that work may be made more effective with greater inclusion of the scientific tenets of human geography.

While migrating is not wholly a modern day occurrence, the overall number of persons migrating at present in the world is quite remarkable. Place attachment, as defined by membership, or lack thereof, in one of the world's nation-states, remains of paramount importance for all persons of the world. J. Bhaba (2009), a migration scholar emphasizes "the mere fortuity" of place of birth as an accidental occurrence but yet citizenship is in the present day the legal correlate for territorial belonging (Zayas, 2016, p. 169). In this era of the more often stated possibilities for "global citizenship" (Abrahamian, 2015), it is impossible to overstate the importance of place attachment, either possessed, in transition, or lost for all people of the world.

Human geographers define the concept of diffusion as a process by which a characteristic spreads from one (physical) space to another, and relocation diffusions as the spread of a characteristic through the bodily movement of people from one place to another. Migration is a specific type of relocation diffusion most often expressed with the inclusion of a sense of permanence to the movement. Over the last 100 years, the scale and speed of movement have increased dramatically. Human geographers document where people migrate to and from across the space of the Earth; migration is a form of mobility. *Emigration* is a migration from a location, whereas *immigration* is a migration to a location (Rubenstein, 2014, pp. 82 and 83).

Human geographers benefit from a strong historical and theoretical foundation for their considerations of migration, and much of that is owed to the work of one geographer, E. G. Ravenstein. It has been 100 years since Ravenstein's first paper on the laws of migration was published in 1876 in the *Geographical Magazine*. His later but better known articles appeared in the *Statistical Journal* in 1885 and 1889. His work laid the foundation for decades of subsequent research on migration, and claims have been made that while thousands of migration studies have been conducted, few additional generalizations have been added (Grigg, 1977).

Again, it is not that social workers were without theoretical notions about their work with immigrant and refugee groups. But in contrast to human geographers who theorized about location transfer and place attachment of immigrants, early social workers rather theorized more on applied problem solution–both at the individual and community level. A good example is the work of the American pragmatist and early social worker Jane Addams. Her work had a powerful activist feature to it. As a representative of the First Chicago School, she was all about solving problems that immigrants faced within and outside their neighborhoods. She wrote and spoke extensively in an attempt to counter eugenics and social Darwinism as a means to explain racial inferiority and the social problems linked to immigration (Lewis-Kraus, 2016).

Ravenstein himself was an international migrant. He was German by birth, but he lived most of his life in England. He worked as a cartographer for that country's War Office from 1854 to 1872. After his retirement he was an active member of the Statistical Society, the Royal Geographical Society, the International Geographical Union, and the British Association for the Advancement of Science. He wrote on many topics, but his best work was on the history of exploration and on population (Grigg, 1977).

The "laws" of migration—Ravenstein also referred to them as "principles" and "rules"—help us understand the why and how of migrant movement (see Fig. 8.5). The laws in Ravenstein's revised form included the following:

1. The majority of migrants go only a short distance.
2. Migration proceeds step by step. [Ravenstein wrote in 1885 "... the inhabitants of the country immediately surrounding a town of rapid growth flock into it; the gaps thus left in the rural population are filled up by migrants from more remote districts, until the attractive force of one of our rapidly growing cities makes its influence felt, step by step, to the most remote corner of the Kingdom." An almost identical statement had appeared in 1876, with the significant omission of the phrase "step by step."]
3. Migrants going long distances generally go by preference to one of the great centers of commerce or industry.
4. Each current of migration produces a compensating countercurrent.
5. The natives of towns are less migratory than those of rural areas.
6. Females are more migratory than males within the Kingdom of their birth, but males more frequently venture beyond.
7. Most migrants are adults: Families rarely migrate out of their county of birth.
8. Large towns grow more by migration than by natural increase.
9. Migration increases in volume as industries and commerce develops and transport improves.
10. The major direction of migration is from the agricultural areas to the centers of industry and commerce.
11. The major causes of migration are economic.

Ravenstein's laws were based on the place of birth tables published in the British Censuses of 1871 and 1881, together with, in the 1889 paper, similar data from Censuses of North America and Europe (Grigg, 1977). Ravenstein's migration "laws" written in the late 19th century have formed a strong theoretical basis for contemporary geographic migration studies for human geographers, but this could also be used for social workers if used more fully. In an attempt to achieve further utility, Ravenstein's migration laws can be organized into three groups: (1) the distance that migrants typically travel, (2) the reasons migrants move, and (3) the characteristics of migrants (Rubenstein, 2014). By looking at distance of movement, human geographers can denote everything from internal migration within a nation-state, regional migration, interregional migration, all the way to long-distance international

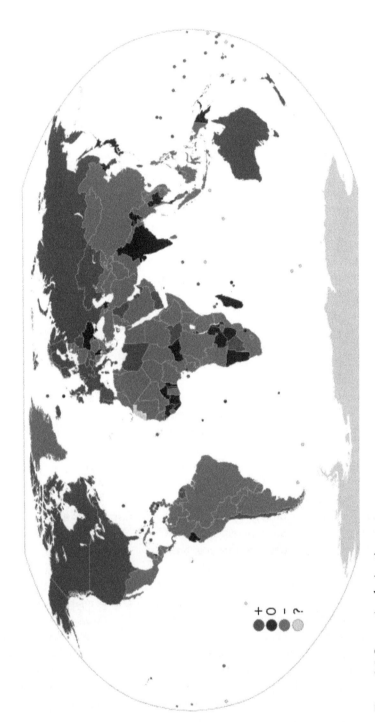

Figure 8.5 International migration routes

migration—all the while focused on positionality, location transfer, and place attachment (Manzo & Devine-Wright, 2013). And the tools of human geography, in this case mapping, can easily help with understanding (Rubenstein, 2014).

And the impact of a present-day migrant crisis owing primarily to the Civil War in Syria and the generalized violence and chaos in parts of central and northern Africa (whereby thousands of persons are flowing into Europe; Bixler, 2005; Rawlence, 2016) can also be understood better by viewing a map (see Fig. 8.6).

Recognizing the multitudes of people in the world who migrate only a short distance helps us understand better how the world has become immensely urbanized. For example, in the United States people living in urban areas increased from 5% in 1800 to 50% in 1920 to 80% in 2010. The reasons migrants move are understood as quite varied but generally are categorized as political push-and-pull factors, environmental push-and-pull factors, and economic push-and-pull factors. And the demographic characteristics of migrants, often times referred to as population demographics and consisting of such variables as gender, family structure, educational attainment, formal labor market participation, life expectancy, birth rate, and death rate, are invaluable tools for understanding the impetus for the movement of people about the world (Rubenstein, 2014). While social worker researchers and practitioners have been aware of these theoretical notions inherent in the study of demographics, they have not embraced them as strongly as have human geographers. For example, human geographers have been much more adept than social workers at understanding how demographic and environmental factors have combined to play a strong part in pushing persons from one location to another location even at times overcoming people's strong attachment to place (Manzo & Devine-Wright, 2013).

If the reader recalls, this chapter began with a brief description of the massive impact of the essay on principles of population by Malthus and the question of the relationship between the Earth and its population. That question has been on our minds ever since. Responders to the question, a number of whom have been prominent human geographers, are either pessimistic in answering the question, like Malthus, or optimistic decrying the fears of the doomsayers. What is important here is that social workers could benefit by emulating human geographers and their more sophisticated use of population numbers and demographics. It is important to understand, if social workers want to play a part in such important issues as what population can the Earth sustain and how will population growth impact global warming and climate change, that knowledge of demographics needs to be used in a more informed manner. For example, social work students, at any level, often do not know the world's present population. Nor can they say much about the pace at which the world's population reached nearly 7.5 billion people. The distribution, fertility, mortality, and migration of people will dramatically change the world's population structure over the next few decades. Demography will help to shape the future in many ways: socially, economically, and, not the least, in our use of the Earth's resources and in magnifying the need to address a range of environmental impacts, in particular, global warming. The 20th century saw unprecedented rates of world population growth. For almost all of world history, population growth was generally slow, albeit with some periods of more rapid growth associated with technological

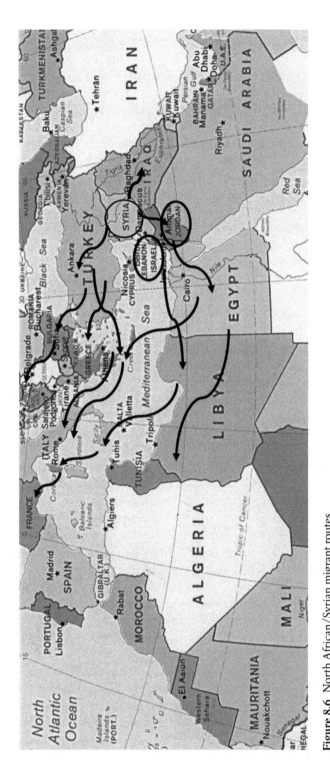

Figure 8.6 North African/Syrian migrant routes

SOURCE: Authors' creation.

and social breakthroughs. A world population of 1 billion people was reached early in the 19th century, 2 billion was not reached until the 1920s, and 3 billion was reached around 1960. After World War II, population growth rates increased and by the mid-1960s had reached 2.1% a year, the fastest rate ever recorded. This rate of growth represents a doubling time of 35 years—and indeed, world population reached 6 billion in 1999. By this date, rates of increase had slowed, but now the population total was so large that even small rates of increase yielded huge increases in absolute numbers. In 2011, 7 billion was reached, and by 2013 the population total was estimated at 7.2 billion (Hall, 2015).

Human geographers use the study of demography and attempt to detect the impact of a political or social intervention by studying changes in population characteristics, particularly noting trends in those characteristics over time (Rubenstein, 2014). No better example exists than the US's own Immigration and Nationality Act of 1965. Sometimes referred to as the Brothers and Sisters Act, the Immigration and Nationality Act radically shifted US immigration policy away from selecting immigrants by national origin. Until 1965, the national-origins quotas created a preference for immigration from countries in Northwestern Europe, partially restricted immigration from Southern and Eastern Europe, and fully restricted immigration from Asia, Africa, and the colonized Caribbean. For example, the 1929 immigration quotas gave 51,227 of the overall 150,000 annual slots to Germans, 100 to Greeks, and 0 to Chinese. The 1965 law eliminated the national-origins quotas and instead relied on a preference system focused on immigrants' family relationships with US citizens or legal permanent residents, or their employment/labor skills. It established an annual cap of 170,000 visas for immigrants from the Eastern Hemisphere, with no country in the hemisphere allowed more than 20,000 visas. The act also for the first time established a cap for immigrants from independent countries of the Western Hemisphere, with an annual limit of 120,000 visas. Spouses, minor children, and parents of adult US citizens were exempted from the new caps (Fitzgerald & Cook-Martin, 2015; Koed, n.d.). The demographics of the United States were quickly altered. For example, the European and Canadian share of legal immigrants fell from 60% in the 1950s to 22% in the 1970s. By contrast, the Asian share of legal immigration rose from 6% in the 1950s to 35% by the 1980s and 40% in 2013. The demographic diversity of the US population today in many ways is the direct result of the 1965 legislation (Fitzgerald & Cook-Martin, 2015).

CONCLUSION

The major tenets of the science of human geography can make the social work knowledge base scientifically stronger. Hopefully, social work readers, be they academics, students, or practitioners, are now a bit more willing to consider the viability of such a notion. Using human migration as a focus, this chapter demonstrated how the concepts and tools of human geography can be applied to a greater understanding of why and how people move about the world—all the while influencing the place around them and being influenced by that place. The argument is not made in the chapter that social work educators, students, and practitioners should abandon their appreciation for and use of the person-in-environment model (Zastrow & Kirst-Ashman, 2006), but rather the argument is made that by adding scientific elements of human geography the field of social work might then be made scientifically stronger. It is hoped that greater specificity in measurement and the use of instrumentation, from the simple presentation of a compass to the more complex workings displayed in a GIS layered map (Rubenstein, 2014), might now seem more plausible as a way to enrich research and practice conducted by social workers.

REFERENCES

Abrahamian, A. A. (2015). *The cosmopolites: The coming of the global citizen.* New York, NY: Columbia Global Reports.

Allman, D. (2013). The sociology of social inclusion. *Sage Open, 3*(1). Retrieved from https://doi.org/10.1177/2158244012471957

Bhabha, J. (2009). The "mere fortuity" of birth? Children, mothers, borders and the meaning of citizenship. In S. Behhabib & J. Resnicik (Eds.), *Migration and mobilities: Citizenship, borders, and gender* (pp. 187–227). New York, NY: New York University Press.

Bixler, M. (2005). *The Lost Boys of Sudan: An American story of the refugee experience.* Athens, GA: University of Georgia Press.

Egbert, R. L., & King, J. E. (2003). *The GPS handbook: A guide for the outdoors.* Short Hills, NJ: Burford Books.

Fitzgerald, D. S., & Cook-Martin, D. (2015). The geopolitical origins of the US Immigration Act of 1965. *Migration Policy Institute, 5.* Retrieved from https://www.migrationpolicy.org/article/geopolitical-origins-us-immigration-act-1965.

Gibson, C. (2009). *Human geography.* University of Wollongong, Wollongong, NSW, Australia: Elsevier.

Grigg, D. B. (1977). EG Ravenstein and the "laws of migration." *Journal of Historical Geography, 3*(1), 41–54.

Hall, R. (2015). Population and the future. *Geography (Sheffield, England), 100*(1), 28–36.

Hawking, S. W. (1998). *A brief history of time.* New York, NY: Bantam Dell.

Koed, B. (n.d.). *The politics of reform: The Immigration Act of 1965.* PhD diss., University of Michigan.

Kuhn, T. S. (2012). *The structure of scientific revolutions.* Chicago, IL: University of Chicago Press.

Lewis-Kraus, G. (2016). The trials of Alice Goffman. *The New York Times Magazine, 12.* Retrieved from https://www.nytimes.com/2016/01/17/magazine/the-trials-of-alice-goffman.html

Malthus, T. R. (1798). *An essay on the principle of population, as it affects the future improvement of society* (Vol. 2). Retrieved from https://quod.lib.umich.edu/e/ecco/004860797.0001.000?rgn=main;view=fulltext

Manzo, L. C., & Devine-Wright, P. (2013). *Place attachment: Advances in theory, methods and applications.* New York, NY: Routledge.

Rawlence, B. (2016). *City of thorns: Nine lives in the world's largest refugee camp.* New York, NY: Picador.

Rubenstein, J. M. (2014). *The cultural landscape: An introduction to human geography* (11th ed.). London, UK: Pearson.

Weiner, E. (2016). *The geography of genius: A search for the world's most creative places from ancient Athens to Silicon Valley.* New York, NY: Simon and Schuster.

Zastrow, C., & Kirst-Ashman, K. (2006). *Understanding human behavior and the social environment.* Chicago, IL: Cengage Learning.

Zayas, L. (2016). *Forgotten citizens: Deportation of children and the making of American exiles and Orphans.* New York, NY: Oxford University Press.

9

Social Work and the Science of the Life Cycle

Nature and human life are as various as our several constitutions.
—HENRY DAVID THOREAU

T he human life cycle is a complex web of constant developmental and physical changes mediated through the various biological systems, the consumption and use of energy, and interactions with the environment. A complete
declination of the stages of the human life cycle will include, at a minimum, the
following: pregnancy, infancy, toddlerhood, childhood, puberty, older adolescence, adulthood, middle age, old age, and end of life. Each of these stages presents
unique opportunities for a social worker or helping professional to play a vital role
in encouraging positive change, growth, and successful completion of significant
developmental milestones.

This chapter first includes a discussion of issues in the academic area of human
development by briefly describing some of the major theories and providing an
overview of trends in human development research methodologies. The chapter
then focuses on the scientific underpinnings of the five selected stages of pregnancy, childhood, adolescence, adulthood, and old age, and following from texts
on human development (Erikson & Erikson, 1998; Kail & Cavanaugh, 2016) progresses in an overview, from pregnancy through end of life, with brief discussions
of scientific topics of interest and relevance to social work practice. It is important,
however, to note that it would be an arduous task and would result in an extremely
lengthy book if an effort was made to analyze science and each life cycle stage as
mentioned earlier. If the social work reader is interested in pursuing such an endeavor, the author highly recommends Kail and Cavanaugh's (2015) *Essentials of
Human Development.*

It is important for students and practitioners who are interested in pursuing
specialized social work practice with a specific developmental population to note
that information provided in this chapter is, for reasons of concision, broad and
general in nature. The chapter does not focus on the inclusion of any sort of listing
of all the possible observable developmental milestones, but rather points out
scientific underpinnings that may inform the social work practitioner's thought

process, curiosity, and ideas of discovery in regards to the life cycle. A concerted effort has been made to provide the reader with resources and references within the chapter to further her reading and provide more specific insights into social work across the life span. It is important to remember that the science of the life cycle is incomplete. More is scientifically unknown than known about how persons mediate the complexities of living, particularly as they move through the different stages of life.

DEFINING THE LIFE CYCLE

The terms *life cycle, life span,* and *life course* are used, sometimes with great distinctive difference but at other times with casual interchangeability. The concept of a life cycle is used here as it has been used generally in other scientific disciplines: as a means to describe a series of distinct, bounded life stages that are socially or biologically determined. With a bit of shaded difference the concept of the life span used in psychology assumes that development and aging form a continuous process from birth to death. The distinction between *life span* and *life course,* the latter term used more commonly in sociology, is mainly a matter of scientific history (Kuh, Ben-Shlomo, Lynch, Hallqvist, & Power, 2003).

And now we turn to a brief review of some recurring issues in the work of human development scholars focused on the life cycle. These recurring issues include but are not limited to the following:

1. *Nature vs. nurture.* This is a massive idea and subject of scientific debate that may never be settled. How much of who you are and how you present to and react to the world around you is a function of your birth and genetic heritage and how much of you is a function of the family, community, and world you are born into and the associated experiences. Of particular note are the nurturing aspects of the interactive elements of one's environment and in some cases the impact of interactive elements that are not so nurturing, maybe even harmful to a person's development.
2. *Continuity vs. discontinuity.* Again, a scientific debate continues about the idea that you are early determined in the life cycle and that your development flows along a continuum post that early determination. Or do the experiences of life, both internal and external to you as a person, create a discontinuity? Is the course of human development as the life cycle progresses altered by a person's lived experiences?
3. *Universal or context specific.* The basic tenet of universality is that all people develop in the same way as they progress through the life cycle. The basic tenet of universality is challenged by the proposition that, yes, there is some universality, but that context-specific environmental variation shapes people's progression through the stages of the life cycle in a unique way. Scientific knowledge expressed about the life cycle can often be judged as to whether universality or culture specificity is granted the primary

position or how sequencing based on prominence of the two has been
achieved.

4. *Basic biopsychosocial elements.* The key here is how much weight is to be
given to the idea that there are basic forces, generally viewed from within
categories, such as biological, psychological, and sociocultural, that have
a major impact on human development, including both a force within
a category alone and/or in combination with other forces in the same
category or in combination with force(s) in other categories. Biological
forces in human development are believed to include such things as genetics
and health. Psychological forces that influence human development are
believed to include such things as cognition, emotions, personality, and
perceptions. Sociocultural forces in human development are believed
to include, as at minimum, such things as race, ethnicity, and culture.
Discrimination of every kind, racism, and oppression are also included and
of great current interest as sociocultural influencers of human development.

Also now included is the scientific awareness and knowledge generated in the field
of neuroscience, an in-depth study of the functioning of the brain and nervous
system. One of the exciting features of neuroscience is its ability to help with the
concept of the interaction effect of all these different forces/elements in developmental research (Kail & Cavanaugh, 2015). In fact, now the term *biopsychosocial
assessment* in social work practice is often augmented with the inclusion of neuro-
biopsychosocial (Carbajal & Aguirre, 2013).

MAJOR THEORETICAL AREAS

Those social work students, scholars, and practitioners wishing to consume, pursue,
produce, and/or extend scientific knowledge in the concept of the life cycle generally choose to base their work in one of the major theoretical areas. These include,
but, again, are not limited to the following:

1. *Psychodynamic theory*—associated often with the psychosocial theory
developed by Erik Erikson, whereby personality develops as sequential
stages and their accompanying tensions are addressed and hopefully
resolved in an adaptive manner (see Fig. 9.1).
2. *Behavioral theory*—associated most often with B. F. Skinner, behaviorism
posits that it is the consequences of a behavior that determine if the
behavior will be repeated in the future (see Fig. 9.2).
3. *Social learning theory*—associated most often with Albert Bandura
and posits that it is the action of simply watching/observing others
that determines behavior; imitation and modeling are key theoretical
components of social learning theory (see Fig. 9.3).
4. *Cognitive-development theory*—associated with the central concept
that thought processes and construction of knowledge are primary to

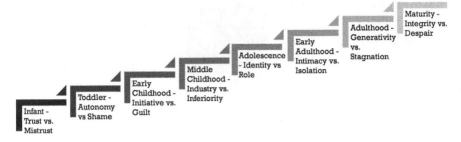

Figure 9.1 Erikson's stages of development Authors' creation

development in the life cycle. Most social work students and educators link the cognitive-development theory to Piaget and his stage theory of cognitive development (see Fig. 9.4).

5. *Ecological and systems perspective*—the developmental theory that social workers most align with is Bronfenbrenner's (1986) ecological perspective (see Fig. 9.5). The ecological theory/perspective posits that there are a myriad complex environments that interact and impact on development of the individual (Kail & Cavanaugh, 2015).

The psychosocial theories of development and their relationship to the life cycle are summarized in Table 9.1. It is important to remember that most theories of development through the life cycle tend to do little with adulthood, even though there is increasingly more attention (particularly as the baby boomer generation ages) on later developmental stages. As Kail and Cavanaugh explain (2015), theoretical study of the life course itself has begun to emerge as a distinct field of study and has made several marked contributions to scholarly approaches to human behavior.

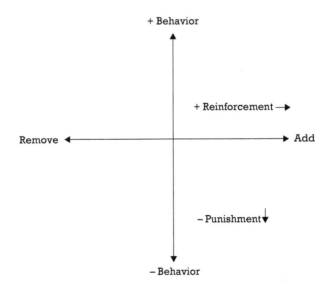

Figure 9.2 Skinner's operant conditioning Authors' creation

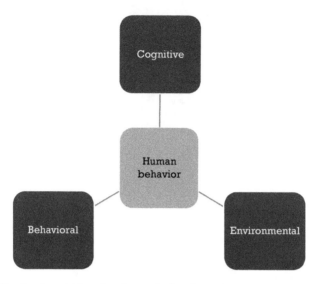

Figure 9.3 Bandura's social learning theory Authors' creation

While scholars in the field of human development and the life cycle use myriad research techniques and work within a number of paradigms, including the scientific method and interpretivist perspectives (sometimes broadly described as quantitative and qualitative, respectively), there are a number of noted trends and tendencies in choices about research design, data collection methods, and data analytic tools. Within the broad area of measurement, as it plays out in human developmental research, we see repeated use of systematic observation and the sampling of behavior as assigned tasks are completed. We see in cross-sectional research the use of categories of age as the basis of comparison. In the studies with a longitudinal design we see the use of different points in the life cycle as the key research descriptor. While the ethical considerations are important in all developmental research where research data are collected from people, the use of experimental designs in developmental research raises additional concerns—particularly with the testing of interventions that are considered to have a positive impact on the ability

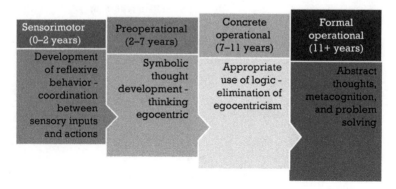

Figure 9.4 Piaget's stage theory Authors' creation

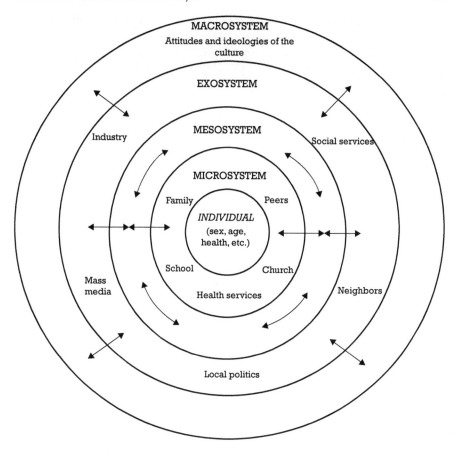

Figure 9.5 Bronfenbrenner's ecological theory of development

of an individual, or another occurring configuration of people, to move in an adaptive manner through the life cycle (Kail & Cavanaugh, 2015).

THE SCIENCE OF EVOLUTION AND THE LIFE CYCLE

Belief in the veracity of evolutionary theory is strong and of long standing in the scientific community. Of course, it is not as well accepted in the last few years in the general public—note that a number of candidates for president in the last few elections have denied their belief in the theory of evolution. Nonetheless, the authors of this text believe social work educators, students, and practitioners can benefit from knowing and understanding the basics of evolutionary theory. While social work students and practitioners need not be experts in the nuances of the theory of evolution, it is important to understand some of the basics, particularly as applied to a scientific review of the life cycle. The reason is because for multicellular organisms like human beings, most major evolutionary change moves forward by alterations

Table 9.1 DEVELOPMENTAL THEORIES AND THEIR RELATIONSHIP WITH LIFE
CYCLE: SOME EXAMPLES

Theory	Perspective/ Type	Relationship to the Life Cycle
Erikson's stages of psychosocial development	Psychodynamic	Emphasis on social and psychological forces; nature and nurture interactions; similar life stages but difference in rate of growth; life cycle forces are critical
Skinner's operant conditioning	Learning	Emphasis on environment (modeling and observing); focus on nurturing; less emphasis on life cycle
Bandura's social learning	Learning	
Piaget's cognitive development	Cognitive development	Emphasis on nature: biological and social forces; less on life cycle; development of thinking in stages
Bronfenbrenner	Ecological and systems	Emphasis on social; less emphasis on psychological and life cycle; nature and nurture interactions

Authors' creation

in life cycles, that is, the patterns of growth, development, and maturation (Bogin & Smith, 1996).

Ironically, one of the more well-accepted and controversial ideas in evolutionary theory is that the shared features of growth, development, and maturation among mammals are, for the most part, due to a common evolutionary origin. Commonalities in developmental biology and behavior were a source of support for Charles Darwin's hypotheses on human evolution. Darwin (1872) wrote of the similarities of humans and other mammals in a host of ways, but he also wrote extensively of development features novel to humans. In his book, *The Expression of Emotions in Man and Animals*, Darwin (1872) wrote of "Special Expressions of Man: Suffering and Weeping" (p. 147). Darwin was one of the first scientists to include photographs in his books, and these included photographs of human infants crying and screaming. Based on the information available at the time, Darwin believed that only human infants and children expressed distress via long bouts of screaming and crying. Darwin wrote that this special behavior of people is due to human features of anatomy and cognition, which are not shared by other mammals. Since Darwin's time, it has been confirmed that other species of mammals do scream and cry.

Darwin, although a bit mistaken about the uniqueness of crying to humans, did help originate the present idea that the human place in nature, as viewed by evolutionary theorists, balances the physical and behavioral characteristics that are shared with other species against those that are found only in the human species (Bogin & Smith, 1996). Major points are integral to both the science of the life cycle and evolutionary theory that have direct application to social work theory and practice. They include but are not limited to the following:

1. Human beings have a relatively long period of gestation and four stages of growth and development between birth and adulthood. These postnatal stages are infancy, childhood, juvenile, and adolescence.
2. Human childhood and adolescence evolved because they confer reproductive advantages, increasing the fertility of parents and reducing the mortality of their offspring (this is classic natural selection and central to evolutionary theory).
3. Adolescence may also have evolved by sexual selection, in which sex-specific features of adolescent girls and boys enhance opportunities for survival and mating. The biology and behavior of human adolescence also promote an apprenticeship-type system of learning and practice of the wide variety of economic, social, political, and sexual skills needed in adulthood and for successful reproduction.
4. Also, and as social workers promote, the way a human being grows is the product of interactions between the biology of our species, the physical environment in which we live, and the social, economic, and political environment that every human culture creates; and because alteration in the pattern of growth, development, and maturation is a major mechanism of evolutionary change. Human growth and development, therefore, reflect the biocultural nature and evolutionary history of people.
5. The basic pattern of human growth is shared by all people.

BASIC PRINCIPLES OF HUMAN GROWTH AND DEVELOPMENT

Human beings begin life as a single cell, the fertilized ovum, via sexual reproduction. In normal human conception and development, the genetic information provided by each parent, the phenotypic environment of the mother's ovum, and the biocultural environment in which the mother lives interact in complex ways to guide the fertilized ovum to divide, grow, differentiate, and develop through many stages, including embryo and fetus, prior to birth. Although growth and development may occur simultaneously, they are distinct biological processes. Growth may be defined as a quantitative increase in size or mass. Measurements of height or weight indicate how much growth has taken place in a child. Development is defined as a progression of changes, either quantitative or qualitative, that lead from an undifferentiated or immature state to a highly organized, specialized, and mature state. Maturity is measured by functional capacity. An example is the development of motor skills from crawling to toddling in an infant to mature human walking in a juvenile (Bogin & Smith, 1996).

The life cycle of an organism includes stages of growth, development, and maturation from conception to death. Many of the basic principles of human growth, development, and maturation are best presented in terms of the key events that take place during the life cycle. One of the many possible orderings of events is given in Table 9.2, in which growth periods are divided into developmentally functional stages. It is important to keep in mind, however, that the table's contents are only one possible ordering, because declaring that one moment, for example fertilization, is the beginning of life is arbitrary in a continuous cycle that passes through fixed stages in each individual person and in generation after generation.

A biocultural perspective of human development is a perspective focused on the constant interactions taking place during all phases of human development, both between genes and hormones within the body and with the sociocultural environment that surrounds the person, no matter what age. Research from social anthropology, developmental psychology, endocrinology, primate ethology, physical anthropology, and human biology shows how the biocultural perspective enhances our understanding of human development. Even though social workers as a professional group, in fact, may not be attuned to the science of the life cycle, nor evolutionary theory, social work practitioners do apply themselves in their work to what life cycle theorists consider risks of the newer stages, childhood and adolescence, of human development. This is especially the case for the social work practitioner when these stages impact with culture change. Malnutrition, child abuse, and neglect of both infants, children, and the elderly are some of the most prominent risks during human development (Bogin, 1999; Bogin & Smith, 1996), and all clearly fall within the purview of social work practice (Beach, Carpenter, Rosen, Sharps, & Gelles, 2016; Dickens, Berrick, Pösö, & Skivenes, 2016; Seipel, 1999).

The Early Life Cycle

Social workers work largely with families and children, often very young children. In the United States, much of that social work is conducted through the state public child welfare agencies that are typically part of state departments of human services or social welfare (Ginsberg, 2000). And the issues that social workers deal with in their work with children and families can be quite complex, and scientific knowledge can help them be more effective in their work. For example, a component of pregnancy and birth issues is family planning, an area of social work practice for many social workers and social agencies. Pregnancy and childbirth are among the more complex and significant issues of family life and, human development scholars would claim, a platform for all later development (Kail & Cavanaugh, 2015; Lindberg & Kost, 2014).

Planning for the eventualities associated with a pregnancy with clients or helping them avoid pregnancy altogether are crucial issues in much of social work practice. Social workers who work with children and families know that adequate prenatal care for mothers, their fetuses, and young children is critical. There are many complications of pregnancy that may be prevented by available and quality prenatal care. The overall health of mothers is generally important in determining the outcome of

Table 9.2 ORDERING OF LIFE-CYCLE EVENTS

Stage	Period	Life-Cycle Events
PRENATAL DEVELOPMENT		
Fertilization	1st trimester	Embryogenesis (fertilization to 12th week)
	2nd trimester	Growth in length (4th through 6th lunar months)
	3rd trimester	Growth in weight and organ development (7th lunar months until birth)
BIRTH		
POSTNATAL DEVELOPMENT		
Neonatal	Birth to 28 days	Transition from uterine environment to external world
Infancy	2nd month to 36 months	Steep deceleration in in growth rate; gradual introduction of food along with feeding; developmental milestones
Childhood	3 to 7 years	Dependent on others for care and feeding, permanent molar and incisor tooth eruption, moderate growth rate
Juvenile	7 to 12 years	7–10 years for girls and until 12 for boys, slower growth rate, self-dependency in feeding, and cognitive transition
Puberty		Short duration (some days to a few weeks), increase in secretion of sex hormones from genitals
Adolescence	13 to 19 years	Growth in height and weight, permanent tooth eruption almost complete, social maturity, increase in interests pertaining to adult behaviors
ADULTHOOD		
Prime and transition	18 to 55 years	For women: until 45 years; for men: 21 to 55 years. Completion of skeletal growth, physiology, cognition, and behavior
Old age and senescence	End of child-bearing until death	Decline in the function and abilities to repairs many body components
DEATH		

pregnancy and the lifelong outcomes for a new child. A disease or other disabling health condition may complicate the pregnancy or the birth of the child. Although the aforementioned is an issue of social welfare policy rather than science, which is the focus of this textbook, it is clear that the positive and negative scientific facts of pregnancy and childbirth are important to addressing issues related to prenatal and child care.

Fortunately, scientific knowledge about procreation is extensive and important to all families as well as adolescents as they reach maturity. Social workers working in schools, public health departments, and social services agencies have important obligations in having a basic grasp of the scientific knowledge and an ability to communicate this information. Of course, the authors of this textbook hope their work might serve as one additional asset to the social work practitioner. While much is known about pregnancy, scientifically much has yet to be determined.

For example, as recently as late 2016, researchers have attempted to ascertain changes that occur in pregnant women's brains during pregnancy. Pregnancy is described as a physiological process that may, in fact, change a woman's brain, altering the size and structure of areas of the brain involved in perceiving the feelings and perspectives of others. Reportedly, these changes remained 2 years after giving birth, at least into the babies' infant years. The more pronounced the brain changes, the higher the mothers scored on a measure of emotional attachment to the babies (Belluck, 2016). The study, which took more than 5 years, involved 25 women approximately 30 years of age in Spain who had never been pregnant. Their brains were scanned before becoming pregnant and within a few months after giving birth. Another group of 20 women who had never been pregnant was created to give the study a strong basis of comparison and increase the internal validity in design and thus greater strength of possible meaning in the results. The women who had never been pregnant had their brains scanned twice, about the same number of months apart as the women who did experience a pregnancy and gave birth. Only the pregnant women showed gray matter reduction, thinning, and changes in the surface area of the cortex in areas thought to be related to social cognition. Hoekzema and colleagues (2016) did not claim they knew exactly what was being reduced in size—neurons, other brain cells, synapses, or other parts of the circulatory system (Belluck, 2016; Hoekzema et al., 2016).

The researchers also scanned the brains of 17 men who were not fathers and 19 first-time fathers before and after the pregnancies of their partners. In the two male groups, those with and those without partners with an experience of pregnancy, no differences were found in brain volume. Six months after giving birth the mothers completed the Maternal Postnatal Attachment Scale, used to measure a woman's emotional attachment, pleasure, and hostility toward her baby. The degree of changes in size and structure of the brain areas under study predicted the degree of hostility and attachment (Belluck, 2016; Hoekzema et al., 2016).

This research exemplifies the scientific possibilities available to neuroscientists and cognitive scientists as they study something as germane to the life cycle as what happens to a mother's brain as a function of an experienced pregnancy. The research team concluded that their current findings indicate that the human pregnancy is associated with substantial long-lasting alterations in brain structure, which may serve an adaptive purpose for pending motherhood. But, as with all good scientific-based research, the researchers caution the reader that the findings should be considered "first insights" into the profound impact of pregnancy on the gray mater architecture of the human brain. For the social worker reader, this this type of theory of mind research can possibly help in the achievement of greater understanding into other periods of the life cycle such as adolescence and the aged.

Pregnancy, Gestation, and Birth Outcomes

Of course, the early life cycle, dominated by ideas of conception, gestation, and pregnancy, has also been studied from a psychological perspective. Dunkel Schetter (2011) makes the claim that psychological research on pregnancy is advancing rapidly. Of note to social workers is that the research includes strong consideration of social support, coping, and resilience as discerning variables with strong impact on pregnancy outcome. Dunkel Schetter (2011) explicitly recommends a multilevel approach to understanding health outcomes in the early part of the life cycle, including attention to individual attributes, social relationships, sociocultural aspects, and community levels of analysis. Relationship-level analyses might include variables such as social network, social support, partner relationship, family, and intergenerational influences. Sociocultural-level analysis includes race/ethnicity, nativity and immigration status, acculturation/adaptation, socioeconomic status, and cultural norms and values. Community-level factors include physical environment characteristics of neighborhoods, health care access and quality, and other geographical features of one's environment.

Dunkel Schetter's (2011) description of this psychologically focused research sounds a lot like the early work of the social work pioneer, Jane Addams. Dunkel Schetter (2011) labels the study of coping in pregnancy an open area of opportunity in the study of pregnancy, gestation, and outcomes such as low birth rate. Strong consideration is given for including psychological research on the early life cycle, pregnancy, gestation, and theory and birth outcomes (Dunkel Schetter, 2011).

Dunkel Schetter (2011) summarizes the strongest points about psychological research on the early life cycle by emphasizing the following empirically derived findings:

1. Stress during pregnancy is implicated as a risk factor for adverse birth outcomes.
2. Pregnancy anxiety, defined as anxiety and fears specifically linked to a particular pregnancy, is emerging as an independent risk factor for spontaneous preterm birth.
3. Chronic stress and depressive symptoms appear to predict fetal growth and risk of low birth weight.
4. The mechanisms for these effects involve multilevel interacting processes, including neuroendocrine, immune, and behavioral processes.
5. Prenatal stress and pregnancy anxiety have been shown to have extensive and far-reaching developmental effects on the fetus, newborn, infant, child, and adolescent and are the focus of much current inquiry.
6. Sociocultural processes, including social support, partner relationship, and a woman's cultural milieu, appear to be direct contributors to infant birth

weight, although social support has not improved birth outcomes in most past randomized controlled trials.

Dunkel Schetter (2011) addresses avenues for further research into the relationship and impacts of stress during pregnancy, including the following:

1. To test the antecedents and correlates of high pregnancy anxiety and determine how high pregnancy anxiety influences onset of labor
2. To investigate the roles that specific resilience factors play in modifying the processes linking pregnancy anxiety to preterm birth
3. To examine chronic stressors, such as racism and discrimination, including the role of depressive symptoms, as they influence fetal growth and low infant birth weight and to determine the ways in which these pathways are similar to and different from those involved in pregnancy anxiety and preterm birth
4. To design innovative and evidence-based intervention research to improve birth outcomes and the experience of pregnancy for women as well as to reduce major disparities in these outcomes and to conduct randomized controlled trials to establish efficacy (Dunkel Schetter, 2011, p. 550).

An interesting and quite complex element of psychological distress in the early life cycle that connects strongly with social work practice with families and children is medical neglect. In an era when most of the more serious childhood illnesses can be prevented with inoculations, failure to protect children by arranging for them to have these preventive services can constitute medical neglect. In recent years, controversies emerged about the possible dangers of inoculations or the substances through which they are delivered. A campaign on the Internet and in other outlets suggests there is a correlative relationship between a child being inoculated and developing autism. Scientists who have studied the matter thoroughly deny any such correlation. Granted some children who have inoculations do develop autism or conditions on the autism spectrum, but the rate at which they occur is not statistically significant and those developments do not appear to be related to the inoculations in any causal or correlative way. Scientific findings and knowledge, even though convincing, can and are set aside by some parents or caregivers. The work of a practicing social worker in the child welfare field is made more difficult with this repudiation of science in regard to inoculations and vaccinations. A very small number of parents deny the science and hold the belief that inoculations might harm their children. Thus, this repudiation of science makes implementing science-based public health measures such as requiring preventive inoculations as a condition of school enrolment quite difficult for the social work practitioner. The controversy is significant for more than just the condition of autism and may even contribute to some recurrence of illnesses such as rubella and mumps (Taylor et al., 1999).

Medical neglect may also develop from parental unwillingness or incapacity to take their ill children to health care practitioners. Failure to do so may constitute neglect. Similarly, parents may refuse to allow their children to be treated with medical procedures that may save a child's life. That is especially true of blood transfusions that some religious belief communities believe are prohibited by Scripture. Medical scientists conclude that blood transfusions are often a matter of life and death. Parental objection to transfusion cases often go to litigation in courts. Generally, the courts, citing scientific knowledge, have required that children receive the transfusions or other procedures that their parents may oppose on religious grounds. Courts in the United States have both upheld the rights of parents to care for their children as they please but have also required that children in danger of severe illness or death, which can be prevented by blood transfusion, be provided the transfusions, even against parental objections (Diekema, 2004; Wadlington, 1994). In contrast, adults who refuse transfusion, even at the peril of dying, are not generally required by the courts to have such transfusions (Pattakos et al., 2012).

Environmental Risks in the Early Life Cycle

Although the research is to varying degrees inconclusive, there is mounting scientific evidence to show that there are environmental risks associated with the early stages of the life cycle. These risks may have a deleterious impact on a person's ability to conceive or her ability to maintain a pregnancy with enough gestational length to avoid such adverse outcomes as pregnancy loss, premature delivery, and/ or low birth weight. Evidence appears to suggest that environmental tobacco smoke is a risk factor for reduced birth weight and preterm delivery. Outdoor air pollution is believed to be associated with reduced term birth weight and preterm delivery. Suggestive evidence associates pesticides and other chemically laded products with decreased fetal growth and length of gestation. Stronger evidence, primarily occupational, links certain birth anomalies with exposure to organic solvents and certain types of herbicides. Evidence suggests other chemicals in a person's living environment could be associated with pregnancy loss. Exposures in utero can also increase the risk of developmental delays, such as impaired neurological function; adult chronic illnesses, such as heart disease, diabetes, and cancer; and next-generation effects, such as reduced reproductive capacity (Stillerman, Mattison, Gidudice, & Woodruff, 2008).

　　While it is important to keep in mind that the primary causes of a number of adverse pregnancy outcomes are not well understood scientifically, there is growing body of scientific evidence that the environment can play an important role. It is also important to note the concept of the environment is quite broad, but most would agree in regard to the early life cycle it is appropriate to consider such environmental factors as nutrition, adequacy of prenatal care, smoking and alcohol use, maternal age, and socioeconomic status, as well as less familiar environmental factors including pollution and chemical agents encountered both indoors and outdoors. And in many cases, two or more environmental factors may be interrelated or synergistic in their impact. Environmental factors may also be magnified or otherwise affected by varying genetic characteristics unique to the individual (Stillerman et al., 2008).

A number of drinking water contaminants, including selenium, arsenic, and nitrates, have been associated with loss of pregnancy and other adverse birth outcomes. Perhaps the most common drinking water contaminants to be linked with pregnancy loss in the United States, however, are byproducts of routine chemical drinking water disinfection. Disinfection byproducts form when chlorine or other disinfectants react with organic material from the decomposition of leaves and other vegetation naturally found in drinking water sources. They are often found at elevated levels, depending on the disinfection method and other variables, in municipal drinking water supplies. People are exposed to these byproducts through not only ingestion of drinking water but also through skin-based absorption and inhalation from showering and other water usages. The scientific evidence to date suggests a variety of links between environmental pollutants and a range of adverse birth and pregnancy outcomes.

Finally, as social work maintains and intensifies its professional relationship with public health, it is important to promote public health policies that will improve birth outcomes at a community-based systems level. Advocacy at the national and state level might even include increasing the scientific knowledge base about the potential harm of chemicals before exposure occurs in utero, similar to policies that govern introduction of new pharmaceuticals into the market place. From a social work perspective, it is important to keep in mind that while early life cycle adverse outcomes can have a devastating emotional impact on a person and/or a family, nuclear or extended, there can be a myriad of other impacts, such as financial, both in the short and long term. While the physical environment is oft a seemingly overwhelming factor in life and encompasses such expansive factors as air, water, food, and soil, the list of environmental factors that something can be done about might include the more mundane, such as a host of consumer products and other substances that individuals come into direct contact with each day. The latter might include environmental tobacco smoke, air pollutants from motor vehicles and industrial facilities, pesticides, heavy metals, plasticizers, flame retardants, chemical byproducts of drinking water disinfection, and pharmaceuticals that are incompletely removed from drinking water (Stillerman et al., 2008).

CHILDHOOD AND THE LIFE CYCLE

Childhood is a stage of life considered to be of utmost importance, particularly considering the platform that childhood provides for all the stages of the life cycle to follow. Social workers can rightfully lay claim to a long-standing and sustained interest in the early years of children. Our history is particularly strong with its pervasive representation of social work professionals in the field of child welfare (Barth, Lloyd, Christ, Chapman, & Dickinson, 2008; Ellett, 2009). Scientific research about early childhood has identified a number of important contributory and deficit variables, and they are discussed in this section. A good deal of science focused on early childhood includes consideration of the availability and quality of childhood development programs. And the need for further consideration of what

is and what is not important scientifically to young children is important domestic-
ally and internationally to social workers as a professional group.

According to child development researchers, early childhood development
programs vary internationally in coordination and quality, with inadequate and
inequitable access, especially for children younger than 3 years. New estimates,
based on proxy measures of stunting and poverty, indicate that 250 million children (43%) younger than 5 years in low-income and middle-income countries are
at risk of not reaching their developmental potential. There is therefore a need to
increase multisectoral coverage of quality programming that incorporates the critical variables of health, nutrition, security and safety, responsive caregiving, and
early learning. From a macro social work perspective, early childhood policies and
programs are crucial for meeting sustainable development goals, and from a micro
practice perspective, implementation of policies via programming is essential for
individual children to develop the intellectual skills, creativity, and well-being required to become healthy and productive adults (Black et al., 2016).

Black and colleagues (2016) provide a thorough examination of recent scientific
progress and summaries of global commitments to early childhood development
programs. Material in the piece demonstrates substantial advancements since 2000,
including new neuroscientific evidence linking early adversity and nurturing care
with brain development and function throughout the life course. Key messages in
the work of these applied social scientists include but are not limited to the following:

1. The proportion of children younger than 5 years in low-income and
   middle-income countries at risk of not attaining their developmental
   potential because of extreme poverty and stunting remains high (43%).
2. The accumulation of adversities, beginning before conception and
   continuing throughout prenatal and early life, can disrupt brain
   development, attachment, and early learning. Developmental delays are
   evident in the first year, worsen during early childhood, and continue
   throughout life.
3. Despite substantial progress in early childhood development research,
   programs, and national policies since 2000, services are of varying quality
   with uncoordinated and inequitable access, especially for children younger
   than 3 years.
4. Children's early development requires nurturing care—defined as
   health, nutrition, security and safety, responsive caregiving, and early
   learning—provided by parent and family interactions, and supported by an
   environment that enables these interactions.
5. Coordination, monitoring, and evaluation research are needed across
   sectors to ensure that high-quality early childhood development services
   are available throughout early childhood and primary school, up to the age
   of 8 years (Black et al., 2016).

The social work reader is cautioned, however, to keep in mind that population-
level assessments measure the developmental status of populations and are used for

monitoring global targets, such as the sustainable development goals of the United Nations. Stunting and extreme poverty serve as proxy measures because they are (1) associated strongly with children's development; (2) are measured globally using uniform methods, and (3) are responsive to environmental and economic changes. We in the world of social work maintain an interest in direct population-level assessments. Direct population-level assessments are advantageous due to their sensitivity to variations in children's development and responsiveness to programmatic interventions. However, direct assessments are often costly and time-consuming to measure, and most often they require at least consideration of developmental and cultural adaptations. Initial analyses using UNICEF's caregiver reported *Early Childhood Development Index* found that 36.8% of 3-year-olds and 4-year-olds in 35 low- and middle-income countries do not attain basic cognitive and socioemotional skills, such as following directions and inhibiting aggression. Efforts are underway to validate population-level measures that can be applied globally and used for monitoring progress in meeting targets from the sustainable development goals for children under 3 years of age (Black et al., 2016).

Applied social science research, including consideration of anecdotal, observational, and experiential data, has established that childhood development is a maturational and interactive process, resulting in a hoped-for ordered progression of perceptual, motor, cognitive, language, socioemotional, and self-regulation skills. Although the developmental process is similar across cultures, progression rates can vary as children acquire culture-specific skills. The acquisition of skills and learning in middle childhood, throughout adolescence, and into adulthood builds on foundational capacities established between preconception and early childhood, with multigenerational effects. Children reach developmental potential when they acquire developmental competencies for academic, behavioral, socioemotional, and economic accomplishments. Multiple factors influence the acquisition of competencies, including health, nutrition, security and safety, responsive caregiving, and early learning; these domains interact with each other and can be mutually reinforcing through the process of development. All are necessary for nurturing care and occur through bidirectional interactions, initiated by both children and caregivers, and sustained by their environments (Black et al., 2016).

Despite remarkable progress in early childhood development research, programs, and policies, services for young children are inadequate and inequitably distributed. The burden of children not reaching their developmental potential remains high. The lack of attention to nurturing care as a comprehensive concept is a major concern, especially during the period of rapid brain development and learning, and the formation of caregiver–child attachments that characterizes children under 3 years. The conceptual basis of early childhood development has been well established and is displayed in Figure 9.6. The underlying science of early childhood development and the life course framework illustrate the crucial part that early childhood development plays, enabling children to become healthy and productive citizens with the intellectual skills, creativity, and well-being to reduce global inequities and ensure sustainable global development. However, the application of policy heuristics to existing evidence has shown that implementation of early childhood development

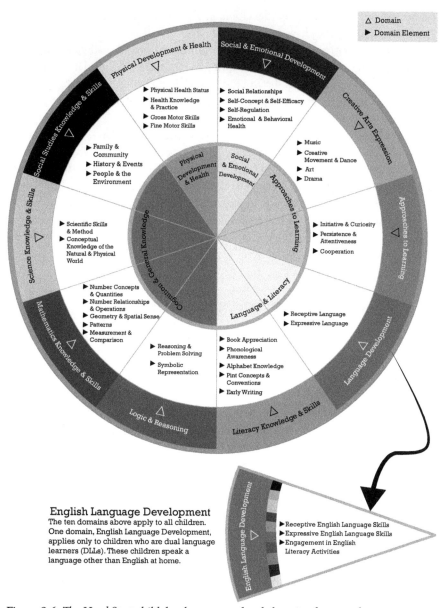

Figure 9.6 The Head Start child development and early learning framework
SOURCE: Office of Head Start: The Head Start Child Development and Early Learning Framework; https://www.acf.hhs.gov/ohs/resource/hs-child-development-early-learning-framework

programs is fragmented and lacks coordination, especially for children under 3 years.

Investment in early childhood development is increasing through advances in the health, nutrition, and social protection sectors, through programs that promote survival, nutritional adequacy, and poverty reduction, respectively. Although these interventions provide benefits for early childhood development, they do not ensure that children reach their developmental potential. The advances in personal and societal equity that have been attributed to early childhood development require that interventions also include opportunities to promote all components of nurturing care through the family. Nurturing care in early childhood is the essential foundation for human capital development and should be followed by high-quality schooling, support for at-risk youth, and programs to facilitate the school-to-work transition.

Early childhood development services are necessary to address the enormous global burden of children in low- and middle-income countries who are not reaching their developmental potential and who will experience lifelong disparities in health, academic achievement, and earning potential. There is an urgent need for population-level indicators of child development, especially for the youngest children, to enable ongoing monitoring and improvement in quality. Achieving sustainable development goals depends on ensuring adequate health, nutrition, security and safety, responsive caregiving, and early learning opportunities for the youngest children.

ADOLESCENCE AND THE LIFE CYCLE

Several theorists have studied and recorded varying developmental tasks of adolescence. In additional to the biological and physical changes that take place, a number of cognitive, behavioral, and social changes have their beginnings within the ages of 11 to 21 years. Piaget, in his theory of cognitive development described earlier, believed that at a certain age children become capable of abstract thinking and hypothesis testing using logical reasoning (Amsel & Smetana, 2011). This is juxtaposed with Erikson's theory of psychosocial development that purports adolescence as a time of identity formation, beginning at age 12 and continuing into early adulthood. Adolescence is also a time of great learning and achievement of several educational and vocational milestones, as well as greater social cohesion.

Puberty signals the onset of adolescence with a series of hormonal and neuro-chemical changes. Adolescence seems to foster a number of changes within the brain, on the cellular and biochemical level (Blakemore & Choudhury, 2006; Roenneberg et al., 2004). The culmination or termination of many of these processes and changes will signal the end of adolescence and the beginning of adulthood, from a biological perspective, but social and behavioral changes may last considerably longer (Arnett, 2014).

Adolescent development is often examined according to three age delineations: early adolescence, aged approximately 10–14 years; middle adolescence, aged approximately 15–17 years; and late adolescence, aged approximately 18–21 years (Smetana, Campione-Barr, & Metzger, 2006). These age groups differ significantly across all of the biological, cognitive-emotional, and social indicators, and a developmental trend or progression can be ascertained throughout each distinctive period to the other (Lerner & Steinberg, 2009; Steinberg, 2014).

Early Adolescence

The onset of puberty (from approximately 10 to 14 years of age) dominates the early adolescent period. Physical changes that are the hallmarks of adolescence (i.e., growth of body hair, increased perspiration, voice change, growth in height and weight, increased oil production in hair and skin) are the key developmental changes for this area of the life cycle. As Tanner (1981) noted, these differences are compounded by an approximate 2-year difference between male and female adolescents, with adolescent girls developing at a faster rate than boys (Tanner, 1981, p. 43). In addition, changes in hormone levels such as testosterone, estrogen, and progesterone may contribute to changes in sleep patterns, emotion regulation, and sexual maturation (Swerdloff & Odell, 1975). Coupled with these biological changes are changes in the neurology and neurochemistry of the brain, which may impact abstract thinking and executive functioning, personal identity, and exploration of roles of parents and friends (Erikson & Erikson, 1998; Göllner et al., 2016).

Middle Adolescence

As shown in Figure 9.7, middle adolescence after puberty focuses on four broad domains. These include achieving independence and autonomy in thinking and feeling, developing a sense of one's physical self, or "body image," after the changes of puberty, developing and maintaining robust peer relationships, and beginning to identify and act out on one's sexuality. During middle adolescence, as physical growth changes associated with early adolescence culminate or terminate (again, subject to sex differences), the effects of these changes come to the fore as adolescents continue to adjust and grow from a cognitive, behavioral, social, and interpersonal perspective. Sexual experiences and development of sexual and romantic relationships are common in middle adolescence.

The literature on middle adolescent development indicates that crucial linkages are formed with regard to cognition, executive functioning, and school-based outcomes (Blakemore & Choudhury, 2006; Roeser & Eccles, 1998). Within the emotional domain, middle adolescents forming decision-making skills, minimizing risk behaviors, and developing communication skills that facilitate positive relationships with parents, peers, and others are at a crucial state to avoid problematic behavior and relationships (Steinberg & Morris, 2001).

Late Adolescence

Late adolescence is typified by a slowing down of the physical and chemical side of development while social and interpersonal development begins to increase and broaden. As such, hormonal fluctuations decrease, mood swings are less frequent, and sleep habits tend to comport with normative circadian rhythm (Dahl & Lewin, 2002). While young women are typically fully developed by late adolescence,

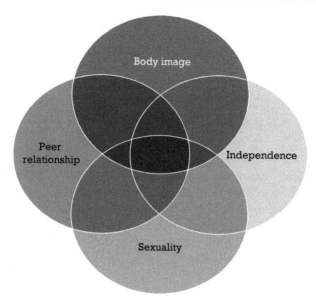

Figure 9.7 Focus of middle adolescence Authors' creation

young men continue to experience physical growth and brain changes into age 20 to 24 (Sawyer et al., 2012). Normative development at this stage is ascertained by observation of sense of identity, emotion regulation, and the development of significant and romantic relationships with a sexual component (Cooper, Shaver, & Collins, 1998).

Late adolescents frequently take on more and more adult responsibilities, including planning for higher education, entering the workforce, and planning for or securing independent living arrangements. Moreover, social interactions in late adolescence have many characteristics in common with adult living, including a secure, established base of friends and acquaintances, independence in decision making, role development, and individuation (Erikson & Erikson, 1998). As Gardner and Steinberg (2005) noted, incorporation into a wider social milieu also signals the greater influence that peers have on decision making in middle to late adolescence. This influence can be made manifest in greater risk-taking behaviors and higher instances of peer conformity in the transition from adolescence to adulthood or "emerging adulthood" (Arnett, 2014; Gardner & Steinberg, 2005; Parsons, Siegel, & Cousins, 1997).

Social work students, scholars, and practitioners can recognize within the developmental pathways of adolescence the roots and early manifestations of many issues of significance to social work practice and many areas that would benefit from social work intervention should circumstances merit it. Onset of mental illnesses, including depression, body dysmorphism, or anxiety, may manifest during adolescence (Mayville, Katz, Gipson, & Cabral, 1999; Petersen et al., 1993; Woodward & Fergusson, 2001). Moreover, disorders which may have their roots earlier in development, such as dyslexia, or from within the social environment (such as substance abuse) may complicate achievement of developmental goals in adolescence

(Snowling, Bishop, & Stothard, 2000). In addition, the rapid increase in social activity and communication with individuals (e.g., parents, friends, romantic partners) and systems (e.g., school, work, home) also present opportunities for social work professionals to engage with adolescents and provide needed services during an important developmental stage within the life cycle.

ADULTHOOD AND THE LIFE CYCLE

Although there is no physical change like puberty to signal the onset of adulthood and scholars like Arnett (2014) challenge whether adulthood can stand alone as a developmental stage of the life cycle, there are some generally accepted notions of adulthood. In Western, industrialized nations, adulthood is roughly tied to the average life span, that is, approximately 71 years (according to the *United Nations World Population Prospects*, 2015), and is demarcated into two basic stages of early and middle adulthood. As Sierles (1982) noted:

> People have noticed that there are stages of adulthood. Adults at one stage are different from adults in other stages in knowledge, problem-solving ability, attitudes, priorities, health, and physical capacities [...] Young adults respect the experienced, seasoned, less-harried, "mellow" qualities of some of their elders, although they appreciate their own youth when older people are cynical, insufficiently inquisitive, or forgetful. Older adults respect the idealism, vigor, good health, and inquisitiveness of their juniors, but appreciate their own age when younger adults are naive or arrogant. Although you are an adult now, you are not quite the same person that you will be years later. (p. 297)

Although clear delineations are not agreed upon in the literature, early adulthood is often considered from 20 to 40 years of age and middle adulthood approximately 40 to 65 years of age (Chopik, Edelstein, & Fraley, 2013; Diehl, Elnick, Bourbeau, & Labouvie-Vief, 1998). A third stage of older or later adulthood remains a discrete developmental stage and is discussed in a later section.

Early Adulthood

In early adulthood, the developmental tasks that have their formation in middle to late adolescence come to fruition. Among these are establishing close interpersonal relationships, completing education and entering or continuing in the workforce, and "putting down roots" in terms of maintaining a stable residence and making considerations for raising a family (Roisman, Masten, Coatsworth, & Tellegen, 2004; Shulman, Feldman, Blatt, Cohen, & Mahler, 2005). Educational, professional, and work-related tasks lead to greater financial independence from family or other supports, while educational and professional goals further establish greater individuation, leading to establishment of close romantic relationships and overt planning for the future, including dating, cohabiting prior to marriage, marriage, and family planning (Lichter, Michelmore, Turner, & Sassler, 2016).

Workforce development figures indicate that career planning is a paramount force in early adulthood, with the 20- to 40-year age group representing the largest percentage of the existing workforce in the United States (Fry, 2018). As Johnson (2001) noted, values about jobs and careers that begin in adolescence may change and solidify during the transition into early adulthood, as individuals seek out stability, independence, and the means to provide for their own well-being and that of potential partners, spouses, or children. Full integration into adult society extends, however, beyond the workplace, as attempts must be made to balance work, family obligations, and socialization or leisure time. Many studies indicate that this "work-life balance" is a central aspect of adult functioning within the broader multisystem environment (Gröpel & Kuhl, 2009; Higgins, Duxbury, & Lee, 1994). Often when these systems are out of equilibrium, social workers may intervene to assist with areas of work or marital dissatisfaction that arise from the imbalance.

Middle Adulthood

Middle adulthood constitutes a two-fold effort at maintaining the developmental achievements of early adulthood while providing for the welfare of future generations. Erikson and Erikson (1998) refer to the problem posed at this stage as generativity versus self-absorption. As Havighurst (1956) noted, the major developmental tasks in middle adulthood include the following:

1. Accepting and adjusting to physiological changes, such as menopause
2. Reaching and maintaining satisfaction in one's occupation
3. Adjusting to and possibly caring for aging parents
4. Helping teenage children to become responsible adults
5. Achieving adult social and civic responsibility
6. Relating to one's spouse as a person
7. Developing leisure-time activities

As with early adulthood, achieving a balance of these key tasks is often difficult and can lead to what many psychologists have termed the "midlife crisis" (Gutmann, 1976; Jaques, 1965). Thoughts and feelings around life choices as well as what may be left undone by the time that an individual reaches old age can often preoccupy individuals still seeking to fulfil work and family responsibilities and achieve sought-after goals. While a condition like this is likely not due to any persistent physical or psychological ailment, it is important for social work practitioners to recognize the long-ranging psychological effects that aging can have on individuals and be prepared to assist in ways that are strengths-based and promote positive communication and relationships.

It is important to note that the delineation between the developmental stage of middle adulthood and older adulthood, from the life span perspective, coincides, not coincidentally, with the average age of retirement from the workforce. Preparing for retirement is not just in furtherance of financial security but also sets the stage for a more productive and fulfilling older adulthood for individuals and their families (James, Matz-Costa, & Smyer, 2016).

OLDER ADULTHOOD AND THE LIFE CYCLE

Social workers are but one professional group that has increasingly turned its attention to aging as a function of the life cycle. Late-life stage, old age, and senescence follow the prime years of adulthood. The aging period is one of gradual or sometimes rapid decline in the ability to adapt to environmental stress. Importantly, the pattern of decline varies greatly between individuals. Although specific molecular, cellular, and organismic changes can be measured and described, not all changes occur in all people. Unlike the biological regulation of growth and development prior to adulthood, the aging process appears to follow no species-specific uniform plan. There are many theories about the aging process and most show that aging is a multicausal process. An overarching theoretical/philosophical question that not only goes unanswered but most often not even asked is why people must age at all. Put simply, aging is a function of all cells losing their ability to renew, expand, and repair damage (Bogin & Smith, 1996; Haselwandter et al., 2015).

Older adults are the fastest growing, yet least active, segment of the population. It is estimated that by 2050, there will be 88.5 million Americans aged 65 and older and, of these, 19 million will be among the "oldest old" (i.e., aged 85 and up). The increase in the aging population will have a number of consequences, such as a rise in health care costs since health care spending increases with age. Health care costs have risen over the past 30 years, from $714 billion in 1990 to more than $2.3 trillion in 2008. These rising costs have alarmed policy makers and individuals alike, and they provide an incentive to prioritize successful aging, including reduced burden from chronic diseases and greater functional independence.

Current physical activity recommendations for older adults in the United States are identical to recommendations for all adults: to achieve at least 150 minutes a week of moderate-intensity aerobic activity, 75 minutes of vigorous-intensity aerobic activity, or an equivalent mix of both moderate- and vigorous-intensity activity. The benefits of physical activity for older adults are wide ranging and include the following: preserving muscle and bone mass; reducing rates of functional decline; and improving glucose control, cardiovascular health, balance, and stability. Increasing physical activity in this population is very likely to support successful aging, which includes limiting disease and disease-related disability, ensuring physical and cognitive functioning is maintained, and preserving an older adult's ability to engage actively in life (Haselwandter et al., 2015).

One aspect of successful aging is aging in place, or the ability to live in one's own home confidently and comfortably. It is possible that a supportive built environment will both enhance one's physical functioning and also make one's home more comfortable for continued living. Researchers hypothesize that built environment effects likely differ by age and physical abilities, and that the built environment can have both facilitating and constraining effects on the activities of older adults. The role that the built environment could play in successful aging calls for a focus on determining which specific elements enhance the health and well-being of older adults, and identifying those factors that may impede older adults from activity. Maintaining mobility and independence are high priorities for older adults, and so it is crucial to determine which environmental factors could encourage these outcomes, and thereby prevent them from moving from more independent or assisted living conditions to nursing home facilities (Haselwandter et al., 2015). Figure 9.8 graphically displays a conceptual framework of aging and the built environment.

Clearly, services for aged persons with cognitive impairments and challenges (e.g., Alzheimers, dementia) can be quite complex, and aged persons may require extensive and intensive help from a social work practitioner to make plans for care, functioning, and almost every element of daily living. Nursing personnel and aides may assist with activities of daily living in a care facility but also in a client's personal residence. Social workers often are engaged in arranging such services and in working with families as well as social service agencies to provide help to the aged client in need. Services to older adults is one of the more rapidly growing fields of practice for social workers in the United States. Another professional concern for social workers is the development of regulations for facilities and services for older adults and the enforcement of those regulations through licensing inspections and other examinations of services for older people (Armstrong, Armstrong, & MacLeod, 2016). A major dimension of social work practice with aged persons, and really true of all areas of social welfare planning, is advocacy on behalf of clients. Social workers in macro practice positions are often engaged in developing services and policies or laws that benefit older persons and patients with major cognitive impairments.

Scientifically based information on older adults is relatively well developed, largely because of government programs for older people such as Social Security. Several US and other national governments collect and analyze information on older adults and services for them. Extensive portions of government budgets are dedicated to services for older persons. Work with the aging is a significant specialization in social work. It is often, however, not initially considered as a professional preference by the majority of social work students. As the overall US population

Figure 9.8 Framework of aging

SOURCE: Recreated from Haselwandter et al. (2015); Haselwandter, E. M., Corcoran, M. P., Folta, S. C., Hyatt, R., Fenton, M., & Nelson, M. E. (2015). The built environment, physical activity, and aging in the United States: A state of the science review. Journal of Aging and Physical Activity, 23(2), 323–329.

ages, it is likely to be a major focus of social services programs and social work employment for the remainder of the current century.

End of Life

End of life is both the culmination of the many developmental pathways occurring through the life cycle as well as a transformative experience for those who may be grieving the loss of a loved one. For individuals who are actively dying or near death, there is a great time for reflection and taking stock of one's own life. For those who are grieving the loss of a parent, sibling or other loved one, there is also the consideration that they, themselves, are undergoing a significant developmental milestone (Barner & Rosenblatt, 2008; Umberson, 2003). As with many of the stages discussed in this chapter, there are particular tasks that are salient to the end of life and its relationship to older adulthood. In Table 9.3, Byock (1996) provides a summary of developmental tasks significant to the end of life.

These developmental landmarks and tasks are key to understanding the work of hospice social workers and other practitioners dealing with end of life. Social workers can provide a much-needed bridge to achieving what Meier and colleagues (2016) describe as a "good death"—that is, a developmentally significant moment for both the dying individual and the family and others who are left to grieve (Meier

Table 9.3 END-OF-LIFE DEVELOPMENTAL TASK

Landmark	Taskwork
World affairs	Fiscal, legal, and social responsibilities
Relationship with community	Closure of relationships at employment, commerce, organizational, and congregational
Meaning of one's life	Reflection about actions (or life review), sharing stories, knowledge and wisdom transfer
Experienced love of self and others	Self-acknowledgment, self-forgiveness, acceptance of worthiness
Relationship with family and friends	Reconciliation, fullness of communication, and closure in important relationships
Accepting finality of life	Acknowledging totality of personal loss and experiencing personal pain of existential loss, emotional withdrawal, and acceptance of dependency
Development of personhood	Developing self-awareness beyond personal loss
Meaning of life in general	Recognizing transcendence, comfort with chaos
Letting go	Surrendering to the transcendent, doer and "taskwork" are one

Source: Authors' creation

et al., 2016). Hospice and palliative care social work are specialized disciplines within the social work field of practice and require specific skills and training, but they are areas of significant growth within the profession, as the population ages overall (Paul, 2016).

CONCLUSION

Understanding the life cycle and the scientific theories that frame its development are crucial to social workers designing a framework for understanding some of the common themes which have affected individuals throughout evolutionary history and which affect individuals throughout their lives in the present day. However, it is an important caveat that social workers must treat each individual's life cycle as unique and interpreted only through her or his own narratives. Scientific studies and theoretical models provide the social worker with the normative guidelines for practice, but they are no substitute for the practice itself, which is interpersonal, subjective, and informed by both human behavior and the social environment.

This chapter has been constructed to provide knowledge acquisition regarding the science of the life cycle and to point to areas where social work practitioners may utilize this knowledge to best intervene with clients and families who may be working through one or more of the developmental stages discussed. A clear combining of powerful scientific knowledge and informed practice can yield tremendous change in the lives of clients throughout all of the many and varied stages of life.

REFERENCES

Amsel, E., & Smetana, J. (2011). Constructivist processes in adolescent development. In E. Amsel & J. Smetana (Eds.), *Adolescent vulnerabilities and opportunities: Development and constructivist perspectives* (pp. 1–20). Cambridge: Cambridge University Press. https://doi.org/10.1017/cbo9781139042819.003

Armstrong, P., Armstrong, H., & MacLeod, K. K. (2016). The threats of privatization to security in long-term residential care. *Ageing International, 41*(1), 99–116. https://doi.org/10.1007/s12126-015-9228-0

Arnett, J. J. (2014). *Emerging adulthood: The winding road from the late teens through the twenties* New York, NY: Oxford University Press. https://doi.org/10.1093/acprof:oso/9780199929382.001.0001

Barner, J., & Rosenblatt, P. (2008). Giving at a loss: Couple exchange after the death of a parent. *Mortality, 13*(4), 318–334. https://doi.org/10.1080/13576270802383899

Barth, R. P., Lloyd, E. C., Christ, S. L., Chapman, M. V, & Dickinson, N. S. (2008). Child welfare worker characteristics and job satisfaction: A national study. *Social Work, 53*(3), 199–209. https://doi.org/10.1093/sw/53.3.199

Beach, S. R., Carpenter, C. R., Rosen, T., Sharps, P., & Gelles, R. (2016). Screening and detection of elder abuse: Research opportunities and lessons learned from emergency geriatric care, intimate partner violence, and child abuse. *Journal of Elder Abuse & Neglect, 28*(4–5), 185–216. https://doi.org/10.1080/08946566.2016.1229241

Belluck, P. (2016, December 20). Pregnancy changes the brain in ways that may help mothering, study finds. *The New York Times*, A15.

Berrick, J., Dickens, J., Pösö, T., & Skivenes, M. (2016). Parents' involvement in care order decisions: A cross-country study of front-line practice. *Child & Family Social Work, 22*(2), 626–637. https://doi.org/10.1111/cfs.12277

Black, M. M., Walker, S. P., Fernald, L. C. H., Andersen, C. T., DiGirolamo, A. M., Lu, C., ... Grantham-McGregor, S. (2017). Early childhood development coming of age: Science through the life course. *The Lancet, 389*(10064), 77–90. https://doi.org/10.1016/s0140-6736(16)31389-7

Blakemore, S.-J., & Choudhury, S. (2006). Development of the adolescent brain: Implications for executive function and social cognition. *Journal of Child Psychology and Psychiatry, 47*(3–4), 296–312. https://doi.org/10.1111/j.1469-7610.2006.01611.x

Bogin, B. (1999). *Patterns of human growth* (2nd edition) (Vol. 23). Cambridge, UK: Cambridge University Press.

Bogin, B., & Smith, B. H. (1996). Evolution of the human life cycle. *American Journal of Human Biology, 8*(6), 703–716. https://doi.org/10.1002/(sici)1520-6300(1996)8:6<703::aid-ajhb2>3.0.co;2-u

Bronfenbrenner, U. (1986). Ecology of the family as a context for human development: Research perspectives. *Developmental Psychology, 22*(6), 723–742. https://doi.org/10.1037//0012-1649.22.6.723

Byock, I. R. (1996). The nature of suffering and the nature of opportunity at the end of life. *Clinics in Geriatric Medicine, 12*(2), 237.

Carbajal, J., & Aguiree, R. T. P. (2013). Traumatic stress response transactions on development. In H. Matto, J. Strolin-Goltzman & M. Ballan (Eds.), *Neuroscience for social work: Current research and practice* (pp. 69–86). New York, NY: Springer.

Chopik, W. J., Edelstein, R. S., & Fraley, R. C. (2013). From the cradle to the grave: Age differences in attachment from early adulthood to old age. *Journal of Personality, 81*(2), 171–183. https://doi.org/10.1111/j.1467-6494.2012.00793.x

Cooper, M. L., Shaver, P. R., & Collins, N. L. (1998). Attachment styles, emotion regulation, and adjustment in adolescence. *Journal of Personality and Social Psychology, 74*(5), 1380–1397. https://doi.org/10.1037//0022-3514.74.5.1380

Dahl, R. E., & Lewin, D. S. (2002). Pathways to adolescent health sleep regulation and behavior. *Journal of Adolescent Health, 31*(6), 175–184. https://doi.org/10.1016/s1054-139x(02)00506-2

Darwin, C. (1872). *The expression of the emotions in man and animals*. London, England: John Murray. https://doi.org/10.1037/10001-000

Diehl, M., Elnick, A. B., Bourbeau, L. S., & Labouvie-Vief, G. (1998). Adult attachment styles: Their relations to family context and personality. *Journal of Personality and Social Psychology, 74*(6), 1656–1669. https://doi.org/10.1037//0022-3514.74.6.1656

Diekema, D. (2004). Parental refusals of medical treatment: The harm principle as threshold for state intervention. *Theoretical Medicine and Bioethics, 25*(4), 243–264. https://doi.org/10.1007/s11017-004-3146-6

Dunkel Schetter, C. (2011). Psychological science on pregnancy: Stress processes, biopsychosocial models, and emerging research issues. *Annual Review of Psychology, 62*(1), 531–558. https://doi.org/10.1146/annurev.psych.031809.130727

Ellett, A. J. (2009). Intentions to remain employed in child welfare: The role of human caring, self-efficacy beliefs, and professional organizational culture. *Children and Youth Services Review, 31*(1), 78–88. https://doi.org/10.1016/j.childyouth.2008.07.002

Erikson, E. H., & Erikson, J. M. (1998). *The life cycle completed (extended version).* New York, NY: WW Norton & Company.

Fry, R. (2018). Millennials are the largest generation in the U.S. labor force. Retrieved from the *Pew Research Center* website: https://pewrsr.ch/2GTG00o.

Gardner, M., & Steinberg, L. (2005). Peer influence on risk taking, risk preference, and risky decision making in adolescence and adulthood: An experimental study. *Developmental Psychology, 41*(4), 625–635. https://doi.org/10.1037/0012-1649.41.4.625

Ginsberg, L. (1998). *Careers in social work* (2nd ed.). New York, NY: Pearson.

Göllner, R., Roberts, B. W., Damian, R. I., Lüdtke, O., Jonkmann, K., & Trautwein, U. (2016). Whose "storm and stress" is it? Parent and child reports of personality development in the transition to early adolescence. *Journal of Personality, 85*(3), 376–387. https://doi.org/10.1111/jopy.12246

Gröpel, P., & Kuhl, J. (2009). Work-life balance and subjective well-being: The mediating role of need fulfilment. *British Journal of Psychology, 100*(2), 365–375. https://doi.org/10.1348/000712608x337797

Gutmann, D. (1976). Individual adaptation in the middle years: Developmental issues in the masculine mid-life crisis. *Journal of Geriatric Psychiatry, 9*(1), 41–59.

Haselwandter, E. M., Corcoran, M. P., Folta, S. C., Hyatt, R., Fenton, M., & Nelson, M. E. (2015). The built environment, physical activity, and aging in the United States: A state of the science review. *Journal of Aging and Physical Activity, 23*(2), 323–329. https://doi.org/10.1123/japa.2013-0151

Havighurst, R. J. (1956). Rewards of maturity for the teacher. *The Educational Forum, 20*(2), 145–150. https://doi.org/10.1080/00131725609340264

Higgins, C., Duxbury, L., & Lee, C. (1994). Impact of life-cycle stage and gender on the ability to balance work and family responsibilities. *Family Relations, 43*(2), 144. https://doi.org/10.2307/585316

Hoekzema, E., Barba-Müller, E., Pozzobon, C., Picado, M., Lucco, F., García-García, D., ... Vilarroya, O. (2016). Pregnancy leads to long-lasting changes in human brain structure. *Nature Neuroscience, 20*(2), 287–296. https://doi.org/10.1038/nn.4458

James, J. B., Matz-Costa, C., & Smyer, M. A. (2016). Retirement security: It's not just about the money. *American Psychologist, 71*(4), 334–344. https://doi.org/10.1037/a0040220

Jaques, E. (1965). Death and the mid-life crisis. *The International Journal of Psycho-Analysis, 46*, 502.

Johnson, M. K. (2001). Change in job values during the transition to adulthood. *Work and Occupations, 28*(3), 315–345. https://doi.org/10.1177/0730888401028003004

Kail, R. V, & Cavanaugh, J. C. (2016). *Essentials of human development: A life-span view.* Boston, MA: Cengage Learning.

Kuh, D., Ben-Shlomo, Y., Lynch. J., & Hallqvist, C. (2003). Life course epidemiology. *Journal of Epidemiology & Community Health, 57*(10), 778–783. https://doi.org/10.1136/jech.57.10.778

Lerner, R. M., & Steinberg, L. (2009). *Handbook of adolescent psychology, volume 1: Individual bases of adolescent development* (Vol. 1). Hoboken, NJ: John Wiley & Sons.

Lichter, D. T., Michelmore, K., Turner, R. N., & Sassler, S. (2016). Pathways to a stable union? Pregnancy and childbearing among cohabiting and married couples. *Population Research and Policy Review, 35*(3), 377–399. https://doi.org/10.1007/s11113-016-9392-2

Lindberg, L. D., & Kost, K. (2013). Exploring U.S. men's birth intentions. *Maternal and Child Health Journal, 18*(3), 625–633. https://doi.org/10.1007/s10995-013-1286-x

Mayville, S., Katz, R. C., Gipson, M. T., & Cabral, K. (1999). Assessing the prevalence of body dysmorphic disorder in an ethnically diverse group of adolescents. *Journal of Child and Family Studies, 8*(3), 357–362. https://doi.org/10.1023/a:1022023514730

Meier, E. A., Gallegos, J. V, Thomas, L. P. M., Depp, C. A., Irwin, S. A., & Jeste, D. V. (2016). Defining a good death (successful dying): Literature review and a call for research and public dialogue. *The American Journal of Geriatric Psychiatry, 24*(4), 261–271. https://doi.org/10.1016/j.jagp.2016.01.135

Parsons, J. T., Siegel, A. W., & Cousins, J. H. (1997). Late adolescent risk-taking: Effects of perceived benefits and perceived risks on behavioral intentions and behavioral change. *Journal of Adolescence, 20*(4), 381–392. https://doi.org/10.1006/jado.1997.0094

Pattakos, G., Koch, C. G., Brizzio, M. E., Batizy, L. H., Sabik, J. F., Blackstone, E. H., & Lauer, M. S. (2012). Outcome of patients who refuse transfusion after cardiac surgery. *Archives of Internal Medicine, 172*(15), 1154–1160. https://doi.org/10.1001/archinternmed.2012.2449

Paul, S. (2016). Working with communities to develop resilience in end of life and bereavement care: Hospices, schools and health promoting palliative care. *Journal of Social Work Practice, 30*(2), 187–201. https://doi.org/10.1080/02650533.2016.1168383

Petersen, A. C., Compas, B. E., Brooks-Gunn, J., Stemmler, M., Ey, S., & Grant, K. E. (1993). Depression in adolescence. *American Psychologist, 48*(2), 155–168. https://doi.org/10.1037/0003-066x.48.2.155

Roenneberg, T., Kuehnle, T., Pramstaller, P. P., Ricken, J., Havel, M., Guth, A., & Merrow, M. (2004). A marker for the end of adolescence. *Current Biology, 14*(24), R1038–R1039. https://doi.org/10.1016/j.cub.2004.11.039

Roeser, R. W., Eccles, J. S., & Sameroff, A. J. (1998). Academic and emotional functioning in early adolescence: Longitudinal relations, patterns, and prediction by experience in middle school. *Development and Psychopathology, 10*(2), 321–352. https://doi.org/10.1017/s0954579498001631

Roisman, G. I., Masten, A. S., Coatsworth, J. D., & Tellegen, A. (2004). Salient and emerging developmental tasks in the transition to adulthood. *Child Development, 75*(1), 123–133. https://doi.org/10.1111/j.1467-8624.2004.00658.x

Sawyer, S. M., Afifi, R. A., Bearinger, L. H., Blakemore, S.-J., Dick, B., Ezeh, A. C., & Patton, G. C. (2012). Adolescence: A foundation for future health. *The Lancet, 379*(9826), 1630–1640. https://doi.org/10.1016/s0140-6736(12)60072-5

Seipel, M. M. O. (1999). Social consequences of malnutrition. *Social Work, 44*(5), 416–425. https://doi.org/10.1093/sw/44.5.416

Shulman, S., Feldman, B., Blatt, S. J., Cohen, O., & Mahler, A. (2005). Emerging adulthood. *Journal of Adolescent Research, 20*(5), 577–603. https://doi.org/10.1177/0743558405274913

Sierles, F. S. (1982). Alcoholism. *Clinical Behavioral Science*. In F. S. Sierles (Ed.), *Clinical behavioral science* (pp. 127–138). Jamaica, NY: Spectrum. https://doi.org/10.1007/978-94-011-7973-7_10

Smetana, J. G., Campione-Barr, N., & Metzger, A. (2006). Adolescent development in interpersonal and societal contexts. *Annual Review of Psychology, 57*(1), 255–284. https://doi.org/10.1146/annurev.psych.57.102904.190124

Snowling, M., Bishop, D. V. M., & Stothard, S. E. (2000). Is preschool language impairment a risk factor for dyslexia in adolescence? *Journal of Child Psychology and Psychiatry, 41*(5), 587–600. https://doi.org/10.1017/s0021963099005752

Steinberg, L. (2014). *Age of opportunity: Lessons from the new science of adolescence.* New York, NY: Houghton Mifflin Harcourt.

Steinberg, L., & Morris, A. S. (2001). Adolescent development. *Journal of Cognitive Education and Psychology, 2*(1), 55–87. https://doi.org/10.1891/194589501787383444

Stillerman, K. P., Mattison, D. R., Giudice, L. C., & Woodruff, T. J. (2008). Environmental exposures and adverse pregnancy outcomes: A review of the science. *Reproductive Sciences, 15*(7), 631–650. https://doi.org/10.1177/1933719108322436

Swerdloff, R. S., & Odell, W. D. (1975). Hormonal mechanisms in the onset of puberty. *Postgraduate Medical Journal, 51*(594), 200–208. https://doi.org/10.1136/pgmj.51.594.200

Tanner, J. M. (2009). Growth and maturation during adolescence. *Nutrition Reviews, 39*(2), 43–55. https://doi.org/10.1111/j.1753-4887.1981.tb06734.x

Taylor, B., Miller, E., Farrington, C. P., Petropoulos, M.-C., Favot-Mayaud, I., Li, J., & Waight, P. A. (1999). Autism and measles, mumps, and rubella vaccine: No epidemiological evidence for a causal association. *The Lancet, 353*(9169), 2026–2029. https://doi.org/10.1016/s0140-6736(99)01239-8

Umberson, D. (2003). *Death of a parent: Transition to a new adult identity.* Cambridge, UK: Cambridge University Press.

United Nations, Department of Economic and Social Affairs, Population Division (2015). *World population prospectus: The 2015 revision, key findings and advance tables* (Working paper no. ESA/P/WP.241). Retrieved from http://www.un.org/en/development/desa/publications/world-population-prospects-2015-revision.html.

Wadlington, W. (1994). Medical decision making for and by children: Tensions between parent, state, and child. *University of Illinois Law Review, 2*, 311–336.

Woodward, L. J., & Fergusson, D. M. (2001). Life course outcomes of young people with anxiety disorders in adolescence. *Journal of the American Academy of Child & Adolescent Psychiatry, 40*(9), 1086–1093. https://doi.org/10.1097/00004583-200109000-00018

10

Social Work and the Science of Execution

Participation in capital trials has ethical implications for the helping professions (e.g., social work and medicine) that operate under a do-no-harm ethic. Execution is antithetical to the do-no-harm mandate and creates difficult professional challenges for social workers who practice with so-called vulnerable populations, such as those groups specially designated in human subjects research (e.g., persons with intellectual disability and children, who for this very reason are constitutionally protected from execution, and prison inmates).

Patterns in execution rates raise significant questions regarding the fair distribution of justice in US society. Predictors of who is most likely to be executed include wealth and income status; the skill set of the legal representation; geographic location; and race of the victim. Moreover, people of color are significantly more likely to be executed than are White people—with this being especially true if the victim is White. In addition to these findings, advances in deoxyribonucleic acid (DNA) testing have shown us that persons who are innocent of the crime for which they stand accused continue to be sentenced to death. Since 1973, more than 156 people have been removed from death row in 26 states due to a finding of innocence; and across the United States, approximately 10% of those sentenced to death have been exonerated (American Civil Liberties Union, 2012).

From a structural perspective, these trends betray the historical and present-day biases of American institutions that result not only in the systemic and systematic denial of rights but also in the state-sanctioned taking of a person's life—even if cruel and unusual. To this point, science plays an integral role in social work's relationship with capital punishment, for when states and state actors fail to apply science to policy appropriately, this can result in a lingering and painful, and therefore unconstitutional, death. In this way, botched executions present opportunities for social work professionals and others to come together in order to challenge existing death penalty laws.

THE HISTORY OF CAPITAL PUNISHMENT IN THE UNITED STATES

Capital punishment, also commonly referred to as the death penalty (and here used interchangeably), has persisted for nearly four centuries on American soil

(Latzer & McCord, 2011). The term "capital" derives from the Latin word *caput*, meaning "head," and suggests that capital punishment may have originally referred to decapitation or beheading (Latzer & McCord, 2011). Capital punishment, now a relic of the UK criminal justice system, came to the American colonies beginning in the 1600s as part of the British legacy (Latzer & McCord, 2011). According to Latzer and McCord (2011), at best estimate, there have been roughly 20,000 executions in the United States since this time. Although early in its nationhood the United States renounced much of the British punishment legacy, including cruel and unusual methods for dispensing criminal justice (Morris & Rothman, 1995), capital punishment itself retained a legitimate role in the early US criminal justice system. The topic of the death penalty continues to grow more controversial over time, as reflected by diminishing public support captured by the Gallup Poll.

From colonial times until the 1800s, a majority of states imposed the penalty of death for all homicides and many felonies (Meany, 2004). By 1820, states had either abolished the death penalty except for the crime of first-degree murder or had strictly limited use of the death penalty to only the most serious of crimes (Morris & Rothman, 1997). A small number of states retained the death penalty for nonhomicide crimes such as rape, kidnapping, and armed robbery; however, rarely, if ever, did states invoke the death penalty for such crimes, with notable exceptions occurring in the South (Latzer & McCord, 2011). In the southern states, capital punishment functioned as a state-sanctioned expression of racial bias. For example, an African American man who stood accused of raping a Caucasian American woman in the South could be lynched or hanged without trial (Latzer & McCord, 2011).

The period from 1890 to present day represents a crucial era in the transformation of America's capital punishment from its traditional to its more modern form vis-à-vis the continued centralization and professionalization of execution (Sarat, 2014). By 1950, about one quarter of the states—but none in the South—had abolished the death penalty (Latzer & McCord, 2011). During this time, criminal defendants also gained considerable procedural protections that included (1) an expansion of federal constitutional rights; (2) more consistent assistance of defense lawyers; and (3) greater availability of appellate review (Latzer & McCord, 2011). From 1950 to 1968, the United States saw a decline in death sentences and executions (Latzer & McCord, 2011). The reason for this decline was threefold: (1) the expansion of rights of criminal defendants; (2) waning public support; and (3) the civil rights movement (Latzer & McCord, 2011).

In the period following the nation's one and only moratorium on the death penalty (from approximately 1972 to 1976, with varying estimates as to how long states actually refrained from the practice), death sentencing and execution have fallen even more dramatically over the last decade in the United States. In fact, the United States now imposes fewer death sentences and executes fewer people than at any time in the past 25 years (Sarat, 2014). With over half of Americans still favoring capital punishment, the death penalty remains a contemporary and controversial topic of interest. As a general practice, capital punishment is under continued scrutiny by the US Supreme Court, thanks to questions raised about the method of execution and the ability to precisely identify those whom society deems categorically and fundamentally undeserving of the death penalty. In 2015, the US Supreme Court approved the execution drug midazolam (linked with "botched" executions and argued to violate the Cruel and Unusual Punishments Clause of the Eighth Amendment) in a five-to-four decision. In their dissenting opinions, Justices Breyer and Ginsberg questioned the constitutionality of the death penalty itself. As 2018 approaches, some death penalty states such as Nevada and Nebraska will begin to use the controversial opioid, fentanyl, as part of their lethal injection protocol. A synthetic painkiller, fentanyl has been the driving force behind the nation's opioid epidemic and has been linked to the overdose deaths of tens of thousands of Americans in 2016. Medical doctors and human rights activists are concurrently working to oppose the use of fentanyl for execution, citing that the untested use of fentanyl could lead to painful and botched executions.

The Role of Social Work in Capital Proceedings

As we will discuss later, mental health experts, such as social work professionals, are playing an increasingly important role in the adjudication process. For example, in capital cases, social work professionals may testify as expert witnesses in the clinical determination of intellectual disability (i.e., a protected class of capital defendants since 2002); serve as mitigation experts; or work therapeutically with capital defendants and/or their family members (Beck, Britto, & Andrews, 2007). Not only is there a practical application of social work to capital proceedings, but there is also an ethical application. As promulgated by the National Association of Social Workers (NASW)—the largest membership organization of professional social workers in the world that works to enhance the professional growth and development of its members, to create and maintain professional standards, and to advance sound social policies—the social work profession is rooted in an ethic of "inherent dignity and worth of the person" and "centrality of human relationships" (NASW, 2008), which is seemingly violated in the instance of capital punishment. It should come as no surprise, then, that the official stance of the NASW opposes use of the death penalty in all cases. Box 10.1 is an official policy statement issued by the NASW in August 2002 titled *Social Workers Oppose Death Penalty and Capital Punishment*. It may also be retrieved electronically at http://www.socialworkers.org/da/da_2002/policy_statements/policy3.asp.

Defining the Science of Execution

For the purpose of this chapter, the science of execution will broadly focus on the two following scientific pursuits: (1) the science of developing and implementing fair capital adjudication procedures; and (2) the science of developing and

Box 10.1

NASW OFFICIAL POLICY STATEMENT 2002

Social Workers Oppose Death Penalty and Capital Punishment
The National Association of Social Workers (NASW) opposes the death penalty and supports a life sentence as an alternative. NASW maintains that the integrity of human life and well-being are among the highest values to which a society aspires. The death penalty is a violation of human rights that belong to every human being, even those who have committed crimes.

According to research, data show that capital punishment is not a deterrent to homicide. In other countries where the death penalty has been abolished, their homicide rate is still lower than that of the United States. NASW also disagrees with the argument that capital punishment is a more cost-effective solution than life in prison. According to numerous studies, the criminal justice system would be less costly if there were no death penalty, because the costs are higher in a capital murder case, both in terms of the initial trial and appeals.

The death penalty has always been and continues to be differentially applied to people who are poor, disadvantaged, of limited mental or intellectual capacity, and people from ethnic or racial minority groups. The US General Accounting Office, on the basis of a review of 28 empirical studies, reported a pattern of racial disparities at all levels: charging, sentencing, and imposition of the death penalty.

Additionally, about 90% of people facing the death penalty cannot afford their own attorney and no state has met the standards developed by the American Bar Association (ABA) for appointment, performance, and compensation of counsel for indigent prisoners.

Therefore, NASW agrees with evidence that shows the application of the death penalty is too arbitrary, too prone to error, and unfairly administered supporting the argument that the system cannot be reliable enough to ensure the principle of life.

---

perfecting humane execution methods. As some scholars maintain, the issues of fair adjudication procedure and humane execution method serve to philosophically distinguish—at least ostensibly—capital punishment from capital murder.

CAPITAL ADJUDICATION PROCEDURES: THE SCIENCE OF FAIRNESS

Presently, the death penalty is considered to be an increasingly outlier practice (Leading Cases, Harvard Law Review, 2014). As of June 2015, 31 states sanctioned the use of the death penalty; 19 states did not (this figure includes four states with a governor-imposed moratorium) (Death Penalty Information Center, 2016a). Figure 10.1 is a map of death penalty states (coded in red) in 2016. According to the American Civil Liberties Union, over 66% of all capital convictions and sentences are reversed "because of serious error during trial or sentencing" (American Civil Liberties Union Capital Punishment Project, 2015).

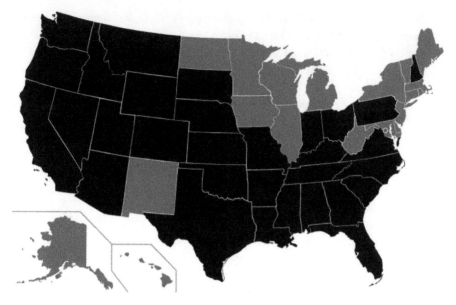

Figure 10.1 Map of death penalty states
SOURCE: By JayCoop - Own work - STATES AND CAPITAL PUNISHMENT - National Conference of State
Legislatures, CC BY-SA 4.0, https://commons.wikimedia.org/w/index.php?curid=56019685

THE FOUR-YEAR NATIONAL MORATORIUM

From 1972 until 1976, there was a national *moratorium* (i.e., temporary prohibition) against the death penalty in the United States. The two cases that started and ended the temporary prohibition against capital punishment in the United States both originated in Georgia. Just 4 years apart, the respective cases were *Furman v. Georgia* (1972) and *Gregg v. Georgia* (1976).

Furman v. Georgia

In the 1972 *Furman v. Georgia* decision, the US Supreme Court overturned existing death penalty laws on the grounds that, as they were currently being implemented, the laws violated the Eighth Amendment's Cruel and Unusual Punishments Clause (Feluren, 2013). A further explanation of the Cruel and Unusual Punishments Clause follows in a later section. Supreme Court Justices representing the majority opinion reasoned that the then extant death penalty laws resulted in a disproportionate and arbitrary application of the death penalty, effectively discriminating against persons earning low income and those who were non-Caucasian American (Latzer & McCord, 2011). The decision of the US Supreme Court was seemingly influenced by a substantial decrease in death sentences and executions beginning in the 1930s, as well as by the outright abolition of the death penalty by several states in the 1950s and 1960s (Latzer & McCord, 2011). As they further point out:

Three characteristics typified death sentencing in the United States before the Furman case. First, in most jurisdictions a broad variety of murders [...] were eligible for death sentences. Second, most jurisdictions used a "unitary trial" which meant that the issue of punishment was submitted to the jury along with the issue of guilt [...] Third, jurors were typically given little or no guidance regarding how to decide whether the penalty should be death or imprisonment. (Latzer & McCord, 2011, p. 37)

While Justices Brennan and Marshall expressly contended that the death penalty was unconstitutional in and of itself in the *Furman* (1972) decision, Justices Stewart and White rejected their absolutist position, making it possible that future statutes could be enacted with sufficient potential for reduced arbitrariness so as to withstand federal judicial review (Latzer & McCord, 2011). In the year prior, by a 6–3 vote, the US Supreme Court rejected a claim in *McGautha v. California* that the death penalty was unconstitutionally arbitrary under the Due Process Clause of the Fifth and 14th Amendments. Yet the US Supreme Court accepted similar arguments in a 5–4 vote in *Furman v. Georgia* (1972) under the Eighth Amendment. Latzer and McCord (2011) attribute this difference in outcome to the fact that Justices Stewart and White "switched sides" (p. 37). After the *Furman* (1972) decision and resultant confusion, 35 states rewrote their death penalty statutes in an effort to comply with the US Supreme Court ruling. Although some states enacted mandatory death penalty laws in response to *Furman* (1972), such laws were deemed unconstitutional (*Woodson v. North Carolina*, 1976). In the same year that the US Supreme Court ruled against mandatory death sentences, it also reinstated the death penalty (*Gregg v. Georgia*, 1976).

Gregg v. Georgia

The US Supreme Court reinstated capital punishment in light of *Gregg v. Georgia* (1976), finding that, as a penalty for the crime of murder, the sentence of death was not excessive, and therefore not in violation of Eighth Amendment protections (Feluren, 2013). The Court also held the death penalty was not a constitutional violation per se, as it could serve the social purposes of retribution and deterrence. To satisfy the goal of retribution, it was ruled that the crime committed must be serious enough to warrant the punishment exacted (Feluren, 2013). In its decision, the US Supreme Court upheld Georgia's new capital sentencing procedures, reasoning that the Georgia rules sufficiently addressed the concern for arbitrary application (*Gregg v. Georgia*, 1976). The Georgia statute approved in *Gregg* (1976) provided that aggravating and mitigating factors must be proved during a separate penalty proceeding (the sentencing phase of the trial)—a phase to be conducted *only after* the guilt/innocence phase of the trial and *only upon* a finding of guilt. Named for its two separate phases, Georgia's model is a type of bifurcated trial procedure. The bifurcated trial requires juries to engage in a separate sentencing phase during capital trials, and it ultimately affirms the critical role of mental health experts (e.g., psychologists, psychiatrists, and clinically licensed social workers) in the mitigation phase of death penalty cases (DeMatteo, Marczyk, & Pich, 2007). The Georgia statute became the model for other death penalty states (Latzer & McCord, 2011).

THE ADJUDICATION PROCESS

Beginning in the mid-1800s, American jurisdictions abandoned mandatory death sentencing in favor of allowing jurors to choose between death and imprisonment (Latzer & McCord, 2011; Meany, 2004). A primary reason for abandoning mandatory death sentencing was *jury nullification*. This was the process by which jurors acquitted guilty defendants in order to avoid sending such persons to the gallows to be hanged (Latzer & McCord, 2011). It was also during the 1800s that an appeals process was instated (Latzer & Mccord, 2011), providing capital defendants with additional legal recourse. This provision seemed fair, as a procedural error resulting in death is arguably a gross miscarriage of justice. The current stages in capital cases include pretrial (investigating, charging, plea bargaining), trial (jury selection, guilt/innocence phase, sentencing phase), direct appeal, certiorari petition to the US Supreme Court, state post conviction remedy, federal habeas corpus, and executive clemency (Latzer & McCord, 2011). Special attention is paid to the pretrial and trial stages. Despite some consistency across states with regard to procedure, it is important to note that rules regarding evidence and expert testimony vary from state to state, as do many—but certainly not all—of the statutory mitigating factors (Andrews, 1991).

Aggravation

During the sentencing phase of a capital trial, aggravating and mitigating evidence is presented to the jury. An aggravating factor is any fact or circumstance that increases the severity or culpability of a criminal act (Cornell University Legal Institute, n.d.a). In general, such factors include simultaneous felonies; previous conviction for violent offenses; crimes committed in remuneration or hire; lack of remorse; and characteristics of the victim such as youth or status as a law enforcement official (Andrews, 1991). The state must prove *beyond a reasonable doubt*, or to the degree of moral certainty, the presence of at least one aggravating factor before the death sentence can be imposed (Andrews, 1991).

Mitigation

A mitigating factor is any fact or circumstance that lessens the severity or culpability of a criminal act (Cornell University Legal Institute, n.d.d). Unlike aggravating factors, mitigating factors are not limited to any given set of circumstances and need not be proved *beyond a reasonable doubt* (Andrews, 1991). However, it is important to note that one state, Georgia, is the only state to require that mitigating factors be proved beyond a reasonable doubt—the highest of three standards of proof. Of the 31 death penalty states, 25 states currently implement the lowest standard (*a preponderance of the evidence*) and five states implement the intermediary standard (*clear and convincing evidence*). Although mitigating factors may vary from state to state, they typically include the defendant's youth; emotional or mental disability; intellectual disability; the victim's participation in the crime; chronic maltreatment during childhood; remorse; capacity for rehabilitation in prison; posttraumatic stress disorder resultant from military service; intoxication and chemical dependency; and efforts to contribute prosocially to society (Andrews, 1991).

Social Work and Mitigation

In the 1978 *Lockett v. Ohio* decision, the US Supreme Court ruled that in death penalty adjudication procedures, the defense be permitted to present mitigating evidence such that would warrant a punishment less than death (Andrews, 1991). For decades social workers have been increasingly recognized by courts as expert witnesses in a variety of court proceedings (Andrews, 1991; Gothard, 1989). For instance, social work professionals are well positioned to function as mitigation experts in capital cases: that is, they have the skill set to thoroughly and reliably conduct, analyze, and report social history findings that may be considered to warrant a lesser punishment than death (Andrews, 1991).

Individuals who commit the offense of capital murder typically have a complex social history; themes of deprivation, untreated learning or mental health disorders, early exposure to violence, and severe forms of abuse are pervasive. Social evaluations generally consist of three main parts: (1) a description of findings regarding the defendant's social history and functioning; (2) an interpretation of the findings from a specified theoretical perspective; and (3) an opinion regarding the relevance of the findings of the crime (Andrews, 1991). Owing to this social work professional skill set, defense attorneys are likely to seek social work consultation (Andrews, 1991). Social workers may function in trials as either fact witnesses or as expert witnesses (Andrews, 1991). Whereas fact witnesses have firsthand knowledge of a situation (e.g., a case worker who knows the defendant), expert witnesses are called upon to express a professional, interpretive opinion about the facts of the case (Andrews, 1991). The role of the expert witness is to construct a reliable and holistic description of the defendant. In mitigation, these facts presumably support a sentence lesser than death.

As discussed earlier, findings of intellectual disability and youth function as mitigating factors; however, they are much more than this, for they also preclude defendants' eligibility for death sentencing de facto. As of 2002 and 2005, respectively, individuals who have been found to have intellectual disability and individuals who commissioned a capital crime while under the age of majority (i.e., 18 years) may not lawfully be executed. Such an execution, according to the evolving standards of decency as found by the US Supreme Court in 2002 and 2005, would constitute an instance of cruel and unusual punishment—which is to say, such an execution would be a violation of the Eighth Amendment of the US Constitution. Before discussing the two protected classes of defendants, what follows next is a brief overview of the Cruel and Unusual Punishments Clause of the Eighth Amendment.

CRUEL AND UNUSUAL PUNISHMENTS CLAUSE

Ratified in 1791, the provision against Cruel and Unusual Punishments is a clause of the Eighth Amendment of the US Constitution (Latzer & McCord, 2011). The Clause was derived verbatim from the English Bill of Rights of 1689, and it was written in response to King James II, who used barbarous tactics in order to suppress a revolution against him (Latzer & McCord, 2011). The Clause was intended to restrict the federal government from inflicting more pain than was necessary to extinguish life, but not to abolish the practice of capital punishment altogether (Latzer & McCord, 2011). It could be argued by opponents, however, that the death penalty is in fact so inherently psychologically cruel and unusual that protocols standardly require one or more physical barriers to be placed between the inmate and the source of death (e.g., a hood and a canvas in the firing squad method). It is in fact so psychologically disturbing that there is also a strong interest in protecting the executioner/s from the adverse psychological effects (e.g., the canvas and the blank round in the firing squad method). Table 10.1 list important court decisions regarding the Cruel and Unusual Punishments Clause.

Protected Classes of Defendants

In the pretrial stage of a capital case, the prosecution must determine if the murder constitutes a crime at all. In a small number of cases, such as those involving self-defense, homicides are considered justifiable. An even smaller percentage of cases are excused if the person who committed the murder was deemed to have diminished culpability. As was discussed earlier, the Court has held two categories of defendants to be insufficiently blameworthy: capital defendants with intellectual disability and capital defendants who commissioned the crime before reaching the age of majority (Latzer & McCord, 2011). Before discussing the protected classes of capital defendants more in depth, it will be helpful to first address the related issue of competency: namely, the insanity plea and the plea of diminished capacity.

INSANITY
In the legal system, mens rea and actus reus are two general requirements for criminal sanction against an individual (Feuerstein et al., 2005). Mens rea refers to the intent to commit an act and have a desired consequence, and actus reus refers to the act fitting within the criminal statute (Feuerstein et al., 2005). The mens rea requirement is the idea that a person must possess a guilty state of mind and be aware of his or her misconduct (Cornell University Legal Institute, n.d.c). The

Table 10.1 IMPORTANT CRUEL AND UNUSUAL PUNISHMENTS DECISIONS

Court Decision	Year	Decision
In re Kemmler	1890	Punishments are considered cruel and unusual when they involve torture or lingering death
Weems v. United States	1910	Punishments are cruel and unusual that are disproportionate to the offense
Trop v. Dulles	1958	The Eighth Amendment must draw its meaning from the evolving standards of decency of society
Furman v. Georgia	1972	Due to arbitrary applications of the death penalty, it was temporarily prohibited as a form of cruel and unusual punishment
Gregg v. Georgia	1976	The death penalty is not cruel and unusual per se, as the punishment of death is proportionate to the crime of murder, but it does require that arbitrary effects be ameliorated vis-à-vis sound statutes and procedures
Atkins v. Virginia	2002	The sentence of death as handed down to a defendant with intellectual disability constitutes cruel and unusual punishment due to diminished culpability
Roper v. Simmons	2005	The sentence of death as handed down to a defendant who commissioned a capital crime while under the age of majority constitutes cruel and unusual punishment due to diminished culpability

insanity defense derives from the idea that certain mental illnesses such as psychosis can interfere with an individual's ability to form mens rea as required by the law (Feuerstein et al., 2005). A plea of "reason of insanity" is the equivalent of pleading "not guilty" (Cornell University Legal Institute, n.d.b). In a plea of insanity, the defendant acknowledges commission of the crime, but the finding of mental illness such as a psychotic disorder precludes the defendant's legal responsibility (Cornell University Legal Institute, n.d.b). Generally, the defendant must prove that due to mental illness, the defendant did not have knowledge of killing someone, or thought that such conduct was acceptable by society's standards (Latzer & McCord, 2011). According to Latzer and McCord (2011), a defendant who was legally insane at the time of the killing should be acquitted by reason of insanity. In order to determine the validity of an insanity plea, many jurisdictions use a variant of the M'Naughten test for insanity, and only a tiny proportion of cases can satisfy its standards (Latzer & McCord, 2011).

DIMINISHED CAPACITY

Like a plea of insanity, diminished capacity requires a mental competency evaluation (Cornell University Legal Institute, n.d.b). Insanity and diminished capacity differ on the point that a person raising a claim of diminished capacity is merely pleading a lesser crime (Cornell University Legal Institute, n.d.b). Whereas a successful insanity plea is likely to result in a verdict of "not guilty," and the defendant is likely to be commissioned to a psychiatric institution, a plea of diminished capacity is likely to result in the defendant being convicted of a lesser offense (Cornell University Legal Institute, n.d.b). The diminished capacity plea is based on the belief that certain people, because of mental impairment, are not capable of reaching the mental state required to commit a particular crime (i.e., mens rea). For example, a successful plea of diminished capacity in a murder trial is likely to result in the charge being reduced to manslaughter (Cornell University Legal Institute, n.d.b).

DEFENDANTS WITH INTELLECTUAL DISABILITY

In the landmark *Atkins v. Virginia* (2002) decision, the US Supreme Court determined there to be a national consensus that the aims of the criminal justice system (i.e., retribution and deterrence) cannot be penologically fulfilled when capital defendants are evidenced to have intellectual disability (formerly termed *mental retardation*). Deficits in intellectual and adaptive functioning of persons with intellectual disability are understood to preclude or diminish culpability, rendering execution inherently excessive and therefore a violation of the Eighth Amendment's protection against Cruel and Unusual Punishments (Cheung, 2013). Additionally, the Court cited the rationale that defendants with intellectual disability face an increased risk of wrongful execution because they "are less able to give meaningful assistance to their counsel, typically make poor witnesses, and their demeanor may create an unwarranted impression of lack of remorse for their crimes" (Cheung, 2103, p. 319). Although the Court categorically barred the execution of individuals with intellectual disability, it entrusted to states the responsibility of aligning their legal definitions with the national consensus—and generally conforming to widely accepted clinical definitions (i.e., the American Association of Intellectual Disability and the American Psychiatric Association).

In 2014, Blume, Johnson, Marcus, and Paavola reported that, from 2002 to 2013, approximately 7.7% ($n = 371$) of death row inmates and capital defendants raised claims of intellectual disability, and an estimated 55% of such claims were substantiated. Furthermore, they found that in states that significantly deviated from accepted clinical methods for determining intellectual disability (e.g., Florida, Alabama, Georgia, and Texas), death row inmates and capital defendants raising claims of intellectual disability had the lowest success rates (Blume et al., 2014). Wide variance within success rates was shown even within the same region of the country (i.e., the South): North Carolina = 82%, Mississippi = 57%, Georgia = 11%, and Florida = 0% (Blume et al., 2014). This finding raises troubling implications about the role of arbitrary features such as geographic location in the determination of justice—which is to say, the decision to end a person's life.

Mild Intellectual Disability

The diagnosis of mild intellectual disability is a particularly important issue because individuals with mild intellectual disability comprise the largest subcategory of defendants raising the claim of intellectual disability. It is speculated that capital

defendants who fall within the mild spectrum will prove the hardest group to legally protect given their near-threshold functioning that results in *social invisibility*.
In general, confounders to the assessment and diagnostic processes are attributed to
a variety of factors: (1) frequent overlap of symptoms across diagnostic categories;
(2) diagnoses are frequently comorbid; and (3) information about etiology is frequently missing (Greenspan, Harris, & Woods, 2015). Between-state variation
and imprecision in diagnosis have led advocates to charge that, without a national
model of standards, states cannot adequately effectuate the categorical ban against
the execution of persons with intellectual disability—leaving such persons vulnerable to rights violations and unlawful execution (Cheung, 2013). Of course, as
critics argue, a uniform standard does not guarantee a fair standard, and any attempt
to secure a national model should be met with caution.

YOUTH DEFENDANTS

In the 2005 *Roper v. Simmons* decision, the US Supreme Court determined that
the execution of nonadult offenders is unconstitutional. The Court's 2005 decision
drew precedence from the 2002 *Atkins* decision, linking deficits in cognitive development with diminished culpability. As was done in the 2002 *Atkins* decision, the
US Supreme Court made this determination through a national consensus that ascertained the evolving standards of decency. Although there are now two protected
classes of capital defendants (i.e., persons who commissioned a crime while a minor
and persons with intellectual disability), the criteria by which a person is said to
meet the definition of the respective classes is strikingly different. While all states
recognize 18 years as the age of majority or adulthood—and this, even if accidental
represents a national standard—states vary on their definitions of intellectual disability and the procedures by which this claim is said to be met. This alone renders
accidents of geography as being fundamentally salient in life-and-death determinations of justice for persons with intellectual disability, but not for youth defendants.

METHODS OF EXECUTION: THE SCIENCE
OF HUMANE PUNISHMENT

Since the beginning, "American execution practices have been designed to differentiate law's violence from violence outside the law—to sharply set capital punishment apart from the crimes the law condemns. This was especially true in the 20th
century, when enormous efforts were made to put people to death quietly, invisibly,
and bureaucratically" (Sarat, 2014, p. 4). In contrast to the new era of executions,
those prior to 1890 were always centrally about the display of the sovereignty's
power to decide who lives and who dies, who is punished, and who goes free (Sarat,
2014). As French philosopher Michel Foucault wrote about the early functionings
of capital punishment:

The public execution has a juridico-political function. It is a ceremonial by
which a momentarily injured sovereignty is reconstituted [...] The public

execution, however hasty and everyday, belongs to a whole series of great rituals in which power is eclipsed and restored [...] There must be an emphatic affirmation of power and its intrinsic superiority. And this superiority is not simply that of right, but that of the physical strength of the sovereign beating down upon the body of his adversary, and mastering it [...] Not only must the people know, they must see with their own eyes. Because they must be made afraid, but also because they must be witnesses, the guarantors of the punishment, and because they must to a certain extent take part in it. (Foucault, 1995, pp. 48–49, 58)

By the end of the 1800s, executions conducted at a central location within the state became closed events to which only a few invited guests were admitted (Latzer & McCord, 2011). The last public execution in the United States took place in 1936 (Latzer & McCord, 2011). Austin Sarat (2014), professor of jurisprudence and political science at Amherst College, operationally defines the new era of capital punishment as occurring post-1890. In this new era, the death penalty has been transformed from:

[D]ramatic spectacle to cool, bureaucratic operation [...] Capital punishment has become, at best, a hidden reality. It is known, if it is known at all, by indirection. What was public is now private. What was high drama has been reduced to a matter of technique [...] Whereas the technologies of killing deployed by the state were once valued precisely because of their gruesome effects on the body of the condemned, today we seek a technology that leaves no trace. (Sarat, 2014, p. 9)

All death penalty jurisdictions authorized the execution method of lethal injection. Up to four alternative methods are legally available at this time, depending on the jurisdiction: hanging, firing squad, electrocution, and lethal gas. Hanging was the most widely used method until its replacement in the first half of the 1900s in many jurisdictions by the method of electrocution; less common, hanging was replaced by method of lethal gas (Latzer & McCord, 2011). This section addresses the history of, and science behind, the different execution methods, and then asks us, in the context of botched executions, *what happens when the science of execution fails?*

THE HANGING METHOD

Death by hanging was the primary method of execution in the United States since the founding of the American colonies (Sarat, 2014), and it remained so until the late 1890s–early 1900s (Death Penalty Information Center, 2016b; Latzer & McCord, 2011; see Fig. 10.2). In the 1600s and 1700s, hanging was a public and solemn spectacle, attended by men, women, and children alike (Latzer & McCord, 2011). The aim of public execution was threefold: (1) it intended to provide justice to the accused in the form of *retribution*; (2) it intended to frighten others in order to prevent

Figure 10.2 The hanging execution of Mary Surratt, Lewis Powell, David Herold, and George Atzerodt, who were all convicted for involvement with the assassination of former President Abraham Lincoln
SOURCE: Library of Congress: Hanging hooded bodies of the four conspirators; crowd departing; http://loc.gov/pictures/resource/cwpb.04230/

crime in the form of *deterrence*; and (3) it intended to give the condemned an opportunity to repent, thereby gaining salvation in the afterlife (Latzer & McCord, 2011). However, hangings were known to go gruesomely wrong, sometimes ending in decapitation and sometimes leaving the accused dangling for unacceptably long periods of time, which resulted in a slow and painful death by asphyxiation as opposed to the intended goal of death by a broken neck (Latzer & McCord, 2011). Today, only Delaware and Washington authorize the use of hanging (Death Penalty Information Center, 2016a).

The Science of Hanging

Hanging procedure dictates that inmates may be weighed the day prior to the execution and a rehearsal should be performed using a sandbag of equal weight (Death Penalty Information Center, 2016b). The measurement of the inmate's weight is integral to determining the length of drop necessary to ensure a quick death (Death Penalty Information Center, 2016b) so that the Cruel and Unusual Punishments Clause is not violated. If the rope is too long, the inmate may be decapitated; if too short, the hanging may result in strangulation, a process that could take up to 45 minutes (Death Penalty Information Center, 2016b). Specifications for the rope include that it should be 3/4-inch to 1-1/4-inch in diameter and that, prior to use, the rope must be boiled and stretched to eliminate spring or coiling, and lubricated with wax or soap (Death Penalty Information Center, 2016b). Immediately before the execution, the inmate's hands and legs are secured, eyes are blindfolded, and the noose is placed around the neck, with the knot behind the left ear (Death Penalty Information Center, 2016b). The execution occurs when a trap door is opened and the inmate falls through, attached at the neck to the noose. Although the science of hanging hypothesizes that the inmate's weight should cause a rapid fracture-dislocation of the neck, instantaneous death rarely occurs (Death Penalty Information Center, 2016b; Weisberg, 1991). Variables that may preclude successful hanging (i.e., rapid fracture-dislocation) and result in slow asphyxiation include the following: if the inmate has strong neck muscles; if the inmate is very light in weight; if the drop is too short; and/or if the noose has been wrongly positioned (Death Penalty Information Center, 2016b). If death by slow asphyxiation occurs, the face becomes engorged, the tongue protrudes, the eyes pop, the body defecates, and violent movements of the limbs occur (Death Penalty Information Center, 2016b; Weisberg, 1991).

THE FIRING SQUAD METHOD

Death by firing squad was unanimously upheld by the US Supreme Court as a method of execution in *Wilkerson v. Utah* (1879) (Latzer & McCord, 2011). As of 2015, Utah is the only state to reauthorize the firing squad as a viable execution method, and this is if, and only if, the state is unable to obtain the drugs necessary to carry out a lethal injection execution (Death Penalty Information Center, 2016b). Prior to Utah's 2015 reauthorization, the firing squad was only a method of execution if chosen by an inmate before lethal injection became the sole means of execution (Death Penalty Information Center, 2016b). The most recent execution by firing squad was of Ronnie Gardner, who chose this method ostensibly by his own volition in June 2010 (Death Penalty Information Center, 2016b).

The Science of the Firing Squad

For this method, the inmate is usually bound to a chair in front with leather straps across the waist and head (Death Penalty Information Center, 2016b). Sandbags to absorb the inmate's blood surround the chair and a black hood is pulled over the inmate's head (Death Penalty Information Center, 2016b). After locating the inmate's heart with a stethoscope, a medical doctor pins a circular white cloth target over it (Death Penalty Information Center, 2016b). Standing in an enclosure 20 feet away, five shooters are armed with .30 caliber rifles (see Fig. 10.3; Death Penalty Information Center, 2016b). Each rifle is loaded with a single round, and one of the five shooters is given a blank (Death Penalty Information Center, 2016b). Each of the shooters aims the rifle through a slot in an oval-shaped canvas that separates shooter from inmate, and proceeds to fire at the human target (Weisberg, 1991). The cause of death is blood loss caused by rupture of the heart or a large blood vessel, or tearing of the lungs (Death Penalty Information Center, 2016b). Whether with intention or by accident, if the shooters miss the heart, the prisoner bleeds to death slowly (Hillman, 1993; Weisberg, 1991).

THE ELECTROCUTION METHOD

Electrocution was thought to be a more reliable and swift method than hanging, and therefore more humane (Latzer & McCord, 2011). In 1888, the New York state legislature was the first to mandate the electrocution method of execution (Latzer & McCord, 2011). Two years later in 1890, William Kemmler was the first man to be electrocuted in the nation's first-built electric chair in New York (see Fig. 10.4). Despite Kemmler's botched electrocution (Drimmer, 2014), the method was upheld by the US Supreme Court in *In re Kemmler* (1890). By 1913, 14 additional states authorized this method (Latzer & McCord, 2011). Before abolishing the death penalty in 2015, Nebraska utilized electrocution as the sole method of execution before the State Supreme Court ruled the method unconstitutional in 2008 (Death Penalty Information Center, 2016b). Today, no state authorizes electrocution as the sole method of execution (Death Penalty Information Center, 2016b).

The Science of Electrocution

Standard electrocution protocol requires that inmates be shaved and strapped securely to a chair using belts that cross the chest, groin, legs, and arms (Death Penalty Information Center, 2016b). A metal cap formed to the crown of the head called an electrode is fastened to the shaved scalp and forehead regions over a saline-moistened sponge (Death Penalty Information Center, 2016b). Saline water contains a significant concentration of dissolved salts (e.g., NaCl) and is a good conductor of electricity. An electrode (i.e., the metal cap) functions as a conductor through which electricity enters and leaves an object,

Figure 10.3 Image of 7.62 mm caliber, commonly known as the imperial unit equivalent, .30 caliber

Figure 10.4 "Old Sparky," the electric chair used at the Sing Sing maximum-security prison in New York
SOURCE: Public Domain, https://commons.wikimedia.org/w/index.php?curid=555946

substance, or region (Oxford English Dictionary, n.d.)—or, in this case, a human body. Therefore, a saline-moistened sponge causes the electricity to transfer more efficiently, resulting in a quicker and (ostensibly) less painful execution (Death Penalty Information Center, 2016b). However, if the sponge is too wet, the saline short-circuits the electric current; if too dry, the electrical resistance becomes very high and causes the body to cook. To further lower resistance, an additional electrode is moistened with conductive jelly and attached to the shaved portion of the inmate's leg (Death Penalty Information Center, 2016b). After blindfolding the inmate, the execution team inhabits an observation room and the warden signals the executioner, who then connects the power at between 500 and 2,000 volts for approximately 30 seconds (Death Penalty Information Center, 2016b). After the initial surge, the body slumps; doctors must wait for the body to cool before checking the inmate's heartbeat. If the doctor determines that the inmate is not yet dead, this process continues until a time of death is established (Death Penalty Information Center, 2016b). Violent movement of the limbs can result in dislocation and fractures (Death Penalty Information Center, 2016b). Additionally, electrocutions often result in the swelling of tissue, defecation, smoking, and the smell of burning

(Hillman, 1992; Weisberg, 1991). Autopsy is delayed until the internal organs have cooled.

THE LETHAL GAS METHOD

Beginning in 1921, 11 states adopted the lethal gas method of execution; as was the case for electrocution, lethal gas was also adopted in response to hanging for humanitarian reasons (Latzer & McCord, 2011). Of the 11 states, Nevada was the first to use cyanide in 1924, and it attempted to execute inmate Jon Gee in his cell as he slept (Death Penalty Information Center, 2016b). Whereas the lack of a seal around his cell prevented his successful execution, it also led to the construction of the first gas chamber (Bohm, 2017).

The Science of Lethal Gas

The inmate is strapped to a chair in a sealed chamber that sits atop a pail of sulfuric acid (Death Penalty Information Center, 2016b). In order to establish and pronounce a time of death, a medical doctor typically affixes a long stethoscope to the inmate before the room is sealed airtight (Death Penalty Information Center, 2016b). Upon receiving a signal from the prison warden, the executioner uses a lever to release crystals of sodium cyanide into the pail beneath the chamber. The chemical reaction between the sulfuric acid in the pail and the crystals of sodium cyanide releases hydrogen cyanide gas (Weisberg, 1991). The inmate is instructed to breathe deeply in order to hasten the process (Death Penalty Information Center, 2016b). Eventually, the inmate dies from lack of oxygen to the brain (i.e., hypoxia) (Weisberg, 1991; see Fig. 10.5). Following death, an exhaust fan pulls the lethal gas from the chamber, and the corpse of the inmate is neutralized with ammonia (Death Penalty Information Center, 2016b). In April 2015, Oklahoma authorized death by nitrogen as an alternative to lethal injection if the necessary drugs cannot be obtained or if lethal injection itself is found to be unconstitutional (Death Penalty Information Center, 2016b).

THE LETHAL INJECTION METHOD

Oklahoma became the first state to adopt the lethal injection execution method in 1977 (Death Penalty Information Center, 2016b). In 1982, Texas performed the first lethal injection execution on Charles Brooks (Death Penalty Information Center, 2016b). Like the methods that came before it, lethal injection was—and perhaps still is—thought to be a step forward for the science of humane execution, worthy of securing the normative distinction between capital punishment and the crime of capital murder. In the case of *Baze v. Rees* (2008), the US Supreme Court rejected a claim that Kentucky's protocol for lethal injection constituted cruel and unusual

Figure 10.5 The former gas chamber at New Mexico State Penitentiary; it was used one time in 1960 before being replaced by lethal injection.
SOURCE: By Shelka04 at en.wikipedia, CC BY 3.0, https://commons.wikimedia.org/w/index.php?curid=16086046

punishment by creating unnecessary risk of pain (Latzer & McCord, 2011). Of the three-drug protocol, Baze argued that an insufficient dose of the first drug puts the inmate at risk for severe pain resulting from the second and third drugs—which would be undetectable due to the effects of the first. The US Supreme Court upheld the Kentucky protocol, but it is anticipated that further challenges will continue to come forward (Latzer & McCord, 2011).

The Science of Lethal Injection

Typical lethal injection protocol requires the inmate to be strapped to a gurney; then a member of the execution team positions heart monitors on the inmate's skin (Death Penalty Information Center, 2016b). A primary needle and a secondary, back-up needle are inserted into usable veins usually in the arms (Death Penalty Information Center, 2016b). Long tubes link the needle to intravenous drips through a hole in a cement wall (Death Penalty Information Center, 2016b). Before receiving the three-drug protocol (now a one-drug protocol in some states), the inmate receives a nonlethal injection of saline solution (Death Penalty Information Center, 2016b). Following the warden's signal, a curtain is raised that exposes the inmate to the witnesses—if any—who watch from an adjoining room (Death Penalty Information Center, 2016b). Once the curtain is pulled, the inmate receives the initial injection, an anesthetic that puts the inmate to sleep (Death Penalty Information Center, 2016b). The inmate then receives the second injection, which paralyzes the muscle system and lungs (Death Penalty Information Center, 2016b). Finally, the third injection of potassium chloride stops the inmate's heart, and death results from anesthetic overdose and respiratory and cardiac arrest (Death Penalty Information Center, 2016b; Weisberg, 1991). Although medical doctors participate in executions in a peripheral way (e.g., certifying time of death), medical ethics prevent them from participating in executions directly (Death Penalty Information Center, 2016b). Due to lack of medical participation, inexperienced technicians or orderlies must perform the injections (Death Penalty Information Center, 2016b). If the drugs are injected into a muscle instead of a vein or if the needle becomes clogged, severe pain can result (Death Penalty Information Center, 2016b; see Fig. 10.6).

BOTCHED EXECUTIONS

It is estimated that of the total US executions that took place between 1890 and 2010, approximately 3% were classified as botched (Sarat, 2014). Botched executions occur when there is a breakdown in, or departure from, the execution method protocol (Sarat, 2014). The protocol may be established informally or formally by the "norms, expectations, and advertised virtues of each method or by the

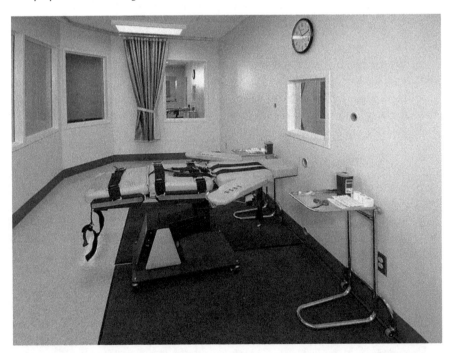

Figure 10.6 The lethal injection execution room at San Quentin State Prison in California
SOURCE: By CACorrections (California Department of Corrections and Rehabilitation) - https://www.flickr.com/photos/37381942@N04/4905111750/in/set-72157624628981539/, Public Domain, https://commons.wikimedia.org/w/index.php?curid=11627466

government's officially adopted execution guidelines" (Sarat, 2014, p. 5). Botched executions include those with unanticipated challenges or delays that caused unnecessary agony for the inmate or reflect gross incompetence of the executioner (Sarat, 2014). As was determined in *In re Kemmler* (1890), the state may choose to spare or to extinguish life, but it cannot force the accused to linger between life and death (Sarat, 2014).

If, as Sarat (2014) reminds us, the legitimacy of state killing depends on humane methods of execution, then "when executions go wrong, they signal a break in the ritualization and routinization of state killing" (p. 4). In doing so, botched executions present a direct challenge to the state's presentation of capital punishment as humane, sterile, and proficient (Greer, 2005). Additionally, botched executions make visible the inherent violence of the death penalty, presenting opponents with an opportunity to mobilize support against the use of capital punishment (Greer, 2005). Despite this seemingly constitutional violation, botched executions have played only a minor role in efforts to end the death penalty in the recent era of capital punishment (Sarat, 2014).

DISCUSSION

Capital punishment is a controversial and contemporary issue. It is a mechanism of our criminal justice system that deserves our ethical consideration as to whether it is a reliable, or even a desirable, manifestation of justice. A British relic and an American tradition, the death penalty is reserved for only the most heinous of crimes—presumably only for the most "deserving" of defendants. However, as the National Association of Social Workers explains, capital punishment is antithetical to treating people in a manner that presumes their inherent dignity and worth. It also precludes the centrality of human relationships. Plainly, the death penalty is inconsistent with the professional ethics of social work, as well as with other helping professions (e.g., medicine). As Liat Ben-Moshe reminds us (2013, p. 123):

From the 19th Century, the webs of the medical and the judicial start to intertwine with the rise of a hybrid discourse, according to Foucault (2003). Its hybridity lies not just in the sense of amalgamation of several discourses (legal, medical) but also in the creation of a new power/ knowledge structure in which "doctors laying claim to judicial power and judges laying claim to medical power" (2003).

1. To what extent is our participation in capital adjudication procedures an endorsement of a practice that is antithetical to our professional ethics?
2. To what extent does our participation implicate us in the extinguishing of—botched and otherwise—human life?
3. And conversely, if we elect not to participate, are we failing those who arguably need our talents the most?

Foucault's medico-judicial hybrid discourse elicits serious ethical considerations for those who work in the helping profession and who participate in death penalty cases:

These are questions not only for individual practitioners to contend with, but perhaps as well for the national and state chapters of professional organizations. Regardless, these are questions that should never overlook, and that are in fact largely relegated to, the space of failed science.

REFERENCES

American Civil Liberties Union. (2012). The case against the death penalty. Retrieved from https://www.aclu.org/other/case-against-death-penalty.

American Civil Liberties Union Capital Punishment Project. (2015). Reason #1 to support a national moratorium on executions. Retrieved from https://www.prisonpolicy.org/scans/aclu_dp_factsheet1.pdf

Andrews, A. B. (1991). Social work expert testimony regarding mitigation in capital sentencing proceedings. *Social Work, 36*(5), 440–445.

Baze v. Rees, 553 US 35 (2008). Retrieved from https://www.supremecourt.gov/opinions/boundvolumes/553bv.pdf.

Beck, E., Britto, S., & Andrews, A. (2007). *In the shadow of death: Restorative justice and death row families.* New York: Oxford University Press.

Ben-Moshe, L. (2013). "The institution yet to come": Analyzing incarceration through a disability lens. In L. J. Davis (Ed.), *The disability studies reader* (5th ed.), 119–130. New York: Routledge.

Blume, J. H., Johnson, S. L., Marcus, P., & Paavola, E. (2014). A tale of two (and possibly three) Atkins: Intellectual disability and capital punishment twelve years after the Supreme Court's creation of a categorical bar. *William & Mary Bill of Rights Journal, 23,* 393.

Bohm, R. M. (2017). *Deathquest: An introduction to the theory and practice of capital punishment in the United States* (5th ed.). Philadelphia, PA: Taylor & Francis.

Cheung, N. (2013). Defining intellectual disability and establishing a standard of proof: Suggestions for a national model standard. *Health Matrix, 23,* 317.

Cornell University Legal Information Institute. (n.d.a). Aggravating factor. Retrieved from https://www.law.cornell.edu/wex/aggravating_factor

Cornell University Legal Information Institute. (n.d.b). Insanity defense. Retrieved from https://www.law.cornell.edu/wex/insanity_defense

Cornell University Legal Information Institute. (n.d.c). Mens rea. Retrieved from https://www.law.cornell.edu/wex/mens_rea.

Cornell University Legal Information Institute. (n.d.d). Mitigating factor. Retrieved from https://www.law.cornell.edu/wex/mitigating_factor

Death Penalty Information Center. (2016a). States with and without the death penalty. Retrieved from http://www.deathpenaltyinfo.org/states-and-without-death-penalty

Death Penalty Information Center. (2016b). Descriptions of execution methods. Retrieved from http://www.deathpenaltyinfo.org/descriptions-execution-methods?scid=8&did=479

DeMatteo, D., Marczyk, G., & Pich, M. (2007). A national survey of state legislation defining mental retardation: Implications for policy and practice after Atkins. *Behavioral Sciences & the Law, 25*(6), 781–802.

Drimmer, F. (2014). *Executions in America: Over three hundred years of crime and capital punishment in America.* New York, NY: Skyhorse Publishing.

Electrode. (n.d.). *Oxford English Dictionary.* Retrieved from http://www. oxforddictionaries.com/us/definition/american_english/electrode

Feluren, J. V. (2013). Moving the focus away from the IQ score towards the subjective assessment of adaptive functioning: The effect of the DSM-5 on the post-Atkins categorical exemption of offenders with intellectual disability from the death penalty. *Nova Law Review, 38,* 323.

Feuerstein, S., Fortunati, F., Morgan, C. A., Coric, V., Temporini, H., & Southwick, S. (2005). The insanity defense. *Psychiatry (Edgmont), 2*(9), 24.

Foucault, M. (1995). *Discipline and punish: The birth of the prison.* New York, NY: Vintage Books.

Foucault, M. (2003). *Abnormal: Lectures at the College de France, 1974-1975.* New York: Picador.

Gothard, S. (1989). Power in the court: The social worker as an expert witness. *Social Work, 34*(1), 65–67.

Greenspan, S., Harris, J. C., & Woods, G. W. (2015). Intellectual disability is "a condition, not a number": Ethics of IQ cut-offs in psychiatry, human services and law. *Ethics, Medicine and Public Health, 1*(3), 312–324.

Greer, C. (2005). Delivering death: Capital punishment, botched executions and the American news media. In P. Mason (Ed.), *Captured by the media* (pp. 84–102). London: Taylor & Francis.

Hillman, H. (1993). The possible pain experienced during execution by different methods. *Perception, 22*(6), 745–753.

Latzer, B., & McCord, D. (2011). *Death penalty cases: Leading US Supreme Court cases on capital punishment* (3rd ed.). Burlington, MA: Elsevier.

Leading Cases (2014). Eighth amendment – cruel and unusual punishments – defendants with intellectual disability – Hall v. Florida. *Harvard Law Review, 128*(1), 271–280. Retrieved from http://www.jstor.org/stable/24643929.

Meany, K. A. (2004). Atkins v. Virginia: The false finding of a national consensus and the problems with determining who is mentally retarded. *Widener Law Review, 11,* 137.

Morris, N., & Rothman, D. J. (1995). *The Oxford history of the prison: The practice of punishment in Western society.* New York, NY: Oxford University Press.

Sarat, A. (2014). *Gruesome spectacles: Botched executions and America's death penalty.* Palo Alto, CA: Stanford University Press.

Weisberg, J. (1991). This is your death. *New Republic, 1,* 23–27.

Workers, N. A. (2008). *NASW Code of Ethics (Guide to the everyday professional conduct of social workers).* Washington, DC: NASW. Retrieved from https://www.socialworkers. org/About/Ethics/Code-of-Ethics/Code-of-Ethics-English.

Court Cases

In re Kemmler, 136 U.S. 436 (1890).

Trop v. Dulles, 356 U.S. 86 (1958).

Atkins v. Virginia, 536 U.S. 304 (2002).
Weems v. United States, 217 U.S. 349 (1910).
Furman v. Georgia, 408 U.S. 238 (1972).
Roper v. Simmons, 543 U.S. 551 (2005).
Gregg v. Georgia, 428 U.S. 153 (1976).

11

Social Work and the Science of Medical

Prevention and Treatment

There is no human condition and no human service that is more fundamental than health promotion and the prevention of illness.

—Leon H. Ginsberg

According to the National Association of Social Workers (NASW), since the early 1900s, the social work profession has been integral to the US health care system, and indeed it continues to play an important role in the psychosocial aspects of health care (NASW, 2016). Social worker professionals provide services to individuals and families throughout the life span by addressing the full range of biopsychosocial and environmental issues that affect individual well-being (NASW, 2016). Social work's unique strengths-based and person-in-environment perspectives provide the contextual focus that is, according to the NASW, necessary for person- and family-centered care (NASW, 2016). The social work profession's commitment to health and well-being focuses in great part on historical and extant health care inequalities in the United States. According to the NASW (2016):

> People living in poverty and communities of color continue to experience disproportionately higher rates of acute and chronic illness, due to unequal access to health care services, lack of health insurance coverage, poverty, discrimination, and other social determinants of health. Therefore, professional medical social workers not only consider the biopsychosocial needs of individuals and families, but as well, they recognize the systemic issues that contribute to poor health outcomes. (NASW, 2016)

The NASW authors and promulgates the Standards for Social Work Practice in Health Care Settings (2016). According to the NASW, these standards articulate the necessary knowledge and skills that medical social workers should possess in order to (1) deliver competent and ethical services in today's health care environment; (2) provide benchmarks for quality social work practice for use by

Table 11.1 SPECIFIC GOALS OF THE STANDARDS FOR SOCIAL WORK PRACTICE
IN HEALTH CARE SETTINGS

No.	Specific Goal
1	Ensure that social work practice in health care settings is guided by the NASW Code of Ethics
2	Enhance the quality of social work services provided to clients and families in health care settings
3	Advocate for clients' rights to self-determination, confidentiality, access to supportive services and resources, and appropriate inclusion in decision making that affects their health and well-being
4	Encourage social work participation in the development, refinement, and integration of best practices in health care and health care social work
5	Promote social work participation in system-wide quality improvement and research efforts within health care organizations
6	Provide a basis for the development of continuing education materials and programs related to social work in health care settings
7	Promote social work participation in the development and refinement of public policy at the local, state, federal, and tribal levels to support the well-being of clients, families, and communities served by the rapidly evolving US health care system
8	Inform policymakers, employers, and the public about the essential role of social workers across the health care continuum

health care employers; and (3) assist policymakers, other health professionals, and the public in understanding the role of professional social workers in health care settings (NASW, 2016). Table 11.1 presents the specific goals of the standards. Currently, social workers are present in settings across what is referred to as the health care continuum, which include (1) prevention and public health; (2) primary and acute care; and (3) specialty care, rehabilitation, home health, long-term care, and hospice (NASW, 2016). In this vein, this chapter explores implications for medical social workers in the health care continuum with regard to the science, and ethics, of medical prevention and treatment.

SOCIAL WORKERS AND MEDICAL SCIENCES

Devices for diagnosing health problems as well as the scientific devices and procedures used in treating illness are among the subjects covered in this chapter. Many of the devices used in diagnosing and treating illness are based on the learnings of fields such as chemistry and physics. In addition, the chapter covers some other basic medical issues such as the specializations practiced by physicians. Ancillary services that are often an important part of the treatment of a patient are also discussed. Such critical issues as nutrition, scientific findings about specific illnesses, the causes of death in the United States, and mortality are also covered. Complementary and alternative health services such as acupuncture and chiropractic care are also discussed.

Perhaps the most important applications of science that are of interest to social workers are those involving medicine and other forms of health care. Science plays a major role in health care, including the care that involves social workers. Although medicine and health care are not consistently or exclusively scientific, they rely on scientific knowledge as their bases. But health care also involves the art of medical practice and other dimensions that affect the ways in which health care providers interact with patients.

Ideally, health care practices are based on scientifically determined facts about the human body and its functioning. However, not all health care practices are informed by scientifically determined principles, as discussed earlier. Practices are carried out because they seem to be reasonable even if not scientifically proven to be effective—or even nonharmful. And much of health care is an art that often depends upon the skills and preparation of the physician and other health care personnel. For every medical procedure and intervention, there is a document that the patient or the patient's family must sign which absolves the health care organization and its practitioners of any blame for any negative outcomes. The science of medicine is complicated and results cannot be predicted with perfect accuracy.

Scientific discoveries change medicine frequently. Perhaps one of the most dramatic changes in recent years was the discovery that ulcers, which had been treated with bland diets and sometimes surgery, were actually infections that could be treated with antibiotics. Today's ulcer treatments are likely to be courses of antibiotics drugs, which have proven to cure them (Mayoclinic.org/ulcers).

The sciences that most affect health care are biology and its various components, such as anatomy, physiology, genetics, and pharmacology. Health care practices usually have some connection with human biological concepts and principles, which are covered in the authors' earlier text, *Human Biology for Social Workers* (Ginsberg, Nackerud, & Larrison, 2003). The sciences, especially chemistry and physics, are the basis for many commonly used diagnostic and treatment services in health care as discussed in Chapter 3.

X-ray (Parker, 2016) is the original and most important resource in examining the interior of the human body. It was originally developed by Marie Curie and to a lesser extent by her husband, Pierre. X-rays use radiation to examine the interior organs and bones. The process is commonly used in much of medical care and in dentistry for finding cavities and other dental problems. X-ray and its later applications, such as computerized tomography (CT) scans (Parker, 2016), were made possible through the research in physics.

CT (Parker, 2016) is a relatively new procedure for examining the human body, especially the internal organs but also the skeletal structure. A specialized X-ray machine takes multiple images of the body and its organs. It can provide a three-dimensional picture of the whole body or of any organ.

X-ray processes and those diagnostic means based on X-ray expose the patient to radiation that can lead to illnesses such as cancer. Readers will recall that when they are given X-rays, the X-ray technician may activate the X-ray machine from another room, isolated from the patient. In dental X-rays, patients ordinarily are fitted with lead covering to prevent the collection of radiation from building up and causing illness. Radiation is also used in the treatment of diseases. Radiation is focused on cancers and is designed to destroy cancer cells.

Magnetic resonance imaging (MRI) (Parker, 2016) is a procedure used to examine the internal body organs with powerful magnets. The magnets provide images of the body and its organs. It does not use radiation but, instead, uses the electronic power of magnets to diagnose illnesses.

Chemotherapy (Parker, 2016) is used in treating cancer. It works by focusing strong chemicals on cancer cells in order to destroy them. The chemicals used in chemotherapy are developed by chemists and physicists.

The diagnostic mechanisms, X-ray, MRI, and CT scans (Beers & Berkow, 1999), are commonly used in health care diagnosis and the planning of treatment for a variety of health problems. Those tools that use radiation pose some threat to the health of technicians. Health physicists, discussed in more detail in Chapter 3, work to insure safety from radiation and monitor exposure to radiation in health care facilities, nuclear power plants, and nuclear waste disposal sites. The MRI procedures do not involve radiation.

It is important for social workers, especially those in health care services, to know about these diagnostic and treatment resources. They may need to help interpret the tools for patients and their families. For some of these procedures, especially chemotherapy and radiation therapy, there may be physical effects after they are administered with which the patient, family members, and social workers, as well as health care providers, should become familiar.

Chemistry and Diagnostic Tests

Chemistry lends itself to many diagnostic and treatment services. Almost every illness can be associated with blood tests (Clayman, 1989), many of which are developed by chemists. The results are also interpreted by a variety of specialists, often using learnings from chemistry in determining the meanings of tests. Each test also has norms for determining the extent to which the test indicates illness. It is worthwhile for social workers to be familiar with these tests and the meanings of the results.

THE STRUCTURE OF MODERN HEALTH CARE

People with health problems or needs are served by a variety of health science professionals, all of whom play roles in diagnosing and treating those problems. Care can be preventive, restorative, or designed to help patients (and their families) maintain satisfactory health.

The most obvious personnel in health care are, of course, physicians, who are divided into a number of specialized categories. Primary care is the fundamental source of service for patients. Primary care physicians who may be specialists in family practice, the most general form of medical practice, or specialists in internal medicine, who are experts in diagnosis and treatment by means that are nonsurgical, provide much of it. In some cases, the primary care provider may be a physician's assistant, a profession for which college-level education is available, or a nurse, especially a nurse practitioner, a specialist within the profession of nursing (Clayman, 1989; www.abms.org).

Primary care providers operate out of many different kinds of settings. Many have private practice offices. Others conduct their work as part of hospital systems. Still others are primarily employed within hospitals and provide primary care to patients who come to emergency rooms or who are otherwise patients in hospitals. Increasingly, primary care is provided within clinics associated with pharmacies or in independent clinics that are licensed, as are all primary care sites, to provide care for people who are ill, people in need of health certifications such as children enrolling in camps or schools, and for preventive services such as the infant inoculations for the various childhood illnesses and polio. Inoculations are usually administered by injections (Centers for Disease Control and Prevention, n.d.).

Some inoculations are also used for adults. Adults who are planning to travel away from the United States may obtain inoculations for conditions such as yellow fever and Hepatitis A and B. These are not likely to affect people in the United States but in some overseas environments they may cause illness (Clayman, 1989).

Insect-borne illnesses are also a concern of public health programs, although there are fewer in the United States than in other parts of the world (Sharma, 2015). Another emerging public health problem is the Zika virus, which became known in 2015. Spread by mosquitoes, most of those who are bitten by an insect carrying the virus do not become ill and if they do the problems are usually minor. However, pregnant women infected with the virus may deliver children with severe developmental difficulties, including microcephalus or a very small head and brain (https://medlineplus.gov/zikavirus.html).

Often public health departments provide inoculations in addition to or instead of private practitioners. Disease-preventive inoculations are an important function of local health departments, especially in their operation of "well baby" services (Clayman, 1989).

In many cases health care is provided by the primary care practitioner. The practitioner may write prescriptions for the patient to use in treating his or her condition. He or she may administer inoculations for the prevention of diseases or inoculations as a form of treatment. Such treatment is within the authority of primary care providers. Many primary health care providers employ social workers either full or part-time to assist patients with the social components of their conditions such as finances and other nonmedical services (Ginsberg, 2000).

When the primary care provider does not believe he or she can effectively address the patient's condition, the patient may be referred to a medical specialist or an ancillary care provider such as physical, occupational, or speech therapists. In some cases, when the patient's problem seems to be more emotional or psychological, the primary care provider may refer the patient for counseling with a social worker, counselor, or psychologist.

LICENSING AND REGULATION

State governments as well as other organizations regulate health care providers at all levels. Professionals are required to have the basic professional education required by the field of practice. The numbers of professions regulated by states varies as do the criteria for providing the professional credentials. In many states, the professional boards also evaluate and give credentials to professional education institutions such as medical, nursing, physical therapy, psychology, and social work schools. Boards regulate nurses, physicians, social workers, physical therapists, and many other providers of health services. The boards consist of members of the profession or specialty and also usually have citizen representatives who are not members of the regulated practitioners. In most states the boards are appointed by governors with requirements that they represent various regions of the state and not all the members can be of one political party membership (www.abms.org).

Most professional practice boards require practitioners to participate in postprofessional education courses. Each state has its own regulations for what is called continuing education. The intention is to ensure that practitioners remain currently educated in their fields and that they are knowledgeable about developing trends in the scientific bases of their professions.

In addition to the credentialing of individual practitioners, validation of professional degrees is also done through the accreditation of educational programs. Schools of medicine and most other health care educational programs are also evaluated by accrediting bodies. These bodies are not always part of state government but rather are usually voluntary organizations financed by the professional schools. Processes of "peer review," somewhat like the peer review of research mentioned earlier, determine the professional education program's conformity to standards set by the accrediting bodies. In some professions in some states, governing boards determine the educational program's viability and license graduates of those programs it approves—and denies licenses for those who complete educational programs at schools the board does not recognize.

In general, several different levels of credentials are provided. Nurses tend to have the most diverse sets of credentials—from credentials just short of professional to specialist education such as nurse practitioners. Nurse practitioners may provide primary care and some specialized care in much the way physicians do; they may be licensed to write prescriptions or administer anesthesia, for example, depending on the state's laws (Parker, 2016). Credentialing for health care professionals is a diverse and complicated subject that varies from state to state and from profession to profession. In some cases, there are conflicting credentialing organizations as well as some that purport to provide valid approval or licensing even when they are not generally recognized by practitioners and educators to determine the validity of a professional's education. In much of the world, professional credentials are regulated and awarded by the national or regional government with only a minimum of involvement of voluntary organizations. In order to understand professional qualifications, it is necessary to study precisely what is required for practice. For example, some states license psychologists to write prescriptions for mental health medicines while others do not. In some states a physician must authorize all prescription medicines. In other states, physician assistants and some nurses may have the authority to write prescriptions for pharmaceuticals (Clayman, 1989).

ANCILLARY SERVICES

There are many nonphysician or nursing services that may be where patients are referred if they need help that is beyond the scope of health care providers. For young children, there are early interventionists who help determine the extent and nature of conditions presented by young children.

Increasingly, physicians rely on diagnostic tests to determine health and illness conditions. Scientific advances in health care develop diagnostic tests regularly, many of which are based on blood chemistry. Specialists in almost all medical fields rely on phlebotomists, specialists in drawing blood from patients, to obtain blood samples that are then studied by medical technicians to determine major elements of the patient's health or disease.

X-ray technicians of various kinds, as discussed in Chapter 3, make X-rays of the patient's body to determine the nature, if any, of a patient's illnesses or traumas. Therefore, modern medical practitioners rely on laboratory personnel to evaluate patient conditions and suggest remediation of illnesses.

Physical therapists assist patients who have difficulties with their physical functioning through prescribed exercises and treatments, sometimes with electrical devices. Speech therapists often specialize their efforts around language and speech problems that are presented by patients, but they also assist with the diagnoses and treatment of physical problems that impede speech. Occupational therapists help patients restore their skills in manual tasks or in other conditions associated with employment or day-to-day life tasks (Clayman, 1989).

Exercise science is another element of treatment of patients. One of the venerable concepts in exercise came in the 1960s from the work of Kenneth Cooper (1968, 1983), who developed, for the Air Force, a system of exercise for adults that translated many exercise activities into "aerobic points," and suggested that healthy adults should earn a prescribed number of points regularly. His book, *Aerobics* (1968, 1983), was augmented many times and many of his later books are in print. However, the basic theory continues. Public, nonprofit, and commercial gymnasia throughout the world provide facilities for the kinds of activity Cooper developed, sustained continuous activity that exercises the heart, blood vessels, and lungs. Running and many cardiovascular fitness machines all support his theories for maintaining health. The activities also go by the name of "cardio or cardio-pulmonary" activities. Physicians often "prescribe" exercise programs and physical therapy. Cooper's ideas are one of the few supported by scientific data.

All of these ancillary services are tied to professional education in community colleges through baccalaureate, master's, and doctoral studies. Those with credentials in the service learn the procedures for diagnosing and helping patients overcome problems, usually with scientifically based concepts that are part of the research in those fields and curricula based on the research.

Nutrition education and use are among the many ways in which medicine hopes to help patients prevent or treat various illnesses. Although there are many books, magazine articles, and nutrition specialists who try to help patients maintain ideal weight, the scientists of nutrition often seem to provide conflicting information. There are diets of all kinds, and new books or theories often seem to be daily occurrences. All of them have their advocates and detractors. Of the types of diets, perhaps the two main examples are the Ornish diet (Ornish, 2000) that focuses on low-fat and low-food consumption as a means for improving health. The Atkins diet (Atkins, 2009) is almost the opposite. It suggests low carbohydrate, sometimes high fat, and some restraint on consuming calories. Both types of nutrition have their advocates among health care providers and both appear to be successful in helping patients control their weight. Recent reports on weight control and weight loss suggest other processes in the quest for healthy weight. A popular television program, *The Biggest Loser*, features competition for losing weight. Its participants often exhibit major weight loss—sometimes hundreds of pounds for people who begin as terribly obese. However, follow-up studies of those participants question the longevity of the weight loss (Aamodt, 2016). Many of the successful biggest losers regained much of their weight shortly after losing it. There may be "set points" in the physiology of individuals that encourage those who lose pounds to return to their set points by changes in metabolism and other factors.

The US Department of Agriculture (USDA) publishes and periodically revises a "food pyramid," suggesting the proportion of various dietary substances for healthy living. It is fairly well agreed that relying heavily on plant foods and less on animal products can assist in maintaining healthy weight. But the key element in most diets and in most nutrition education is to keep one's weight down.

A former dentist was critical of the food pyramid and other nutrition advice promoted in recent years. Dr. Cristin Kearns noted an emphasis on reducing dietary fat as a way to reduce body weight. However, Dr. Kearns believes that the sugar industry promoted the concerns about fat while neglecting emphasis on sugar as a dietary problem. Many low-fat foods actually substitute sugar for fat, which causes obesity (Sifferlin, 2016).

PHYSICIAN SPECIALIZATIONS

Perhaps the most complicated array of specializations are those in the medical profession. An online search of medical specializations will yield dozens of specialties and subspecialties. Even a search of most telephone directories will provide alphabetical listings of many medical specialties.

In general, patients reach medical specialists through referral by their primary care physician, usually a family practitioner or a specialist in internal medicine, as discussed earlier. In some cases, patients self-refer to specialists who are experts in a health problem they are experiencing.

Family practitioners have the most varied lists of services they provide. They may care for children, although the specialization of pediatrics is designed for serving children; they may provide surgery, although general surgeons and specialized surgeons such as neurosurgeons may provide most of the specialized surgery; and they may prescribe medicine and treatments in a variety of fields that are also covered by specialists such as ear, nose, and throat problems, communicable diseases, nutrition, and mental health care.

Family practitioners may offer and perform more medical services in areas with few health care practitioners and specialists such as rural communities. In metropolitan areas patients are more likely to be served by a range of medical specialists.

There are also differences in the credentials of physicians to use hospitals. Hospitals grant physicians "admitting" privileges, which means they may place a patient in a hospital and follow up on the patient's care during hospitalization. And hospitals are varied as well. Smaller communities may have primary care hospitals, which handle more routine care which is not always critical and is within the scope of knowledge of primary care physicians. Secondary hospitals care for more complex care and more complicated surgery. Tertiary care hospitals address the most complex of problems and the more complicated forms of treatment, including surgery. The differences are often the levels of nursing practitioners on the hospital staff and the complexity of the equipment in the hospital. Lower level hospitals often resolve their inability to handle the most complex cases by having access to ambulances and helicopters to transport more complicated cases to higher level hospitals.

DIMENSIONS OF US HEALTH CARE

Because this book is about science and its impact on social work practice, a detailed discussion of modern health care is beyond the scope of the book. But it is important for social workers to understand that modern health care in the United States is often confusing and difficult to understand and use.

For example, the model of a primary care physician who provides a "medical home" for patients is not always followed. Patients may self-refer to specialists that they know about or that their friends or relatives may recommend. Primary care in physician offices is less common than it once was. Today's primary care may be provided by a hospital emergency room, a free-standing neighborhood clinic, or a clinic located in a pharmacy. Staff in primary care facilities may be physicians but also may be other professionals. In hospital emergency rooms, emergency room practitioners may be the first point of contact between a patient and the health care system.

Increasingly, advertising of health services drives the use of the health care system. Once rare or unheard of, physicians and physician practices may now advertise themselves in magazines, newspapers, and on radio and television.

HEALTH INSURANCE

An important skill of professional social workers in the medical setting is the ability to navigate the health care system with, and on behalf of, clients. Not only is health insurance directly linked with client access to services but clients' ability to afford the cost of needed services can impact client quality of life (e.g., anxiety associated with financial stress can exacerbate pre-existing anxiety associated with the medical condition itself). While this text is not focused on social welfare policy and programs, it is still important to understand the massive research efforts that produce dataset after dataset of science-based empirical evidence that undergirds the major social welfare programs overseen by the Centers for Medicare and Medicaid Services (CMS). The scope of the work of the CMS is massive, as more than 100 million persons in the United States are ongoing beneficiaries of their major programs: Medicare, Medicaid, Children's Health Insurance Program (CHIP), and the Health Insurance Market Place, which was established in support of the Patient Protection and Affordable Care Act (commonly referred to as the Affordable Care Act [ACA] and "Obama Care"). Given the coverage of CMS programs and the persons who access them as beneficiaries, CMS is easily claimed as a federal agency with great prominence to social workers. Just to refresh our memories and to set the stage for a more in-depth review of the research and science production of the CMS, let's first look at a bit of history and milestones of CMS and the major social welfare programs that rest under the umbrella of the CMS. Table 11.2 presents selected historical milestones.

History

Written and published by CMS is a nicely constructed timeline: *Medicare & Medicaid Milestones 1937–2015*. The timeline (see Table 11.2) includes the major milestones of their major programs, but the selected entries presented here focus more on program development, design, implementation, and the call for impact evaluation over the past 50 years. CMS policy and procedures are most often supported by evaluative and/or impact research and the accompanying policy analysis prior to any changes taking place. In the selections from the Milestones timeline, please note the use of the following terms: *demonstration projects, oversight, quality performance requirements*, and *standards and testing of innovative practices*. All indicate the existence of accompanying evaluative research and empirical data production. It is the accompanying research and empirical data production that helps CMS achieve its

Table 11.2 Selected Milestones of the Major CMS Programs

Year	Description of Milestone
1937	US Surgeon General Thomas Parran proposed that National Health Insurance first cover Social Security beneficiaries.
1939	The Federal Security Agency was created to administer federal organizations dealing with health, education, and social insurance, including the Social Security Board, Public Health Service, and Office of Education.
1965	Medicare and Medicaid were enacted as Title XVIII and Title XIX of the Social Security Act, providing hospital, posthospital extended care, and home health coverage to almost all Americans aged 65 or older (e.g., those receiving retirement benefits from Social Security or the Railroad Retirement Board), and providing states with the option of receiving federal funding for providing health care services to low-income children, their caretaker relatives, the blind, and individuals with disabilities. At the time, seniors were the population group most likely to be living in poverty; about half had health insurance coverage. To implement the Health Insurance for the Aged (Medicare) Act, the Social Security Administration (SSA) was reorganized and the Bureau of Health Insurance was established on July 30, 1965. This bureau was responsible for the development of health insurance policy. Medicaid was part of the Social Rehabilitation Service (SRS) at this time.
1966	Medicare was implemented and more than 19 million individuals enrolled by July 1.
1967	An Early and Periodic Screening, Diagnosis, and Treatment (EPSDT) comprehensive health services benefit was established for all children getting Medicaid. Medicare was also given authority to conduct demonstration projects.
1972	Medicare eligibility was extended to individuals under age 65 with long-term disabilities and to individuals with end-stage renal disease (ESRD). Medicare was given additional authority to conduct demonstration programs. Medicaid eligibility for elderly, blind, and disabled residents of a state was linked to eligibility for the newly enacted Federal Supplemental Security Income (SSI) program.
1973	The HMO Act provided start-up grants and loans for the development of health maintenance organizations (HMOs). HMOs meeting federal standards relating to comprehensive benefits and quality were established and under certain circumstances had the right to require an employer to offer coverage to employees. The Medicare statute was also amended to provide for HMOs to contract to provide Medicare benefits to beneficiaries who choose to enroll.

(continued)

Table 11.2 CONTINUED

Year	Description of Milestone
1977	The Health Care Financing Administration (HCFA) was established to administer the Medicare and Medicaid programs.
1980	Coverage of Medicare home health services was broadened. Medicare supplemental insurance, also called "Medigap," was brought under federal oversight.
1986	The Emergency Medical Treatment and Labor Act (EMTALA) required hospitals participating in Medicare that offer emergency services to provide appropriate medical screenings and stabilizing treatments. Medicaid coverage for pregnant women and infants (up to 1 year of age) up to 100% of the Federal Poverty Level (FPL) was established as a state option.
1988	The Medicare Catastrophic Coverage Act of 1988 was enacted, which included the most significant changes since enactment of the Medicare program, improved hospital and skilled nursing facility benefits, covered mammography, and an outpatient prescription drug benefit and a cap on patient liability. The Medicare Catastrophic Coverage Act also provided for Medicaid coverage for pregnant women and infants up to 100% of the FPL was mandated; special eligibility rules were established for institutionalized persons whose spouses remained in the community to prevent "spousal impoverishment." The Qualified Medicare Beneficiary (QMB) program was established to pay Medicare premiums and cost-sharing charges for beneficiaries with incomes and resources below established thresholds. The Clinical Laboratory Improvement Amendments (CLIA) of 1988 strengthened quality performance requirements for clinical laboratories to ensure accurate and reliable laboratory tests and procedures.
1989	Medicaid coverage of pregnant women and children under age 6 up to 133% of the FPL was mandated; expanded Early and Periodic Screening, Diagnostic, and Treatment (EPSDT) requirements were established.
1990	Phased-in Medicaid coverage of children ages 6 through 18 under 100% of the FPL was established, and a Medicaid prescription drug rebate program was created. A specified low-income Medicare beneficiary eligibility group (SLMBs) was also established for Medicaid programs to pay Medicare premiums for beneficiaries with incomes at least 100% but not more than 120% of the FPL and limited financial resources. Additional federal standards for Medicare supplemental insurance were enacted.
1995	Social Security Administration became independent of the Department of Health and Human Services (HHS).

Table 11.2 CONTINUED

Year	Description of Milestone
1996	Welfare Reform: The Aid to Families with Dependent Children (AFDC) entitlement program was replaced by the Temporary Assistance for Needy Families (TANF) block grant; the welfare link to Medicaid was severed; a new mandatory low-income group not linked to welfare was added to Medicaid; and enrollment in/termination of Medicaid was no longer automatic with receipt of welfare cash assistance.
1997	The Balanced Budget Act of 1997 (BBA): The Children's Health Insurance Program (CHIP) was created; limits on Medicaid payments to disproportionate share hospitals were revised; new Medicaid managed care options and requirements for states were established. BBA also made changes to Medicare, including testing and other innovative approaches to payment and service delivery through research and demonstrations.
2001	Secretary Tommy Thompson renamed the Health Care Financing Administration (HCFA) the Centers for Medicare & Medicaid Services (CMS).
2003	The Medicare Prescription Drug, Improvement, and Modernization Act (MMA) made the most significant changes to Medicare since the program began.
2009	On February 4, 2009, President Obama signed the Children's Health Insurance Program Reauthorization Act of 2009 (CHIPRA). This legislation marked a new era in children's coverage by providing states with significant new funding, new programmatic options, and a range of new incentives for covering children through Medicaid and the Children's Health Insurance Program (CHIP).
2010	The Patient Protection and Affordable Care Act (ACA), commonly known as the "Affordable Care Act," was signed into law by President Barack Obama on March 23, 2010, for the first time prohibiting health insurance companies from denying or charging more for coverage based on an individual's health status, providing for expansion of the Medicaid program, and subsidies for insurance purchased through state-based Marketplaces to ensure that private insurance is affordable. The ACA also provided a variety of other insurance reforms, like new preventive benefit requirements and prohibitions on dollar limits, and expanded Medicare drug and preventive services benefits.
2013	The Health Insurance Marketplace opened on October 1, 2013.
2014	During the first open enrollment for the Health Insurance Marketplace, 8 million people signed up for private insurance. Three million young adults gained coverage by being able to stay on their parents' plan. Up to 129 million Americans with pre-existing conditions gained access to health insurance coverage, and the lifetime limit on benefits in many health insurance plan was prohibited.

overall goals of reduction in the lived experience of poverty, lowered health care costs for all (but in particular vulnerable populations), and improved health of the overall population in the United States.

RESEARCH AND SCIENCE PRODUCTION OF THE CENTERS FOR MEDICARE AND MEDICAID SERVICES

One of the most important, but most often overlooked, sectors of CMS work is labeled "Research, Statistics, Data, and Systems." Included in this sector's work and output is in-depth analysis and interpretation of demonstration projects, evaluation reports, and scholarly publications. It is impossible to understate the enormity of the research and scientific-based work of the CMS. For example, their data and reports page currently lists 293 entries. Examples of report titles listed in Table 11.3 reveal the import of this work to the work of social workers.

Table 11.3 EXAMPLES OF CMS REPORTS THAT ARE BENEFICIAL TO SOCIAL WORK PROFESSIONALS

Title of CMS Report	Author(s) of Report
Access to Care for Medicaid Beneficiaries and Disability in Rural Kentucky	Mitchell, J. B., Hoover, S., & Bir, A.
American Indian and Alaska Native Eligibility and Enrollment in Medicaid, SCHIP, and Medicare Estimates	Langwell, K., Cox, D., Schur, C., & Bell, T.
End-Stage Renal Disease (ESRD) Disease Management Demo Evaluation Report: Findings from 2006–2008	Arbor Research Collaborative for Health
Estimating the Impacts of Medicaid Managed Care in Rural Minnesota	Long, S. K., Coughlin, T. A., & King, J.
Health Disparities: Measuring Health Care Use and Access for Racial/Ethnic Populations	Bonito, A. J., Eicheldinger, C. R., & Lenfestey, N. F.
National Evaluation of the State Children's Health Insurance Program: A Decade of Expanding Coverage	Rosenbach, M., Irvin, C., Merrill, A., Shulman, S., Czajka, J., Trenholm, C., Williams, S., Limpa-Amara, S. S., & Katz, A.
Questionnaire Development and Cognitive Testing Using Item Response Theory (IRT)	Uhrig, J. D., Squire, C., McCormack, L.A., Bann C., Hall, P. K., An, C., & Bonio, A. J.
Utilization of Health Care Services Related to Cancer Prevention for Women in the Medicaid Program	Kulas, E., Adamache, W., & Mitchell, J.B.

Additionally, CMS has a scholarly journal. For 30 years the Health Care Financing Review (CMS used to be called the Health Care Financing Administration) was the publishing site for the research work of policy analysts sponsored by the CMS. The archive of the Health Care Financing Review (HCFR) has 1,236 past articles listed. Many, if not most, of the articles contain achieved evidence that helps health care researchers, policy analysts, and others collect and gain access to data analytics compiled by and stored within the CMS. By adhering a bit closer to the scholarly concept of peer review, these articles have a bit more scholarly feel to them than the demonstration projects and evaluation reports listed earlier. Two exemplary titles of HCFR articles again demonstrate the applicability of this work to social work practice and include (1) *Measuring and Improving Health Outcomes in Medicare: The HOS Program* by Haffer and Bowen and (2) *Chronic Conditions: Results of the Medicare Health Outcomes Survey, 1998–2000* by Ellis, Shannon, Cox, Aiken, and Fowler. In 2010, the Health Care Finance Review (HCFR) was renamed the Medicare and Medicaid Research Review (MMRR). An exemplary titles in the MMRR is *Trends in Complicated Newborn Hospital Stays & Costs, 2002–2009: Implications for the Future* by Fowler et al. It is noteworthy that all the archived material and current editions of the Medicare and Medicaid Review are available to all as open-access material. CMS asks only that a citation of record be provided when social work students, social work educators, or social work practitioners use their material.

CMS also has a strong legacy of creating and storing descriptive datasets based on classic variables used by policy analysts as a means to create a basis of comparison in their work—particularly over time and between population groups within a dataset. The two most prominent variables in these datasets are enrollment in program and trends in enrollment. Demographic variables, such as race, ethnicity, gender, socioeconomic status, and geographic location, are also widely used in the CMS datasets and most often included in the reference booklet. Figure 11.1 is exemplary of the use of those variables.

The CMS reference booklet section actually starts out with this description of its population-based data sets:

> For Medicare, statistics are based on persons enrolled for coverage. Original Medicare enrollees are also referred to as fee-for-service enrollees. Historically, for Medicaid, recipient (beneficiary) counts were used as a surrogate of persons eligible for coverage, as well as for persons utilizing services. Current data systems now allow the reporting of total eligibles for Medicaid and for Children's Health Insurance Program (CHIP). Statistics are available by major program categories, by demographic and geographic variables, and as proportions of the U.S. population. Utilization data organized by persons served may be found in the Utilization sections.

CMS offers researchers and other health care professionals a broad range of quantitative information on their programs, from estimates of future Medicare and

Demographic Characteristic	Part A and/or Part B	Part A and Part B	Part A	Part B
Total	55,496,222	50,414,746	55,153,316	50,757,651
Age				
Under 65 Years	8,865,269	8,016,178	8,864,796	8,016,651
65 Years and Over	46,630,952	42,398,568	46,288,520	42,741,000
Under 18 Years	1,716	1,499	1,714	1,500
18-24 Years	108,143	99,271	108,121	99,293
25-34 years	633,073	576,529	633,012	576,590
35-44 Years	1,159,117	1,043,606	1,159,035	1,043,688
45-54 Years	2,425,079	2,181,321	2,424,957	2,181,443
55-64 Years	4,538,142	4,113,953	4,537,957	4,114,138
65-74 Years	26,168,937	22,822,997	25,999,527	22,992,407
75-84 Years	13,971,883	13,367,776	13,862,756	13,476,903
85-94 Years	5,815,990	5,613,351	5,762,590	5,666,751
95 Years and Over	674,142	594,444	663,647	604,940
Sex				
Male	25,257,685	22,430,984	25,142,108	22,546,561
Female	30,238,537	27,983,762	30,011,208	28,211,090
Race				
Non-Hispanic White	41,684,261	38,293,941	41,568,585	38,409,616
Black (or African-American)	5,749,061	5,214,643	5,701,168	5,262,536
Asian/Pacific Islander	1,721,038	1,430,121	1,638,590	1,512,569
Hispanic	4,993,061	4,356,756	4,918,811	4,431,006
American Indian/Alaska Native	251,940	217,836	248,429	221,347
Other	464,115	400,800	458,699	406,216
Unknown	632,747	500,650	619,034	514,362

Figure 11.1 Variables frequently used in Centers for Medicare and Medicaid Services (CMS) reports
SOURCE: Already in the chapter

Medicaid spending to enrollment, spending, and claims data, and a broad range of consumer research. CMS also conducts demonstration projects to explore alternative policies of health care coverage and delivery. These demonstration projects typically cover a limited time frame, geographic area, and scope of coverage (Center for Medicare and Medicaid—Research, 2017).

The evaluative research and scientific evidence production work of CMS is of importance to the social work student, practitioner, and researcher. The efficacy of the CMS-sponsored programs and the exploration of the intended and unintended outcomes of their development and modification in program design, coverage, financing, fidelity of implementation, and impact have major consequences for persons in the United States. Social workers know firsthand that the persons who are sometimes referred to as clients are included in massive numbers in populations with descriptors such as aged, persons with a physical or mental disability, person with end-stage renal disease, a person with limited fiscal assets or resources, a child with special needs, a child living in a family with low income, and individuals or groups of persons with a pre-existing medical condition who are in need of health insurance coverage. The following sections provide a cursory overview of the Medicare and Medicaid programs, and the Affordable Care Act.

Medicare

There are three eligibility categories for Medicare beneficiaries: (1) persons who are age 65 years and older; (2) persons who are under the age of 65 years and who qualify as having a disability (e.g., people who qualify for Social Security Disability benefits should receive a Medicare card in the mail when the required time period has passed); and (3) persons of all ages who carry a diagnosis of end-stage renal disease (i.e., people with permanent kidney failure who require dialysis or transplantation for medical treatment). There are three parts of Medicare. The first part (i.e., Part A) is hospital insurance. Part A covers inpatient care in hospitals, including critical access to hospitals and skilled nursing facilities (however, not custodial or long-term care facilities). Part A also helps to cover the cost of hospice and some home health care. The second part of Medicare (i.e., Part B) is medical insurance. Part B helps to cover doctor services and outpatient care. Part B also helps to cover some medically necessary services not covered under Part A, such as portions of physical and occupational therapy and some home health care. The third part of Medicare is prescription drug coverage. This part is insurance. A beneficiary selects a prescription drug plan offered by a private insurance provider and pays a monthly premium.

Medicaid

CMS is the federal agency that works with state Medicaid agencies to make sure they are complying with federal regulations. Medicaid is administered at the state level, and states therefore vary according to the established eligibility criteria, though eligibility will be generally tied to financial and citizenship status. Importantly for social workers who work in the field of mental health, Medicaid is the single largest payer for mental health services in the United States, and it is increasingly playing a

Table 11.4 MANDATORY AND OPTIONAL MEDICAID BENEFITS

Mandatory Benefits	Optional Benefits
2. Inpatient Hospital Services	3. Prescription Drugs
4. Outpatient Hospital Services	5. Physical Therapy
6. Early and Periodic Screening, Diagnostic, and Treatment Services	7. Occupational Therapy
8. Nursing Facility Services	9. Speech, Hearing, and Language Disorder Services
10. Home Health Services	11. Respiratory Care Services
12. Physician Services	13. Other Diagnostic, Screening, Preventive, and Rehabilitative Services
14. Rural Health Clinic Services	15. Podiatry Services
16. Federally Qualified Health Center Services	17. Optometry Services
18. Laboratory and X-Ray Services	19. Dental Services
20. Family Planning Services	21. Dentures
22. Nurse Midwife Services	23. Prosthetics
24. Certified Pediatric and Family Nurse Practitioner Services	25. Eyeglasses
26. Freestanding Birth Center Services (When Licensed or Otherwise Recognized by the State)	27. Chiropractic Services
28. Transportation to Medical Care	29. Other Practitioner Services
30. Tobacco Cessation Counseling for Pregnant Women	31. Private Duty Nursing Services
	32. Personal Care
	33. Hospice
	34. Case Management
	35. Services for Individuals Age 65 or Older in an Institution for Mental Disease (IMD)
	36. Services in an Intermediate Care Facility for Individuals With Intellectual Disability (ID)
	37. State Plan Home and Community-Based Services—1915(i)
	38. Community First Choice Option–1915(k)
	39. Tuberculosis (TB) Related Services
	40. Inpatient Psychiatric Services for Individuals Under 21
	41. Other Services Approved by the Secretary
	42. Health Homes for Enrollees With Chronic Conditions—Section 1945

larger role in the reimbursement of substance use disorder services. Because states also vary with regard to Medicaid benefits offered, the Table 11.4 presents both mandatory and optional benefits.

The Affordable Care Act

The Affordable Care Act (ACA) actually refers to two separate pieces of legislation: (1) the Patient Protection and Affordable Care Act and (2) the Health Care and Education Reconciliation Act. Together, the two 2010 Acts expand Medicaid coverage to millions of low-income US residents and espouses numerous improvements to both Medicaid and the Children's Health Insurance Program (CHIP). The Affordable Care Act attempted to put in place comprehensive health insurance reforms aimed at expanding coverage; making insurance companies accountable; lowering health care costs; providing beneficiaries with more market options; and enhancing quality of care. However, public reception of the Affordable Care Act has remained a sharp point of political division within the United States in the 21st century. In 2016, US President-elect Donald Trump ran on the platform "repeal and replace" after an October 2016 report by the federal government revealed a marked increase in health care premiums. The federal government estimated that the average midlevel plan under the Affordable Care Act, the most popular choice, would cost approximately 22% more in 2017 than it did in 2016 (Abelson & Sanger-Katz, 2016). Presently, it remains uncertain as to how much of the Affordable Care Act will be repealed and/or replaced under the Trump administration.

Since the Affordable Care Act was enacted in March 2010, CMS has worked together with state partners to identify key implementation priorities and to provide guidance to prepare for the significant changes to Medicaid and CHIP that took effect on January 1, 2014. In 2012, CMS released two final rules defining the eligibility and enrollment policies needed to achieve a seamless system of coverage for individuals who became eligible for Medicaid in 2014. These final rules were intended to establish the framework for states' implementation of the eligibility expansion going forward. A description of all of the major Medicaid and CHIP-related provisions of the Affordable Care Act as well as related policy guidance are presented in Table 11.5.

In December, 2018, a federal judge held that the Act is unconstitutional, based on changes in the U.S. tax structure. The constitutionality of the Act was being litigated in the courts at the time of publication of this book.

MEDICINES, PHARMACEUTICALS, AND SCIENCE

Among the most important tools of modern medicine are medicines, especially prescription medicines. Medicines and substances such as chemicals for treating cancer, as discussed in Chapter 3, are typically the primary tool available to patients (Edwards, 2016).

Table 11.5 AFFORDABLE CARE ACT (ACA) PROVISIONS AND DESCRIPTIONS

ACA Provision	ACA Provision Description
Eligibility	Fills in current gaps in coverage for the poorest Americans by creating a minimum Medicaid income eligibility level across the country.
Financing	Beginning in 2014, coverage for the newly eligible adults will be fully funded by the federal government for 3 years. It will phase down to 90% by 2020.
Information Technology Systems and Date	Policy and financing structure designed to provide states with tools needed to achieve the immediate and substantial investment in information technology systems that is needed in order to ensure that Medicaid systems will be in place in time for the January 1, 2014, launch date or the new Affordable Insurance Exchanges as well as the expansion of Medicaid eligibility.
Coordination With Affordable Insurance Exchanges	This system enables individuals and families to apply for coverage using a single application and have their eligibility determined for all insurance affordability programs through one simple process.
Benefits	People newly eligible for Medicaid will receive a benchmark benefit or benchmark equivalent package that includes the minimum essential benefits provided in the Affordable Insurance Exchanges.
Community-Based Long-Term Services and Supports	Includes a number of program and funding improvements to help ensure that people can receive long-term care services and supports in their home or the community.
Quality of Care and Delivery Systems	Improvements will be made in the quality or care and the manner in which that care is delivered while at the same time reducing costs.
Prevention	Promotes prevention, wellness and public health and supports health promotion efforts at the local, state, and federal levels.
Children's Health Insurance Program (CHIP)	Extends funding for the Children's Health Insurance Program (CHIP) through FY 2015 and continues the authority for the program through 2019.
Dual Eligibilities	A new office will be created within the Centers for Medicare & Medicaid Services to coordinate care for individuals who are eligible for both Medicaid and Medicare ("dual eligibles" or Medicare-Medicaid enrollees).

Table 11.5 CONTINUED

ACA Provision	ACA Provision Description
Provider Payments	States will receive 100% federal matching funds for the increase in payments.
Program Transparency	Promotes transparency about Medicaid policies and programs, including establishing meaningful opportunities for public involvement in the development of state and federal Medicaid waivers.
Program Integrity	Includes numerous provisions designed to increase program integrity in Medicaid, including terminating providers from Medicaid that have been terminated in other programs, suspending Medicaid payments based on pending investigations or credible allegations of fraud, and preventing inappropriate payment or claims under Medicaid.

Again, it is not within the scope of this book to describe the whole process of developing and dispensing pharmaceuticals. It is important to know that physicians are aware of the medicines that may serve their patients' needs. In many ways, almost all physicians are experts in the use of medicines.

The other components of the pharmaceutical continuum are the pharmaceutical companies that finance and market medicines, which is an international industry. Professionals trained in the field of pharmacology do the actual development of pharmaceuticals, or the more common term "drugs." Chemistry is the science that underlies much of what is done in pharmaceutical research. Researchers carry on the fundamental work of creating the drugs, often with grants from the federal government and private foundations. Before a drug can be sold for the treatment of patients, the substances must be carefully tested and determined to be helpful in treatment and not harmful to patients. The process is complicated and involves tests with human subjects to determine the effectiveness and safety of the drugs.

For the first few years the drugs are marketed, the company that owns them is protected from duplication of the substances. After the patent on the drugs ends, other companies may manufacture duplicate medicines called generics. Sometimes the original patent holders also manufacture and market the generic equivalents of their original, patented medicines.

Pharmacists are the professionals who fill the prescriptions written by health care providers. Pharmacists are other professionals in the health care field. They may be employed by pharmacies, hospitals, and clinics. Their professional preparation and licensing are also governed by the state governments in many ways that are similar to the ways that nurses and physicians are provided credentials.

Laws generally cover the ways in which pharmaceuticals are provided. For example, those that are "controlled" substances, usually those that can be addictive, have special rules governing their dispensing. Of course, any drug can be dangerous if used incorrectly or if used to cure a condition for which it is not appropriate. The scientific bases for pharmaceuticals and the use of medicines is one of the more consistently scientific elements of the health care industry. The validity of the substances is determined by careful and documented research often over periods of years.

The US government's Food and Drug Administration (part of the Department of Health and Human Services) governs the approval of medicines and establishes the rules for their distribution. Details on the possible side effects of drugs are provided to patients along with cautions about their misuse.

It is interesting that not all drugs are governed by the FDA. Substances that manufacturers describe as curative medicines are exempt from the research and evaluation scrutiny of the FDA. Such substances are sold "over the counter," with prescriptions, in pharmacies, grocery stores, and other retailers. The US Congress exempted these substances from the intense scrutiny of the FDA. They include the whole range of vitamins and minerals, many pain killers, and treatments for respiratory problems.

Alternative Medicine

Homeopathic medicines are among those exempt from FDA approval. Homeopathic medicine is a long-standing alternative to prescription drugs, based on the belief that exposing the patient to a very low, diluted dose of the problem condition can cure illnesses. For example, homeopathic practitioners may believe that injecting a patient with a highly diluted dose of the influenza virus could prevent or cure a case of influenza. Most scientific students of health and medicines reject the idea as having never been proven. However, the homeopathic medicines may be purchased in various places, including health food retailers and grocery stores. Homeopathy is studied by the National Center for Complementary and Integrative Health, a part of the National Institutes of Health, which deals with acupuncture and chiropractic, as discussed elsewhere in this chapter.

Sometimes pharmaceuticals that were originally dispensed by prescription only become over-the-counter generics, often at lower dosages than the original product. These over-the-counter products are not allowed to make claims that they heal illnesses. They can argue that they enhance health but not that they are cures. If they are implicated in causing illnesses and other health problems, the manufacturers and distributors may be subject to lawsuits for the damages they are accused of causing. For details on the FDA rules and regulations for prescription drugs and supplements, see www.fda.gov. There are multiple subsections on the FDA's control of medicines, supplements, and foods.

EXPERIMENTS AND TRIALS

In addition to the care patients seek and regular health care clinics provide, some of medicine's treatments involve experimental approaches and trials. Experiments attempt to address or cure a specific condition with methods that are based on experiments—hypothesized approaches to addressing health condition for which there are no known or consistently successful treatments. It is through experiments and trials of treatments associated with the experiments that scientists become involved in health care. Representatives of many scientific professions engage in experiments about treatment for medical conditions. As is the case with pharmaceuticals, laws require that experimental treatments not be harmful to patients. However, some experiments provide waivers for the experimenters so that they are able to provide their experimental treatments with appropriate warnings that the treatment may not be effective or even harmful. The subjects of such experiments must agree to the treatment and demonstrate, in writing, that they are aware of the potential dangers.

PROTECTION OF SUBJECTS

The protection of human subjects became a central issue in the American government over the Tuskegee experiments (Centers for Disease Control and Prevention, n.d.). In those experiments, which began in 1932 and continued for another 40 years, African American men in Tuskegee, Alabama, were recruited for a study of their health to determine some facts about "bad blood." A group of over 200 men who had syphilis were given regular medical checkups, travel to medical facilities for the study of their conditions, and burial insurance. A somewhat smaller group of men who were not affected by the disease were also recruited and studied. The upshot of the experiment was that during the years of the study, cures were found for syphilis—penicillin became a reliable and simple treatment for the condition. However, the infected subjects were never informed that there was treatment and were not given penicillin to cure their disease. In the 1970s, the experiments ended and payment was made to the subjects. Their health care continued (Centers for Disease Control and Prevention, n.d.).

Since the time of the Tuskegee experiments, federal law has required documented informed consent from subjects of potentially dangerous research of any kind. Research organizations, government agencies, and universities all operate under strict procedures for providing protection of human research subjects and informed consent to participate in the experiments.

Experiments vary and incorporate multiple approaches, based upon an experimenter's studies or observations of interventions. There are always large numbers of experimental approaches being used to determine their effectiveness. That is especially true of conditions for which there are no known cures and for which traditional interventions appear to be without useful consequences. Experimenters have attempted to treat ALS (Lou Gehrig disease) with injections of toxic snake venom; cancer with injections of disease substances such as the polio virus and HIV. Press reports (CBS News, *60 Minutes*, May 15, 2016) may suggest that the treatments are effective.

Some experimental treatments are financed by the federal government through the National Institutes of Health or by private grants, often through pharmaceutical companies. Often the efforts involve trials of the treatment, involving patients whose reactions to the treatments are studied and evaluated. Some of the trial subjects may be prisoners who constitute an available and consistent population for study.

ALTERNATIVE AND COMPLEMENTARY HEALTH CARE

A major set of practices throughout the world are those of alternative and complementary health care—approaches that differ significantly from mainstream, science-based health care. These include a variety of practices such as homeopathy (described earlier); chiropractic; naturopathy; acupuncture; and Ayurvedic medicine, a traditional healing process with a long history in India; and even such common health offerings as massage, faith-based healing, and medical practices that are part of the tradition of populations such as Native Americans. Many of these traditional healing programs include using herbs as medicines. Some herbs, with and without the health care processes that use them, are demonstrably useful for some conditions and less so for others.

One science encyclopedia (Philip, 1999) says that acupuncture, a Chinese traditional medical practice, which involves placing long needles into a patient's body, enables surgeons to perform operations on people who are awake but whose pain is overcome through the acupuncture. The same encyclopedia says that this procedure defies scientific explanation. However, the National Center for Complementary and Integrative Health (NCCIH; https://nccih.nih.gov/health/acupuncture/introduction) says that the science is still unclear and that factors other than the insertion of needles such as expectations and beliefs may play a role in the observed effectiveness of acupuncture.

The National Institutes of Health includes the NCCIH. The website of the NCCIH describes the wide range of alternative and complementary health services. Many of these approaches have long histories of use in the United States as well as training institutions and clinics that offer services based on their approaches.

In general, the NCCIH explains in its materials, these alternative practices have usually not been proven effective or necessarily safe. The NCCIH cautions people to avoid dropping other, more scientifically based health care, in favor of the alternative and complementary services (Nahin, Boineau, Khalsa, Stussman, & Weber, 2016).

Although many of the alternative approaches suggest that their treatments are scientifically based and proven safe and effective, the research designs used and the conclusions reached are often not in keeping with generally accepted scientific methods. There are still, nevertheless, thousands of people who swear by the effectiveness of their alternative treatments. Books, newspaper advertisements, and television commercials present testimonies from satisfied users of these practices.

LIFE EXPECTANCY AND CAUSES OF DEATH

According to the National Center for Health Statistics, Division of Vital Statistics, life expectancy for the United States is 78.8 years, for people born in 2013. For

White people, life expectancy was 79.1 years and for women 81.2. For Black people, life expectancy is 75.5 years and for Hispanics 81.6 years. The death rate is 731.9 deaths per 100,000 populations. These figures were for 2013, the most recent date for which data are available. Of course, the death rates vary by age—the older age groups have much higher death rates than the younger population.

In 2016, the first decline in US life expectancy was recorded in many years. (Tavernise, 2016). Details of the reasons for the decline are still being developed but speculation was that suicide, increased availability of illegal drugs, and perhaps other factors were being considered.

The Division of Vital Statistics also provides information on the leading causes of death. The top 15 are as follows:

1. Diseases of heart (heart disease)
2. Malignant neoplasms (cancer)
3. Chronic lower respiratory diseases
4. Accidents (unintentional injuries)
5. Cerebrovascular diseases (stroke)
6. Alzheimer's disease
7. Diabetes mellitus (diabetes)
8. Influenza and pneumonia
9. Nephritis, nephrotic syndrome, and nephrosis (kidney disease)
10. Intentional self-harm (suicide)
11. Septicemia
12. Chronic liver disease and cirrhosis
13. Essential hypertension and hypertensive renal disease (hypertension)
14. Parkinson's disease
15. Pneumonitis due to solids and liquids

Again, there are major variations according to age. Heart disease, cancer, and stroke, for example, all affect the elderly much more than they do other age groups. Parkinson's disease and Alzheimer's disease are practically nonexistent among the young and are therefore not causes of death. There are also differential rates of death from the various cancers with some affecting primarily older people and rarely young people. Accidents are a major cause of death among younger men and women and suicide, by rate, is higher among older White adult males than among other groups. The federal vital statistics data break down death rates by ethnicity (Black, White, Hispanic, Native American, and Alaska Native) and by age.

The second leading cause of death, malignant neoplasms, or cancer, may actually be a collection of causes rather than a single cause. There are many different kinds of cancers in various sites. Some quickly kill their victims; others are more like chronic diseases. Some are readily discovered through ongoing tests such as breast cancer and mammograms, while others are so unlikely to be diagnosed, such as pancreatic cancer, for example, that the patient dies before he or she or the doctors know what the illness is.

CONCLUSION

Covered in this chapter are some of the issues for which social workers need special awareness—the ways in which health care and medicine are practiced in the United States. It also covers some of the issues in public health, which is also a major site for employment of social workers. Prevention of illness, treatment for illness, life expectancy, and the incidence of diseases in the nation are all discussed.

Medicine and health care are among the most important applications of science for social workers. Knowing about the science behind illness and health is especially crucial for social work practitioners. Being conversant with the science issues in health care is important for most social workers and of special importance to those engaged in medical social work or other forms of social work in health settings.

REFERENCES

Aamodt, S. (2016, May 6). Why you can't lose weight on a diet. *New York Times*, pp. SR1. Retrieved from https://www.nytimes.com/2016/05/08/opinion/sunday/why-you-cant-lose-weight-on-a-diet.html.

Abelson, R., & Sanger-Katz, M. (2016). A quick guide to rising Obamacare rates. *New York Times*, pp. A19.

Atkins, R. D. C. (2009). *Dr. Atkins' new diet revolution*. New York, NY: Harper.

Beers, M. H., & Berkow, R. (1999). *The Merck manual of diagnosis and therapy*. Whitehouse Station, NJ: Merck and Co.

Centers for Disease Control and Prevention (n.d.). U.S. Public Health Service study of syphilis at Tuskegee. Retrieved from https://www.cdc.gov/tuskegee/index.html.

Clayman, C. B. (1989). *The American Medical Association encyclopedia of medicine*. New York, NY: Random House.

Cooper, K. N. (1983). *Aerobics*. New York, NY: Bantam. (Original work published 1968)

Edwards, H. S. (2016, May 30). Why do drugs cost so much? *Time*, 38–43.

Ginsberg, L., Nackerud, L., & Larrison, C. (2003). *Human biology for social workers*. New York, NY: Pearson.

Ginsberg, L. (2000). *Careers in social work* (2nd ed.). New York, NY: Pearson.

Mayo Clinic. (2016). Ulcers. Retrieved from www.mayoclinic.org/ulcers

Nahin, R. L., Boineau, R., Khalsa, P. S., Stussman, B. J., & Weber, W. J. (2016). Evidence-based evaluation of complementary health approaches for pain management in the United States. *Mayo Clinic Proceedings, 91*(9), 1292–1306. doi: 10.1016/j.mayocp.2016.06.007

NCCIH. (n.d.). *Acupuncture: In depth*. Retrieved from https://nccih.nih.gov/health/acupuncture/introduction

Ornish, D. (2000). *Eat more, weigh less: Dr. Dean Ornish's life choice program for losing weight safely while eating abundantly*. New York, NY: Harper Collins.

Parker, S. (2016). *Medicine: The definitive illustrated history*. New York. NY: DK Publishing.

Philips, G. (1999). *Philip's Science & Technology Encyclopedia*. London, UK: Octopus Publishing.

Sharma, S. (2015, September 20). Mosquito-borne illnesses. *Hindustan Times*. Retrieved from https://www.hindustantimes.com/columns/

you-should-know-5-deadliest-mosquito-borne-diseases-in-india/story-HVE7pprbScppKyqClE5GoN.html

Sifferlin, A. (2016, December 19). Dr. Cristin Kearns. *Time*. Retrieved from http://time.com/4606066/dr-cristin-kearns/.

Tavernise, S. (2016, June 1). First rise in U.S. death rates in years surprises experts. *New York Times*, pp. A10. Retrieved from https://www.nytimes.com/2016/06/01/health/american-death-rate-rises-for-first-time-in-a-decade.html.

US Department of Health and Human Services/Centers for Medicare & Medicaid Services/Office of Enterprise Data and Analytics (2017). *2016 CMS statistics* (CMS Pub. No. 03513). Washington, DC. Retrieved from https://www.cms.gov/Research-Statistics-Data-and-Systems/Statistics-Trends-and-Reports/CMS-Statistics-Reference-Booklet/index.html.

12

Social Work and the Science of Substance Use

As social workers, when we think about alcohol and substance use, we typically focus on a subset of individuals who experience significant problems with life because of alcohol and/or substance abuse. Neuroscience, genetics, and chemistry researchers have greatly expanded our understanding of alcohol and substance use to move beyond clinical judgments typically discussed by social workers. By adding information from these three fields of science to the traditional social work teachings on substance abuse, we hope to expand social workers' knowledge about this common and confusing human behavior and to move beyond the clinical focus of abuse. Discussions of alcohol and substance use and abuse have always been controversial. We hope to capture some of this tension and then move beyond it by examining the basic definitions of terms related to substance use and the contributions of chemistry, neuroscience, and genetics to our understanding of why human beings use substances.

WHAT IS TYPICAL HUMAN BEHAVIOR IN REGARD TO ALCOHOL AND SUBSTANCE USE?

Writer and gonzo journalist Hunter S. Thompson once said famously: "I hate to advocate drugs, alcohol, violence, or insanity to anyone, but they've always worked for me." Others like William Penn, founder of Pennsylvania, have viewed drug and alcohol use with a more jaundice eye: "All excess is ill, but drunkenness is of the worst sort. It spoils health, dismounts the mind, and unmans men. It reveals secrets, is quarrelsome, lascivious, impudent, dangerous and mad." And some people start in one place like Alex Huxley, who saw drugs as a tool utilized by a dystopian government to control people in his book *Brave New World* (1932) but then moved to view drugs as a way of creating a utopian society in *Island* (1962). Drugs have even been strategically used by militaries from around the world. *Blitzed: Drugs in Nazi Germany* (Ohler, 2014) outlines the extensive use of stimulants and opioids by Nazi leadership and military personnel. Additionally, the US Air Force has used "Go Pills," which are stimulants since World War II (Bonne, 2003). Needless to say, throughout history the relationship between human beings and mind-altering substances, whether it is opioid painkillers or a cup of coffee, has been a contentious one.

At the heart of the controversy is the double-edge sword of positive benefits (e.g., a cup of coffee makes people more alert as well as provides a number of other health benefits) with the dark possibility of misuse that results in negative life outcomes, including ill health, loss of family and employment, and even premature death. This fine line between positive and negative can been seen dramatically in the growing opioid epidemic that started to gain speed in the mid-2000s and coincided with the expanded prescribing of opioids to address pain problems ranging from chronic back pain to pain associated with knee surgery to cancer-related pain. If you have ever known someone recovering from cancer, think about the role of opioids in decreasing the almost unbearable pain created by invasive surgeries, radiation, and chemotherapy. However, these same prescribing practices that help cancer patients have resulted in an opioid and heroin epidemic that has decreased the life expectancy of White males in rural communities across the United States because of overdoses, suicides, and chronic health problems associated with long-term opioid use.

Identifying when alcohol and substance use requires intervention is not easy. In fact, the use of alcohol and other substances is fairly widespread in the general population. Some examples include (1) caffeine—it is estimated that 80% to 90% of adults consume caffeine on a daily basis with 50% consuming more than 300 mg a day (an 8 oz cup of coffee has between 95 and 200 mg; Mayo Clinic Staff, 2017); (2) nicotine—24.6% of individuals 12 years or older use nicotine products (Center for Behavioral Health Statistics and Quality, 2015); (3) alcohol—more than 55% of adults (18 years or older) in the United States reported drinking alcohol in the past month, 71% in the last year, and nearly 88% have tried alcohol at some point in their life (NIAAA, 2016); and finally, (4) marijuana, which is considered the most widely used illegal substance worldwide. In the United States, 43% of people over the age of 12 have tried marijuana and 13% use it regularly (Center for Behavioral Health Statistics and Quality, 2015). See Figure 12.1 from the Center for Behavioral Health Statistics and Quality, (2015) to get a sense of the illicit substance use the United States.

Of the people who are exposed to substances, a minority of individuals develop behaviors that become problematic or rise to a clinical level. For example, among adults using alcohol, approximately 7.2% have an alcohol use disorder (AUD; NIAAA, 2016). This is not to underestimate the significance of the personal, public health, economic, and social problems that are experienced by the 17 million adults living in the United States with AUD, but to instead to differentiate between use and abuse of alcohol. Figure 12.2 from the Center for Behavioral Health Statistics and Quality provides a nice graphic breakdown of alcohol use and abuse.

In general, if you find yourself drinking a cup of coffee a day, occasionally have a beer or glass of wine, or even periodically indulging in marijuana, then you are part of a significant part of the human population that enjoys the chemical reaction substances create in the human brain. The relationship between the chemicals in alcohol and other substances, and the brain seems to become broken for a minority of individuals when the cognitive rewards created by the alcohol or other substances encourage an escalating cycle of use that leads to abuse. This relationship between a chemical (i.e., alcohol and other substances), the brain, and genetics is what we will explore in more detail throughout the rest of the chapter.

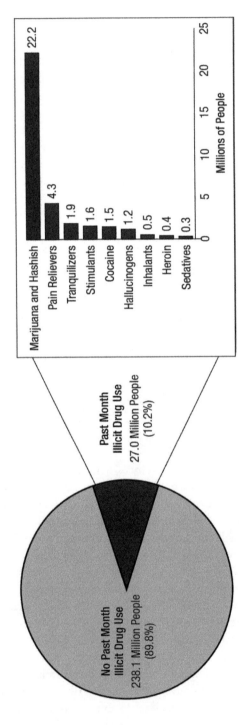

Figure 12.1 Numbers of past month illicit drug users among people aged 12 or older: 2014 (Center for Behavioral Health Statistics and Quality, 2015)

SOURCE: https://www.samhsa.gov/data/sites/default/files/NSDUH-FRR1-2014/NSDUH-FRR1-2014.pdf

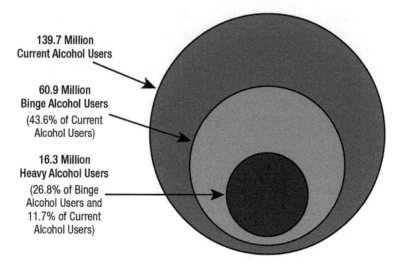

139.7 Million
Current Alcohol Users

60.9 Million
Binge Alcohol Users
(43.6% of Current
Alcohol Users)

16.3 Million
Heavy Alcohol Users
(26.8% of Binge
Alcohol Users and
11.7% of Current
Alcohol Users)

Figure 12.2 Current, binge, and heavy alcohol use among people aged 12 or older: 2014 (Center for Behavioral Health Statistics and Quality, 2015)
SOURCE: https://www.samhsa.gov/data/sites/default/files/NSDUH-FRR1-2014/NSDUH-FRR1-2014. htm#fig24desc

BASIC DEFINITIONS

Before going any further, let's try to pin down some definitions for "substance," "alcohol," and "drug" as well as identify the distinction between what is considered typical behavior (i.e., use) with what is clinical behavior (i.e., abuse). The definitions will help us to appreciate the importance of chemistry in understanding alcohol and substance use. In the most basic terms, all of the substances we introduce into the biology of our bodies are chemicals. The distinction between use and abuse provides an entree to understanding the neuroscience and genetic aspects of alcohol and substances.

Substance is a word usually describing anything that has physical presence. When used by social workers in a clinical context, the word refers to drugs and alcohol. *The Diagnostic and Statistical Manual of Mental Disorders*, fifth edition (*DSM-5*; 2013) has 10 separate substance classes: (1) alcohol; (2) caffeine; (3) cannabis; (4) hallucinogens (with separate categories for phencyclidine [or similarly acting arylcyclohexylamines] and other hallucinogens); (5) inhalants; (6) opioids; (7) sedatives, hypnotics, and anxiolytics; (8) stimulants (amphetamine-type substances, cocaine, and other stimulants); (9) tobacco; and (10) other (or unknown) substances. Some substances are chemical compounds, such as lysergic acid diethylamide (LSD; $C_{20}H_{25}N_3O$) or methamphetamine ($C_{10}H_{15}N$), and others, such as marijuana, contain chemical compounds (tetrahydrocannabinol; THC; $C_{21}H_{30}O_2$) that are released when the plant, food, or compound is consumed.

Sometimes the word *drug* is used to distinguish between illicit and legal substances, but Merriam-Webster's online dictionary offers two definitions of the word *drug* that cover both aspects:

1. A substance used as a medication or in the preparation of medication according to the Food, Drug, and Cosmetic Act (1) a substance recognized in an official pharmacopoeia or formulary (2) a substance intended for use in the diagnosis, cure, mitigation, treatment, or prevention of disease (3) a substance other than food intended to affect the structure or function of the body (4) a substance intended for use as a component of a medicine but not a device or a component, part, or accessory of a device,

2. Something and often an illegal substance that causes addiction, habituation, or a marked change in consciousness. (https://www.merriam-webster.com/dictionary/drug)

Alcohol is a commonly used word in the public discourse that is periodically considered separate from other substances. This distinction is probably because it is the most widely used legal substance. Alcohol is a chemical from the hydroxyl functional group (–OH). Functional groups are specific groupings of atoms that share common chemical reactions. Hydroxyl has a common base of oxygen bonded to hydrogen that is shared by water, alcohols, and carboxylic acid, for example (see Table 12.1 for a complete list of the hydroxyl functional group). For more information about the concepts of functional groups and hydroxyl, please refer to Chapters 2 and 7.

When we think of alcohol consumed by human beings, it is ethanol. Methanol (wood alcohol), the most commonly known other type of alcohol, is poisonous to humans and creates a significantly weaker intoxicating effect than ethanol. This is why drinking methanol is particularly dangerous—it is deadly poisonous and takes large quantities to achieve intoxication. See the molecular models of the two alcohols types in Figure 12.3 to get a sense of their chemical difference differences and similarities (hence the same functional group).

How do social workers typically distinguish use from abuse? There is probably no definition of substance abuse that would gain a universal positive response from social work professionals, but the *DSM-5* provides one perspective that is the result of a substantial amount of thought and debate among a group of substance use experts (Hasin et al., 2013). According to the *DSM-5*, substance use disorders (SUDs) are determined by the number of criteria exhibited by the person, with 2 to 3 criteria indicating mild, 4 to 5 criteria indicating moderate, and 6 or more criteria indicating severe SUD (*DSM-5*, 2013). There are 11 possible criteria:

1. The substance is often taken in larger amounts or over a longer period than was intended.
2. There is a persistent desire or unsuccessful effort to cut down or control use of the substance.
3. A great deal of time is spent in activities necessary to obtain the substance, use the substance, or recover from its effects.
4. Craving, or a strong desire or urge to use the substance.
5. Recurrent use of the substance, resulting in a failure to fulfill major role obligations at work, school, or home.

Table 12.1 HYDROXYL FUNCTIONAL GROUP

Chemical Formula	IUPAC Name	Common Name
MONOHYDRIC ALCOHOLS		
CH_3OH	Methanol	Wood alcohol
C_2H_5OH	Ethanol	Alcohol
C_3H_7OH	Propan-2-ol	Isopropyl alcohol, rubbing alcohol
C_4H_9OH	Butan-1-ol	Butanol, butyl alcohol
$C_5H_{11}OH$	Pentan-1-ol	Pentanol, amyl alcohol
$C_{16}H_{33}OH$	Hexadecan-1-ol	Cetyl alcohol
POLYHYDRIC ALCOHOLS		
$C_2H_4(OH)_2$	Ethane-1,2-diol	Ethylene glycol
$C_3H_6(OH)_2$	Propane-1,2-diol	Propylene glycol
$C_3H_5(OH)_3$	Propane-1,2,3-triol	Glycerol
$C_4H_6(OH)_4$	Butane-1,2,3,4-tetraol	Erythritol, threitol
$C_5H_7(OH)_5$	Pentane-1,2,3,4,5-pentol	Xylitol
$C_6H_8(OH)_6$	Hexane-1,2,3,4,5,6-hexol	Mannitol, sorbitol
$C_7H_9(OH)_7$	Heptane-1,2,3,4,5,6,7-heptol	Volemitol
UNSATURATED ALIPHATIC ALCOHOLS		
C_3H_5OH	Prop-2-ene-1-ol	Allyl alcohol
$C_{10}H_{17}OH$	3,7-Dimethylocta-2,6-dien-1-ol	Geraniol
C_3H_3OH	Prop-2-yn-1-ol	Propargyl alcohol
ALICYCLIC ALCOHOLS		
$C_6H_6(OH)_6$	Cyclohexane-1,2,3,4,5,6-hexol	Inositol
$C_{10}H_{19}OH$	2-(2-propyl)-5-methyl-cyclohexane-1-ol	Menthol

Note. Adapted from "Alcohol", Wikipedia contributors (2018, July 21). *Wikipedia, The Free Encyclopedia*. Retrieved from https://en.wikipedia.org/wiki/Alcohol.

6. Continued use of the substance despite having persistent or recurrent social or interpersonal problems caused or exacerbated by the effects of its use.
7. Important social, occupational, or recreational activities are given up or reduced because of use of the substance.
8. Recurrent use of the substance in situations in which it is physically hazardous.
9. Use of the substance is continued despite knowledge of having a persistent or recurrent physical or psychological problem that is likely to have been caused or exacerbated by the substance.

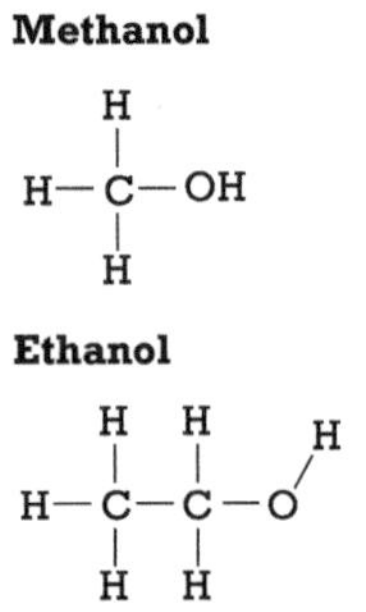

Methanol

$$H-\overset{\displaystyle H}{\underset{\displaystyle H}{C}}-OH$$

Ethanol

$$H-\overset{\displaystyle H}{\underset{\displaystyle H}{C}}-\overset{\displaystyle H}{\underset{\displaystyle H}{C}}-O\diagup{}^{H}$$

Figure 12.3 Molecular models of methanol and ethanol Authors' creation

10. Tolerance, as defined by either of the following:
    a. A need for markedly increased amounts of the substance to achieve intoxication or desired effect.
    b. A markedly diminished effect with continued use of the same amount of the substance.
11. Withdrawal, as manifested by either of the following:
    a. The characteristic withdrawal syndrome for that substance (as specified in the *DSM-5* for each substance).
    b. The substance (or a closely related substance) is taken to relieve or avoid withdrawal symptoms.

Regarding the DSM-5 definition, the Substance Abuse and Mental Health Services Administration (SAMHSA) states:

> The Diagnostic and Statistical Manual of Mental Disorders, Fifth Edition (DSM-5), no longer uses the terms substance abuse and substance dependence, rather it refers to substance use disorders, which are defined as mild, moderate, or severe to indicate the level of severity, which is determined by the number of diagnostic criteria met by an individual. Substance use disorders occur when the recurrent use of alcohol and/or drugs causes clinically and functionally significant impairment, such as health problems, disability, and failure to meet major responsibilities at work, school, or home. According to the DSM-5, a diagnosis of substance use disorder is based on evidence of impaired control, social impairment, risky use, and pharmacological criteria. (https://www.samhsa.gov/disorders/substance-use)

The *DSM*'s new approach captures some of the evolution in language as well as the tension that exists among social workers providing alcohol and substance abuse services.

WHY IS SUBSTANCE USE INTERESTING TO STUDY?

Beyond the terrible human and economic toll taken by SUDs, the basic definitions and the distinction between use and abuse explored in the previous section provide some initial sense of why scientists and social workers are interested in studying substance use and abuse. Substance use represents an appealing mechanism for understanding how a mix of genetics, biology, and environmental cues shapes human behaviors. The substance, an outside chemical introduced into the body, becomes a vehicle for change in behavior and biology. The reasons for taking substances tend to be environmental, and the reasons people develop SUDs tend to be behavioral re-enforcement related to changes in neurology and genetics. We won't be able to cover all of the differences between substances, which can be substantial. Instead, we will explore research within neuroscience and genetics using discrete examples to help us better understand the dynamics that inform substance use and abuse.

Neuroscience

Research utilizing mice and rat models, as well as research on human beings addicted to substances, indicates that long-term substance use creates stable changes in the brain at the cellular and molecular levels (Nestler, 2001). SUDs appear to be linked to positive memories of the experience created by substances that encourage use through environmental cues (Kauer & Malenka, 2007). Think about the role that people, places, and dates play in even casual substance use. For example, some of the authors have New Year's Eve traditions that include specific friends, places, objects, and the responsible consumption of alcohol. Getting together with old friends on the same date, at the same place, and using the same table settings for decades provides powerful cues that could be associated with alcohol consumption. If we were to develop SUDs, there would probably be many more environmental cues to use alcohol that result in usage that impacts the synaptic plasticity among the brain circuits in the mesolimbic dopamine system (Kauer & Malenka, 2007). The mesolimbic dopamine system is associated with the reward and pleasure processes in the brain (Kauer & Malenka, 2007).

Another substance to consider is marijuana and tetrahydrocannabinol (THC), which is a cannabinoid. Cannabinoids are chemical compounds that act on cannabinoid specific receptors in the brain. The body naturally produces similar cannabinoids found in THC. These cannabinoids help with sending messages between cells throughout the nervous systems (Davis, 2018). As a result, cannabinoid receptors are found throughout the brain and are related to memory, concentration, movement and coordination, pleasure, and perception of time (Davis, 2018). This means that using marijuana can impact all of these areas of brain functioning as THC is picked up by the receptors. For example, THC impacts receptors in the hippocampus and orbitofrontal cortex, which are associated with memory and attention as well as the cerebellum and basal ganglia, which are associated with reaction time and physical movement such as balance and posture (Davis, 2018). Like other chemicals found in cocaine and nicotine (for instance), THC increases the release of the neurotransmitter dopamine, which is linked to the euphoric feelings typically associated with substance use (Davis, 2018).

When we move to examining the model for something like opioid abuse, the initial chemical reactions in the brain are similar, but there is limited understanding of the neural mechanisms that move a person from use to SUD. De Vries and Shipenberg (2002) describe this gap and some viable hypotheses in their review of the research. Following is the abstract from that review:

Opiate addiction is a chronically relapsing disorder that is characterized by compulsive drug taking, an inability to limit intake, and bouts of intense drug craving that can be precipitated by the mere presence of people, places, or objects previously associated with drug use. Although knowledge of the neural mechanisms that underlie the transition from casual drug use to addiction is still incomplete, the development of animal models that enable differentiation of the various stages of the addiction process have provided new insights regarding the neural substrates on which opiates act to affect and subsequently control behavior. Data derived from these models are consistent with the hypothesis that opiates, like psychostimulants, are initially abused by virtue of their rewarding or hedonic effects. However, the repeated use of opiates induces alterations in neurotransmitter and neuropeptide systems that regulate incentive–motivation and stress–responsiveness. Increasing evidence indicates that the dysregulation of these systems underlies the compulsive use and loss of control of drug-taking that characterizes opiate and other addictions. (De Vries & Shippenberg, 2002, p. 3321)

Genetics

Two areas of genetics research contribute to our understanding of substance use and abuse. First is research to understand how genetic variation contributes to people being susceptible to substance abuse (Nestler, 2000). This research focuses on identifying specific genes associated with creating vulnerability to substance abuse. In social work, we have believed for a long time that genetics plays at least some role in substance abuse. The client assessment processes we teach in BSW and MSW programs always include questions about family history, implying both environmental exposure as well as genetic susceptibility. This genetic susceptibility is well documented in the research literature. For example, the family members of individuals who have alcohol abuse have significantly higher rates of abuse themselves (Wang, Kapoor, & Goate, 2012). Twin studies and adoption studies untangle some of the environmental and genetic questions. Monozygotic twins have significantly higher risk rates of alcohol abuse than dizygotic twins (Wang, Kapoor, & Goate, 2012). In addition, children from parents with alcohol abuse have higher rates of alcohol abuse than children from parents without alcohol abuse even when both are adopted by families that do not experience alcohol abuse (Wang, Kapoor, & Goate, 2012). Second is research on how substances, like other chemicals that can be toxic, result in damage to the functioning of genes. This research highlights how substance abuse can impact the very biology of human beings.

Genetics research aimed at ascertaining genetic markers associated with substance abuse have found a correlation between the genes that regulate stress, impulsivity, risk-taking behaviors, and substance abuse behaviors (Kreek, Nielsen, Butelman, & LaForge, 2005). However, genome studies related to substance abuse have experienced different levels of success (Wang, Kapoor, & Goate, 2012). In a review of 371 studies associated with gene research related to alcohol, nicotine, cannabis, and cocaine abuse, Bühler et al. (2015) found that there are many more studies replicating findings associated with the genetic mechanisms of alcohol and nicotine abuse than for cannabis and cocaine. Wang, Kapoor, and Goate (2012) do a nice job of identifying genetic variants associated with alcohol abuse:

> The most well-established genetic factors associated with alcohol dependence are in the genes encoding alcohol dehydrogenase (*ADH*), which oxidizes alcohol to acetaldehyde, and aldehyde dehydrogenase (*ALDH2*), which oxidizes acetaldehyde to acetate. Recently emerging genetic studies have linked variants in the genes encoding the α3, α5, and β4 nicotinic acetylcholine receptor subunits to smoking risk. However, the influence of these well-established genetic variants accounts for only a small portion of the heritability of alcohol and nicotine addiction, and it is likely that there are both common and rare risk variants yet to be identified. (Wang, Kapoor, & Goate, 2012, p. 241)

The first part of the discussion fits with a classic understanding of genetics as an underlying biological structure that makes us susceptible to risk. Epigenetics suggests another way of viewing the relationship between the environment and genetics. Typically the term means "any process that alters gene activity without changing the DNA sequence, and leads to modifications that can be transmitted to daughter cells (although experiments show that some epigenetic changes can be reversed)" (Weinhold, 2006, A163). The chemicals that we know as substances/drugs also are suspected of having an epigenetic effect on us. Remember in the previous section the discussion about the gaps in our understanding of the mechanisms that create long-term change in the dopamine reactors that re-enforce substance-taking behaviors leading to SUD. One of the mechanisms is change in gene transcription, in RNA, and protein processing, and in synaptic structure created by long-term substance use (Nestler, 2001). Beyond epigenetics, alcohol toxicity is thought to damage human DNA (Brooks, 1997). This can be seen dramatically in fetal alcohol spectrum disorder (FASD), which occurs sometimes when a mother consumes alcohol during pregnancy introducing an outside chemical to the early development process. The research on epigenetics leaves open the question of whether or not the changes created by substances can be undone, a concern that is important to social workers interested in helping people with SUDs find recovery.

WHAT DOES THE RESEARCH EXPLORED IN THIS CHAPTER MEAN FOR SOCIAL WORKERS?

Three areas of science that are understudied by social work students have readily expanded our understanding of the substance use: chemistry, neuroscience, and genetics. We have examined substance use and abuse through the lens of these three sciences, which unlike most social work research, is far removed from interventions or services for people with substances abuse problems. The goal of this chapter is to view substance use in a fashion that should help us as social workers to better understand the complexity of human behavior involved in the range of substance use, instead of focusing singularly on what are now known as SUDs.

For people experiencing SUDs, the chemical changes occurring in the brain that are studied in neuroscience and the epigenetic effects of studied in genetics research may offer significantly different intervention approaches (Morgenstern et al., 2013). Current interventions tend to focuses almost solely on what are typically identified as the mechanisms of behavior change (MOBCs; Morgenstern et al., 2013). The MOBCs that most social work–based interventions address are related to changes in environmental cues (e.g., clients should stop going to the places where they abuse substances and stop being friends with people who use substances). The research discussed in this chapter suggests that the environmental cues are only part of the reasons for substance abuse. Expanding research in the areas of neuroscience and genetics could offer two ways to advance intervention knowledge for substance abuse. First is to test the impact of current interventions on brain functioning and epigenetic changes associated with substance use. This approach tests the effectiveness of interventions using measureable biological markers, which fits with the desire among researchers and funding sources like the National Institute of Alcohol Abuse and Alcoholism (NIAAA) to move beyond client self-reported and provider observation measures of intervention outcomes. Second is to offer a new model that explains the reasons for substance abuse by combining MOBCs, neuroscience, and genetics (Morgenstern et al., 2013). This new model can already be seen in use with increased focus on drug interventions such as methadone for heroin and morphine, nicotine gum or patches for tobacco, and Antabuse (Disulfiram) for alcohol that assist with more traditional substance abuse interventions, signaling a recognition that the underlying biology of substance abuse is important in treatment.

Overall, social workers interested in assisting people experiencing substance abuse problems are likely to see the interventions they use expand and change as chemistry, neuroscience, and genetics research contribute to our understanding of the underlying mechanisms leading to and maintaining abuse.

REFERENCES

American Psychiatric Association. (2013). *Diagnostic and statistical manual of mental disorders* (5th ed.). Washington, DC.

Bonne, J. (2003, January 9). Go pills: A war on drugs. *NBC News.* Retrieved from http://www.nbcnews.com/id/3071789/ns/us_news-only/t/go-pills-war-drugs/#.WHPvpGM77ww

Brooks, P. J. (1997). DNA damage, DNA repair, and alcohol toxicity—A review. *Alcoholism: Clinical and Experimental Research, 21*(6), 1073–1082.

Bühler, K., Giné, E., Echeverry-Alzate, V., Calleja-Conde, J., Fonseca, F. R., & López-Moreno, J. A. (2015). Common single nucleotide variants underlying drug addiction: More than a decade of research. *Addiction Biology, 20*(5), 845–871.

Center for Behavioral Health Statistics and Quality. (2015). *Behavioral health trends in the United States: Results from the 2014 National Survey on Drug Use and Health* (HHS Publication No. SMA 15-4927, NSDUH Series H-50). Rockville, MD. Retrieved from https://www.samhsa.gov/data/sites/default/files/NSDUH-FRR1-2014/NSDUH-FRR1-2014.pdf.

Davis, K. (2018, August 1). Everything you need to know about marijuana (cannabis). *Medical News Today.* Retrieved from https://www.medicalnewstoday.com/articles/246392.php

De Vries, T. J., & Shippenberg, T. S. (2002). Neural systems underlying opiate addiction. *Journal of Neuroscience, 22*(9), 3321–3325.

Hasin, D. S., O'Brien, C. P., Auriacombe, M., Borges, G., Bucholz, K., Budney, A., … Petry, N. M. (2013). DSM-5 criteria for substance use disorders: Recommendations and rationale. *American Journal of Psychiatry, 170*(8), 834–851.

Kauer, J. A., & Malenka, R. C. (2007). Synaptic plasticity and addiction. *Nature Reviews Neuroscience, 8*(11), 844.

Kreek, M. J., Nielsen, D. A., Butelman, E. R., & LaForge, K. S. (2005). Genetic influences on impulsivity, risk taking, stress responsivity and vulnerability to drug abuse and addiction. *Nature Neuroscience, 8*(11), 1450.

Mayo Clinic Staff. (2017, April 4). Caffeine content for coffee, tea, soda and more. (Healthy Lifestyle: Nutrition and Healthy Eating). Retrieved from https://www.mayoclinic.org/healthy-lifestyle/nutrition-and-healthy-eating/in-depth/caffeine/art-20049372.

Morgenstern, J., Naqvi, N. H., Debellis, R., & Breiter, H. C. (2013). The contributions of cognitive neuroscience and neuroimaging to understanding mechanisms of behavior change in addiction. *Psychology of Addictive Behaviors, 27*(2), 336.

National Institute on Alcohol Abuse and Alcoholism (NIAAA). (2016). Alcohol facts and statistics [Fact sheet]. Bethesda, MD. Retrieved from https://www.niaaa.nih.gov/alcohol-health/overview-alcohol-consumption/alcohol-facts-and-statistics.

Nestler, E. J. (2000). Genes and addiction. *Nature Genetics, 26*(3), 277.

Nestler, E. J. (2001). Molecular basis of long-term plasticity underlying addiction. *Nature Reviews Neuroscience, 2*(2), 119.

Ohler, N. (2017). *Blitzed: Drugs in Nazi Germany.* London, England: Allen Lane/Penguin.

Wang, J.-C., Kapoor, M., & Goate, A. M. (2012). The genetics of substance dependence. *Annual Review of Genomics and Human Genetics, 13*, 241–261.

Weinhold, B. (2006, March). Epigenetics: The science of change. *Environmental Health Perspectives, 114*(3), A160-A167. doi: 10.1289/e[j/114-a160

13

Social Work and the Science of Mental Health

A sick thought can devour the body's flesh more than fever or consumption.

—GUY DE MAUPASSANT

According to the most recent estimates published by the National Alliance on Mental Illness (2015), more than 40 million Americans suffer from a mental illness or mental disorder. Data suggest that, in the United States, approximately 1 in 5 adults (43.8 million individuals or approximately 19% of the current population) experiences mental illness in a given year. Nearly 1 in every 2 individuals with mental disorders fits the criteria for multiple disorders or diagnoses (National Alliance on Mental Illness, 2015).

Approximately 1 in every 25 adults in the United States is so impacted by these illnesses that it substantially interferes with or limits one or more major life activities. Mental illness impacts 1 in 5 youth, with those aged 13–18 years (or approximately 21% of the population) experiencing a severe mental disorder at some point during their life. For children aged 8–15 years, the estimate is 13% of the population (National Alliance on Mental Illness, 2015). As Insell (2008) noted, serious mental illness costs America $193.2 billion in lost earnings per year. Annual mental health care costs are estimated at nearly $57.5 billion (National Alliance on Mental Illness, 2015). Thus, the industry that has grown up around mental health and mental illness—its prevention, intervention, and treatment—is wide-ranging and expansive. To provide some context for the occurrence of mental illness in the United States, Table 13.1 provides the current percentage of the population who have been diagnosed with a disorder from a particular mental illness category.

Since many mental illnesses are not severe and many more go untreated, it is extremely beneficial for practitioners and advocates to understand the science behind what causes mental illness and how it manifests itself in everyday life and a variety of social situations in which a social work practitioner might operate. For example, a report from the US Department of Housing and Urban Development, Office of Community Planning and Development (2011) estimated that 26% of currently homeless adults staying in shelters live with serious mental illness and an estimated 46% live with severe mental illness and/or substance use disorders. Glaze and James

Table 13.1 PERCENTAGE OF US POPULATION BY MENTAL DISORDER CATEGORY

Mental Disorder Category	% of Current US Population
Mood disorders	9.50%
Major depressive disorder	6.70%
Dysthymic disorder	1.50%
Bipolar disorder	2.50%
Anxiety disorders	18.10%
Panic disorder	2.70%
Obsessive-compulsive disorder	1.00%
Posttraumatic stress disorder	3.50%
Generalized anxiety disorder	3.10%
Social phobia	6.80%
Schizophrenia	1.10%

Source: National Alliance for Mental Illness (2015); https://www.nami.org/Learn-More/ Infographics-Fact-Sheets.

(2006) noted that approximately 20% of state prisoners and 21% of local jail prisoners have "a recent history" of a mental health condition and 70% of youth in juvenile justice systems have at least one mental health condition and at least 20% live with a serious mental illness, according to the National Center for Mental Health and Juvenile Justice (2007). The Substance Abuse and Mental Health Services Administration (2015) noted that only 41% of adults in the United States with any diagnosed mental health condition received mental health services in the past year. Among adults with a serious mental illness, 62.9% received mental health services in the past year.

The percentage of Americans receiving treatment for mental illness, according to the National Institute of Mental Health (2015), is lower for children. According to 2015 data, just over half (50.6%) of children aged 8–15 received mental health services in the previous year. As Kessler, Chiu, Demler, and Walters (2005) noted, half of all chronic mental illnesses begin onset by age 14 with three quarters beginning onset by age 24. Despite the availability of effective treatment, there are long delays—sometimes decades—between the first appearance of symptoms and when people get help.

In addition to age, there are also disproportionalities seen across race and ethnicity, with the Agency for Healthcare Research and Quality (2010) reporting that African Americans and Hispanic Americans used mental health services at about one half the rate of Caucasian Americans in the past year and Asian Americans at about one third the rate. As noted by Hernandez, Nesman, Mowery, Acevado-Polakovich, and Callejas (2009), members of many US racial minorities who are in need of mental health services may be less likely to receive services and "even when services are available to members of U.S. racial-ethnic minority groups, they often are not accessible to large subsets of those populations" based on a wide range of factors, including geographic, linguistic, and cultural differences (p. 1046).

Given the incidence and prevalence of mental illness across a variety of social work practice settings and the possibilities that exist to advocate for and improve treatment options, availability, and access, this chapter will begin by reviewing the scientific definitions of mental health and mental illness and address the biological, chemical, and scientific elements of mental disorders. Then, the tools used by practitioners to diagnose mental disorders will be reviewed, along with sections on historical and present-day treatments. Special attention is paid to pharmaceutical treatments for mental illness and the connections between mental health and physical health. The chapter concludes with a brief meditation on instances where mental illness may trigger episodes of self-harm or violent behavior and some conclusions for the social work practitioner working with clients who are living with mental illness.

DEFINING MENTAL HEALTH AND MENTAL ILLNESS

The phrase "mental health" is commonly used in reference to mental illnesses or the related treatment protocols to manage mental illnesses. However, knowledge in the field has progressed to a level that appropriately differentiates mental health as a distinctive phenomenon to the instance of mental illness. Although mental health and mental illness are related, they represent different psychological states. Mental health is defined by the World Health Organization (2001) as "a state of well-being in which the individual realizes his or her own abilities, can cope with the normal stresses of life, can work productively and fruitfully, and is able to make a contribution to his or her community" (p. 1). It is estimated by the US Department of Health and Human Services (1999) that only about 17% of US adults are considered to be in a state of optimal mental health. This is coupled with emerging evidence that positive mental health is associated with improved overall health outcomes (Keyes, 2007). Conversely, mental illness is defined as "collectively all diagnosable mental disorders" using the American Psychological Association's *Diagnostic and Statistical Manual* or "health conditions that are characterized by alterations in thinking, mood, or behavior (or some combination thereof) associated with distress and/or impaired functioning" (US Department of Health and Human Services, 1999, p. 5). These two definitions are important to keep in mind when exploring the scientific nature of mental health treatment, as they set the basis for distinctions in preventative and invasive treatments, acute and chronic symptoms, and ways in which clients, caregivers, and others view the larger environmental and social factors arising from helping someone living with a mental illness.

NEUROSCIENCE, NEUROLOGY, AND NEUROCHEMISTRY

Neuroscience as a category typically encompasses the entirety of the scientific study of the brain and the human nervous system. Traditionally seen as a branch of biology, it is currently viewed as an interdisciplinary science that includes elements of many wide-ranging disciplines, including chemistry, cognitive science, linguistics, and genetics. Numerous other disciplines also inform and are informed by neuroscience, including philosophy, physics, psychology, and sociology. At the center of the disciplinary web of neuroscience is neurology, which is defined as the biological study of the nervous system and the medical diagnosis and treatment of all categories of conditions and disease involving the central nervous system (e.g., the brain) and the peripheral nervous system (e.g., nerves) at the cellular level. The peripheral system is itself subdivided into two smaller systems, the autonomic nervous system and the somatic nervous system. The autonomic nervous system, regulated by a gland called the hypothalamus, controls the actions and interactions between internal organs and is responsible for bodily responses such as heart rate, digestion, and respiration. The somatic nervous system, largely manifest by the network of nerves running through the human body, controls skeletal and muscle movements. The combination of these biological systems and subsystems and their individual and collective interactions with the brain accounts for the majority of human behavior and development.

A previous volume by the authors (see Ginsberg, Nackerud, & Larrison, 2004, pp. 155–176) provided an in-depth study into the biology of the brain and nervous system. That discussion is not replicated in this chapter except to focus on the behavioral indicators at the heart of neurological and neurochemical interaction, resulting in cognitive or behavioral change in the case of mental illness. Many of the scientists who study mental illness believe an imbalance in brain chemicals contributes to the development of many disorders. These chemicals are important for communication between nerve cells, or neurons. Neurons, like many other types of cells, contain a cell body which includes the nucleus, cytoplasm, and organelles. The nucleus contains the deoxyribonucleic acid (DNA) containing the information that the cell needs for growth, metabolism, and repair. Cytoplasm is the substance that fills a cell, including all the chemicals and parts needed for the cell to work properly including small structures called organelles (National Institute of Mental Health, 2015). In addition, a neuron has dendrites, which are small organs branching off from the cell body that allow the neuron to receive chemical and electrical signals called impulses from neighboring neurons. Axons, also branching out from the neuron's cell body, act as antennas to broadcast chemical or electrical messages to other neurons. The spaces between one axon and another dendrite, where a chemical reaction or electrical charge may take place within the brain, is called a synapse. Researchers suspect that chemical imbalances impede the brain's ability to move these chemical or electrical messages from one neuron to another, thus inhibiting normal function within the brain. As a result of this breakdown, the brain may not communicate properly with the body, and a person may begin to show signs of mental illness. There are many different chemicals that have been associated with a variety of mental disorders. Table 13.2 provides examples of these neurochemicals and the mental illness or bodily changes associated with them.

Neurochemicals form what might be called "road maps" of interactions between the brain and the rest of the body. All chemicals have specific purposes that promote both mental and physical health and well-being and, conversely, have the potential to be out of balance, leading the person who may be living with a mental illness down a wrong path, causing aberrant thoughts, emotions, behaviors, or physical symptoms. The process by which these road maps occur is called synaptic transmission or, more commonly, neurotransmission (and the neurochemicals called neurotransmitters). The process begins when neurochemicals are released by a particular nerve cell (called a presynaptic neuron) and bind to and activate the receptors of another type of nerve cell (called the postsynaptic neuron). Neurotransmission is essential for the process of communication between two neurons, and thus for signals to emerge from the brain and travel, via the autonomic and/or somatic nervous subsystems, to facilitate some response from other organs or to signal for other brain activity (including thoughts, feelings, sensations, or bodily reactions) to occur.

A common example of neurotransmission at work is when a person is either awake and alert, or going to sleep. Many neurotransmitters are involved in driving wakefulness and sleep, including histamine, dopamine, norepinephrine, serotonin, glutamate, orexin, and acetylcholine, among others. Histamine exhibits high levels during wakefulness, gradually decreasing and reaching its lowest levels during sleep. Serotonin activity promotes wakefulness, with decreases promoting and encouraging sleep. Acetylcholine activity in the reticular activating

Table 13.2 NEUROCHEMICALS AND MENTAL ILLNESS OR COGNITIVE OR BEHAVIORAL CHANGE

Neurochemical	Associated Mental Illness or Physical, Cognitive, or Behavioral Change
Acetylcholine	Depression Dementia
Adrenaline	Anxiety and anxiety disorders
Dopamine	Schizophrenia Parkinson's disease Attention-deficit/hyperactivity disorder (ADHD)
Epinephrine	Depression
GABA (gamma-amino butyric acid)	Anxiety and anxiety disorders Depression Panic disorders
Glutamate	Autism Obsessive-compulsive disorder (OCD) Schizophrenia Depression
Norepinephrine	Schizophrenia Depression
Serotonin	Depression and anxiety disorders, especially obsessive-compulsive disorder

Source: National Institute of Mental Health (2015).

system of the brain stem stimulates activity in the forebrain and cerebral cortex, encouraging alertness and wakefulness (Schenck, 2007). The amounts of these chemicals released and their interactions within the neurons in the brain and subsequent brain signals throughout the body can determine the type of sleep a person experiences, including its depth, duration, length of time taken to fall asleep, and its restfulness and how refreshed a person feels upon waking (Lockley & Foster, 2012).

The Mind, the Brain, and Science

The greatly expanding knowledge base in both neurology and neurochemistry can tell us much about how mental illness impacts a person. For example, technological advancements in nuclear medicine and the imaging of the brain, such as magnetic resonance imaging (MRI), computerized axial tomography (CAT), or positron emission tomography (PET) scanning techniques, provide health care professionals and the scientific community with a wealth of information on the physical and chemical changes occurring in the brain of a particular person living with a mental or physical illness. Imaging technology is further enhanced by genetic testing to determine if specific genetic markers are present in the person that may predispose them to particular mental disorders, such as autism or depression (Insel et al., 2010). However, these biological indicators are only one piece of a much larger picture of how mental illnesses manifest and how persons who are living with mental illness function within the parameters of a particular disorder.

For social work practitioners and other helping professionals, it is useful to apply the principles of the biopsychosocial model, as theorized by Engel (1980), in their work with those who are living with mental illness (Matto, Strolin-Goltzman, & Ballan, 2013). The model allows for the knowledge-building elements of biologically or medically informed care as seen in much modern neuroscience, while also allowing for a greater spectrum of influence from other areas, including what the person living with mental illness thinks, feels, or perceives, and the greater social context that may be influencing those thoughts, emotions, or perceptions, including cultural or relational factors. The general intelligence on the disorder, depth of understanding of diagnosis and treatment, and the quality of personal relationships are all factors that contribute greatly to how a mental illness manifests, is diagnosed or treated, and how it may be managed in a given society. As such, a practitioner may find it beneficial to differentiate the knowledge of the disorder that originates from the neurology and neurochemistry of a client, and those factors that contribute to the "mindfulness" of that client.

As Uttal (2011) noted, the brain (as an organ) of a client or patient and the mind are not the same. The brain is an organ and part of the visible, tangible world of the body. In contrast, the mind is part of the invisible, transcendent world of thought, feeling, attitude, belief, and imagination. The brain is the physical organ most associated with thoughts and consciousness, but the mind extends outward into the social world: tapping into relationships, beliefs, and various sources of knowledge that are not limited to physical interactions. Practitioner understanding and acceptance of "mindful" approaches to mental health, mental illness, and general well-being will, as the following sections of this chapter will explore, contribute greatly to the scientific approach to diagnosis and treatment of many mental disorders.

THE SCIENCE OF DIAGNOSIS

Diagnosis of mental illness is the central driving force leading to medical treatment. In the process of pursuing diagnosis, facts about the person's specific situation are determined and a diagnostic profile is developed, which may include symptoms and subjective factors about the illness from a personal perspective, or neurological or genetics elements. The diagnostic profile can usually be divided into two categories. The first category includes those factors that are known about the illness itself (or how it "presents" in the person's specific case). Another category may pertain to what is known about the illness, but it may not currently be present in the person's specific case (or the "risk factors"). Part of the profile may refer to the rate of occurrence of the illness at issue or to specific facts about the person or his or her environment. As the following subsections explain, these two categories are combined, when compared to what is generally known about a specific disorder or set of disorders (called a "spectrum"), and then a diagnostic determination is made.

The Diagnostic and Statistical Manual (DSM-5)

The fifth edition of the *Diagnostic and Statistical Manual of Mental Disorders* (*DSM-5*) is the standard diagnostic classification of mental disorders used by mental health providers in the United States. It contains a listing of criteria for diagnosis of every psychiatric disorder recognized by the health care system in the United States. The *DSM* is established by the American Psychological Association (APA), which began codifying diagnoses for mental illness in 1952, with the publication of the first edition of the *DSM*. The publication history of the *DSM* extended to four editions from 1952 to 1994, and a text revision of the fourth edition (known as the *DSM-IV-TR*) in the year 2000.

Work began for the fifth edition of the *DSM* in 1999 with a conference sponsored jointly by APA and the National Institute of Mental Health (NIMH) to set the research agenda and develop work groups of researchers and practitioners to develop and revise the diagnostic systems that make up the *DSM*. There were six work groups, each focusing on broad topics used as subdivisions for the fifth edition of the *DSM*: Nomenclature, Neuroscience and Genetics, Developmental Issues and Diagnosis, Personality and Relational Disorders, Mental Disorders and Disability, and Cross-Cultural Issues (Regier, Narrow, First, & Marshall, 2002). From 1999 until 2007, preliminary articles were published and conferences held for researchers and practitioners to review the work group materials and learn about future directions for the forthcoming edition of the *DSM*.

On July 23, 2007, the APA announced the task force that would oversee the development of fifth edition of the *DSM*. The *DSM-5* Task Force consisted of 27 members who represented research scientists from psychiatry and other disciplines. Scientists working on the revision of the *DSM* had a broad range of experience and interests related to specific psychiatric diagnoses and mental illness treatments as a precondition to appointment to the task force. As part of the task force responsibilities in creating the fifth edition of the *DSM*, experiments were conducted which involved different clinicians doing independent evaluations of the same patient—a common approach to the study of reliability of a particular mental illness diagnosis.

It is important to note that, as a diagnostic system, the fifth edition of the *DSM* is not meant as a replacement for patient care, nor does it attempt to explain all of the elements of a mental illness as it specifically impacts the life of a person. As Kraemer (2007) noted:

> The purpose of any diagnostic system, such as the DSM, is not to say what is "normal" or "abnormal," nor what is or is not "acceptable" in any society ... nor is it an effort to "medicalize" society's problems nor to channel clients to psychiatrists rather than to clinical psychologists, sociologists or other mental health providers ... DSM does not concern "insanity," a legal rather than a medical term, and assuredly does not concern who is "crazy" or "mad," terms that are layman pejorative terms, not necessarily related to mental health disorders. Such terms continue to stigmatize those with mental health problems and are a major factor in the less than adequate care that those with mental health problems continue to receive. (p. 8)

Thus, we can posit that the *DSM* is a systemic tool for the development of more personal and specific diagnostic profiles made by medical professionals for particular persons seeking information and understanding of potential medical conditions impacting their mental functioning. As seen in Table 13.3, the categorical listing of mental illnesses in the *DSM* is, by design, broad and it is the responsibility of the diagnosing professional to move from these broad categories to more specific diagnoses (represented in the *DSM* by individual three-digit, two-decimal codes) and from specific diagnosis to individualized diagnosis and treatment planning.

Axial, Categorical, and Dimensional Assessment of Mental Illness

One of the more far-reaching and controversial changes that came out of the creation of the fifth edition of the *DSM* was a move away from a previous system of classification. In previous editions of the *DSM*, an axial system was used, which involved documentation of diagnoses on five axes in order to present the most complete diagnostic profile. Axis I listed the primary or principal (or "presenting") diagnoses. Axis II contained personality disorders, personality traits, and intellectual disabilities. Axis III was intended for additional medical

Table 13.3 DIAGNOSTIC CATEGORIES OF THE *DSM-5*

Category
1. Neurodevelopmental Disorders
2. Schizophrenia Spectrum and Other Psychotic Disorders
3. Bipolar and Related Disorders
4. Depressive Disorders
5. Anxiety Disorders
6. Obsessive-Compulsive and Related Disorders
7. Trauma and Stressor-Related Disorders
8. Dissociative Disorders
9. Somatic Symptom and Related Disorders
10. Feeding and Eating Disorders
11. Elimination Disorders
12. Sleep-Wake Disorders
13. Sexual Dysfunctions
14. Gender Dysphoria
15. Disruptive, Impulse Control, and Conduct Disorders
16. Substance-Related and Addictive Disorders
17. Neurocognitive Disorders
18. Personality Disorders
19. Paraphilic Disorders
20. Other Disorders

Note: DSM-5 = Diagnostic and Statistical Manual of Mental Disorders (5th ed.).

Source: Adapted from the American Psychiatric Association (2013).

problems that were relevant to the person's mental disorders. Axis IV required diagnosing professionals to indicate which of nine categories of environmental factors might influence treatment, to include (1) problems with primary support group; (2) problems related to the social environment; (3) educational problems; (4) occupational problems; (5) housing problems; (6) economic problems; (7) problems with access to health care services; (8) problems related to interaction with the legal system/crime; and (9) other psychosocial and environmental problems. Axis V included the opportunity to provide a Global Assessment of Functioning (GAF) rating, a number between 0 and 100 intended to indicate overall level of that person's ability to function with a particular diagnosis (American Psychological Association, 2000).

According to the American Psychological Association (2013), with the fifth edition of the *DSM*, the diagnostic system for mental illness "has moved to a nonaxial documentation of diagnosis (formerly Axes I, II, and III), with separate notations for important psychosocial and contextual factors (formerly Axis IV) and disability (formerly Axis V)" (p. 16). The new system of classification completely removes the former axial system in favor of letting diagnoses stand alone, as individual categories, with an addition of a dimensional diagnostic paradigm to supplement some of the categories.

As Kraemer (2007) noted, "a categorical diagnosis has only two values: The patient is either positive (thought to have the disorder) or negative (thought not to have the disorder)" (p. 10). Thus, within the diagnostic system of the fifth edition of the *DSM*, a diagnoses stands on its own once the criteria for administration of that diagnosis have been met by the individual person's profile (such as exhibiting symptoms, having thoughts or feelings, or engaging in behaviors consistent with that particular disorder). In contrast, dimensional scales allow for diagnoses to be more general in character, so that a particular person's disorder might be seen as part of a continuum on which there are various levels of characteristic symptoms, thoughts, feelings, or behaviors. Dimensional diagnosis also maintains the possibility for degrees of severity or intensity for mental illness, as well as differing manifestations of the same mental disorder (Porter & Risler, 2013). For example, within the context of the fifth edition of the *DSM*, the dimensional diagnostic system has been applied to personality disorders, in which particular traits exhibited by the person living with the disorder may manifest across wide groupings or clusters of diagnostic characteristics or traits, as influenced by the person's individual personality or other factors, such as intelligence or cooperation (Morey, Benson, & Skodol, 2016).

The relative merits of diagnostic systems of classification will continue to be subject to debate, scrutiny, and testing within the medical and scientific community. For practitioners working in clinical settings and providing direct diagnostic support or care for persons living with mental illness, it is important to have a comprehensive knowledge of the systems of diagnosis used for particular clients, any subsequent changes in their diagnostic history, and an understanding of all characteristic and traits associated with the diagnosis to provide the best and most informed treatment decisions.

THE SCIENCE OF TREATMENT

As Charney, Buxbaum, Sklar, and Nestler (2013) noted, both the knowledge of brain and nervous system functioning and the tools by which to measure the brain, the genes, and the chemical interactions within the body have grown at an accelerated pace in recent times. However, that increased knowledge and advanced technology has not translated into either more understanding of the mental disorders themselves or advancement in prevention and treatment at the same rate. There may be many reasons for this discrepancy. Treatment of mental illness, much like its diagnosis, is often personalized. Though the same methods may be applied to those suffering from the same or similar disorders, how those individuals react to treatment may vary and, as a result, the treatment may be altered to suit the needs of the person (Rogers & Pilgrim, 2014). For example, it would be difficult to codify advancements for the treatment of depression as a whole because there are many singular ways in which clinical depression manifests and treatments for each person would necessarily be adjusted according to individual needs. Another reason might be related to the time between when researchers in a particular area or illness make a new discovery or development and when that information is put into practice within the clinical setting. The following sections trace how, throughout history and even in the modern era, treatment for mental illness has overcome obstacles and advanced.

Historical Treatments

Attempts to understand the nature of mental disorders have their roots far back into the ancient world and across a myriad of cultures, influencing conceptual developments in religion, philosophy, and social thought. Archeological evidence exists that supports that a form of surgery on the skull and the brain tissues to cure mental ailments, known as trepanation, had been practiced since at least the 5th millennium BCE (Restak, 2000). As Rosen (1968) postulated, ancient societies were alike in their belief that mental illnesses of any kind were related to religious and spiritual practice, with treatments such as prayer and social isolation being promoted to either correct or reduce perceived divine inflictions or "curses" on the ill person. It was not until the Greek epoch, between the 5th and 3rd centuries BCE, that the father of modern medicine, Hippocrates, promoted a hypothesis that the long-held belief of mental illness caused by supernatural or divine intervention was false and was instead a natural phenomenon in the human body, particularly the brain (Hooley, Butcher, Nock, & Mineka, 2016; Foerschner, 2010). Hippocrates promoted this hypothesis of "humors"—four essential fluids of the human body (blood, phlegm, yellow bile, and black bile)—that combined and interacted within the body and brain to produce individual mood and personality, and also, when out of proportion, to cause mental illness or emotional upset. This hypothesis would sustain medical and scientific thought on mental illness and its treatment for centuries, from Greek, Roman, and Persian antiquity until the Middle Ages (Nuland, 2007).

Many ancient ways of treating mental illness were refined from the 14th to 18th centuries CE. Some were directly related to the idea of "humors," and re-establishing an equilibrium between fluids in the body, where others were attempts to offset emotional outbursts and calm the afflicted person. Exsanguination, including bloodletting by small cuts in the arms, wrists, or legs, and the application of leeches to suck blood, was commonly employed to individuals thought to be suffering from a mental illness or other maladies, like epilepsy or other seizure disorders, or migraine headaches, whose causes evaded in-depth medical knowledge at the time (Greenstone, 2010). Immersion in or pouring on of cold or hot water, known as hydrotherapy, had its roots in antiquity but continued well into the 19th century

CE. While hydrotherapy as a therapeutic tool in treatment of mental illness had been supplanted by the early 20th century, water immersion as a tool of relaxation and as a physical therapy tool continues to the present day (Campion, 2001).

By far the most common and widespread of all the treatments for mental illness rooted in antiquity is that of social isolation and therapeutic confinement. Dating back to at least the 8th century CE in the Middle East, and approximately the 10th or 11th centuries in Europe, asylums for the mentally ill served both as a means of confinement for those whose illnesses manifested in violent or socially unacceptable behavior and as a place for therapeutic observation and development of treatment practices. As Foucault (2013) noted:

> Confinement was an institutional creation … an economic measure and a social precaution … seen against the social horizon of poverty, the inability to work and the impossibility of integrating into a social group. It was the moment when it started to be classified as one of the problems of the city. (p. 77)

As urban centers grew and populations increased in the 17th and 18th centuries, state-run asylums were often where many who were living with mental illness were placed. Many of the treatment protocols were advanced during this period, as more became known about the nature and functioning of mental illness, so that simple confinement gave way to more medical auspices, and more emphasis was placed on physical therapies, including exercise regimes, and controlling the sleep and rest habits of patients in the asylums or hospitals. Psychiatric hospitals and retreats still exist today, though their role has mainly, since the mid-20th century, been relegated to crisis stabilization and diagnosis. By the 1880s, however, a discovery was to mark a turn away from older, historical means of treatment and usher in the modern age of mental health diagnosis and treatment.

Modern Treatment

Medical doctor and neurologist Sigmund Freud opened a clinical practice in Vienna, Austria, in 1886. The purpose of this clinic was to attempt a new therapeutic technique with patients who were living with mental illness but were not incapable of living their lives outside of the rigid confines of asylums or private hospitals for the mentally ill. The technique was called psychoanalysis, and it utilized a simple, free-associative dialogue with the patient to attempt to find unconscious or hidden motives for his or her maladaptive thoughts, feelings, or behavior. This "talk therapy" model was to revolutionize how mental illness is diagnosed and treated even today. The popularity and widespread adoption of psychoanalysis throughout America and Western Europe led the charge in a wave of scientific discovery and interest in the relationship between the mind and mental illness. By the early 20th century, the number of patients residing in mental hospitals increased significantly and necessitated an increase in scientific investigation into effective medical treatments (Drake, Green, Mueser, & Goldman, 2003). This culminated in several movements of popular and scientific support for deinstitutionalization of those living will mental illness and a turn away from the asylum model that had dominated the previous two centuries (Goffman, 1961; Mac Suibhne, 2009). New physical therapies were being devised alongside the bourgeoning field of psychoanalysis and the development of other psychotherapies during the early decades of the 20th century, including malarial therapy in 1917, deep sleep therapy in 1920, prefrontal lobotomy in 1931, insulin shock therapy in 1933, cardiazol shock therapy in 1934, and electroconvulsive therapy (ECT) in 1938 (Gay, 2006; Ginsberg et al., 2004; Shorter, 1997). Many of these treatments, such as insulin shock, ECT, and Freudian psychoanalysis, have continued to be refined and modified as treatments today. These treatments, for the most part, corroborated the paths that neurology and neurochemistry were blazing at this time, connecting conditions to potential biological and chemical causes.

A great deal about the scientific understanding of how mental disorders happen has changed since Sigmund Freud first postulated his psychoanalytic theories in the late 19th century, and these discoveries have shaped much of the therapeutic practices that a current practitioner will encounter. There are numerous varieties of "talk therapy" besides the psychoanalytic, including cognitive-behavioral therapy (CBT), dialectical behavioral therapy (DBT), and humanistic therapies, within psychology and other clinical disciplines like social work. These disciplines often work directly from a biologically informed framework, such as the biopsychosocial model, and may involve, in some cases, neuropsychological testing or the use of neurological tools for accurate diagnosis and treatment planning. But perhaps the most notable scientific milieu was the study of how certain drugs interact with the genetic, chemical, and physiological makeup of the individual.

PSYCHOPHARMACOLOGY

Drugs and mental illness have been linked together through the ages. For example, caffeine, cocaine, and opium all have a shared history as potential "cures" for mental ailments (Crocq, 2007). However, the synthesis of new pharmaceuticals expressly for the purposes of treating symptoms of mental illness began in the mid-20th century. These new drugs were the result of new scientific theories about neurochemistry, including the hypothesis that neurotransmitters engage in what is called "reuptake," or absorption back into the body, and that control of this process could ameliorate the neurochemical imbalances that promote mental illness symptoms through the reuptake of particular neurotransmitters. Marketing and prescribing of these drugs began in the early 1950s, setting the foundation for the widespread use of psychoactive drugs in medical settings. In 1954, chlorpromazine (with the brand name Thorazine in the United States) was the first psychoactive drug used to treat schizophrenia. Chlorpromazine, however, had side effects, and researchers and scientists were soon at work synthesizing other compounds that worked along with the complex neural and chemical networks within the body (Rubin, 2007).

Beginning in the 1960s, scientific scrutiny of drug manufacturing and marketing came under the aegis of a new governmental agency. The United States Food and

Drug Administration (FDA) is the arbiter of new scientific discoveries in the area of psychopharmacology, or the interaction between drugs and the nervous system. The FDA is now proactive rather than reactive with regard to new drug development, and the agency has developed a system of scientific testing to ensure the relative safety and effectiveness of a drug before it goes on the market. As Angell (2011) noted:

> When drug companies seek approval from the FDA to market a new drug, they must submit to the agency all clinical trials they have sponsored. The trials are usually double-blind and placebo-controlled, that is, the participating patients are randomly assigned to either drug or placebo, and neither they nor their doctors know which they have been assigned. The patients are told only that they will receive an active drug or a placebo, and they are also told of any side effects they might experience. If two trials show that the drug is more effective than a placebo, the drug is generally approved. (p. 23)

Clinical trials or studies might involve research programs found in universities, government labs, and pharmaceutical companies around the world. As with many aspects of neuroscience, the work is multidisciplinary and may involve aspects of microbiology and chemistry in addition to all of the aspects of the neurosciences and partner disciplines stated earlier. With more emphasis placed on mental illnesses and their treatments throughout the 20th century into the present day, the pharmaceutical industry around mental illness has grown into a multi-billion-dollar industry, with many of the drugs used to treat mental illnesses well known and popularized by advertising today (Greenblat, Harmatz, & Shader, 2011). However, for the social work practitioner, it is important to maintain a general understanding of the types of pharmaceuticals that clients may be taking and how the drugs interact with their respective diagnoses and treatment plans.

Drugs for treatment of mental disorders fall into five general classes: antidepressants, anxiolytics, drugs for attentional disorders, and antipsychotics. While antidepressants are mainly for treatment of depression, they may include mood stabilization drugs or drugs for anxiety or insomnia. Anxiolytics are drugs for anxiety, with the most common drugs being benzodiazepines. Starting in the early 1980s, several drugs were marketed for the treatment of what is now classified as attention-deficit/hyperactivity disorder (ADHD) in children and teens. Methylphenidate (also known as Ritalin), a drug originally synthesized in the 1940s, became a common treatment prescribed to children and teens diagnosed with ADHD symptoms (Lange, Reichl, Lange, Tucha, & Tucha, 2010). There were some controversies around this time regarding the use of drugs Ritalin and other drugs, since they are powerful stimulants and operate on inattention and hyperactivity through what is known as a paradoxical drug effect (Robbins & Sahakian, 1979). While Ritalin remains the most prescribed treatment for attentional disorders, there are both stimulant and nonstimulant treatments being prescribed today (Lange et al., 2010). Antipsychotic drugs address certain symptoms associated with psychotic disorders, like schizophrenia, bipolar disorder, or very severe depression in which there has been some loss of contact with reality, often including delusions or hallucinations. Table 13.4 provides a general listing of the types of pharmaceuticals associated with mental illness, along with representative drugs from each classification.

MENTAL AND PHYSICAL CORRELATES

The physical body responds to directly to your thoughts, feelings, and behaviors. This is often called the "mind/body connectivity" (Cozolino, 2014, p. xi). When stressed, anxious, or depressed, the body may respond in ways that signal some disruption in normal functioning. For example, blood pressure may rise after a particularly stressful event, such as the loss of a job, a divorce, or the death of a close relative. Conversely, while mental illnesses may manifest themselves in a variety of ways for different people, many of the physical symptoms are held in common. It is important for the social work practitioner to be observant of these similarities,

Table 13.4 MEDICATIONS FOR MENTAL ILLNESS BY CLASS AND SUBCLASS

Drug Class	Subclass	Medications
Drugs for Attentional Disorders	Stimulants	Ritalin, Dexadrine, Concerta, Focalin
	Nonstimulants	Strattera, Intuniv, Kapvay
Antidepressants	SSRIs/SSNRIs	Prozac, Zoloft, Cymbalta, Lexapro, Viibryd
	Atypical	Wellbutrin, Nefazodone, Effexor
	TCAs	Tofranil, Amitriptyline, Norpramin
	MAOIs	Marplan, Nardil, Parnate
	Mood stabilizers	Lithium, Symbyax
Anxiolytics	Benzodiazapines	Valium, Xanax, Ativan, Klonopin
	Adrenergics	Inderal, BuSpar, Catapres
Antipyschotics	Atypical	Zyprexa, Abilify, Clozaril, Invega
	Conventional	Haldol, Navene, Orap

Notes: SSRI/SSNRI = selective serotonin reuptake inhibitor/selective serotonin and norepinephrine reuptake inhibitor; TCA = tricyclic antidepressant; MAOI = monoamine oxidase inhibitor.

Source: Adapted from Walker, H. M., & Gresham, F. M. (2013). Handbook of evidence-based practices for emotional and behavioral disorders: Applications in schools. New York: Guilford Publications.

as they can play a crucial role in diagnosis, treatment planning, and monitoring an ongoing treatment plan for the client. Following are examples of somatic or physical symptoms in three common mental health diagnoses: anxiety, depression, and schizophrenia.

Anxiety disorders are frequently associated with physical symptoms. Often these can be acute and fast-acting (such as in "panic attacks" or moments of momentary high stress) or, as in a panic disorder diagnosis, these symptoms can be chronic or prolonged. Rapid heartbeat; a feeling of dizziness or lightheadedness; a burning sensation on the face, neck, ears, scalp, or shoulders; and uncontrollable facial or bodily tics are commonly physical manifestations of anxiety (Kroenke et al., 1994). For depressed clients, the physical manifestation of the disease may start small, with complaints of headaches or back pain, then increase over time to involve oversleeping or insomnia, and marked changes in appetite (Mathew, Weinman, & Mirabi, 1981). In schizophrenia, physical symptoms may include a blank or vacant facial expression, motor skill impairment, insomnia or excessive sleeping, dysfunctional speech or mouth movements, and awkward gait and catatonia (Chapman, 1966).

VIOLENCE, SUICIDE, AND SELF-HARM: CHALLENGES FOR THE PRACTITIONER

Violent behavior, either self- or other-directed, and issues of homicidal and suicidal ideation are particular challenges for mental health professionals. In addition to the ethical responsibility that disclosures of this type place on the social worker or other helper, the threat of physical harm is often unpredictable and uncontrollable. Specialized locales for diagnosis and treatment, such as psychiatric wings of hospitals, residential treatment facilities, or special education classrooms, may have specific policies or treatment models (including physical restraint) for containing any perceived threats from clients who may be experiencing particularly violent episodes of disturbance.

With regard to violence within the mental illness, recent studies suggest that violence among people with mental illnesses is not simply due to the symptoms themselves but also environmental stressors that may exacerbate loss of control or intensify the episodes themselves (Link, Cullen, Agnew, & Link, 2015). Social workers working in direct-care environments are encouraged to pay specific attention to linkages between environmental stressors and symptom presentation with clients living with mental illness, in order to rapidly deescalate situations that might encourage or promote violent responses.

Self-harming behaviors offer a greater challenge, as they are often deliberately hidden from caregivers or professionals. However, these behaviors within the context of other mental disorders have shown significant risk for escalation into suicidal ideation and attempt. As Hawton, Saunders, and O'Connor (2012) noted:

Only small advances have been made in prevention and there is a paucity of evidence for effective treatment interventions. The development and assessment

of new psychosocial and pharmacological interventions to reduce self-harm
and suicide should be a major priority, and should include internet-based
interventions. The improvement of mental health care in adolescents in terms
of both access to and quality of services is essential, especially in low-income
and middle-income countries. Better management of the care pathway of vulnerable young people as they move from child and adolescent to adult services
to ensure continuity of care should reduce the risk of suicide. (p. 2380)

Suicide is the tenth leading cause of death in the United States (Centers for
Disease Control and Prevention, 2015). Suicide and self-harm is the third leading
cause of death for people aged 10–24 (Centers for Disease Control and Prevention,
2014) and the second leading cause of death for people aged 15–24 (Drapeau &
McIntosh, 2015). Studies have shown that more than 90% of children who die by
suicide have been diagnosed with a mental health condition (Swanson, McGinty,
Fazel, & Mays, 2015; US Department of Health and Human Services, 1999). In
addition to disproportionately impacting young people, it is estimated that each
day an estimated 18–22 veterans die by suicide (US Department of Veteran Affairs
Mental Health Services Suicide Prevention Program, 2012). Again, given the un-
predictability of behaviors, it is incumbent upon social work practitioners in direct
care settings to understand both the etiology of the behavior in the given context
of the mental illness as it is diagnosed and within the confines of the general plan
of treatment. As stated in the National Association of Social Worker's *Code of Ethics*
(2008), social workers are entrusted with a "duty to warn":

> Social workers should protect the confidentiality of all information obtained in
> the course of professional service, except for compelling professional reasons.
> The general expectation that social workers will keep information confidential
> does not apply when disclosure is necessary to prevent serious, foreseeable,
> and imminent harm to a client or other identifiable person. (§ 1.07)

Social workers in clinical settings with clients at higher risk for these types of behaviors (e.g., youth and veterans) should make every effort to maintain clear professional boundaries and follow policies and procedures around crisis prevention and
intervention commensurate with their clinical environment.

CONCLUSION

According to the National Association of Social Workers (2000), social workers
provide most of the country's mental health services, with over 60% of the mental
health professionals in the United States as clinically trained social workers, compared to 10% of psychiatrists, 23% of psychologists, and 5% of psychiatric nurses.
Social workers also have the unique ability to work in diversified settings, from hospitals and private clinics to neighborhood associations, nonprofit organizations,
and school systems. Social workers are trained in the biopsychosocial model, which

allows for a complete assessment clients within their environment and takes stock of the relationships and systems that may be most beneficial to treatment.

Given that the science of mental health work is multifaceted and ever-changing, it is incumbent upon social work practitioners to have a basic understanding of the science behind diagnosis and treatment, as well as a willingness to maintain that knowledge and continue their education and training far into their career. Social workers can also utilize their scientific knowledge to advocate for their clients so that new treatments are made available in a timely manner, and structural or social stigmas of those living with mental illness are avoided.

This chapter provided a basic overview of the scientific discourse on mental illness, its potential causes, the history of diagnostic criteria, and both historical and current treatment protocols. The practitioner is provided with a solid foundation in biological processes and medical terminology around mental illness and its course of treatment. However, this material is no substitute for a firm grounding in holistic and acceptable social work practice and ethical social work skills. With both of these, the practitioner is best prepared for the challenges of working with people living with mental illness today and the scientific discoveries of tomorrow.

REFERENCES

Agency for Healthcare Research and Quality. (2010). *National Healthcare Quality and Disparities Reports*. Rockville, MD: Agency for Healthcare Research and Quality. Retrieved from http://www.ahrq.gov/research/findings/nhqrdr/nhdr10/index.html.

American Psychiatric Association. (2000). Diagnostic and statistical manual of mental disorders (4th ed., text revision) (*DSM-IV-TR*). Washington, DC: American Psychiatric Association. https://doi.org/10.1176/appi.books.9780890423349

American Psychiatric Association. (2013). *Diagnostic and statistical manual of mental disorders* (5th ed.). Washington, DC: American Psychiatric Association. https://doi.org/10.1176/appi.books.9780890425596

Angell, M. (2011). The epidemic of mental illness: Why. *The New York Review of Books*, 58(11), 20–22.

Hooley, J. M., Butcher, J. N., Nock, M. K. & Mineka, S. (2016). *Abnormal psychology* (17th ed.). New York, NY: Pearson.

Campion, M. R. (2001). *Hydrotherapy: principles and practice*. Woburn, MA: Butterworth-Heineman.

Centers for Disease Control and Prevention (CDC). (2014). *Suicide prevention*. Retrieved from http://www.cdc.gov/violenceprevention/pub/youth_suicide.html

Centers for Disease Control and Prevention (CDC). (2015). *Suicide facts at a glance*. Retrieved from http://www.cdc.gov/violenceprevention/pdf/suicide-datasheet-a.pdf

Chapman, J. (1966). The early symptoms of schizophrenia. *The British Journal of Psychiatry*, 112(484), 225–251. https://doi.org/10.1192/bjp.112.484.225

Charney, D. S., Buxbaum, J. D., Sklar, P., & Nestler, E. J. (2013). *Neurobiology of mental illness* (4th ed.). New York, NY: Oxford University Press.

Cozolino, L. (2014). *The neuroscience of human relationships: Attachment and the developing social brain*. New York, NY: WW Norton & Company.

Crocq, M.-A. (2007). Historical and cultural aspects of man's relationship with addictive drugs. *Dialogues in Clinical Neuroscience, 9*(4), 355.

Drake, R. E., Green, A. I., Mueser, K. T., & Goldman, H. H. (2003). The history of community mental health treatment and rehabilitation for persons with severe mental illness. *Community Mental Health Journal, 39*(5), 427–440. https://doi.org/10.1023/a:1025860919277

Drapeau, C. W., & McIntosh, J. L. (2015). *USA suicide 2013: Official final data.* Washington, DC: American Association of Suicidology. Retrieved from http://www.suicidology.org/portals/14/docs/resources/factsheets/2013datapgsv2alt.pdf.

Engel, G. L. (1980). The clinical application of the biopsychosocial model. *American Journal of Psychiatry, 137*(5), 535–544. https://doi.org/10.1176/ajp.137.5.535

Foerschner, A. M. (2010). The history of mental illness: From "skull drills" to "happy pills." *Inquiries Journal, 2*(9). Retrieved from http://www.inquiriesjournal.com/a?id=1673.

Foucault, M. (2013). *History of madness.* New York, NY: Routledge.

Gay, P. (2006). *Freud: A life for our time.* London, UK: Little Books.

Ginsberg, L. H., Nackerud, L. G., & Larrison, C. R. (2004). *Human biology for social workers: Development, ecology, genetics, and health.* Boston, MA: Pearson/Allyn and Bacon.

Glaze, L. E., & James, D. J. (2006). *Mental health problems of prison and jail inmates.* Washington, DC: US Department of Justice, Office of Justice Programs, Bureau of Justice Statistics.

Goffman, E. (1961). *Essays on the social situation of mental patients and other inmates.* New York, NY: Doubleday.

Greenblatt, D. J., Harmatz, J. S., & Shader, R. I. (2011). Psychotropic drug prescribing in the United States. *Journal of Clinical Psychopharmacology, 31*(1), 1–3. https://doi.org/10.1097/jcp.0b013e318209cf05

Greenstone, G. (2010). The history of bloodletting. *BC Medical Journal, 52*(1), 12–14.

Hawton, K., Saunders, K. E. A., & O'Connor, R. C. (2012). Self-harm and suicide in adolescents. *The Lancet, 379*(9834), 2373–2382. https://doi.org/10.1016/s0140-6736(12)60322-5

Hernandez, M., Nesman, T., Mowery, D., Acevedo-Polakovich, I., & Callejas, L. (2009). Cultural competence: A literature review and conceptual model for mental health services. *Psychiatric Services, 60*(8). https://doi.org/10.1176/appi.ps.60.8.1046

Insel, T. R. (2008). Assessing the economic costs of serious mental illness. *American Journal of Psychiatry, 165*(6), 663–665. https://doi.org/10.1176/appi.ajp.2008.08030366

Insel, T., Cuthbert, B., Garvey, M., Heinssen, R., Pine, D. S., Quinn, K., … Wang, P. (2010). Research domain criteria (RDoC): Toward a new classification framework for research on mental disorders. *American Journal of Psychiatry, 167*(7), 748–751. https://doi.org/10.1176/appi.ajp.2010.09091379

Kessler, R. C., Chiu, W. T., Demler, O., & Walters, E. E. (2005). Prevalence, severity, and comorbidity of 12-month DSM-IV disorders in the National Comorbidity Survey replication. *Archives of General Psychiatry, 62*(6), 617. https://doi.org/10.1001/archpsyc.62.6.617

Keyes, C. L. M. (2007). Promoting and protecting mental health as flourishing: A complementary strategy for improving national mental health. *American Psychologist, 62*(2), 95–108. https://doi.org/10.1037/0003-066x.62.2.95

Kraemer, H. C. (2007). DSM categories and dimensions in clinical and research contexts. *International Journal of Methods in Psychiatric Research, 16*(S1), S8–S15. https://doi.org/10.1002/mpr.211

Kroenke, K. (1994). Physical symptoms in primary care: Predictors of psychiatric disorders and functional impairment. *Archives of Family Medicine, 3*(9), 774–779. https://doi.org/10.1001/archfami.3.9.774

Lange, K. W., Reichl, S., Lange, K. M., Tucha, L., & Tucha, O. (2010). The history of attention deficit hyperactivity disorder. *ADHD Attention Deficit and Hyperactivity Disorders, 2*(4), 241–255. https://doi.org/10.1007/s12402-010-0045-8

Link, N. W., Cullen, F. T., Agnew, R., & Link, B. G. (2015). Can general strain theory help us understand violent behaviors among people with mental illnesses? *Justice Quarterly, 33*(4), 729–754. https://doi.org/10.1080/07418825.2015.1005656

Lockley, S. W., & Foster, R. G. (2012). *Sleep.* New York, NY: Oxford University Press. https://doi.org/10.1093/actrade/9780199587858.001.0001

Mac Suibhne, S. (2009). Asylums: Essays on the social situation of mental patients and other inmates. *BMJ, 339*, b4109–b4109. https://doi.org/10.1136/bmj.b4109

Mathew, R. J., Weinman, M. L., & Mirabi, M. (1981). Physical symptoms of depression. *The British Journal of Psychiatry, 139*(4), 293–296. https://doi.org/10.1192/bjp.139.4.293

Matto, H. C., & Ballan, M. (2013). *Neuroscience for social work: Current research and practice.* New York, NY: Springer.

Morey, L. C., Benson, K. T., & Skodol, A. E. (2016). Relating DSM-5 section III personality traits to section II personality disorder diagnoses. *Psychological Medicine, 46*(3), 647–655. https://doi.org/10.1017/s0033291715002226

National Alliance on Mental Illness. (2015). Mental health facts in America. Retrieved September 12, 2016, from https://www.nami.org/NAMI/media/NAMI-Media/Infographics/GeneralMHFacts.pdf

National Association of Social Workers. (2000). *Social work speaks* (5th ed.). Washington, DC: NASW Press.

National Association of Social Workers. (2008). *Code of ethics of the National Association of Social Workers.* Retrieved from https://www.socialworkers.org/About/Ethics/Code-of-Ethics/Code-of-Ethics-English

National Center for Mental Health and Juvenile Justice. (2007). *Blueprint for change: A comprehensive model for the identification and treatment of youth with mental health needs in contact with the juvenile justice system.* Delmar, NY: Policy Research Associates.

National Institute of Mental Health. (2015). *Use of mental health services and treatment among children.* Retrieved from http://www.nimh.nih.gov/health/statistics/prevalence/use-of-mental-health-services-and-treatment-among-children.shtml

Nuland, S. B. (2007, July 8). Bad medicine. *New York Times Sunday Book Review.* Retrieved from http://www.nytimes.com/2007/07/08/books/ review/Nuland.html?_r=0

Porter, J. S., & Risler, E. (2013). The new alternative DSM-5 model for personality disorders. *Research on Social Work Practice, 24*(1), 50–56. https://doi.org/10.1177/1049731513500348

Regier, D. A., Narrow, W. E., First, M. B., & Marshall, T. (2002). The APA classification of mental disorders: Future perspectives. *Psychopathology, 35*(2–3), 166–170. https://doi.org/10.1159/000065139

Restak, R. M. (2000). *Mysteries of the mind.* Washington, DC: National Geographic Society.

Robbins, T. W., & Sahakian, B. J. (1979). "Paradoxical" effects of psychomotor stimulant drugs in hyperactive children from the standpoint of behavioural pharmacology. *Neuropharmacology, 18*(12), 931–950. https://doi.org/10.1016/0028-3908(79)90157-6

Rogers, A., & Pilgrim, D. (2014). *A sociology of mental health and illness.* Berkshire, England: McGraw-Hill Education.

Rosen, G. (1968). *Madness in society: Chapters in the historical sociology of mental illness.* Chicago, IL: University of Chicago Press.

Rubin, R. P. (2007). A brief history of great discoveries in pharmacology: In celebration of the centennial anniversary of the founding of the American Society of Pharmacology and Experimental Therapeutics. *Pharmacological Reviews, 59*(4), 289–359. https://doi.org/10.1124/pr.107.70102

Schenck, C. H. (2007). S26.1 Symposium summary. *Sleep Medicine, 8,* S30–S31. https://doi.org/10.1016/s1389-9457(07)70111-9

Shorter, E. (1997). *A history of psychiatry: From the age of the asylum to the era of Prozac.* New York, NY: Wiley.

Substance Abuse and Mental Health Services Administration. (2015). *Results from the 2014 National Survey on Drug Use and Health: Mental health ginding.* NSDUH Series H-50, HHS Publication No. (SMA) 15-4927. Rockville, MD: Substance Abuse and Mental Health Services Administration. Retrieved from http://www.samhsa.gov/data/sites/default/files/NSDUH-FRR1-2014/NSDUH-FRR1-2014.pdf

Swanson, J. W., McGinty, E. E., Fazel, S., & Mays, V. M. (2015). Mental illness and reduction of gun violence and suicide: Bringing epidemiologic research to policy. *Annals of Epidemiology, 25*(5), 366–376. https://doi.org/10.1016/j.annepidem.2014.03.004

US Department of Health and Human Services. (1999). *Mental health: A report of the Surgeon General.* Retrieved from http://profiles.nlm.nih.gov/ps/access/ NNBBJC.pdf

US Department of Housing and Urban Development. (2011). *The Annual Homeless Assessment Report to Congress (2009).* Retrieved from https://www.hudexchange.info/resources/ documents/2010HomelessAssessment Report.pdf

US Department of Veteran Affairs Mental Health Services Suicide Prevention Program. (2012). *Suicide data report, 2012.* Retrieved from http://www.va.gov/opa/docs/Suicide-Data-Report-2012-final.pdf

Uttal, W. R. (2011). *Mind and brain.* Cambridge, MA: The MIT Press. https://doi.org/10.7551/mitpress/9780262015967.001.0001

Walker, H. M., & Gresham, F. M. (2013). *Handbook of evidence-based practices for emotional and behavioral disorders: Applications in schools.* New York, NY: Guilford.

World Health Organization. (2001). *Mental disorders affect one in four people.* Retrieved from http://www.who.int/whr/2001/media_centre/press_release/en/,

14

Social Work and the Science of Intellectual/ Developmental Disabilities

---

Traditionally, the construct "disability" has been viewed from the perspective of the medical model—a model that presents disability as an individual pathology with a physical or organic etiology (Ali, Strydom, & King, 2012). Beginning in the latter half of the 1900s, however, the disability movement embraced the social constructionist approach, a view that focuses on person-in-environment interactions that establish the underpinning structures of a shared social reality (Ali et al., 2012). While the medical model concerned itself with the *what* of disability, the social model sought to understand the *how* of disability. As opposed to rooting disability at the individual level, a social constructionist approach allowed for a critical examination of the ways in which society's institutions limit a person's functionings and capabilities. In this way, and owing to ideas such as labeling and cognitive-behavioral theories, language has played a key role in the disability rights movement—with many terms having been adopted and then discarded for reflecting negative, albeit publicly endorsed, stereotypes about persons with disability. Advocates in the disability community have both recognized the value of combining all disability types within the movement (e.g., intellectual/ developmental, learning, sensory, mental, and physical) and have been skeptical about the impact of this conceptual amalgam. On the one hand, the grouping of individuals across disability classifications is partially credited with the movement's strong momentum; on the other hand, the concern remains that the single label is insensitive to the qualitatively different experiences associated with a particular disability type, and that this lack of sensitivity perpetuates public misconceptions about what persons with disabilities can and cannot do. Contemporary scholars such as Lennard Davis (2013) and Liat Ben-Moshe (2013) suggest that the term *disability* functions as a catchall for those whom society has deemed as nonadherent to prevailing social norms.

While the science of diagnostic labeling is tied to service access, the protection of certain legal rights, and the determination of insurance reimbursement rates, labeling can contribute to the process of stigmatization and the decreased realization of rights vis-à-vis social exclusion.

This chapter will focus on intellectual/developmental disabilities in particular, as well as the relationship between the intellectual and developmental disability constructs. For the purpose of this chapter, science is conceptualized as the clinical diagnosis (i.e., measurement) of intellectual/developmental disabilities, as such a determination will have significant implications for individuals' access to educational, medical, and social services; the experience of social stigmatization; and—as will be discussed later—in the case of capital defendants, significant implications for death sentencing eligibility. For these reasons, challenges to the scientific measurement of intellectual/developmental disabilities impact social work practice and have special implications for social justice. As an aside regarding use of language in this chapter, the term *intellectual disability* is understood as a form of *developmental disability*. While the term *intellectual disability* will imply developmental disability (and may at times be notated as intellectual/developmental disabilities), the converse will not hold true. That is, while intellectual disability will imply developmental disability, developmental disability will not necessarily imply intellectual disability.

CLASSIFICATION AND DIAGNOSIS OF DEVELOPMENTAL DISABILITIES

Presently, *developmental disability* is understood as an umbrella term under which intellectual disability falls. The US Congress formalized the designation *developmental disability* in 1975 (Haydt, Greenspan, & Agharkar, 2014). Originally, developmental disability was used as an overlay to intellectual disability with additional provisions such as autism, cerebral palsy, epilepsy, and other brain-based conditions originating during childhood and adolescence (Haydt et al., 2014). The American Association on Intellectual and Developmental Disabilities presently defines developmental disability as a severe and chronic disability that is likely to be lifelong and can be cognitive, physical, or both. The Association specifies the period of manifestation as occurring prior to age 22 years. While some developmental disabilities are largely physical issues (e.g., cerebral palsy or epilepsy), some individuals may have a condition that includes a physical and intellectual disability (e.g., Down syndrome or fetal alcohol syndrome) (AAIDD, 2013a). Intellectual disability encompasses the cognitive component of the definition (AAIDD, 2013a). Interestingly, despite the fact that intellectual disability is a type of developmental disability, the Association sets the age of onset for intellectual disability at 18 years (i.e., 4 years younger than the age of onset for developmental disability). The American Psychiatric Association, on the other hand, specifies intellectual disability as an intellectual developmental disorder with the age of onset occurring during the nonnumeric *developmental period* (APA, 2013).

ETIOLOGY AND SCREENING

Developmental disabilities have a variety of causes that include, but are not limited to, (1) genetic mutation, additions or deletions; (2) chromosomal abnormalities; (3) exposure to substances/chemicals while in the womb; (4) infections during pregnancy; (5) complications during childbirth including preterm birth; and (6) traumatic brain injury (US DHHS, 2012). Some conditions that lead to developmental disabilities may be diagnosed with a blood test, ultrasound, or other methods (US DHHS, 2012). Tests may be conducted during pregnancy or after birth (US DHHS, 2012). There are two main types of prenatal tests: amniocentesis and chorionic villus sampling (US DHHS, 2012). Amniocentesis is a test that is usually performed to determine whether a fetus has a genetic disorder (US DHHS, 2012). Developmental disabilities that can be detected with amniocentesis include Down syndrome and certain types of muscular dystrophy (US DHHS, 2012). Like amniocentesis, chorionic villus sampling can be used to test for chromosomal disorders such as Down syndrome and other genetic nonnormalities (US DHHS, 2012). While chorionic villus sampling can be done earlier in pregnancy than amniocentesis, it is also associated with a higher risk of miscarriage than amniocentesis (one in 100 cases versus one in 200 cases) (US DHHS, 2012). This technology has serious ethical ramifications, as it may result in the parents' decision to terminate the pregnancy (Davis, 2013). This will necessarily have impact for social workers in the medical setting (e.g., social worker professionals working with parents who are grappling with such decisions).

TREATMENTS

According to the US Department of Health and Human Services, National Institute of Health (US DHHS, 2012), children and adults with Down syndrome, fragile X syndrome, Rett syndrome, and other developmental disabilities can often benefit from therapeutic speech therapy, occupational therapy, and exercises targeted at the improvement of gross and fine motor skills. Social contact and communication are also important (US DHHS, 2012). For children with Down syndrome, surgery can help to correct heart defects that may be present (US DHHS, 2012). Additionally, a variety of treatment options are available to help with the symptoms of autism spectrum disorders: behavioral, occupational, physical, and speech-language therapies (US DHHS, 2012). However, with regard to genetic testing and treatment, Lennard Davis (2013) offers these important words of caution:

> Many would claim that for behaviors like speech, sexual orientation, or intelligence, there can be no single gene or genetic causality. So the premise that we can fix a single gene is itself a problem. Further, the idea of a "mistake" is also problematic. Take the examples I have given of sickle-cell anemia and cystic fibrosis […]. It turns out that people who carry the trait are resistant to malaria (in the case of sickle-cell anemia) and cholera (in the case of cystic fibrosis). If we posit that other "defects" are also protective against pandemic diseases, we can see that the simple elimination of such defects might be a complicated process with a possibly dubious result. (p. 270)

CLASSIFICATION AND DIAGNOSIS OF INTELLECTUAL DISABILITY

Intellectual disability is a form of developmental disability. The definition of intellectual disability has undergone many reconstructions over time, originally referring only to deficits in intellectual functioning (Papazoglou, Jacobson, McCabe, Kaufmann, & Zabel, 2014). It was not until roughly the past decade that the term *intellectual disability* began to replace the term *mental retardation*. The two leading US authorities on intellectual/developmental disabilities, the American Association on Intellectual and Developmental Disabilities and the American Psychiatric Association, adopted the new term in their 2010 and 2013 diagnostic manuals, respectively. Prior to the term *mental retardation*, language such as idiot, imbecile, feeble-minded, and moron prevailed in the 19th and early 20th centuries, reflecting the roots of the present-day classification system (i.e., mild, moderate, severe, and profound) (Haydt et al., 2014; Meany, 2004). Presently, in order to reach a clinical determination of intellectual disability, three criteria, or prongs, must be satisfied: (1) deficits in intellectual functioning; (2) deficits in adaptive functioning; and (3) age of onset/period of manifestation.

Prong 1: Intellectual Functioning

Intellectual functioning is the first of three prongs of intellectual disability and is typically measured by the administration of a standardized intelligence test. According to the American Psychiatric Association, intellectual functioning includes abstract thinking, practical understanding, planning, and problem solving (APA, 2013). The statistical norm in the United States is a score range of between 80 and 120 points (Borromeo, 2001), with approximately 97% of the general population falling within two standard deviations (i.e., 30 points) of the average (Blume, Johnson, & Seeds, 2009). Therefore, it is estimated that less than 3% of the population has intellectual disability (Blume et al., 2009). It has been estimated that the majority of individuals (85%) diagnosed as having intellectual disability fall within the mild spectrum (Blume et al., 2009; Borromeo, 2001). However, alone, IQ scores are not a reliable scientific measure of the upper boundary of intellectual functioning and require clinical judgment by experienced diagnosticians (Ellis, 2003). A skilled evaluator will be aware that not all IQ tests are the same and that scores are not fixed, but instead represent an approximated range of intellectual functioning (Leading Cases, Harvard Law Review, 2014). The literature consistently identifies other issues that can diminish score validity, such as practice effect, the Flynn effect, and inherent cultural biases of the test (Blume, Johnson, Marcus, & Paavola, 2014; Cheung, 2013; Feluren, 2013; Haydt et al., 2014). Moreover, if intellectual disability is a dynamic, malleable, and flexible biopsychosocial condition, individuals will likely have IQ test scores and functions that fluctuate in and out of the designated score range across time (Fabian et al., 2011).

Prong 2: Adaptive Functioning

Adaptive functioning is the second prong of the intellectual disability diagnosis and is assessed using both clinical evaluations and individualized psychometric measures (Feluren, 2013). The American Association on Intellectual and Developmental Disabilities first incorporated adaptive functioning into its definition of intellectual disability in 1961 (Foster, Leland, Nihira, & Shallhass, 1970). However, at this time there were no available scientific measures of adaptive functioning, so that the construct had to be developed by a special program of research (Foster et al., 1970). The current diagnostic manuals define adaptive functioning using three broad domains of skills: (1) conceptual, (2) social, and (3) practical (Cheung, 2013). Conceptual skills consist of language and literacy; money, time, and number concepts; and self-direction (Cheung, 2013). Social skills are comprised of interpersonal skills, social responsibility, self-esteem, gullibility, naiveté, social problem solving, and ability to follow rules/obey laws and to avoid being victimized (Cheung, 2013). Practical skills are conceptualized as activities of daily living: occupational skills, health care, travel/transportation, schedules/routines, safety, use of money, and use of telephone (Cheung, 2013). A salient concern is how social work professionals in the forensic setting are to accurately evaluate the adaptive functioning in individuals with below-average IQ scores who have been "long institutionalized in secure environments" (Brodsky & Galloway, 2003, p. 7).

Prong 3: Age of Onset

The third element of intellectual disability is the age of onset, also referred to as the period of manifestation. The current diagnostic manuals promulgated by the American Association on Intellectual and Developmental Disability and the American Psychiatric Association differ on this point, with the former setting the age of onset at 18 years and the latter during the more nebulous, developmental period (AAIDD, 2013b; APA, 2013). Clinical definitions neither specify nor require that the age of onset be established using a standardized test score (Blume et al., 2009). Instead, evidence of onset is usually established through a social history investigation, including an inventory of school records and medical records, and interviews with witnesses and peers who knew the person in the community (Blume et al., 2009). Intelligence testing, and official documentation of such testing, as well as resultant referrals to appropriate supports and services, is most likely to occur in the public school setting. In this way, and especially in conjunction with compulsory school attendance, the public school system functions as a primary broker of psychosocial and educational support services. However, realistically, not every child in the public school system with intellectual disability will be identified, and others may be misidentified as having an emotional/behavioral disorder or some form of learning disability.

DIAGNOSTIC CONFOUNDERS

Due to variance within the functioning of persons with intellectual disability, diagnosis is a nuanced process that requires professional judgment and experience. In general, confounders to the assessment and diagnostic process are attributed to a variety of factors: (1) frequent overlap of symptoms across diagnostic categories; (2) diagnoses are frequently comorbid; and (3) information about etiology is frequently missing (Greenspan, Harris, & Woods, 2015).

Confounders to the diagnostic process may be owed to the constructs of intellectual and adaptive functioning themselves, as well as to the substantive overlap between intellectual disability, developmental disability, learning disability and mental disability, and sensitivity issues in the detection of mild intellectual disability in particular. Accurate diagnosis has social justice implications and should be the concern of the social work profession. For example, in the *Atkins* (2002) decision, the US Supreme Court determined that the execution of persons with intellectual disability is unconstitutional on the grounds that such an execution violates the Eighth Amendment's protections against cruel and unusual punishment, owing to the diminished culpability of such defendants. As the vast majority of *Atkins* claimants fall within the mild spectrum of intellectual disability (Blume et al., 2014), accurate diagnosis of mild intellectual disability, as explained in the following section, may be difficult. Therefore, when capital defendants raise the claim of intellectual disability and trained mental health professionals (e.g., social workers) are tasked with the scientific assessment of intellectual disability, such professionals may be directly implicated in the resultant life-or-death determinations.

Mild Intellectual Disability

The classification of mild intellectual disability is a relatively new construct, owing much to the creation of IQ tests (Haydt et al., 2014). Prior to IQ tests, individuals were identified informally based on their perceived ability to survive physically and socially in society (Haydt et al., 2014). In general, individuals with mild intellectual disability represent approximately 85% of those who have intellectual disability (Feluren, 2013). Social invisibility remains a salient concern for persons with mild intellectual disability. As a consequence of social invisibility, the class of individuals with mild intellectual disability will prove to be the most difficult to protect because "they come closer to the normal border range" (Feluren, 2013, p. 340), presenting with higher intellectual and adaptive functioning than persons with moderate, severe, and profound deficits in functioning (Fabian, Thompson, & Lazarus, 2011). Persons who experience mild intellectual disability are therefore "unlikely to meet the standards of the stereotype" (Feluren, 2013, p. 355). The issue of social invisibility is further confounded by the finding that "when society envisions people with intellectual disabilities, people typically assume that they are those with physical manifestations of mental disabilities, such as Down Syndrome" (Cheung, 2013, p. 343).

Mental Disability

Commonly, persons with intellectual disability experience a co-occurring psychiatric disorder (Fabian et al., 2011, p. 409; Musso, Barker, Proto, & Gouvier, 2012). Like people with chronic, severe intellectual disability, people with chronic, severe psychiatric disorders typically experience substantial deficits in adaptive functioning (Haydt et al., 2014). However, because they may occur independently, "adequate professional skills to deal with one problem does not assure competency to deal with the other" (US Department of Health, Education and Welfare, 1970, p. 37). One comparative study examined differences between cohorts of forensic and nonforensic patients with intellectual disability, finding that (1) the forensic patients had lower rates of mood disorder; (2) no differences in other mental illnesses; and (3) significantly higher rates in personality disorder (Lindsay, 2013). Personality disorder is considered a risk factor for criminal behavior in all offenders (Lindsay, 2013).

Malingering

Malingering is the term used to designate a person's exaggeration or fabrication of clinical symptoms for the purpose of achieving a secondary gain (Feluren, 2013). As a diagnostic confounder, malingering has played a crucial role in death penalty cases. In the 2002 *Atkins* decision, the US Supreme Court ruled that the execution of persons with intellectual disability is unconstitutional on the grounds that it would violate the Eighth Amendment. In the case of capital defendants raising the claim of intellectual disability, the secondary gain of malingering is, presumably, the categorical ineligibility for execution. On January 27, 2015, Mr. Warren Lee Hill was executed by the State of Georgia despite many advocates claiming that Mr. Hill met criteria for intellectual disability. When the case was first heard, three state medical experts testified that Mr. Hill exhibited signs of malingering, not intellectual disability. Ten years later, however, the three state experts recanted their original testimony. Dr. Thomas Sachy was among them; in his written affidavit, Dr. Sachy stated:

> I felt that my previous conclusions about Mr. Hill's mental health status were unreliable because of my lack of experience at the time [...] (Sachy, 2013). In the psychiatric community, we now know that reliance on the DSM criteria has resulted in an extremely high rate of false findings of malingering [...] I do not believe now that Mr. Hill was deliberately feigning a cognitive disorder in 2000, and I believe that his responses to my questions were consistent with mild mental retardation [sic]. (Sachy, 2013).

Although the concern for potential malingering may be a valid one, it should not preclude the constitutional protection of persons with intellectual disability (Mobbs & West, 2013). Nor should it necessarily preclude a diagnosis of intellectual disability. Although the assessment of malingering is the fundamental task in forensic assessment and should always precede any conclusions drawn (Brodsky &

Galloway, 2003), Blume et al. (2014) remind us that there are currently no formalized, reliable diagnostic assessments designed to capture the feigning of intellectual disability.

ASSUMPTIONS OF THE STANDARDIZED INTELLIGENCE TEST

Intellectual functioning is scientifically measured by the administration of a standardized intelligence test. However, it is noted in the literature that IQ scores are not a reliable measure of the upper boundary of intellectual functioning, and they require clinical judgment by diagnosticians who are experienced with intellectual disability (Ellis, 2003). A skilled evaluator will be aware that not all IQ tests are the same, and that scores are not fixed, but represent only an approximated range of intellectual functioning (Leading Cases, Harvard Law Review, 2014). Regarding capital defendants raising the claim of intellectual disability, a study in 2014 found that between 2008 and 2012, 31% of all unsuccessful claims lost on the first prong of the definition, intellectual functioning. The court's decision to stipulate that only a reliable, individually administered, full-scale IQ score could be considered was the most significant predictor of success on intellectual functioning (Blume et al., 2014). Despite a new focus on adaptive functioning, the measurement of intelligence still plays a key role in the determination of intellectual disability in the legal system.

THE HEREDITARIAN THEORY OF UNITARY INTELLIGENCE

The hereditarian theory of unitary intelligence is rooted in the argument from biological determinism. Biological determinism holds that shared behavioral norms, and social and economic disparities, arise from inherited, innate distinctions—and that social realities are an accurate reflection of biology (Gould, 1996, p. 52). Paleontologist and evolutionary biologist Stephen Jay Gould (1996) identified the logical appeal of a biological and unitary theory of intelligence: "A single gene for normal intelligence removed the potential contradiction between a unilinear scale that marked intelligence as a single, measurable entity, and a desire to separate and identify the mentally deficient [sic] as a category apart" (Gould, 1996, p. 193). Critical of biological determinism, Gould posited that a hereditarian theory of unitary intelligence is guilty of a number of philosophical fallacies, three of which are (1) reductionism (i.e., "the desire to explain partly random, large-scale, and irreducibly complex phenomena by deterministic behavior of the smallest constituent parts"); (2) reification (i.e., "the propensity to convert an abstract concept into a hard entity"); and (3) hierarchy (i.e., "to order items by ranking them in a linear series of increasing worth") (Gould, 1996, p. 27). According to Gould (1996), the history of cognitive testing in the 20th century had two major strands: (1) scaling and ranking by mental age as represented by IQ testing, and (2) analysis and correlations among mental tests, as manifest in factor analysis (p. 46). The latter informs the former (Gould, 1996). A hereditarian theory of unitary intelligence relies on both strands and commits what Gould refers to as the "hereditarian fallacy" (Gould, 1996, p. 186), manifest as the following implications: (1) that "heritable" is the same as "inevitable," and (2) within- and between-group heredity can be explained by, or reduced to, the same phenomenon (Gould, 1996).

Normal Distributions and Category Mistakes

The bell curve (also called a *normal curve* or *normal distribution*) is a graph that shows roughly how much of the general population falls into each quartile of a normal range (Fig. 14.1). Theoretically, if everyone in the world were tested with a traditional IQ test, most people would score in the average range. A smaller number would score moderately below average and moderately above average, and extremely high and low scores would be rare (i.e., outliers) (http://www.investopedia.com/terms/n/normaldistribution.asp). Bell curves arise when:

> Variation is distributed randomly around the mean—equally in both directions, with greater probability of values near the mean [...] Specific pathologies do not fall on the bell curve, but usually form clumps or clusters far from the curve's mean value and apart from the normal distribution. The causes of these exceptions [pathologies] therefore do not correspond with reasons for variation around the mean of the bell curve itself [...] "Category mistakes" are among the most common errors of human thought: we commit a classic category mistake if we equate the causes of normal variation with the reasons for pathologies. (Gould, 1996, p. 33)

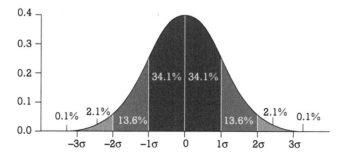

Figure 14.1 Normal distribution
SOURCE: By M. W. Toews - Own work, based (in concept) on figure by Jeremy Kemp, on 2005-02-09, CC BY 2.5, https://commons.wikimedia.org/w/index.php?curid=1903871

Factor Analysis and Spearman's g

Spearman's g is the central claim of the heritable theory of unitary intelligence, and it holds that intelligence is singular, uniform, rankable, genetically based, and a largely fixed entity that exists in the head (Gould, 1996, p. 36). The g factor (i.e., *general factor*) is a variable that summarizes positive correlations among different cognitive tasks in intelligence tests and reflects the fact that an individual's performance on one cognitive task tends to be comparable to performances on other cognitive tasks (Gould, 1996). Intelligence test scores are frequently regarded as estimates of individuals' standings on the g factor (Gould, 1996). Stephen Jay Gould argued that the endeavor of psychometrics has erroneously reified the g factor as a physical entity in the brain, even though it is only the product of factor analysis (1996). Moreover, Gould argued that, historically, the ranking of persons by level of intelligence has been used to justify the oppression of disadvantaged groups of people, and that the preference for one factor solution over another is simply an arbitrary matter of taste (Gould, 1996).

Standardized Measures

Despite documented logical and philosophical issues surrounding the upper boundaries of IQ scores, the validity of IQ tests continues to be broadly accepted (Silverman et al., 2010). Historically and currently, one of most widely used instruments in the United States to assess intelligence is the Stanford-Binet Intelligence Scale (Silverman et al., 2010). In 1904, the minister of public education commissioned French psychologist Alfred Binet to develop techniques for identifying children whose lack of success in normal classrooms suggested the need for some form of specialized education (Gould, 1996, p. 179). Binet rejected the hereditarian interpretation of intelligence, wanting to only use his test as a device to identify children who were in need of intervention (Gould, 1996, p. 40), and expressed concerns that his test could be used to apply an ineffaceable label rather than as an assessment tool to identify children who did not perform well in the general classroom (Gould, 1996). Because of his concern, Binet had three cardinal principles for using his tests: (1) scores are a practical device; they do not buttress any theory of intellect; they do not define anything innate or permanent; (2) the scale is a rough, empirical guide for identifying children with learning disability and mild intellectual disability; it is not a device for ranking [statistically] normal children; (3) low scores shall not be used to mark children as innately incapable (Gould, 1966, p. 185).

However, American psychologists introduced the Binet-Simon Intelligence Test in June 1905, largely ignoring Binet's cautions regarding how the test should be used. In 1916, a psychologist from Stanford University named Lewis M. Terman introduced the first edition of the Stanford–Binet Intelligence Scale, an individually administered intelligence test that was revised from the original Binet-Simon Scale

(Bain & Allin, 2005; Gould, 1996). Currently in its fifth edition, the Stanford–Binet Intelligence Scale is a cognitive ability and intelligence test that is used to diagnose developmental or intellectual deficits in young children (Beker, 2003Bain & Allin, 2005; Beker, 2003). The test consists of both verbal and nonverbal subtests, and it scientifically measures five weighted factors: (1) knowledge; (2) quantitative reasoning; (3) visual-spatial processing; (4) working memory; and (5) fluid reasoning (Beker, 2003).

PROFESSIONAL ORGANIZATIONS AND THE IMPORTANCE OF RESEARCH

The American Association on Intellectual and Developmental Disabilities and the American Psychiatric Association promulgate two widely used criterion sets for reaching a clinical diagnosis of intellectual/developmental disability (Cheung, 2013; DeMatteo, Marczyk, & Pich, 2007). Publications of the American Psychiatric Association's *Diagnostic and Statistical Manual of Mental Disorders* (*DSM*) have closely followed the lead of the most recent American Association on Intellectual and Developmental Disabilities manual, with differences typically attributed to the fact that the *DSM* manuals have undergone revision less frequently (Haydt et al., 2014). Both manuals undergo revisions informed by changes in evidence-based knowledge and, in turn, inform evidenced-based practices.

THE AMERICAN ASSOCIATION ON INTELLECTUAL AND DEVELOPMENTAL DISABILITIES

Founded in 1876, the American Association on Intellectual and Developmental Disabilities is an interdisciplinary organization of professionals and a leading authority on disabilities research (DeMatteo et al., 2007). It has been the primary organization involved in defining intellectual disability (Obi et al., 2011). Since 1961, the Association has revised its definition of intellectual disability several times (DeMatteo et al., 2007; Ellis, 2003). Definition changes have varied on the point of the adaptive functioning prong (i.e., real-life impact on the individual's life) (Ellis, 2003). In 2010, the American Association on Intellectual and Developmental Disabilities published its 11th and most recent manual. This current edition retains the broader conceptual domains of adaptive functioning (i.e., social, conceptual, and practical) in lieu of the 11 narrower skills-related areas, and it formally replaces the term *mental retardation* with *intellectual disability*. As the Association explains, the term *intellectual disability* is intended to cover "the same population of individuals who were diagnosed previously with mental retardation in number, kind, level, type and duration" (Cheung, 2013, p. 322; Fabian et al., 2011).

THE AMERICAN PSYCHIATRIC ASSOCIATION

The American Psychiatric Association was established in 1844 and is the world's largest psychiatric organization and publisher of the *Diagnostic and Statistical Manual of Mental Disorders* (*DSM*) (Cheung, 2013; Feluren, 2013). The fifth and most recent edition of the Manual departed from the fourth and fourth-text revised editions in the following ways: (1) a name change of the disorder (i.e., mental retardation to intellectual disability and intellectual developmental disorder); (2) revision of the diagnostic criteria (i.e., age 18 onset to during the developmental period; former multiaxial system to a single axis); and (3) changes in the severity specifiers (i.e., IQ score ceiling raised from 70 to 75 points; severity established according to deficits in adaptive, not intellectual, functioning) (Papazoglou et al., 2014). Overall, the *DSM-5* reflects a move away from rigid and somewhat arbitrary IQ ceilings toward a new emphasis on adaptive functioning (Feluren, 2013). The logic of the multiaxial assessment was to help clinicians develop a more comprehensive evaluation of a person by incorporating levels of diagnosis across five axes (Feluren, 2013), which would then establish a primary diagnosis as differentiated from other, nonprimary (i.e., less impairing) diagnoses. This, in conjunction with the use of narrower, adaptive skill areas (i.e., communication, self-care, home living, social/interpersonal skills, self-direction, functional academic skills, work, leisure, health, and safety) (Cheung, 2013), would in turn serve as a more sensitive guide for matching the specific needs of individuals with appropriate psychosocial supports and services. The *DSM* also serves as a tool for the development of treatment plans, and it is used by the insurance industry to determine appropriate reimbursements for psychological treatment (Feluren, 2013).

SCIENCE AND SOCIAL JUSTICE

Good science entails the accurate measurement of intellectual and adaptive functioning in the diagnosis of intellectual/developmental disabilities; it also acknowledges its own limitations (e.g., human error; observer effect; the Standard Margin of Error). In addition to determining eligibility for supports and services, and the rate of insurance reimbursement, a diagnosis of intellectual/developmental disabilities also has real-life impact on a persons' eligibility for death sentencing (e.g., Georgia's 2015 state execution of Warren Lee Hill). In this way, clinical diagnosis is linked to the recognition and protection of legal rights. However, and conversely, such a label may also contribute to the process of social stigmatization, raising concerns for social justice. Social justice is one of six ethical principles endorsed by the National Association of Social Workers:

> Social workers pursue social change, particularly with and on behalf of vulnerable and oppressed individuals and groups of people. Social workers' social change efforts are focused primarily on issues of poverty, unemployment, discrimination, and other forms of social injustice. These activities seek to promote sensitivity to and knowledge about oppression and cultural and

ethnic diversity. Social workers strive to ensure access to needed information, services, and resources; equality of opportunity; and meaningful participation in decision making for all people. (NASW, 2008)

The science of clinical diagnosis of intellectual/developmental disabilities has important social justice implications for persons receiving and living with the diagnostic label. These considerations include the protection of rights and the facilitation of social inclusion at the substantive level—challenges rightfully taken up by the social work profession.

STIGMA, STEREOTYPES, AND RIGHTS

Clinical diagnosis impacts stigma, stereotypes, and rights. Stigma is the process whereby certain groups of people are marginalized by society because the group norms differ from those of the dominant cultural group, with power differentials being exacerbated by socioeconomic and political differences (Ali et al., 2012). It is a process consisting of stereotypes, prejudice and discrimination (Ali et al., 2012; Werner, 2015). Public stigma is conceptualized as the attitudes of the general public toward stigmatized individuals and groups, and it can diminish participation and inclusion in the community, including a decreased realization of rights (Werner, 2105). Diminished expectations that result from and perpetuate stigma frequently lead to discrimination and diminished rights of persons with intellectual/developmental disabilities because these individuals are viewed by the general public as being incapable of making autonomous decisions (Werner, 2015). Related yet different, self-stigma refers to the process whereby a member of a stigmatized group psychologically internalizes the attitudes and behaviors of those upholding negative stereotypes about the group (Ali et al., 2012). In this form of stigma, the individual comes to endorse the cultural stereotypes in reference to his or her group membership and label avoidance may occur (Ali et al., 2012). For this and other reasons, the American Association on Intellectual and Developmental Disabilities warns that the use of self-rating scales is not a reliable scientific measure of intellectual disability (Fabian et al., 2011).

Stereotypes refer to knowledge structures or attitudes about a group of people (Werner, 2015). Although people with intellectual/developmental disabilities are often able to hold jobs, drive cars, support their families, achieve vocational skills, and live independently/interdependently, this does not typically align with the public perception. One study found that college students are likely to conceptualize mild intellectual disability as more severe and easily identifiable than would clinically be the case (Musso et al., 2012). Overall, and especially for individuals with intellectual disability, the rights to have children, to receive medical treatment only after consent, and to vote were found to be the most challenging rights to realize, owing to public stigma—a construct that is linked to the decreased realization of rights and community inclusion (Werner, 2015). In a 2015 study, Shirli Werner examined the relationship between public stigma and the perception of rights as they relate to persons with intellectual disability. Werner found the following: (1) more negative stereotypes, greater social distance, and greater withdrawal behaviors were evidenced toward individuals with intellectual disability than persons with a physical disability; (2) lower support of rights toward people with intellectual disability versus those with a physical disability; and finally, (3) a lower degree of acceptance and a higher perception of dangerousness were associated with greater social distance, which correlates with the diminished perception of rights (Werner, 2015).

Inclusion

Research supports a hierarchy of acceptance among disability groups, with intellectual disability frequently being the least socially accepted (Werner, 2015). While public perception of dangerousness of persons with intellectual disability is often used as a criterion to withhold rights and individual autonomy, acceptance and positive perceptions of individuals may enhance their inclusion and rights status (Werner, 2015). In the early 1900s, Henry H. Goddard and Lewis Terman translated the Stanford-Binet IQ test for use in the United States (Haydt et al., 2014). Goddard used the scientific measure and its construct, intelligence, to argue for a number of popular policy initiatives: (1) placing people with mild intellectual disability into non-coed institutions; (2) adopting enforced sterilization laws; and (3) restricting immigration from parts of Europe and Asia (Haydt et al., 2014). Exclusionary and segregationist practices were upheld on grounds of public safety and concern for the greater good. However, as the hereditarian theory of intelligence and morality/criminality gave way to a more social constructionist approach, greater emphasis was placed on the role of the social environment—and, perhaps in combination with fiscal motives, the deinstitutionalization of persons with disabilities gained momentum. Legislation in the 1990s and 2000s has been aimed at the further inclusion of persons with intellectual disabilities in the employment and education settings.

Execution

In 2002, the US Supreme Court found that the execution of persons with intellectual disability is unconstitutional on the grounds that such an execution violates the Eighth Amendment's protections against cruel and unusual punishment, owing to the diminished culpability of defendants with intellectual disability. The *Atkins* (2002) decision created a special category of defendants exempt from capital punishment, with inclusion in that class established vis-à-vis clinical diagnosis (Haydt et al., 2014)—and when the US Supreme Court left the determination of intellectual disability to state-level discretion, it simultaneously left this task to trained mental health professionals such as social workers (Feluren, 2103). Psychological understanding of criminal offense "and the extent to which [intellectual disability] is a disability" (p. 106) is not necessarily strong among the general public (who may serve as jurors in capital cases) and, importantly, by lawmakers (Lindsay,

2013). There is strong potential that, in jury cases, the determination of intellectual disability may ultimately fall to the discretion of 12 lay people who, in addition to having a lack of mental health training, are provided with contradictory expert testimony (Musso et al., 2012). One pause for consideration is that, from 2002 to 2014, 22 of the total 23 jury determinations of intellectual disability (96%) ruled against the finding of intellectual disability; this is contrasted with an overall success rate of 43% (Blume et al., 2014). Because of a lack of training and experience, and prevailing stereotypes about disability, court officials and jurors alike may understand intellectual disability in a way that is inconsistent with the mild category of the diagnosis (Cheung, 2013), further substantiating the import of mental health professionals (i.e., social workers) in legal proceedings involving the determination of intellectual disability. However, a point of caution is that, although some mental health professionals may have specific experience in the clinical evaluation of persons with intellectual disability, most do not (Ellis, 2003). In any legal proceeding involving an assessment of intellectual disability, the evaluator "must not only be skilled in the administration and interpretation of psychometric (IQ) tests, but also in the assessment of adaptive behavior and the impact of intellectual impairment in the individual's life" (Ellis, 2003, p. 11).

CONCLUSION

The focus of this chapter was the scientific measurement, or clinical diagnosis, of intellectual/developmental disabilities and implications for the practice of social work. While some developmental disabilities are largely physical issues, some individuals may have a condition that includes a physical and intellectual disability. Intellectual disability encompasses the cognitive component of the definition and is measured in three prongs: (1) intellectual functioning, (2) adaptive functioning, and (3) age of onset. Advances in science have resulted in the ability to test for developmental disabilities during pregnancy. However, this technology has serious ethical implications, as it may result in the parents' decision to terminate the pregnancy. This will necessarily have impact for hospital social workers. Furthermore, science by way of statistical analysis is used to measure intellectual disability using standardized intellectual and adaptive functioning tests. For individuals with intellectual disability, diagnostic labeling is a double-edged sword: on the one hand, a label provides access to educational, medical, and social services, as well as the protection of certain legal rights; on the other hand, labeling can contribute to the process of stigmatization and the decreased realization of rights vis-à-vis social exclusion. The scientific measurement (i.e., clinical diagnosis) of intellectual/developmental disabilities, therefore, has important implications for persons who receive, and who do not receive, the diagnostic label. These considerations include the securement of legal rights, access to services (including insurance reimbursement), and social inclusion at the substantive level. Challenges to the scientific measurement of intellectual/developmental disabilities impact social work practice and have special implications for social justice.

REFERENCES

Ali, A., Hassiotis, A., Strydom, A., & King, M. (2012). Self stigma in people with intellectual disabilities and courtesy stigma in family carers: A systematic review. *Research in Developmental Disabilities, 33*(6), 2122–2140.

American Association on Intellectual and Developmental Disabilities. (2013a). Frequently asked questions on intellectual disability. Retrieved from https://aaidd.org/intellectual-disability/definition/faqs-on-intellectual-disability#.VraBOylEwZg

American Association on Intellectual and Developmental Disabilities. (2013b). Definition of intellectual disability. Retrieved from https://aaidd.org/intellectual-disability/definition

American Psychiatric Association. (2013). *Diagnostic and statistical manual of mental disorders,* text revision *(DSM-V)*. Washington, DC: Author.

Atkins v. Virginia, 536 U.S. 304 (2002).

Bain, S. K., & Allin, J. D. (2005). Book review: Stanford-Binet intelligence scales. *Journal of Psychoeducational Assessment, 23*(1), 87–95.

Becker, K. A. (2003). *History of the Stanford-Binet Intelligence Scales: Content and psychometrics* (Stanford-Binet Intelligence Scales, Fifth Edition Assessment Service Bulletin No. 1). Itasca, IL: Riverside Publishing.

Ben-Moshe, L. (2013). The institution yet to come: Analyzing incarceration through a disability lens. *The Disability Studies Reader, 4,* 132–145.

Blume, J. H., Johnson, S. L., Marcus, P., & Paavola, E. (2014). A tale of two (and possibly three) Atkins: Intellectual disability and capital punishment twelve years after the Supreme Court's creation of a categorical bar. *William & Mary Bill of Rights Journal, 23,* 393.

Blume, J. H., Johnson, S. L., & Seeds, C. (2009). An empirical look at Atkins v. Virginia and its application in capital cases. *Tennessee Law Review, 76,* 625.

Borromeo, A. D. (2001). Mental retardation and the death penalty. *Loyola Journal of Public Interest Law, 3,* 175.

Brodsky, S. L., & Galloway, V. A. (2003). Ethical and professional demands for forensic mental health professionals in the post-Atkins era. *Ethics & Behavior, 13*(1), 3–9.

Cheung, N. (2013). Defining intellectual disability and establishing a standard of proof: Suggestions for a national model standard. *Health Matrix, 23,* 317.

Davis, L. J. (2013). The end of identity politics: On disability as an unstable category. In L. J. Davis (Ed.), *The disability studies reader* (5th ed.) (pp. 263–277). New York, NY: Routledge.

DeMatteo, D., Marczyk, G., & Pich, M. (2007). A national survey of state legislation defining mental retardation: Implications for policy and practice after Atkins. *Behavioral Sciences & the Law, 25*(6), 781–802.

Ellis, J. W. (2003). Mental retardation and the death penalty: A guide to state legislative issues. *Mental & Physical Disability Law Report, 27,* 11.

Fabian, J. M., Thompson IV, W. W., & Lazarus, J. B. (2011). Life, death, and IQ: It's much more than just a score: Understanding and utilizing forensic psychological and neuropsychological evaluations in Atkins intellectual disability/mental retardation cases. *Cleveland State Law Review, 59,* 399.

Feluren, J. V. (2013). Moving the focus away from the IQ score towards the subjective assessment of adaptive functioning: The effect of the DSM-5 on the post-Atkins categorical exemption of offenders with intellectual disability from the death penalty. *Nova Law Review, 38,* 323.

Gould, S. J. (1996). *The mismeasure of man.* New York, NY: WW Norton & Company.

Greenspan, S., Harris, J. C., & Woods, G. W. (2015). Intellectual disability is "a condition, not a number": Ethics of IQ cut-offs in psychiatry, human services and law. *Ethics, Medicine and Public Health, 1*(3), 312–324.

Leading Cases (2014). Eighth amendment – cruel and unusual punishments – defendants with intellectual disability – Hall v. Florida. *Harvard Law Review, 128*(1), 271–280. Retrieved from http://www.jstor.org/stable/24643929.

Haydt, N., Greenspan, S., & Agharkar, B. S. (2014). Advantages of DSM-5 in the diagnosis of intellectual disability: Reduced reliance on IQ ceilings in Atkins (Death Penalty) cases. *UMKC Law Review, 82,* 359. Retrieved from https://ssrn.com/abstract=2416659

Leland, H., Nihira, K., Foster, R., & Shellhaas, M. (1970). *The demonstration and measurement of adaptive behavior.* In M. Schreiber (Ed.), *Social work and mental retardation* (pp. 137–143). New York, NY: John Day Company.

Lindsay, W. R. (2013). Criminal behavior, offending and pathways into forensic intellectual disability services. In R. M. Hodapp (Serial Ed.), R. Hastings & J. Rojahn (Vol. Eds.), *International Review of Research in Developmental Disabilities, Vol. 44. Challenging behavior* (pp. 105–142). Elsevier. Retrieved from https://doi.org/10.1016/B978-0-12-401662-0.00004-X

Meany, K. A. (2004). Atkins v. Virginia: The false finding of a national consensus and the problems with determining who is mentally retarded. *Widener Law Review, 11,* 137.

Mobbs, K., & West, S. (2013). Burden of proof for mental retardation. *Journal of the American Academy of Psychiatry and the Law Online, 41*(4), 585–588.

Musso, M. W., Barker, A. A., Proto, D. A., & Gouvier, W. D. (2012). College students' conceptualizations of deficits involved in mild intellectual disability. *Research in Developmental Disabilities, 33*(1), 224–228.

National Association of Social Workers. (2008). *NASW Code of Ethics: Ethical principles.* Retrieved from https://www.socialworkers.org/About/Ethics/Code-of-Ethics/Code-of-Ethics-English

National Institute of Health. (2012). Intellectual and developmental disabilities. Retrieved from https://www.nichd.nih.gov/health/ topics/idds/conditioninfo/Pages/treatment.aspx

Obi, O., Van Naarden Braun, K., Baio, J., Drews-Botsch, C., Devine, O., & Yeargin-Allsopp, M. (2011). Effect of incorporating adaptive functioning scores on the prevalence of intellectual disability. *American Journal on Intellectual and Developmental Disabilities, 116*(5), 360–370.

Papazoglou, A., Jacobson, L. A., McCabe, M., Kaufmann, W., & Zabel, T. A. (2014). To ID or not to ID? Changes in classification rates of intellectual disability using DSM-5. *Mental Retardation, 52*(3), 165–174.

Sachy, T. (2013). Affidavit of Thomas H. Sachy M.D., MSc. Jones County, GA. Retrieved from http://s3.documentcloud.org/documents/603976/warren-hill-sachy.pdf Google Scholar

US Department of Health, Education and Welfare, Secretary's Committee on Mental Retardation (1970). The distinction between mental retardation and mental illness. In

M. Schreiber (Ed.), *Social work and mental retardation* (p. 37). New York, NY: John Day
   Company.

U.S. Department of Health and Human Services, National Institute of Health. (2012).
   Intellectual and Developmental Disabilities. Retrieved from https://www.nichd.nih.gov/
   health/ topics/idds/conditioninfo/Pages/treatment.aspx

Silverman, W., Miezejeski, C., Ryan, R., Zigman, W., Krinsky-McHale, S., & Urv,
   T. (2010). Stanford-Binet and WAIS IQ differences and their implications for adults
   with intellectual disability (aka mental retardation). *Intelligence, 38*(2), 242–248.

Werner, S. (2015). Public stigma and the perception of rights: Differences between
   intellectual and physical disabilities. *Research in Developmental Disabilities, 38*, 262–
   271. Retrieved from https://doi.org/10.1016/j.ridd.2014.12.030

15

Conclusions

S
ocial work's commitment to scientific inquiry and the use of science in its practice began with the creation of the profession and its entry into the world of human problem solving. More than 100 years ago, the beginnings of social work were synonymous with the desire to understand social problems such as financial dependency, family dissolution, child development, substance abuse (especially alcoholism in the profession's early days,) and crime from scientific viewpoints. In many ways, social work's development was an alternative to moral judgments and arbitrary punishments of behavior deemed socially unacceptable. Instead, social work's pioneers wanted to know why and how social problems existed. They wanted to devise methods, based on scientific inquiry, to deal with those problems. That is why research is a fundamental and historically critical factor in social work practice and theory.

Of course, 19th-century understandings of human behavior had lengthy developmental needs. The scientific study of human intelligence, human biology, immunology, and modern medicine also have roots in the 19th century along with social work. Much of what the world sees now in health care, especially surgery, education, and family life, were an earlier era's science fiction as well as being among the mandates of the profession of social work.

Although the associations between science and social work may seem modest, even unlikely, in fact social work's developments in science, especially those dimensions of science that are closely related to human and social behavior, have moved in parallel increments. The discovery of immunizations to prevent illnesses, as well as the medical and surgical interventions that extend life, move in direct relationship with social work. Social workers are part of the health care systems throughout the world. Dealing with social work's absolute desire to prevent childhood and adult illnesses as well as coping with the social consequences of evolving health care are, in some ways, as much a part of disease prevention and treatment as are more readily identified health care professions such as medicine and nursing. Helping society deal with family dissolutions and the scourges of domestic violence and child maltreatment are primary historical concerns of social work. Other professions have often played secondary roles in comparison to social work.

So this book about the application of science concepts to social work practice is in the long tradition of social work. Although it has not always been identified as such, social work's commitment to understanding and using science is as old as the profession.

Several examples may suffice to illustrate the associations. When new illnesses— AIDS is a major example—begin to affect humans, social workers are typically among the earliest agents dealing with their consequences. AIDS, not unlike other health problems, has multiple social effects. In many ways, the social consequences of AIDS are as serious as the physical.

In other examples, when science began finding ways to extend the life span, social workers began developing programs for the aging, an entirely new role for the profession, which had traditionally been concerned with children and their parents. Social workers are now heavily involved in day programs, home care, nursing homes, and other forms of service for the elderly. When it became clear that many people with serious illnesses could not be effectively treated but needed to end their lives with dignity, social work, along with other professions, developed hospice programs to serve people in their last stages of life. When engineers and other scientists began developing modern approaches to limb replacement and mobility devices, social workers were among the most important professionals helping accident victims, congenitally disabled people, and wounded veterans learn to function with prostheses. Engineers and physicists, as well as other professionals, play major roles in artificial body parts but social workers are heavily involved in helping patients learn to use them in rehabilitation programs and veterans' services.

Although health and medical issues are the most obvious examples, social work's associations with science move far beyond health and disease. Much of what is now known about substance abuse relies on relatively clear understandings of chemistry concepts. Knowledge of family planning, an historically important element in much of social work practice, evolved through the sciences of chemistry and pharmacology. So social workers must often learn about and serve as experts on services that are largely based on chemistry (see Chapter 2).

Execution of violators of the law, an historically common practice which social work, as a profession, generally opposes, has evolved from hanging and similar forms of taking lives of those convicted of crimes such as murder to modern and perhaps more humane execution methods such as the use of lethal injections. Execution was employed, as recently as the last century, for crimes such as espionage and treason. Chapter 10 details the evolution of execution in the United States and the methods for achieving it from scientific perspectives but also from the legal and social policy dimensions.

Social work is not only a clinical profession. It also takes serious responsibilities in social welfare policy and services. Environmental issues such as air pollution, climate change, and waste disposal often attract and make use of social work knowledge about bringing such issues to the attention of the public and advocating for solutions to them. Issues such as housing, health care facility design, budgeting, and financial planning and administration are all of special interest to social workers and involve many members of the profession as full-time advocates as well as volunteers. Some of the most severe human problems result from natural disasters such as floods and earthquakes. Chapters 6 through 8 contribute to that element of social work practice. In the coming years, these "macro" issues may have the most important impact on social work practice.

Issues of mental disability are understood much differently and are more informed by scientific concepts than they were when social work began. Social workers have been in the forefront of such steps as deinstitutionalization and mainstreaming of people with mental limitations. The same is true of people with mental illnesses. Throughout much of the world, large institutions for housing people with mental disabilities have been abandoned because of major changes in the ways they are treated. Much of the better understanding of mental problems and alternative solutions for those who suffer from them are a product of social work's as well as other professions' knowledge and application of the science which demands and demonstrates more effective ways of helping people with mental limitations live within and contribute to the larger society.

This book also provides some information on science fundamentals. Even those that are not immediately applicable to social work practice such as astronomy and physics have special relevance to life on Earth. These basic sciences affect the ways in which people live. Some solutions to issues of human need are likely to be associated with sciences that are important for every professional's background. Life in outer space, which already has some commercial initiatives, may be one of the realities of this and future centuries. And knowing about basic sciences is a necessity for any well-educated person.

While this book was being written, issues about science became unexpectedly important. Some of America's top officials promoted the idea that science and scientists were suspect, especially when they suggested the climate is changing in ways that are detrimental to life on Earth—and that human activity caused and could redress the damaging effects of the warming of the world's climate. Rising sea levels, often sufficient to make low-lying areas uninhabitable, floods in places and of magnitudes that were not seen before, frequent earthquakes in areas that had no history of them, were all evidence of human impact on the climate, most scientists agreed.

Some of the proposed measures for dealing with climate change seemed to have economic consequences for the United States. The use of fossil fuels, especially petroleum, seemed to have deleterious effects on the atmosphere. But fossil fuel production is one of America's largest businesses. The use of "fracking," a method for extracting petroleum from previously unreachable sites, appeared to be associated with earthquakes in Oklahoma, a petroleum-producing state that began relying on fracking in recent years. Foregoing the production and use of fossil fuels became the conflict issue of the times.

Critics of the climate-change arguments of scientists counter that the world's climate has always changed and that there is no proof of a direct relationship between human activity and the worst environmental challenges. Activists trying to minimize climate change have pressed for the replacement of fossil fuel generation with the use of energy drawn from the sun and the wind. Science, which had previously been less controversial, was likely to continue growing as the source of extensive political conflict. The issues raised in this volume are likely to affect family and economic life, including employment, the growth or decline of communities, industries as varied as agriculture, transportation, and manufacturing, and the distribution of wealth. Science, broadly defined, may be the most important human issue of the 21st century. As such, science is of increasing importance to social work.

The authors hope this volume is helpful to its readers in thinking about and using science concepts in their learning about and practicing of social work. In some ways, the topic and the framework for understanding science's contributions to social work is designed to help social workers—teachers, students, and practitioners— better employ scientific knowledge in their work. We hope that this brief text will help social work grow and improve as it increases and uses its awareness of science concepts.

GLOSSARY OF KEY TERMS

Activities of daily living (ADLs): Basic self-care, such as being able to move from one place to another, bathing, and eating. Loss of the ability to perform ADLs is often the basis for long-term care placement or services.

Acupuncture: A procedure used in or adapted from Chinese medical practice in which specific body areas are pierced with fine needles for therapeutic purposes or to relieve pain or produce regional anesthesia.

Adaptive functioning: Adaptive functioning is one of three criteria, or prongs, used to diagnose intellectual disability, and it refers to impairments in daily functioning. Three broad domains of skills currently comprise this clinical construct: conceptual, social, and practical.

Addiction: A condition involving use of a substance, such as a drug or alcohol, or engagement in a behavior, such as gambling, in which a person has strong cravings, is unable to stop or limit the activity, continues the activity despite harmful consequences, and experiences distress upon discontinuance.

Aggravation: Aggravation refers to any fact or circumstance that increases the severity or culpability of a criminal act. Aggravating factors typically include the following: simultaneous felonies; previous conviction for violent offenses; crimes committed in remuneration or hire; lack of remorse; and characteristics of the victim such as youth or status as a law enforcement official. To impose a penalty of death, the state must prove beyond a reasonable doubt the presence of at least one aggravating factor.

Algorithm: A finite set of unambiguous instructions that, given some set of initial conditions, can be performed in a prescribed sequence to achieve a certain goal and that has a recognizable set of end conditions.

Allergies: Sensitivity to substances in the environment such as animal dander and insect stings that would not cause problems for most people. Some allergies for people with great sensitivity to specific items such as peanuts or insect stings may induce serious reactions or even death.

Anecdotal: Based on casual observations or indications rather than rigorous or scientific analysis.

Anthropocene: The period of time during which human activities are thought to have had a significant impact on the global environment, regarded as having begun sometime between 8,000 years ago, with the spread of agriculture, and 200 years ago, with the advent of industrialization. The Anthropocene has been proposed as a new epoch of geologic time, following the Holocene.

Artificial intelligence: The ability of a computer or other machine to perform those activities that are normally thought to require intelligence.

Asthma: A health condition in which the airways are blocked or constricted, interfering with breathing.

Astrology: Study of the movement and positions of celestial objects from which conclusions about human affairs are drawn. It is generally an unproven, mythical phenomenon that is sometimes confused with astronomy.

Astronomy: The scientific study of matter and phenomena in the universe, especially in outer space, including the positions, dimensions, distribution, motion, composition, energy, and evolution of celestial objects.

Atkins diet: Diet regimen that focuses on restricting carbohydrates.

Atom: A part or particle considered to be an irreducible constituent of a specified system.

Bioinformatics: The use of computer science, mathematics, and information theory to organize and analyze complex biological data, especially genetic data.

BIPAP: Bilevel positive airway pressure machine, used for patients with sleep apnea.

Black holes: described by NASA as a place in space where gravity pulls so much that even light cannot get out. The gravity is so strong because matter has been squeezed into a tiny space. This can happen when a star is dying. Because no light can get out, people can't see black holes. They are invisible. Space telescopes with special tools can help find black holes. The special tools can see how stars that are very close to being labeled as black holes act differently than other stars.

Body image: The subjective picture or mental image of one's own body.

Body Mass Index (BMI): A measure of someone's weight in relation to height; to calculate one's BMI, multiply one's weight in pounds and divide that by the square of one's height in inches; overweight is a BMI greater than 25; obese is a BMI greater than 30.

Botched execution: Botched executions occur when there is a breakdown in, or departure from, the execution method protocol that results in unnecessary agony for the inmate or reflects gross incompetence of the executioner. It is estimated that approximately 3% of executions in the United States between 1890 and 2010 were botched.

Braille: Raised characters that people who are blind can write and read. Many documents, including magazines and newspapers, are printed in braille.

Byte: A unit of data equal to eight bits. Computer memory is often expressed in megabytes or gigabytes.

Calculus: The mathematics discipline that deals with change.

Capital punishment: Capital punishment is the state- and federal-level practice of imposing a sentence of death upon inmates who have presumably committed a crime so heinous that the sentence of death is not disproportionate to the offense. Although controversial, capital punishment is traditionally upheld on the philosophical grounds that it fulfills the penological aims of deterrence and retribution. All 31 death penalty states currently sanction the lethal injection method; a handful of these states also sanction one or more of the following alternative methods: firing squad, hanging, lethal gas, and/or electrocution.

CAT scan: an X-ray image obtained by examination with a CAT scanner.

Celiac disease: The condition that is a reaction to gluten in the diet, which can cause severe illness, even death.

Celsius: Of or relating to a temperature scale that registers the freezing point of water as 0° and the boiling point as 100° under normal atmospheric pressure.

Centers for Disease Control and Prevention: A federal government agency that tracks health problems and their consequences. It conducts both data collection and research on health problems.

Cerebral palsy: Any of a group of disorders of varying severity caused by brain injury usually at or before birth, resulting in impairment of muscle movement that may include spasticity, involuntary movement, or problems maintaining balance.

Chemistry: The branch of science that deals with the identification of the substances of which matter is composed; the investigation of their properties and the ways in which they interact, combine, and change; and the use of these processes to form new substances.

Chemotherapy: The use of chemical substances to treat health problems, especially to kill cancer cells.

Child welfare: The array of public and private agencies that work to improve life for and care for children in programs such as child abuse and neglect, adoption, foster care, and institutional services.

Climate: The meteorological conditions, including temperature, precipitation, and wind, that characteristically prevail in a particular region.

Climatology: The meteorological study of climates and their phenomena.

Clinical trial: a rigorously controlled test of a new drug or a new invasive medical device on human subjects; in the United States it is conducted under the direction of the FDA before being made available for general clinical use.

CMS: The Center for Medicare and Medicaid Services, a federal agency which directs the two largest health care programs, Medicare and Medicaid, and others such as the Children's Health Insurance Program (CHIP).

Cochlear implant: Devices implanted in the brains of people with deafness to assist their hearing.

Compound: A substance that is composed of two or more separate elements; a mixture.

Computerized tomography: A procedure and equipment that take multiple X-rays of the body. Can provide three-dimensional images of organs. Often referred to as a "CT scan."

Contaminant: The presence of an unwanted constituent or impurity in a material, physical body, or the natural environment.

Cooper aerobics: The Kenneth Cooper plan for improving and maintaining health through exercise.

Cosmology: The study of the physical universe considered as a totality of phenomena in time and space.

CPAP: Continuous positive airway pressure. A machine used for people who have sleep apnea. Patients breathe through a mask and tube connected to a positive airway machine that prevents them from having sleep apnea.

Cruel and unusual punishments: Cruel and unusual punishments refers to a clause of the Eighth Amendment and was ratified in 1791. The clause was intended to restrict the federal government from inflicting more pain than necessary to extinguish life. Punishments that are constitutionally considered cruel and unusual include those that involve torture or a lingering death; those that are disproportionate to the offense; those that do not meet evolving standards of decency; those that are applied arbitrarily/are procedurally nonadherent; those that are inflicted upon persons who are not deemed fully culpable due to diminished cognitive functioning and development (e.g., persons with intellectual disability and youth offenders).

Cystic fibrosis: A genetic disorder of the lungs in which mucus blocks the respiratory functions.

Dark matter: Matter in the universe, in addition to planets and other known objects that are unidentified.

Data: Facts that can be analyzed or used in an effort to gain knowledge or make decisions; information.

Data mining: The extraction of useful, often previously unknown information, from large databases or data sets.

Demography: The study of the characteristics of human populations, such as size, growth, density, distribution, and vital statistics.

Development: The pattern of change that begins at conception and continues through the life cycle.

Developmental disability: Developmental disability is severe and chronic disability that is likely to be lifelong and can be cognitive, physical, or both, with the period of manifestation occurring before age 22. While some developmental disabilities are largely physical issues, some individuals may have a condition that includes a physical and intellectual disability.

Diagnosis: The act or process of identifying or determining the nature and cause of a disease or injury through evaluation of patient history, examination, and review of laboratory data.

Diffusion: The spread of linguistic or cultural practices or innovations within a community or from one community to another.

Double blind: A testing procedure designed to avoid biased results by ensuring that at the time of the test neither the administrators nor the subjects know which subjects are receiving a test treatment and which belong to a control group.

Ecosystem: An ecological community together with its environment, functioning as a unit.

Electron microscope: A microscope that illuminates objects through accelerated electronics rather than light alone. Such microscopes are able to help scientists see small materials that would be in visible with ordinary microscopes.

Electronic health record (EHR): An electronic health record is an evolving concept defined as a systematic collection of electronic health information about individual patients or populations. It is a record in digital format that is theoretically capable of being shared across different health care settings. In some cases this sharing can occur by way of network: connected, enterprise-wide information systems and other information networks or exchanges. EHRs may include a range of data, including demographics, medical history, medication and allergies, immunization status, laboratory test results, radiology images, vital signs, personal statistics like age and weight, and billing information.

Element: Substances that cannot be chemically interconverted or broken down into simpler substances and are primary constituents of matter. Each element is distinguished by its atomic number, that is, the number of protons in the nuclei of its atoms.

Emigration: To leave one country or region to settle in another.

Empirical: Empirical evidence is a source of knowledge acquired by means of observation or experimentation. Empirical evidence is information that justifies a belief in the truth or falsity of an empirical claim. In the empiricist view, one can only claim to have knowledge when one has a true belief based on empirical evidence.

Energy: The conversion of mass such as an object to a force. Energy is a result of mass multiplied by time squared or, in the famous Einstein equation, E (energy) equals M (mass) times time (C) squared ($E = MC^2$).

Engineers: Professionals who apply scientific and mathematical knowledge to structures, programs, and designs. A scientist may discover the effects of chemical therapy on treating cancer. Engineers would design the methods for using that knowledge in treating patients.

Epidemic: Spreading rapidly and extensively by infection and affecting many individuals in an area or a population at the same time.

Epidemiology: The branch of medicine that deals with the study of the causes, distribution, and control of disease in populations.

Euclidean geometry: Geometry based upon the postulates of Euclid, especially the postulate that only one line may be drawn through a given point parallel to a given line.

Evidence-based practice: Social work assessment of clients and services to them based on evidence from the sciences and from data collected about the client as part of the service plan as opposed to a priori service based on theories and conventions that do not build on systematically developed evidence about the client and the services available to assist him or her.

Fahrenheit: Of or relating to a temperature scale that registers the freezing point of water as 32° and the boiling point as 212° at one atmosphere of pressure.

Fracking: A method of releasing oil or gas from rock by forcing liquid at high pressure into the rock.

Gene: A hereditary unit consisting of a sequence of DNA that occupies a specific location on a chromosome and is transcribed into an RNA molecule that may function directly or be translated into an amino acid chain.

General theory of relativity: Albert Einstein's basic and revolutionary theory about the forces of gravity and its impact on things and planets, the curvature of space, and the curvature of time.

Geology: The scientific study of the origin, history, and structure of the Earth.

Geometry: The mathematics of shape and sizes.

Germ theory: The theory that all infectious diseases are caused by microorganisms.

Global warming: Recent increases in the world's temperature, which are believed to result from the increase in greenhouse gases. The causes appear to be large-scale factory farming, manufacturing, and other activity that releases carbon into the atmosphere. Global warming has been much greater in recent years than in the past and preventing catastrophes may require substantial reductions in the production of greenhouse gases.

The political argument is whether this warming is a result of human activity or other reasons such as the cyclical changes in temperature.

Gluten: The protein in wheat and related grains that holds the grain together. Some people have an intolerance to gluten and suffer from Celiac disease, which can be debilitating and can even cause death. For most people, gluten is not harmful.

GMO foods: Genetically modified organisms, in this case genetically modified foods. A source of health concern for some people; in 2016, the federal government announced that there is no evidence that GMO foods are harmful to people.

Gram: A metric unit of mass equal to one thousandth (10^{-3}) of a kilogram.

Gravity: The natural attraction between physical bodies, especially when one of the bodies is a celestial body, such as the Earth.

Greenhouse gases: Gases that affect the climate and are associated with global warming, which include water vapor, carbon dioxide, methane, nitrous oxide, and ozone.

Health physicist: A profession that concerns itself with the prevention of radiation damage to patients of health care facilities as well as workers in nuclear power plants and nuclear waste disposal sites.

Hearing aids: Electronic devices that increase the volume of sounds for people who are deaf or hard of hearing.

Heat: Energy as it passes among systems to its surroundings.

HIV/AIDS: Human immunodeficiency virus infection and acquired immune deficiency syndrome. Although there is no cure and many patients die from the syndrome, there are now pharmaceutical interventions that can slow or stop the damage done by the syndrome.

Hormones: Powerful chemical substances secreted by the endocrine glands and carried through the body by the bloodstream.

Human genome: The human genome is the complete set of genetic information for humans. The Human Genome Project produced the first complete sequences of individual human genomes.

Hydrology: The scientific study of the properties, distribution, and effects of water on the Earth's surface, in the soil and underlying rocks, and in the atmosphere.

Immigration: The movement of nonnative people into a country in order to settle there.

Individuation: A process of transformation whereby the personal and collective unconscious are brought into consciousness (e.g., by means of dreams, active imagination, or free association) to be assimilated into the whole personality. It is a completely natural process necessary for the integration of the psyche.

Intellectual disability: Formerly termed "mental retardation," intellectual disability is a type of developmental disability that manifests as impairments in adaptive and intellectual functioning, with the age of onset specified as either occurring prior to age 18 or the broader concept of during the developmental period.

Kilometer: A designation of 1,000 meters, equal to 0.621371 miles.

Latitude: The angular distance north or south of the Earth's Equator, measured in degrees along a meridian, as on a map or globe.

Lethal injection: Lethal injection is currently the primary method of execution sanctioned in all 31 death penalty states and by the US federal government. First adopted by Oklahoma in 1977, lethal injection was first used by Texas in 1982. In the three-drug protocol, the initial injection is an anesthetic; the second paralyzes the muscle system and lungs; and the third injection of potassium chloride stops the inmate's heart. Medical professionals cannot perform lethal injections due to their professional mandate to do no harm.

Liberal arts: Term originally used to designate the arts or studies suited to freemen. It was applied in the Middle Ages to seven branches of learning, the trivium of grammar, logic, and rhetoric, and the quadrivium of arithmetic, geometry, astronomy, and music. During the Renaissance, the term was interpreted more broadly to mean all of those studies that impart a general, as opposed to a vocational or specialized, education.

Life cycle: The series of changes in the life of an organism, including reproduction.

Light: The speed of light is 299,792,458 meters per second or 186,000 miles per second. These figures are absolute constants, but the measurement would have to apply to light in a vacuum.

Limb reanimation: A procedure for placing an implant in the brain that allows otherwise disabled people to move their limbs.

Liter: A metric unit of volume equal to approximately 1.056 liquid quarts, 0.908 dry quart, or 0.264 gallon.

Longitude: Angular distance on the Earth's surface, measured east or west from the Prime Meridian at Greenwich, England, to the meridian passing through a position, expressed in degrees (or hours), minutes, and seconds.

Longitudinal study: A study conducted over time.

Long-term care: Services for individuals who are not able to perform the activities of daily living. It includes nursing homes, home health care, and various other programs that help sustain people when they are or become disabled.

Macro practice: Social work practice with larger systems, for example, community.

Magnet resonance imaging (MRI): A procedure conducted with a special machine that examines the body and/or specific organs with magnets and computers to obtain detailed information on a patient.

Mass: The size of a material. However, weight is a different phenomenon, which is the force exerted on an object by gravity. In space, objects may be weightless because of the absence of the force of gravity on the object.

Measurement: The dimension, quantity, or capacity determined by measuring.

Metric system: System of weights and measures planned in France and adopted there in 1799; it has since been adopted by most of the technologically developed countries of the world. It is based on a unit of length, called the meter (m), and a unit of mass, called the kilogram (kg).

Microbiology: The branch of biology that deals with microorganisms.

Microsurgery: Procedures that surgeons use to conduct operations through small body incisions rather than complete exposure of the body's internal organs. Microscopes and specially designed small instruments are used in the process of treating illnesses surgically.

Migrant: A person who is moving, generally from one country to another.

Milligram: One thousandth of a gram.

Mitigation: A mitigating factor is any fact or circumstance that lessens the severity or culpability of a criminal act. Mitigating factors typically include the defendant's youth; emotional or mental disability; intellectual disability; the victim's participation in the crime; chronic maltreatment during childhood; remorse; capacity for rehabilitation in prison; posttraumatic stress disorder resultant from military service; intoxication and chemical dependency; and efforts to contribute prosocially to society. Social workers may function as mitigation experts in capital trials by conducting, analyzing, and reporting social history findings that would presumably warrant a punishment less than death.

Moratorium: A moratorium is a temporary prohibition. From 1972 until 1976, there was a national moratorium against the death penalty in the United States arising from concerns that demonstrated arbitrariness constituted cruel and unusual punishment. The two cases that started and ended the temporary prohibition against the death penalty in the United States originated in Georgia: *Furman v. Georgia* (1972) and *Gregg v. Georgia* (1976).

Natural sciences: Collectively, the branches of science dealing with objectively measurable phenomena pertaining to the transformations and relationships of energy and matter; includes biology, physics, and chemistry.

Neurology: The branch of medicine that deals with the diagnosis and treatment of diseases and disorders of the nervous system.

Neuroscience: In medicine, the study of the anatomy, physiology, biochemistry, and pharmacology of the nervous system.

Newtonian mechanics: A system of mechanics based on Newton's laws of motion.

Nuclear energy: The energy released by a nuclear reaction, especially by fission or fusion.

Ocular character recognition: A device developed by Ray Kurzweil which translates written materials into raised letters so that people who are blind can "read" handwritten, printed, or computer: generated materials by touch without the necessity to translate the materials into braille.

Optics: A branch of physics that studies light and its interaction with matter. Telescopes, microscopes, and other scientific instruments rely on the learnings of physicists who study optics.

Ornish diet: Developed by Dean Ornish with a focus on restricting the consumption of fat and reducing calorie consumption.

Ornithology: The branch of zoology that deals with birds.

Pacemaker: An electronic device implanted in the heart of a patient whose heart rhythms are inconsistent with healthy heart functions. Pacemakers help regulate the heart so that the rhythms are more healthful.

Peer review: The evaluation by fellow specialists of research that someone has done in order to assess its suitability for publication or further development.

PET scan: Position emission tomography uses X-rays with multiple images, usually when the patient is inserted with dyes, to examine organs and identify diseases.

Physical sciences: Any of the sciences, such as physics, chemistry, astronomy, and geology, which analyze the nature and properties of energy and nonliving matter.

Physics: The basic science discipline that explores matter, motion, mass, and related concepts such as time. It is the study of how the universe behaves. Several other sciences developed from it examine smaller pieces of the subject such as biology and chemistry.

Pollutant: A substance or energy introduced into the environment that has undesired effects, or adversely affects health, well-being, or natural conditions.

Population: All of the people inhabiting a specified area.

Postmodern: Of or relating to an intellectual stance often marked by eclecticism and irony and tending to reject the universal validity of such principles as hierarchy, binary opposition, categorization, and stable identity.

Psychopharmacology: The branch of pharmacology that deals with the study of the actions, effects, and development of psychoactive drugs.

Puberty: A period of rapid skeletal and sexual maturation that occurs mainly in early adolescence.

Quantum: A unit that cannot be subdivided. (Plural is *quanta*)

Quantum mechanics or quantum theory: The science of the very small: the body of scientific principles that explains the behavior of matter and its interactions with energy on the scale of atoms and subatomic particles.

Radiology: The branch of medicine that deals with diagnostic images of anatomic structures made through the use of electromagnetic radiation or sound waves and that treats disease through the use of radioactive compounds. Radiological imaging techniques include X-rays, CT scans, PET scans, MRIs, and ultrasonograms.

Radiation treatment: The use of intense radiation to kill cancer cells.

Random: Having no specific pattern, purpose, or objective.

Random clinical trial: Research studies in which one or more groups are formed by random assignment to treatments and controls. Allows groups to be more equivalent when comparing he effects of treatment.

Relativity theory: Actually the two theories for which Einstein is most famous. Special relativity states that nothing can travel faster than the speed of light, the speed identified by Einstein. It explains how matter can be converted to energy and energy to matter. The second, general relativity, redefines gravity and creates the concept of space-time.

Reliability: The degree of stability exhibited when a measurement is repeated under identical conditions.

Replicability: The quality or state of being replicable in research.

Sample: A set of data or elements drawn from a larger population and analyzed to estimate the characteristics of that population.

Search engine: A website whose primary function is providing a search engine for gathering and reporting information available on the Internet or a portion of the Internet.

Sleep apnea: A condition in which people have periodic cessation of breathing, often many episodes every hour, which can lead to medical problems as well as the more common event, loud snoring.

Social inclusion: Broadly, social inclusion refers to a theoretical orientation that is concerned with the full and meaningful participation of all members of society, and the mechanisms by which individuals and groups who do not adhere to prevailing social norms are formally or substantively excluded from participation vis-à-vis political, social, and economic oppression and exploitation.

Social invisibility: Social invisibility refers to persons with mild intellectual disability in particular who may be at risk for rights violations; they often suffer social stigmatization that frequently results in non-self-disclosure, which may leave such persons unseen by the general public.

Social model of disability: In contrast to the medical model of disability, which roots disability at the individual level, the social model of disability is concerned with the processes by which society's institutions and the underpinning social structures that constitute our shared social reality limit a person's functionings and capabilities.

Social stigma: Social stigma is severe social disapproval and can diminish participation and inclusion in the community. Stigmatization is the process whereby certain groups of people are marginalized by society because the group norms differ from those of the dominant cultural group, with power differentials.

Space junk: Materials that were part of now defunct satellites that continue to orbit the Earth.

Spina bifida: A hereditary malformation of the spine that often makes it impossible for children with this condition to walk and engage in other physical activities.

Statistics: The mathematics of the collection, organization, and interpretation of numerical data, especially the analysis of population characteristics by inference from sampling.

STEM: Science, technology, engineering, and mathematics.

Stryker frame: A specialized rolling cart for patients who must lie prone. It allows for rotation and is used to help patients avoid bedsores.

Synapse: The junction across which a nerve impulse passes from an axon terminal to a neuron, muscle cell, or gland cell.

Tai chi: A traditional Chinese medicine movement process.

Technician: A worker in a field of *technology* who is proficient in the relevant skills and techniques, with a relatively practical understanding of the theoretical principles.

Temperature: The degree of hotness or coldness of a body or environment.

Theory: A set of statements or principles devised to explain a group of facts or phenomena, especially one that has been repeatedly tested or is widely accepted and can be used to make predictions about natural phenomena.

Tide: The periodic variation in the surface level of the oceans and of bays, gulfs, inlets, and estuaries, caused by gravitational attraction of the moon and sun.

Time and place sampling: A type of sampling where the individual items of the population cannot be enumerated and instead location and time are the variables substituted to aid in creating a representation of the research interest.

United Nations Climate Change Summit The conference was held in 2015 and the participating nations agreed to hold climate change to 2 degrees Celsius or 35.6 degrees Fahrenheit, compared to preindustrial levels.

Weather: The state of the atmosphere at a given time and place, with respect to variables such as temperature, moisture, wind velocity, and barometric pressure.

X-ray: Use of radiation to examine the internal organs and bones of a patient.

INDEX

Tables, figures, and boxes are indicated by an italic t, f, and b following the page/paragraph number